The 'One Plar

The 'One Planet' Life demonstrates a path for everyone towards a way of life in which we don't act as if we had more than one planet Earth. The difference between this approach and others is that it uses ecological footprint analysis to help to determine how effective our efforts are. Much of the book is a manual – with examples – on how to live the 'good life' and supply over 65 per cent of your livelihood from your land with mostly positive impacts upon the environment.

It examines the pioneering Welsh policy, One Planet Development, then considers efforts towards one planet living in urban areas. After a foreword by BioRegional/One Planet Living co-founder Pooran Desai and an introduction by former Welsh environment minister Jane Davidson, the book contains:

- An essay arguing that our attitude to planning, land and development needs to change to enable truly sustainable development
- Guidelines on finding land, finance, and creating a personal plan for one planet living
- Detailed guides on: sustainable building, supplying your own food, generating renewable energy, reducing carbon emissions from travel, land management, water supply and waste treatment
- 20 exemplary examples at all scales – from micro-businesses to suburbs – followed by Jane Davidson's Afterword.

The book will interest anyone seeking to find out how a sustainable lifestyle can be achieved. It is also key reading for rural and built environment practitioners and policy makers keen to support low-impact initiatives, and for students studying aspects of planning, geography, governance, sustainability and renewable energy.

David Thorpe is a writer and consultant on sustainability issues. He is a Special Consultant on Sustainable Cities Collective, the primary website for urban leaders globally; a founder and core group member of the One Planet Council; and the author of several books on sustainability, including: *Energy Management in Buildings*, *Energy Management in Industry*, *Solar Technology* and *Sustainable Home Refurbishment*, all in The Earthscan Expert Guide series. Prior to this he was the News Editor and Opinion Writer of the UK's *Energy and Environmental*

Management magazine for 13 years. Before that he was director of publications at the Centre for Alternative Technology.

On a lighter front, he has also written comics, including Marvel Comics, been an editor of graphic novels for several publishers, and is a novelist – the winner of a HarperCollins contest to find a major new children's writer with his science-fiction dystopia for young adults, *Hybrids*. His novel *Stormteller* is on a related theme to this book. He lives in south Wales with his wife, the musician and composer Helen Adam. For more information, see his website: www.davidthorpe.info.

"David Thorpe's new book is a timely reminder that we have only one planet to live on – and that this fact needs to be reflected how we live, and everything we do. But as well as making the irrefutable case for 'one planet living', it provides a wealth of practical detail on how to actually do it, and this is surely where the book's greatest value lies for a new generation of one planet pioneers determined to lead the transition to new ways of living, that tread lightly upon the Earth and sustain her natural riches." – Oliver Tickell, editor, *The Ecologist* magazine and author of *Kyoto2: How to Manage the Global Greenhouse*

"David Thorpe outlines, in fastidious detail, the journey to a new life that is not only lower impact, but is also delightful and fun – and he is quite prepared to fully address the multiple bureaucratic and technical challenges and along the way. This book is an excellent and immensely practical step by step guide, illustrated with copious examples, for everyone ready to make that change." – George Marshall, founder of the Climate Outreach Information Network and author of *Don't Even Think About It: Why Our Brains Are Wired to Ignore Climate Change*

"Over the last 30 years economists have had to reassess how improvements to human welfare are measured. Unfettered growth in household demands causes local and global problems. Measures such as the ecological footprint seek to assess the 'planet' consequences of our consumption activities. Practically what it means to live a 'one-planet' lifestyle is rarely considered in terms of the benefits and challenges, and this book is therefore a welcome reckoning. A key theme is the fact that maximising consumption activity should not be confused with maximising human welfare." – Professor Max Munday, Director of the Welsh Economy Research Unit, Cardiff Business School

The 'One Planet' Life

A blueprint for low impact development

David Thorpe

Routledge
Taylor & Francis Group

LONDON AND NEW YORK

earthscan
from Routledge

First published 2015
by Routledge
2 Park Square, Milton Park, Abingdon, Oxon OX14 4RN

and by Routledge
711 Third Avenue, New York, NY 10017

Routledge is an imprint of the Taylor & Francis Group, an informa business

British Library Cataloguing-in-Publication Data
A catalogue record for this book is available from the British Library

Library of Congress Cataloging-in-Publication Data
Thorpe, Dave, 1954-
The 'one planet' life : a blueprint for low impact development / David Thorpe.
pages cm
Includes bibliographical references and index.
1. Sustainable living. 2. Sustainable development. 3. Sustainable agriculture. 4. Sustainable living--Wales--Case studies. 5. Sustainable development--Wales--Case studies. 6. Sustainable agriculture--Wales--Case studies. I. Title.
GE196.T56 2014
338.9'27--dc23
2014011741

ISBN: 978-0-415-73854-5 (hbk)
ISBN: 978-0-415-73855-2 (pbk)
ISBN: 978-1-315-75503-8 (ebk)

Typeset in Frutiger by
Servis Filmsetting Ltd, Stockport, Cheshire

'Clear evidence shows that we are living beyond our means on a planet, using resources we will never be able to replace.'

Phil Barton, chief executive of Keep Britain Tidy

'The collective ecological footprint of humanity now significantly exceeds the regenerative capacity of the earth.'

Herbert Girardet[1]

'This can and must be the moment for governments to set a new course toward sustainability.'

Jim Leape, Director General, WWF International

---

1 *Towards the Regenerative City*, Herbert Girardet (with Stefan Schurig, Anna Leidreiter and Fiona Woo), Expert Commission on Cities and Climate Change of the World Future Council, 2014.

Contents

List of Figures and Tables

Tables

How to use this book

The purpose of this book is to encourage a transition by everyone to the One Planet Life; in other words, a way of life in which people don't act as if we had more than one planet Earth. It advocates and gives many practical examples and advice for most aspects of life. The difference between this approach and others is that it uses a powerful new tool – ecological footprint analysis – to help evaluate the success of one's practice. Measuring success using this tool will help us find out if we are not wasting our time.

This book recognises that ahead of us lies a long journey, but a necessary one. It uses the example of a pioneering Welsh policy in particular, One Planet Development, but also that of BioRegional and other urban case studies. At the moment it is easier for people to attempt to live this life in rural areas, although that is difficult enough in itself. So most of the examples are from rural case studies. There are urban examples and I anticipate future editions will include more.

We recognise that most people will not be able to do all of the things suggested in this book, but will take from it whatever they find beneficial and applicable in their own circumstances.

After the forewords by Pooran Desai and Jane Davidson, this book is divided into four parts. You can skip any of the sections if you wish:

1 A call for change: An essay which sets out the case for one planet living. It argues that our attitude to planning, land and development needs to change to incorporate the ecological footprint analysis tool that should be applied to every planning decision in order to ascertain whether it is sustainable.
2 Chapters Two and Three: how to find land, finance, and construct a management plan.
3 Chapters Four to Nine: detailed information and further reading on: land management, water, energy, building, food and transport.

4 **Chapter Ten:** Exemplary examples at all scales, followed by a conclusion and Jane Davidson's Afterword.

During the writing of this book a group of us set up the One Planet Council, to help further the principles and practices in this book, details of which are given close to the end of Part One.

Acknowledgements

From my experience of the 1970s' 'alternative society' – which tried to imagine another way of life; activism and cycling in London during the 1980s; working at the Centre for Alternative Technology in the 1990s publishing proven grass-roots eco-solutions; and as an environmental journalist, writer and researcher working with corporate, national and local leaders in the twenty-first century, I've learned a huge amount at all social and geographical scales, much of which has been distilled into this book. There's been remarkable progress in many areas, and at the same time a curious hesitation, until recently, to monitor and measure the results of our innovations. But in the last decade or more, this has changed.

And we've discovered that it's not just – or even – about the technology. It's about people, and the way they want to and can and dare to live their lives. There are so many people I would like to thank from whom I have learned, and not just during the active part of the research for this book. If I've left anybody out, I am sorry, but it does not mean you are forgotten.

First, a big thanks to Jane Davidson, former Environment Minister for Wales and probably the best Environment Minister the UK has ever had – what a shame she wasn't in Westminster – for prompting me to write the book. At the initial meeting were also Paul Wimbush and Rachel Shiamh, who have also been extremely helpful and contributed much of their special wisdom.

From Lammas, One Planet Development pioneers and the founding members of the burgeoning One Planet Council, who have provided case studies and feedback, as well as tolerating my presence on their sites, special thanks to: Hoppi Wimbush, Cassie and Nigel, Melissa, Andy and Jane, Jasmine and Simon Dale, all at Lammas, plus Tom next door, Welsh godfather of LID Tony Wrench at Brithdir Mawr, Samara Hawthorne, John Hargreaves, Tracey Styles and Mel Robinson at Cornerwood, Stefan Cartwright, Pete Linnell, Peter Barker, Dan and Sarah Moody, Bill at Hockerton Housing Project, Phil Corbett, Jay Andrews and Tom O'Kane.

Then there's organic smallholding and farming practitioners such as: John Gaffney and Steve Brown, Peter Mitchell, James and Tilla Waters, and all the people introduced to me by Gerry Gold of A World to Win and Transition Town Llandeilo. Mark Waghorn of Calon Cymru. The English godfather of LID: Simon Fairley.

I'd especially like to thank Ian Mitchell for teaching me much about organic growing, and Peter Harper, Cindy Harris, Pat Borer and many others too numerous to mention at the Centre for Alternative Technology. Peter also gave valuable feedback on the draft. Andy Rowland of Ecodyfi and the Dyfi Biosphere Reserve. George Monbiot, who put up with me and taught me much during our time together in Machynlleth. The varying staff at *Energy and Environmental Management* magazine down the years, including Charles Harkness and David Allaby for the break. The staff at Sustainable Cities Collective on the US east coast, for creating that amazing platform. Rob Hopkins of the Transition Town Network, tireless visionary; similarly, Pooran Desai of BioRegional.

My editors at Earthscan, Alice Aldous and Nicki Dennis, with a special thanks to Frank Jackson in Berlin, an old friend and colleague. Zoe Wangler of the Ecological Land Cooperative, whose members are already proving with ecological footprint analysis that the methods in this book work.

My wife, the wonderful and inspirational Helen Adam, who has already done much of what is in this book, for sense and sensibility.

Glen Peters of Tŷ Solar. Kelly Carter at the National House Building Council for further case studies. Andreas Delleske in Freiburg for his amazing work there. Peter Davies, Sustainable Development Commissioner for Wales, for listening (and talking). Sam Minas, for feedback. Karolina Rietzler for permission to use her thesis. Amanda Jackson for the beautiful photographs. And last, but not least, various officials who did not want to be named.

About the author

David is a writer and consultant on sustainability issues. He is a Special Consultant on Sustainable Cities Collective, the primary website for urban leaders globally; a founder and core group member of the One Planet Council; and the author of several books on sustainability, including: *Energy Management in Buildings*, *Energy Management in Industry*, *Solar Technology*, and *Sustainable Home Refurbishment*, all in The Earthscan Expert Guide series. Prior to this he was the News Editor and Opinion Writer of the UK's *Energy and Environmental Management* magazine for 13 years. Before that he was director of publications at the Centre for Alternative Technology.

On a lighter front, he has also written comics, including for Marvel Comics, been an editor of graphic novels for several publishers, and is a novelist – the winner of the HarperCollins contest to find a major new children's writer, with his science-fiction dystopia for young adults, *Hybrids*. His 2014 new novel, *Stormteller*, is on a related theme to this book. He lives in south Wales with his wife, the musician and composer Helen Adam. For more information, see his website: www.davidthorpe.info.

'Whoever said the world is not enough forgot that less is more.'

Foreword by Pooran Desai

In 2002, in partnership with The Peabody Trust, BioRegional completed our Beddington Zero (fossil) Energy Development, or BedZED, in south London. Designed with architect Bill Dunster, the 100-home development aimed to create a whole sustainable lifestyle. It has led to major environmental savings such as reducing electricity and water consumption by half and private car use by almost two thirds. Not everything has worked, like the wood-fired combined heat and power system – but it remains an inspiration. It was our analysis of BedZED, and measuring its performance against ecological footprint, which enabled us to coin the term 'one planet living' and lead a process to create a framework which is now being used around the world.

It has been a personal as much as a professional journey. I have lived at BedZED, together with BioRegional co-founder and my wife, Sue Riddlestone, and a number of our staff, since it was built. The sense of community is highlighted by the statistic that the average person here knows 20 of their neighbours by name – about four times the UK average. With more people walking and cycling than using their cars, I am sure it is delivering health benefits as well. There is a sweet spot where environmental, social and health benefits coincide.

The year 2002 was also the year in which Johannesburg, South Africa, hosted the World Summit on Sustainable Development. Working with Johannesburg EcoCity, we built an eco-community centre and demonstration eco-homes in Ivory Park Township on the outskirts of the city. Welsh First Minister Rhodri Morgan visited Ivory Park Township and our demonstration. We were able to tell him about one planet living and he invited me to present our experiences to him and some of his colleagues at the Welsh Parliament, which I did. I hope it helped sow a seed, along with the hard work of others in Wales, which has allowed the One Planet One Wales and One Planet Development concepts to germinate.

As I write this, the storms and floods which had battered or submerged so much of Wales and Southern England, have subsided but have left a mark on our consciousness. Scientists have been predicting warmer, wetter and stormier winters. The impacts of climate change are starting to hurt and will, in all probability, get worse. Science tells us we need to reinvent our relationship with the planet – the metrics of ecological footprint and planetary boundaries must be fundamental to our way of life. Now is the time to create new models. We have no option.

In rising to the challenge, we can make things better for ourselves. Technology can help us, alongside putting values of social and environmental stewardship at the heart of society. These aspirations are embodied in the Welsh commitment to a One Planet Future and are world-leading. The job in hand is to translate these aspirations into practical ways to live high-quality, happy and healthy lives within the environmental limits of the planet. It will be a journey with its challenges but also its joys.

This thought-provoking book summarises some of the approaches which can help us on the journey – so please read, learn, practise and share. There are many already on the journey and we can, together, co-create a better future.

Pooran Desai OBE HonFRIBA, co-founder, BioRegional and
One Planet Living.

Introduction by Jane Davidson

Why I believe we should all live 'One Planet Lives'

One of the key challenges for those of us who advocate living the One Planet Life is to sell the concept to our friends and families, neighbours and communities in a way that demonstrates a positive lifestyle change that enhances rather than diminishes our and their quality of life. Throughout this book you will read how those who have embraced this lifestyle feel fully liberated by their choice: they have reconnected with nature; they understand the seasons and where food comes from and the limitations of what can/cannot be grown or reared where they live; they can offer a different, more sustainable future to their offspring. Not everyone will want to take the great leap into the unknown, but all of us can use this book to help us demonstrate the principles of one planet living in one or more parts of our lives.

The community of people who want to live one-planet lives is growing daily across the world. Through social media, books, meetings, forums, real and virtual conversations, each lends another tips and hints for better lifestyles – this is a world of global cooperation rather than a world of competition, a world where your skills and my skills blend together to make a whole greater than the sum of its parts, and when you magnify that by the opportunity to exchange with more and more others then together we can create a community of interest that can easily demonstrate love and belonging, esteem and self-actualisation, as described by Maslow's hierarchy of needs. The highest needs of morality, creativity, spontaneity, problem solving, lack of prejudice and acceptance of facts are in fact much easier in a world built on empirical evidence and mutual self-esteem on a day to day basis, where you have to find solutions to your own problems yourself. But what there will be in abundance, is plenty of friendly advice and ideas from the previous pioneers – just the sort of friendly advice and support that will help you develop your own problem-solving skills.

Maslow's hierarchy of needs puts physiological needs – such as breathing, food, water, sex, sleep, homeostasis and excretion – at the base of everything human beings must satisfy. The next layer is safety – security of body, of resources, of employment, of family, of morality of health, of property. These basic needs are satisfied in a far more satisfying way in One Planet Lifestyles, because they are earned and actively contribute to an individual and mutual sense of self-esteem. For years, highly paid managers have been sent on team-building exercises – often in the country – to develop cooperative, innovative, imaginative, problem-solving skills to improve their business or service delivery back in the city; now not a day goes past that I don't have to exercise those skills in my daily life – with an enormous sense of achievement, of belonging and self-esteem. To reach self-actualisation, I would contend, is far easier living a One Planet Life, because those living such a life act accordingly; know what their impacts are and take decisions that reflect that. This is a huge contrast to traditional consumerist measures of success: respect on the basis of the size of your house, the amount you earn, the car you drive, the number of holidays you take abroad. Such measures of success are unsustainable as they encourage greater consumerism. In the absence of a coherent values system, it is no surprise that people who consume the most will discuss the importance of recycling and re-use while waiting for a flight. It is no surprise either, but a little more encouraging, that as energy prices rise, larger houses are becoming less popular – but there is still a long way to go before reducing our consumerism, for example through measuring our ecological footprint, will become the measure of success it needs to be for the future.

I don't live a One Planet Life, yet, but I'm on the way. I live in a refurbished eighteenth-century barn and have a full-time job looking after

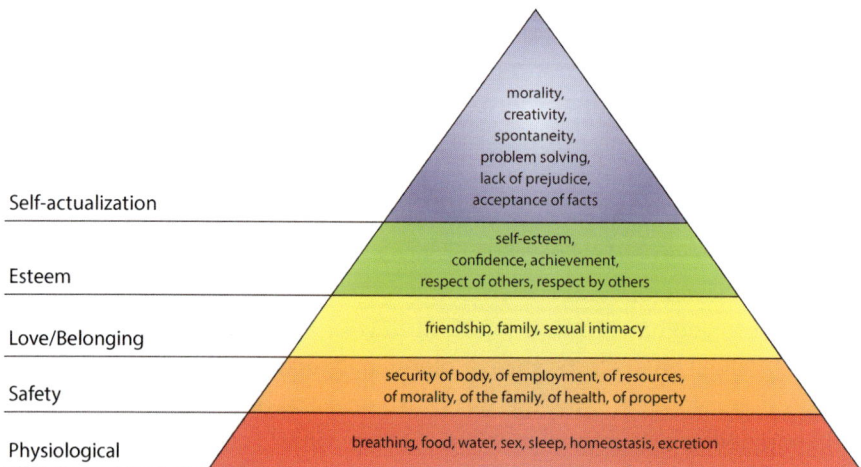

Self-actualization	morality, creativity, spontaneity, problem solving, lack of prejudice, acceptance of facts
Esteem	self-esteem, confidence, achievement, respect of others, respect by others
Love/Belonging	friendship, family, sexual intimacy
Safety	security of body, of employment, of resources, of morality, of the family, of health, of property
Physiological	breathing, food, water, sex, sleep, homeostasis, excretion

Maslow's hierarchy of needs

sustainability in a university some 30 miles away by car, but I do my best to live a one-planet lifestyle at home – and that choice is available to all of us irrespective of our accommodation. This is a fundamentally important point as most of us live in houses more than 20 years old – the new housing market contributes less than 1 per cent of housing needs a year – so what we do in our current houses will make a revolutionary change to the overall ecological and carbon footprint of the country we live in. My family's electricity costs (using Good Energy because it provides renewable energy) are matched by the income from our solar PV panels and we heat the house using fuel from our own woodland using a wood-fuelled range and underfloor heating.

In the three years my husband and I have managed our ten acres (6 acres woodland for fuel, 2 acre paddock, 1.5 acre allotment and 0.5 acre garden) we have now reached the point that we have fresh vegetables all year round, fresh or frozen fruit all year round, we trade hen and duck eggs for wine; we trade our vegetables for others we haven't grown; throughout the year we eat our own jams and jellies and drink our own cordials, sloe gin, redcurrant brandy, homemade grape wine, cider and apple juice. This year, we grew everything for our Christmas dinner apart from the turkey and the goose, and we are remedying that for next year. We could not have done this on our own: our neighbours give us their grass cuttings for compost, we give them eggs; we've traded firewood for horse manure and the loan of a chicken-house for a broody hen; the long-term loan of a trailer is also paid for in eggs. Neighbours and friends look after our ducks and chickens in return for similar services. This sense of community and shared purpose definitely gives us a better quality of life. As my husband also works away from home, we have not branched out into bigger animals yet, but that day will come as we definitely want to move into pigs and sheep and I am particularly tempted by the idea of homemade buffalo mozzarella.

In order to turn the self-sufficiency dream into a reality, you can't just plan it on paper, you have to make sure that you or someone in your family is physically strong enough to deliver on your changed lifestyle or that you can trade for those skills. Having lived on the edge of a city for 20 years, where we'd grown fruit and vegetables and kept chickens and ducks for much of that time, we knew we had those skills but no woodland management or chainsaw skills – which meant we could have fallen at Maslow's first hurdle.

If you are living a One Planet Life, the development of a management plan – excellent guidance is available from the Welsh Government Planning website in relation to One Planet Developments – will enable you to think your way through your basic needs, but if you are wanting to start this journey where you live now, some of the other things you need to think about are how you gain the skills you will need, such as learning how to grow or using a saw. Are you prepared to cut/collect /store/transport firewood in all weathers? We need 12 tons a year to keep us warm – that is a lot of wood! There are key lifestyle choices as well. Are you prepared to get up early to release your fowl from their fox-proof sleeping roosts, feed them and collect their eggs? Do you have enough time to look after animals well around your other commitments? Are you prepared to have low-carbon holidays – such as walking, cycling and rail travel – and only outside the growing season, unless you have neighbours/friends who can help you to keep going in your absence?

One-planet lifestyles are not life-choices for the fainthearted, but they will take you straight to the top of Maslow's hierarchy – you will have chosen to have an exciting, curious, ever-changing life to look forward to; a life regulated by the seasons and by light, a life that will leave you too exhausted to do anything other than crawl into bed in the growing season, but give you wonderful, fresh-tasting food free of chemicals; that will daily throw up wonderful surprises – I've just looked up while I'm writing to see a pheasant walk majestically past my field gate.

I was immensely privileged to be the Minister for Environment, Sustainability and Housing in Wales when the opportunity came along in 2009 to enshrine in the Welsh national planning system the idea of 'One Planet Developments' defined in the Welsh Government's Technical Advisory Note 6: 'Agricultural and Rural Development'. The development of this policy at national level is a testimony to the determination of the pioneering families at Lammas, the first planned eco-village in the UK, described later as a case study. Planning decision-making processes rely on custom and practice about what is acceptable in local areas over many years. I hoped that making such a policy national – i.e. across the whole of Wales – would normalise it and would encourage a range of One Planet Developments across Wales that would have local characteristics reflecting local circumstances, but would be part of a bigger government vision to encourage a national debate about low-impact lives. From my perspective, this was about a clear direction of travel – all future buildings and lifestyles should be low-impact and the pioneers of low-carbon, low-ecological-footprint lifestyles should be supported and encouraged as they forged a way forward in ways that would help others learn lessons in their wake and demonstrate positive responses to our ecological and carbon challenges.

Being granted permission to create a One Planet Development is a privilege. The successful applicant is being given permission to live on agricultural land when others cannot; the 'system' has designated him/ her an appropriate guardian of the earth, a teacher and leader of others, a prophet and scientist for future generations, a pioneer testing what will work for a better future in our carbon-constrained world. Achieving this privilege is not easy. Successful applicants have often felt bruised by the process, but each obstacle overcome is another problem solved, another hurdle crossed. Every planning application for low-impact development that is put in anywhere in the UK enables local planning officers to understand the issues better. Every application that is agreed contributes towards a better future for us all.

Good planning is key to success in gaining permission to create a One Planet Development; if you are the applicant, the management plan is your targets, action points and business plan, without which your land-use planning application will fail, but is also your principal tool to communicate your vision. The Welsh Government guidance – all 77 pages of it – can help applicants anywhere choose appropriate sites. Importantly, even though that guidance requires you in Wales to demonstrate how you will move from an ecological footprint of 2.4 global hectares per person to 1.8 global hectares per person over a maximum of five years, you don't have to account for any impacts as a result of other work you do that is separate from your livelihood from the site – so you can have another source of income or job, as my husband and I both do. This is really important in mainstreaming the idea of one-planet lifestyles.

What buildings look like is also a matter of taste. As you will see from the exemplary examples, that can be anything from a 'hobbit house', using naturally bent wood, to rammed earth or a modular construction on a timber frame. One Planet Developments can test the boundaries of building performance, while meeting building regulations and being zero-carbon over their lifetime. Just as the construction industry has had to demonstrate rigorous testing and monitoring of attempts to achieve zero-carbon new homes and refurbishments to establish what works and what doesn't, so One Planet houses can break new boundaries. You don't have to build your own house if you haven't the skills, although self-build may well be cheaper and is a much more common practice in Europe. What is exciting is that all zero-carbon homes use passive solar design – harnessing as much of the sun's light and heat into free energy as possible. Imagine living in a house with large south-facing windows, with your water heated by the sun through solar heating panels, with your electricity coming from the sun through PV panels and with a large south-facing conservatory. The first rule of energy is to use as little of it as possible and the second is to use nature first. All the features I've just described are often put forward by estate agents as positive features in large, expensive homes but come as standard in a One Planet Development.

From my perspective, the idea of national planning guidance supporting One Planet Developments was not to build 'hobbit houses' across Wales but for builders and developers to be experimental with local materials. There is nothing to stop a One Planet Development looking like any other house built from local materials, as you will see in the exemplars described in this book. Only last year, Tŷ Solar (Solar House) was built out of local wood as a demonstration house in north Pembrokeshire, according to Welsh Government space standards for social housing.

Slowly, and I hope surely, the revolution is starting. There are still major challenges; despite the One Planet Development policy being in place since 2010, most applications at the time of writing are still being turned down; the interface between planning and building regulations for low-impact developments needs to be resolved, as does insurance for non-traditional buildings in the age of the computer-programmed insurance market. But these issues are solvable. The Welsh Government's higher environmental standards are already paying off in terms of public buildings. The big challenge now is to ensure that those who want to be the pioneers of 'one planet living' are given a fair wind and that their planning applications are of the highest possible standard, taking into account all the relevant issues.

This book should be read by planners, by policymakers and by applicants. You will be challenged, but you will also be helped to make the best possible planning application to live lightly on the land. There is an increasing amount of support out there. The Lammas website is a huge resource for anyone wanting to go on this journey: www.lammas.org.uk. A new One Planet Council is being established as I write. The One Planet Council supports those who are making the transition to this more sustainable way of life by providing guidance and tools. It aims to work together with all those with an interest in One Planet Developments: Local Planning Authorities, policymakers, academics, landowners, and those already living on and planning to live on One Planet Development sites.

I hope this book will make every reader think about the maximum they can do in their lives to create a one-planet lifestyle – and if that does result in putting forward a successful planning application, don't keep your lessons to yourself. The more we share, the better our stewardship of our one planet will be.

John Rawls, the American philosopher, said that we should do unto future generations what we would have past generations do unto us. I am optimistic that just as my memories of my grandparents are memories of helping bring in produce from their gardens, that I will be able to teach my grandchildren similar values and skills, just as we've taught our children. As the anthropologist Margaret Mead said, *'The solution to adult problems tomorrow depends on large measure upon how our children grow up today'*. The more children who grow up in a 'One Planet Life', the better all our lives will be. The next big challenge is to reflect such commitments in the education system. What we can all do is resolve to be greener this year than we were last year, and next year than we were this year.

Jane Davidson
March 31st 2014

Jane Davidson *is the Director of a INSPIRE (Institute for Sustainability Practice, Innovation and Resource Effectiveness) at the University of Wales Trinity Saint David, which has introduced sustainability content into all students' experiences from 2013.*

From 2007 to 2011, she was Minister for Environment, Sustainability and Housing in Wales, where she was responsible for the Welsh Government agreeing to legislate to make sustainable development its central organising principle, the creation of the Wales coastpath, legislation on waste which has seen Wales come from behind the rest of the UK to be the lead recycling country in Britain, low-carbon planning requirements and the introduction of a charge on single-use carrier bags.

Part One
A call for change

We ask:

1   That to aim towards one planet living should become an underlying principle of planning and official policy as *de facto* the only objectively verifiable sustainable strategy.

2   That the same set of social and environmental criteria should be used to assess all planning applications to create a level playing field.

3   That these criteria, amongst others, should be informed by ecological footprint analysis, which enables all projects to be compared for their environmental impact.

4   That official attitudes to land use should change to help rural areas use one planet living methods to become more productive and more populated, and urban areas more green.

We make this call for the following reasons, which we substantiate below:

The One Planet Life

1   Results in more productive land use, with far fewer environmental impacts.
2   Creates more employment than conventional agriculture.
3   Promotes greater physical and mental health and well-being, reducing the burden on the welfare state and health service.
4   Requires no agricultural subsidies, unlike some conventional farming.
5   Improves the local economy, resilience and food security.
6   Therefore is more sustainable and gives excellent value.

1 We only have one planet!

Just one. Obviously. But the way some people carry on you'd think we had five – in some cases even eight – wonderful blue, vibrant orbs just like planet Earth, rotating round our life-giving sun. Perhaps they imagine these worlds – duplicates of ours except minus human beings – are hiding on the far side of the sun. Sitting there conveniently, so that when we've used up all the resources on this planet, we can go and tap into those. How simple the future might be if we could. We'd probably need more than one extra planet. But hey, you never know what might turn up.

As far as I know, astronomers haven't detected any more earth-like planets in the attainable vicinity.

What a shame.

The problem is, that with a human population projected to rise up to nine billion or so by 2050, we already use up more resources provided by the Earth's land surface and bodies of water than are being naturally replaced. Coincidentally, I'm writing this on 20 August 2013, dubbed by the Global Footprint Network and the New Economics Foundation as 'Earth Overshoot Day'[1] for this calendar year. This marks the date when humanity as a whole has exhausted nature's budget for the year, assuming we start each one with a fresh balance sheet. From this point on for the rest of the year, humanity is operating in overdraft, creating an ecological deficit by drawing down local resource stocks, polluting the land and seas, and accumulating carbon dioxide in the atmosphere.

The ecological footprint

We know this thanks to an amazing tool. Ecological footprint analysis is a resource-accounting tool that helps countries understand their ecological balance sheet and gives them the data necessary to manage their resources and secure their future. The unit used is global hectares (gha) per capita, that is to say the amount of average quality land area required to provide all the things we need as individuals, not to mention to absorb the pollution we create. It's different for the inhabitants of different countries. It is also different for individuals depending upon their way of life. While it's true that there are concerns[2] about the accuracy of some of the tool's assumptions (for example, the scoring may need tweaking for different types of land-use) there's no denying its general message. Moreover, the methodology behind the numbers is being constantly improved.

The most recent data is from 2010.[3] In that year, the USA had the highest footprint in the world: 8 gha per capita; but it has a biological carrying capacity of 3.9 gha per individual. This gives it a deficit of 4.1 gha per individual. In other words, Americans are using over twice as much as they

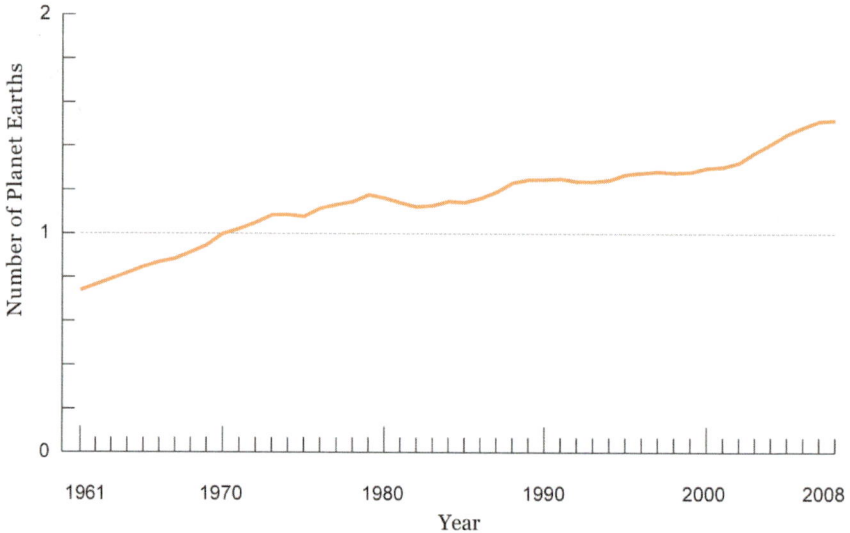

Figure 1.1 The world's ecological footprint since 1961. This is an average amount for every person on the planet. It increases because the population is increasing. As many people consume few resources, it means that the ecological footprint of the middle class and rich, of whom there are more and more, especially in the fast-growing developing countries, is outweighing the 20 per cent of the world's population who live in extreme poverty (under $1.25 per day).
Source: Global Footprint Network, 2011.

can sustainably manage. The United Kingdom has an average ecological footprint of 4.9 hectares, with a biocapacity of 1.3 ha. In other words, British citizens are using more than three and a half times what they can sustainably manage.

Another way of getting your head around this is to divide up the useful land area of average quality that we use on the planet by the population level. Doing this gives an average area of land for each individual of 1.8 ha. But we are using collectively, on average, more than twice as much as this. So, again on average, we are behaving as if we had at least one more planet like this one.

The financial crash of 2008 occurred because banks were lending more than they were receiving and people were borrowing more than they could pay back. This is exactly what's happening now with our global resource use. A potential future ecological crash promises to be much worse than the economic shock of 2008. Because, unless we consume a great deal less and recycle or reuse a lot more raw materials, there's no way we can pay back what we've taken. Just pause for a moment and imagine the consequences of this: refugees, starvation, violence, wars and even more food banks; and the poor will suffer the most.

At least we understand that what we borrow from banks we will have to pay back some day – with interest. We still do not get it, that we borrow – not take – from the natural world. The Global Footprint Network[4] – one of the organisations that works out ecological footprinting – believes us to be on track to require the resources of two planets well before mid-century. Actually, I think this is a severe underestimate, and Fred Pearce, the environmental correspondent of the *New Scientist* magazine, agrees.[5]

So: the future will be sustainable or not at all. This truism implies that humanity as a whole will have to learn to live within its means, otherwise millions – perhaps billions – of us will not be able to survive at all.

This is where the idea of The One Planet Life comes from. We all have to be able to live within the planet's means while affording a good standard of living for everyone. So if we are to lift out of extreme poverty the 1.2 billion people who currently live on under $1.25 per day, the rich will have to consume less, and the way everyone lives will have to change.

This process of change will work on several levels: individuals can reduce their own ecological impacts, using the ideas in this book; businesses, in particular industries, can move towards 'closed-loop' resource use and net zero fossil-fuelled energy use (using a combination of renewable energy, energy efficiency and carbon offsetting); and governments, whether national, regional or local, can use their legislative and planning powers to support

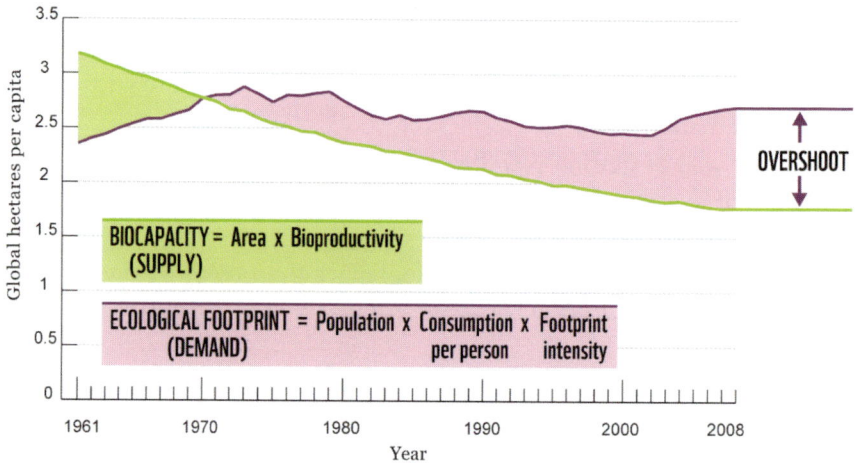

Figure 1.2 The overshoot of the capacity of the world's biological systems to accommodate the consumption levels of humanity is increasing. The pink area shows the environmental deficit.
Credit: Global Footprint Network, 2011.

healthier and more sustainable ways of life for their citizens: to make it easier for them to live the One Planet Life.

The components of the ecological footprint that these governments at every level are able to influence concern things like: the energy performance standards of buildings; the carbon content of energy; the treatment of waste using the Waste Hierarchy (see Chapter 3); managing water catchments better; the provision of subsidised public transport that people want to use; making urban areas walkable and cycle-able and combating car dependency; situating housing near to jobs and shops, schools and hospitals; incorporating nature in cities; preventing pollution; and encouraging the growing of food within and near to the places where it is consumed.

The good news is that things like this are already happening in many places around the world. Some examples are given towards the end of this book. One country has even begun explicitly to use the ecological footprint as a planning tool. That country is Wales, a part of the UK that has jurisdiction only over some of its policy areas and no tax-raising powers. It has chosen the measure of the ecological footprint to help it determine whether some activities are in line with its constitutional aim of securing sustainable development. It has adopted a Sustainable Development Scheme, called 'One Wales: One Planet', that includes an objective that: 'within the lifetime of a generation, Wales should use only its fair share of the earth's resources, and our ecological footprint be reduced to the global average availability of resources – 1.88 global hectares per person in 2003'.[6] In 2006 the ecological footprint for each Welsh citizen was 4.41 global hectares.

The golden thread

'Sustainable development is a golden thread that winds its way through all that we do', asserted the civil servant in charge of planning policy in the Welsh Government, in conversation with me in his office in Cathays Park, Cardiff, in September 2013.[7] Although these words echo strongly those of the UK government's National Planning Policy Framework (cited by Communities Secretary Eric Pickles, see below) I do believe he wasn't being cynical, and that there is a genuine commitment to sustainable development in Wales, even though it is not yet clear what this will mean in practice. This is being embedded in something called a Future Generations (Wales) Bill which, at the time this book went to press, was in the consultation stage. It's the name the government has given to its bill for advancing sustainable development, because they think that by placing the emphasis upon children and their children's children, the people of Wales can begin to understand what sustainable development actually means in practice, rather than being a bit of overused jargon. There has been a popular national conversation in which all citizens were encouraged to participate, and many did.

Ecological footprint analysis will, it is expected, be used as a tool to monitor, in the context of the Act when it is passed, the sustainability of all development that arises as a result of spending by the Welsh government. The idea began, as Jane Davidson explains in her Foreword, with the need to permit low-impact developments on agricultural land. These types of development have come to be called One Planet Developments, and they are where a particular version of the One Planet Life is being trialled. It is partly on the experience of people living in these developments that much of this book is based.

One Planet Developments

So how does this work? One Planet Developments should, according to the Welsh Government guidance, initially 'achieve an ecological footprint of 2.4 global hectares per person or less in terms of consumption and demonstrate clear potential to move towards 1.88 global hectare target over time'.[8] They are assessed using an ecological footprinting tool devised by a different organisation than the Global Footprint Network – the Stockholm Environment Institute (SEI).[9] This body was established in 1989 by the Swedish Government and has a reputation for rigorous and objective scientific analysis in the field of environment and development. It has pioneered the use of ecological footprint analysis (EFA) so that production and consumption can become more sustainable and we can move towards an economy in which there is no waste.

One Planet Development in Wales came as 'an exogenous force from elsewhere', said the civil servant I talked to. He was referring to Jane Davidson, because it 'would not have happened without her'. Her conviction as Environment Minister that it was the right thing to do 'lay behind the revision of Technical Advice Note 6 (known as TAN 6)' – which contains the policy – 'and Planning Policy Wales (PPW)'. This key document says:

> Land-based One Planet Developments located in the open countryside should provide for the minimum needs of the inhabitants in terms of income, food, energy and waste assimilation over a period of no more than five years from the commencement of work on the site. This should be evidenced by a management plan produced by a competent person(s). The management plan should set out the objectives of the proposal, the timetable for development of the site and the timescale for review. It should be used as the basis of a legal agreement relating to the occupation of the site, should planning consent be granted.[10]

One Planet Development as defined by the Welsh government is applicable to new low-impact developments in the open countryside, but TAN 6 leaves open the possibility that they could occur in, or on the edge of, urban areas too. So far, it hasn't done, but there is no reason why it cannot. The Welsh government saw TAN 6 as a way of freeing up the planning system to allow these developments. As the official said:

> It confirms the definition of low-impact development to come forward in a way that is sustainable and does not drive a coach and horses through the planning system, which has a duty to protect the open countryside and environment from unfettered development. So it's a mechanism by which we sought to loosen the policy agenda to allow this kind of development but caveat it very very tightly to make sure that the system is not abused by people who just want homes in the open countryside.

We shall meet this fear of 'unfettered development' again later. Amongst the 8,000 planning applications a year for housing, those for One Planet

Developments are very few. At the time of writing, as far as we are aware, there are 13 applications at various stages.[11] Just one has received permanent planning permission.

Low-impact development and one planet living

One Planet Development as practised at the moment can be seen as a type of low-impact development (LID).[12] This was a term coined by Simon Fairlie (a founding residents of Tinkers Bubble, Somerset, a high profile LID, and a former editor of the *Ecologist* magazine) in his book, *Low Impact Development*.[13] He defined it as 'development that, through its low negative environmental impact, either enhances or does not significantly diminish environmental quality.' But One Planet Development in the future could – and must – take other forms. one planet living, as defined by Pooran Desai of BioRegional in his eponymous book,[14] points to another approach.

Pooran Desai's definition is contained in ten principles: zero waste, zero carbon, the use of sustainable water, transport and materials, restoring biodiversity and using local and sustainable food, and enhancing local community ties, equity, health and happiness. Those signing up to BioRegional's action plans commit to certain targets en route to these aspirations. They largely apply to city dwelling and not rural dwelling.

The criteria for LIDs include: integrated site management and use, reversibility (leaving the land, after use, essentially as it was before), minimised resource consumption, renewable resource use, on-site waste processing, and positive environmental impacts. It typically, but doesn't have to, involves the practice of agroecology, a 'holistic' approach to designing land use, buildings, communities and businesses as sustainable systems.

Low-impact development as practised in the UK and elsewhere have, up till recent years, been characterised by people living in tipis, yurts and roundhouses, or constructions based on wattle-and-daub, pole frames, cob, straw bales, rammed earth, earth-cover and the like, and not necessarily attempting a degree of self-sufficiency. All of these structures are easy and quick to build, low tech, often based on traditional and vernacular architecture, and have low embodied energy/carbon, often sourced from local and/ or reused materials.

This is different in several ways from BioRegional's approach,[15] which is one that will suit most people. While criticising official building regulations for new buildings for not taking embodied energy into account, BioRegional believes that it is better to work within rather than outside of the system. Buildings may therefore include high-tech equipment such as heat pumps and mechanical ventilation with air conditioning, in a level of airtight construction approaching Passivhaus standard. These buildings may well have a higher embodied energy than traditional LIDs and will consume more energy, but it may be renewable energy. Their homes, like BedZed in Sutton, South London (see Chapter 10), are typically in cities, so their inhabitants may require less heating and use public transport, but will grow little of their own food. Their ecological footprint may still be too high. How to bring it down further is the subject of ongoing research.

Self-sufficiency

Another ancestor of the One Planet Life is John Seymour's gospel of self-suf-ficiency, as explained in his seminal book,[16] originally published in 1970 but constantly updated since then. It is no coincidence that the smallholding/farm on which he developed his praxis is located in Pembrokeshire, which is also home to Brithdir Mawr and Lammas, and many other low-impact dwellings and smallholdings. A recently built roundhouse at Brithdir Mawr contains an efficient stove made by Seymour. But nowadays no one believes that it is really possible for a family to be completely self-sufficient and live a reasonable lifestyle. Instead, people take from Seymour's books what they can use in their own lives, something I expect to happen with this one. They will do whatever they can, where they can. Whatever is most appropriate.

One Planet Development is an evolution and improvement upon low-impact living, aimed at encouraging relatively self-sufficient sustainable developments. Some people describe it as having high impact – positive impact that is, on the environment, health and communities where they are located. It is based partly on the belief, for which we will make the case, that the countryside can sustainably support a greater density of population than at present, as it did once in the past. To support a greater population, there needs to be a change in land use that will require more labour and an improvement in soil quality compared to that used for typical grazing land. One Planet Development is just one type of One Planet Life, but the only one that is currently being measured using ecological footprint analysis.

This is what is so powerful, unique and revolutionary about it. It's an exciting, real-life experiment, generating unprecedented data about what really works – and what doesn't – in terms of living within our means. And we hope everybody can learn something from it.

Proponents of the One Planet Life believe that, for example, the UK can in principle supply all its food needs from the land. But could it?

Could the UK feed itself?

To reduce its ecological footprint, the UK must produce more of the food it consumes. Food supply currently comprises 20–25 per cent of the total footprint of a typical city (between 1.12 gha (Leicester) and 1.52 gha (Durham) in 2007).[17] Feeding the entire population would certainly entail changes – in land use, agricultural and horticultural practice, and diet. But would there be any benefits? A report called Zero Carbon Britain (ZCB), published in 2013,[18] says there would be several. It lists: improved health, reduced obesity and vastly reduced greenhouse gas emissions. Other benefits would be reduced pollution from nitrates into watercourses, and increased biodiversity, employment and food security. In total, a reduction in our ecological footprint.

Currently 78 per cent of UK land is given over to agriculture. Agricultural food production is responsible for just under 10 per cent of total UK greenhouse gas emissions, or about $44.8MtCO_2e$ in 2010.[19] Over half (55 per cent) is due to nitrous oxide emissions from fertiliser application. In 2012 we imported about 42 per cent of all the food we ate; this resulted in at least a further 59 $MtCO_2e$ per year. Greenhouse gas emissions from land-use change abroad attributable to food consumption in the UK are up to $100MtCO_2e$ per year. Emissions from the UK food chain amount to 115 $MtCO_2e$, including transporting and processing goods.

The ZCB report concluded that the UK could feed itself – but also foresees a massive change in diet to vegetarianism, and giving over much land to growing biofuels. At present only 3 per cent of the UK population is reported to be vegetarian or vegan and 5 per cent partially vegetarian,[20] so this would be a major cultural shift.

Simon Fairlie[21] has also calculated the ability of Britain to meet its food needs from our available agricultural land. His 2007 article *Can Britain Feed Itself*? evaluated six land-use scenarios, ranging from 'chemical with livestock' to 'vegan permaculture', and again concluded that Britain could feed a population of 60.6 million people with varying degrees of flexibility, but only if its population ate less meat.

A further exercise was conducted by Ed Hamer in the same magazine five years later,[22] by which time the UK's population had increased by a further two million. It found that 'it is still possible to feed 62.3 m people a standard but varied diet with very little change in the way we farm today', and this could create a further 4,000 jobs. He then raised the question: 'how many people could we employ if we radically changed the way we farm?'

This question has been investigated by Vicki Hird from the Sustainable Agriculture Food and Environment Alliance (SAFE – now Sustain)[23]. She concluded that: 'By switching support away from the richest farm sectors (such as arable) and providing support for sustainable agriculture, it is possible to protect the environment, whilst facilitating job creation: a double yield'.

Job creation

An attempt to put a figure on the number of jobs that would be created if we wanted to feed ourselves and reduce our ecological footprint was made by the Soil Association in 2009. It commissioned a report from Reading University that compared yields of indigenous foods that could be produced in England and Wales under organic production (which produces half the greenhouse gas emissions) with the volumes currently produced under 'conventional' (non-organic) production. The report used a subset of data from organic certified farms collected by Defra's Farm Business Survey, and scaled the figures up to national level. It found that over 150,000 jobs would be created, almost a doubling of current levels.

Organic land management, or agroecology in some form or other, is therefore more labour dependent than conventional agriculture. It is also a requirement of One Planet Development. It should come as no surprise that in a more sustainable world we would have to replace excess carbon emissions (energy supplied by fossil fuels) with more manual labour, as well as with renewable energy. We can also replace some of it with animal energy – which itself gives us a useful by-product: manure.

The Spanish example

A sustainable future practising the One Planet Life will therefore value jobs over efficiency. This has been proven in Spain by a very successful village-scale 'one-planet' type development. Marinaleda village in Andalusia hosts a cooperative that manages a farm of 1,200 hectares, deliberately choosing to cultivate crops that create jobs – such as peppers, artichokes, fava beans, olives, green beans and broccoli. All of these require processing in the form of canning, preserving and jarring to create added value and more jobs in factories. 'Our aim was not to create profit, but jobs,' says the mayor, Sánchez Gordillo. His model must be successful since he has been re-elected in every election since the first one he won in 1979 aged 30.

A reporter called Dan Hancox[24] went there to investigate. He wrote: 'The town co-operative does not distribute profits: any surplus is reinvested to create more jobs. Everyone in the co-op earns the same salary, €47 (£40) a day for six and a half hours of work: it may not sound like a lot, but it's more than double the Spanish minimum wage.' The area is now transformed into one of high employment, contrasted with the high unemployment in much of the rest of Spain caused by its economic crisis.

'Paradoxically, in light of Spain's staggering unemployment figures, they still need more people to join their co-operative, and have more farmland than they can currently cultivate,' wrote Hancox. According to Florence, a French woman who lives in Somonte, a village an hour away which has emulated this model, its land was some of the most fertile in Spain, but had for decades been used by the government to grow corn, to bring in European subsidies, 'creating next to no work, and no produce; the corn was left to rot'. As we shall see below, subsidies have distorted land use in Britain as well.

A food revolution

Wales' Commissioner for Sustainable Futures, Peter Davies, is of the view that while it is 'not desirable' for a country, community or a household to be self-sufficient in food,

> There is no question that a significant growth in local food growing and supply is required. There are many benefits in terms of health, wellbeing and social cohesion, and we must accelerate this as there are also clear benefits to local economies. There will still be an export advantage and opportunity for Welsh meat, but we must address the fact we have two parallel universes: sheep and beef and fruit and vegetables. You hardly ever see farmers at gatherings for local food and vice versa. The debate at a policy level is dominated by the dairy and red-meat producers, led by the Welsh Farmers Union, because they are big contributors to the national economy. Some community-supported agriculture schemes (CSAs) cross these boundaries, but they are the exception. The Welsh Farmers Union needs to be brought into the dialogue, while we also need to address a massive shortage of horticulture skills.[25]

The contradictions in our present attitude towards land use are graphically described here by Davies. A food revolution is required. Commercial-scale agriculture is dominated by subsidies, yet it is still considered not to be sufficiently productive, because genetically modified seed producers like Monsanto and Syngenta use the argument that we cannot feed the world's growing population without them in order to promote their patented products. One-planet-living policies alone cannot engender the food revolution. Yet one-planet smallholdings and some Community Supported Agriculture schemes are far more productive than conventional agriculture, without subsidies and using no artificial inputs. Instead, they use organic and agroecology growing techniques. The parallel worlds identified by Davies need to be unified by dialogue and legislation.

Recolonising the countryside

Encouraging one planet living on a wider scale would be one way to provide employment and livelihood so the UK can improve its food security and reduce its ecological footprint. But replacing fertilisers, tractors and pesticides with labour means more people living in the countryside. This is extremely difficult within current planning guidelines and culture. They were not designed to make it easy to obtain planning permission for new residential accommodation in rural areas. The OPD policy is designed to address this failure. OPD thus potentially represents nothing less than an attempt at social engineering; to recolonise and regenerate the countryside.

And why not? Before the heyday of the industrial revolution and the Enclosures Act, the British countryside was much more densely populated. It has since fallen from a maximum of 3.84 million in 1851 to 1.2 million in 2001.[26] By 1911, the population of rural districts in England and Wales had decreased by about half since 1850.[27] By 2010, the population density for Wales was 145 people per square kilometre, with two thirds (slightly under two million) living in urban (greater than 10,000 population) areas, concentrated mostly in the southeast of the country.[28] This is demonstrated by the number of derelict stone hulls sprouting vegetation, former farm labourers' family homes, that can still be seen dotted around the Welsh countryside, despite waves of hippies and wealthier English incomers buying up the most salvageable of them.

Many other remote areas of the British countryside would benefit from higher levels of population density, provided it was introduced in a sensitive and sustainable manner. Many areas (about two thirds, in fact[29]) of Wales are given over to sheep farming – which would not be economic were it not for subsidies. There are two sheep for every three people in the principality: approximately two million. The lamb and mutton currently produced on 3.6 million hectares of rough pasture – approximately 15 per cent of the land area of the UK – represent just 1.5 per cent of our national diet, according to Simon Fairlie.[30] Furthermore, tens of thousands of sheepskin fleeces are burnt every year because there is not a sufficient market demand (although with targeted support this could be created, e.g. for insulation, instead of using polystyrene EPS/XPS).

Sheep farms need subsidies to work, the farmers' union constantly tells us. But One Planet Developments can only be permitted without direct public subsidy. They are more productive, but hard to get planning permission for. Am I the only one to be puzzled by the logic here?

In 2009–2010 the average subsidy for sheep farms on the hills was £53,000, while the average net farm income was £33,000,[31] suggesting that the average sheep farmer subsidised his income to the tune of £20,000. Unsustainable farming practices are heavily supported by subsidy in Less Favoured Areas (80 per cent of the agricultural land area of Wales). The UK National Ecosystem Assessment (NEA)'s chapter on Wales[32] documents that about 37.4 per cent of Wales is Enclosed Farmland, consisting of 34 per cent Improved Grassland and just 3.4 per cent Arable and Horticultural land, a balance which OPD demonstrates can be shifted.

The value of LIDs is undisputed:

> What is most striking is that LID makes positive contributions to all three aspects of sustainability together, without trading them off against each other. In this respect LID appears to be an intrinsically sustainable form of development. LID's weakest contribution is economic, but it is arguable that LID does not set out to make large monetary contributions to the economy, as it is a subsistence-based livelihood. There is little evidence either that residents of LID are an economic burden on society.[33]

The truth is, that because of the EU Common Agricultural Policy (CAP) subsidies, the opposite is true. Enclosed Farmland may have certain value for provisioning and cultural services in Wales, which needs to be recognised, but it also imposes significant disbenefits: greenhouse gas emissions, diffuse water pollution and losses to biodiversity, which the One Planet Life does not.

Each OPD conversion of a sheep farm would therefore save an average of £53,000 of taxpayer's money, as well as making the land more productive, improving biodiversity, and reducing carbon emissions from livestock.

OPDs intrinsically promote a more sustainable level of food production, because whereas farmers constantly complain that they cannot afford to produce fruit and vegetables for resale at a competitive market price, and so do not do so, those choosing to live a low-impact life are happy to do so, and without high levels of artificial input such as nitrogen fertilisers and pesticides which themselves have a global warming effect.

The multiple benefits of OPD

There is, therefore, a double economic benefit, as well as several environmental ones, for switching a certain proportion of rural land use to one planet living. A level of greater population density increases sustainability in the sense that there are economic and social benefits from greater demand for local services. This encourages more young people to stay in the area, with their families, where there is employment, increasing social cohesion and community resilience.

Even in upland areas, where it is thought that less can be grown, in previous centuries land was cultivated using a form of land-use rotation. Simon Fairlie recounts that 'upland areas followed a form of "convertible husbandry" where enclosed fields were grazed by sheep for ten years or more and then were ploughed up for a spell of arable production before being put back to grass'.[34] He observes that 'this cycle could provide enough fertility for the modest output of grain necessary to maintain the local economy without resorting to the more labour intensive business of bringing in nutrients from the outlying saltus'. In other words, the sheep fertilise the soil, and remove the need for imported petrochemical fertilisers; but grazing for too long does deplete soil quality, so rotation has a dual benefit.

This form of upland land management, in the future, could be practised alongside OPD and a modest amount of rewilding, as envisaged in George Monbiot's book *Feral*. Monbiot argues in his book 'against a mass rewilding of high-grade farmland, because of the threat this could present to global food supplies'.[35] One planet living might in this context coexist with 'convertible husbandry' and a level of rewilding, shading into some form of managed woodlands populated by huntable wild mammals such as deer and wild boar, which have useful functions in clearing land for cultivation and nutrient recycling, as well as large wildfowl.

This is a patchwork picture of land use appropriate to its locality that balances the benefits of environmentally friendly management with the need for food security. Just as smallholdings are a micro-patchwork of different vegetable and fruit plots and animal husbandry, as well as barns, workshops and accommodation buildings, so the macro level of land use can become patchwork too.

The advantages of agroecology

This book advocates some form of agroecology as a design and food-providing method (existing residents often call it permaculture, although the terms are not strictly interchangeable). A study,[36] completed in 2012 at Cumbria University into the mixed growing of different vegetables in 24 different sites throughout mainland Britain, found productivity using Permaculture methods was "on average, 3.4 kg harvested from a square-metre of the low diversity plots for every hour of effort put in". 3.5 kg per square metre equates to 35 tonnes per hectare. This is over 4 to 5 times greater than average UK wheat yields of around 7–8 tonnes per hectare on the best soil. While there is little doubt that labour-intensive food production from small plots in developed countries like the UK produces higher yields than conventional dairy or arable agriculture, there is a regrettable lack of academic research that compares the relative benefits of different growing methods and land management to food production, value and the environment, and Permaculture has seemed to resist comparative studies. The data on organic vs. non-organic cultivation is also problematic. In this ongoing debate, the wider impacts of fertiliser and pesticide production are often ignored. Yet a global survey by the UN International Fund for Agricultural Development (IFAD)'s Office of Evaluation has found that small farmers making the shift to organic production yields increased rapidly and revenues grew.[37]

Dr Michel Griffon, Director General, National Research Agency (ANR), France, has developed the concept of "ecologically intensive agriculture"[38] as a solution to feeding the world's growing population. Acknowledging that the ecological and economic costs of the Green Revolution have proved to be considerable, he argues that a more holistic approach is needed that takes into account the productivity of the entire ecosystem. This is what is referred to as integrated agriculture, including the management of soil, water, plants, animals, diseases and pests, and the management of the landscape as a whole. In a study led by Oxford University scientists, 'integrated' farms that maximised crop yields whilst using environmentally-friendly techniques – such as crop rotation, organic fertilisers, over winter cover crops, and minimal use of pesticides – were found to use less energy and generate lower greenhouse gas emissions per unit of production than both organic and conventional farms.[39]

But Dr Griffon argues that ecologically intensive agriculture will go further than integrated agriculture by imitating natural phenomena and using them as an inspiration for the development of new inputs, in particular by enhancing the quality of the soil using many of the techniques cited in the chapters later in this book on growing and land management, such as mulch covering and encouraging earthworms in soil.

The opportunity in Wales

The chance for a land-use change to reduce our ecological footprint is currently more likely in Wales than in England or Scotland. The policy schema *One Wales: One Planet,* which will be updated by the Future Generations (Wales) Bill, is complemented by the Living Wales initiative. This is establishing a Natural Environment Framework for governance in Wales, based on the ecosystem approach. Sustainable development is a central organising principle through which all these polices will be developed and delivered, and by means of which natural capital will be conserved or enhanced.

The Living Wales policy 'recognises the value and importance of the efforts of every individual contributing to a healthy environment, and it aims for prosperous livelihoods, where the provision of public goods and services is well rewarded and where nature thrives... Wales aims to be the first country to explicitly embed the ecosystem approach into governance and grass-roots action, based on sound scientific evidence.'[40]

Jeff Cuthbert, AM, Minister for Communities and Tackling Poverty, is on record as saying that the aim of the Future Generations (Wales) Bill is to tackle poverty through the provision of affordable housing and 'contribute to long-term environmental benefits through consideration of materials and energy efficiency – building more resilient and low-carbon sustainable homes'.[41] He has visited One Planet Developments, one of which is in his constituency, and given them the thumbs up. The Welsh Government has appointed Peter Davies, as Wales' Commissioner for Sustainable Futures, to provide guidance. He has said that the process must be meaningful, and that it is critical that it 'both directly connects to the decision-making process in the public sector and to the wider public', as well as 'to the UN's Global Millennium Development Goals, which will be introduced post 2015, with the intention that all countries will align their contributions towards achieving these goals, and to ecological footprint analysis'.

There is another way in which Wales – along with a part of England and parts of the rest of the world – is helping to lead the world to a more sustainable type of land use.

Biosphere reserves

Nestled on the edge of mid Wales, where I lived for nearly 20 years, is an example of another piece of this emerging jigsaw: the beautiful Dyfi Valley. From its windswept hills down to its coastal wetlands and long, sandy beaches, it is one of 621 so-called biosphere reserves, test beds for

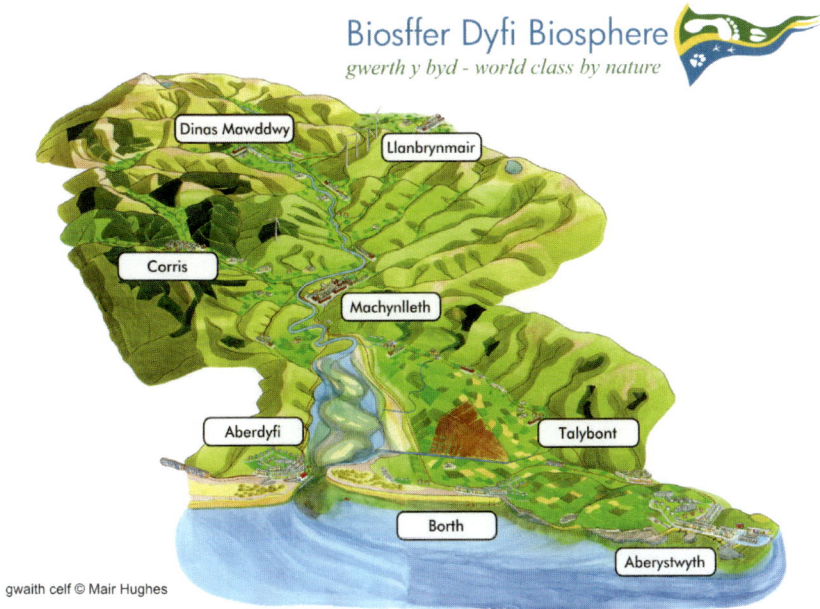

Figure 1.3 Map of the Dyfi Valley Biosphere on the west coast of mid-Wales.
Credit: Mair Hughes.

a new way of living. Surprisingly, this catchment area around the town of Machynlleth shares this status with many World Heritage sites such as the central Amazon, Huanglong in China, Mount Kenya and India's Nanda Devi. It contains a diverse collection of habitats and land use: acid moorland, conifer plantations, mixed woodland, stock grazing pastures, floodplains, rare sand dunes, peat-based wetlands, urban ecologies and more. The status of biosphere reserve is accorded by UNESCO and I believe that the One Planet Development model of land management has a notable analogue in the definition of a UNESCO Biosphere.

UNESCO's World Network of Biosphere Reserves are areas of ecosystems which are internationally recognized within the framework of UNESCO's Programme on Man and the Biosphere (MAB), as explained in its Statutory Framework of the World Network of Biosphere Reserves. Far from being the quarantined nature conservation zones which UNESCO originally supported, these designated locations in the world are, like Lammas, living laboratories of how human beings can successfully and sustainably live alongside nature while preserving and enhancing biodiversity. Lest it be thought that most are in developing countries, there are also examples in Germany, Hungary, Italy, Japan (Yakushima Island), Ayer's Rock and Macquarie Island in Australia, eight locations in Russia and nine in the USA.

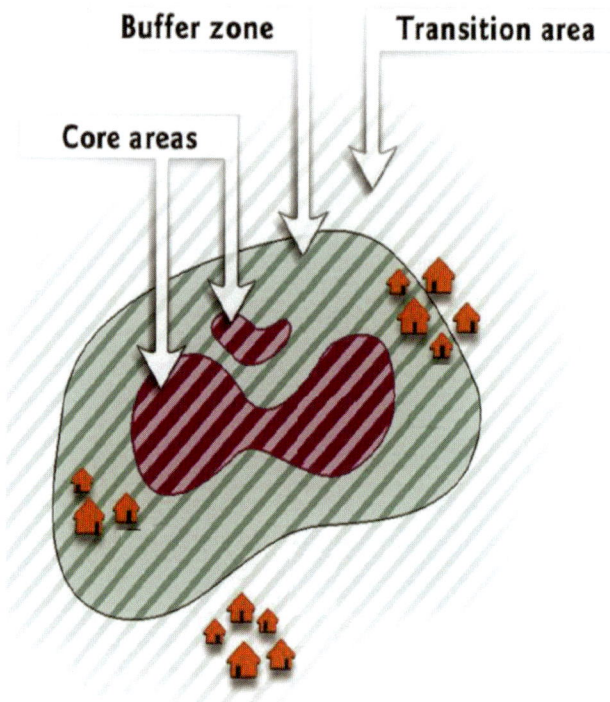

Figure 1.4 Concept of the UNESCO Biosphere. Housing and industry can coexist with conservation except in the core areas, as long as it does so sustainably.
Credit: MAB.

What do these areas have in common? In order to achieve Biosphere status, a region must have a conservation function, to preserve genetic resources, species, ecosystems and landscapes; a development function, to foster sustainable economic and human development, and a logistic support function, to support demonstration projects, environmental education and training, and research and monitoring related to local, national and global issues of conservation and sustainable development.

In practice this means that each reserve contains three elements. First, there are securely protected core areas for conserving biological diversity, monitoring minimally disturbed ecosystems, and undertaking non-destructive research and education. Each of these is surrounded by a clearly identified buffer zone, which is used for cooperative activities, including environmental education, recreation and research. Finally, there is a flexible transition area, which may contain a variety of agricultural activities, settlements, industry and other uses, in which local people work together to manage and sustainably develop the area's resource.[42]

You can see what this has in common with OPDs: both represent an attempt to accommodate the struggle between human needs and the needs of the rest of the planet. Both seek to reconcile humanity's voracious expansion and appetites with the planetary life-support system upon which it depends, but which can exist independently of us, given the chance. Both are developing models and templates for how to do this. Both have an educational role. Both result in an interlocking patchwork of different but complementary land uses.

There we have that word patchwork again. There is a simple reason why a patchwork design for land use is more productive and good for bio-diversity, at whatever scale: it is because the place where two eco-systems or habitats meet (e.g. woodland and meadow) is generally more produc-tive and richer in species than either habitat on its own. In ecology this is called 'ecotone' and is defined as a transition area between two biomes. Maximising the number of edges and their length is therefore a key principle in permaculture/agroecological design.

It is within the context of all of these considerations that One Planet Developments can be seen to represent a valuable and evolving planning tool for governments anxious to reduce their countries' ecological footprints.

To live closer to the earth

In the end, it's down to people. To live closer to the earth is a dream that captivates many, but for all but a minority of those it remains just that: the reality of doing so is either too extreme or too hard to reach for it to be attained. The people who are doing it now, whom I will introduce to you in the later parts of this book, are to be considered pioneers. They are on a par with the first settlers who left from Europe for North America or Australia, except they are settling much closer to home. Consider the analogy with the Centre for Alternative Technology (CAT), near Machynlleth (it's no coincidence that it's within the Dyfi Biosphere: key individuals in the admin-istration of that project were previously employed by CAT). This was an abandoned slate quarry in 1974. Those who colonised it with the dream of creating a living laboratory for what were then termed alternative lifestyles and technologies were considered outliers: radicals, dreamers and certainly pioneers. Yet for some time, CAT has been at the heart of the establishment in Wales and beyond, its views widely sought on how to live sustainably, based on the real experience of doing so. The early settlers in the quarry struggled to create soil, to self-build their homes, to secure a water supply, electricity and power, as well as feed themselves. Many of those who live in low-impact developments now have gained skills and knowledge by either attending courses at CAT or reading their publications based on this experience. As an off-grid settlement itself, it can easily be seen as a forerunner of Lammas and Hockerton. OPDs now are similarly pioneers.

Life can be hard for pioneers. But it doesn't have to be for those who choose the One Planet Life in the future. Parts Two and Three in this book explain some of the required skills, but the real challenge in making it easier for more people to choose this path lies at the institutional level.

Making it easier

The paradigm shift that humanity needs to undergo, in order to survive on this planet, is encapsulated by Herbert Girardet in the concept of regenerative cities.[43] This is advanced by the World Futures Council, of which he is a founder, and stresses the linkages between urban systems and ecosystems. Our expanding cities currently excessively rely on the countryside for food. Correspondingly, greenbelt land is treated differently under planning laws, making it very hard for anyone to secure permission to erect a dwelling even if they are proposing to work the land.

The paradigm shift that is required boils down to a change in attitude towards development and land use: to incorporate nature in cities and more people in nature. To be effective, one planet living has to be a principle that is applied equally everywhere: in city and countryside. Girardet himself is encouraging this in his role as an advisor to the mayor of Bristol and to the Riyadh-based Saudi Sustainability Initiative.

We know that most people like living around nature, that it enhances the quality of life, and health. The first European Quality of Life Survey, which examined 'urban-rural differences', showed that people living in the countryside are likely to be happier than people of the same income level living in the city.[44] Many studies have documented the health benefits of direct contact with nature. Of all the possible types of contact with nature that people can have, the one with the greatest benefit is regular use of their own green space, whether it is a garden or smallholding. In the UK National Ecosystem Assessment (NEA) this type of land use is given the highest of all monetary values (should it even need to be given one to justify supporting the policy) of between £171 and £575 per person.[45]

The UK NEA report lists numerous benefits of contact with nature that would reduce the burden of those living in low-impact developments upon the National Health Service, including: improvements in both self-esteem and mood, recovery from stress, blood pressure, heart rate, vitamin D deficiency, the benefit upon health of consuming fresh food, as well as others such as improved community building. These results are reinforced by a survey of 12,000 people over five years, conducted by the University of Essex on behalf of the mental health charity MIND,[46] who took part in an 'ecotherapy' project comprising green exercise activities. It found that participants reported improved self-esteem, a greater desire to see friends and family, and more drive to become involved in their community. Participants were involved in creating a new wildlife garden, building an outdoor shelter and growing vegetables, or were able to just take the time to relax outside.

> There is a clear link between the amount of accessible greenspace and psychological well-being. The more frequent the visits to nearby green spaces, the lower the incidence of stress. Individuals with easy access to nature are three times as likely to participate in physical activity and, therefore, are 40 per cent less likely to become overweight or obese.[47]

A way out of the planning cul-de-sac

It is surprisingly hard to be able to live and work on the land. But why, given the evidence that it is good for you, and for the planet? To find the answer, we have to peel back the pages of history. Ever since land enclosures began apace in Tudor times, ordinary people have been gradually dispossessed from the land that was theirs by common right, with land ownership concentrated in fewer hands. Such evictions were often accompanied by a loss of common rights and resulted in the destruction of whole villages. Before enclosure, much of the arable land in central England was organised into an open field system, with practices very akin to modern organic growing techniques. There is now only one place in the entire country where an original mediaeval cultivation system remains in place and is still farmed: Laxton in Nottinghamshire. It shows what all one-planet development and organically cultivated areas show: that such labour-intensive horticulture is more productive than widespread farming techniques, and yields greater soil health and biodiversity.

To cut a long story short, the enclosure process culminated in the Labour Government of 1947 passing the Town and Country Planning Act, which was designed to stop ribbon development and unscrupulous capitalist development of the countryside. For example, it preserves greenbelts, and is still the only protection we have to stop large areas of Britain becoming like the Irish countryside, littered with hideous breezeblock dwellings.

But, as Chapter 7's DIY Planning Handbook[48] says, it 'has created a scarcity of building land that has forced low-income people out of the countryside and made rural England, in the words of a recent Cabinet Office report, "the near exclusive preserve of the more affluent sections of society".' Chapter 7 is the planning office of campaign group The Land Is Ours. It 'campaigns for a planning system which actively encourages sustainable, low-impact and affordable homes' and dispenses planning advice to people seeking to/or already embarking upon living on the land, engaged in land-based livelihoods.[49]

The current planning system: illogical and inefficient

The overriding philosophy of land use now is to keep people and greenfield sites separate. Time and again you hear planning officials say that their purpose is to stop 'unfettered development' on greenfield sites. They are, justifiably, frightened that the 'floodgates' (another word they use often) will open to conventional housing; desirable homes for commuters who work elsewhere. This is certainly not in the interests of the environment, but perhaps it is time to re-examine this attitude, to create a new sense of perspective that permits sensitive development of the countryside so that the country as a whole can live within its means.

The contemporary division of land function affects its value, and this is the key driver of development: the price of agricultural land tends to be between £4,000 and £10,000 per acre, whereas land with planning permission attached to it can be as much as £200,000 per acre. Woe betide any planning department that interferes with this pricing arrangement.

In parts of the UK there are people who have acquired some agricultural land, and secretly lived on it for years without planning permission while they did battle with planning officials, sometimes eventually winning retrospective planning permission. This usually comes with conditions attached. For example, Ben Law's[50] is a silvicultural tie, forcing him to run a woodland and charcoal-burning business on the land. What is more, only Ben Law himself can do this, to prevent him from selling up.

A more reliable and secure route, but one that by no means guarantees a home at the end of years of trying, and which is not open to communities – only households – is to purchase an area of agricultural land and submit an 'agricultural prior notice consent form' to the planning office for an agricultural workshop or barn. Such buildings are known as 'permitted developments', and therefore do not require planning permission. Consent can in theory take as little as 28 days but often takes longer. It is then perfectly legal to situate a temporary mobile home on the land while the workshop is being constructed and the business is being set up, for up to five years. After this period has elapsed, the next step would be to apply for planning permission to construct a permanent dwelling, which involves presenting a cast-iron case that it is necessary to live on site in order both to run the business, perhaps in order to look after livestock all year round, and that the business generates sufficient income to support the household.

In Scotland, while acquiring a croft for rent or purchase is just as expensive as buying developed land, it's now possible to purchase new land for a croft. One applies to the Crofter's Commission and can thereby obtain planning permission for one house on a working croft. This follows the passing of the 2010 Crofting Reform (Scotland) Act, which charged the Commissioners with the task of developing a Plan that would help retain populations in remote communities, through the occupation of crofts. The Crofting Act requires that all tenants and owner-occupier crofters reside on or within 32 km of their crofts and have a duty to cultivate. The guidance says: 'This includes horticulture, keeping livestock including poultry and bees, growing of crops and the planting of trees'.[51] Chrissie Sugden says that it is 'common for crofters in a crofting "township" (a group of crofts) to own/lease "land in common" which is managed by a "Grazings Committee". Grants are available for crofters and Grazings Committees towards the cost of fencing, agricultural buildings and (for crofters) a house.'[52]

Also in Scotland, The National Forest Land Scheme and the Woodland Crofts scheme allow communities to apply to buy land owned by the Forestry Commission in Scotland that falls within their designated boundary, even if the land is not for sale. It is applicable to 'communities of interest' (i.e. groups of people who aren't necessarily resident in the same area), which is often how intentional low-impact communities describe or constitute themselves, and provides an opportunity to create new woodland crofts.

The situation in England

Here, the planning system is riddled with inconsistencies, as witnessed by contrasting Ben Law's judgement with the following. In September 2013, English communities secretary Eric Pickles overruled a planning inspector's rejection of 100 homes on top-quality farmland. The inspector had judged the proposed housing estate to be in conflict with the local plan (decided by local people), unsustainable in transport terms (inadequate roads and public transport) and prejudicial to development of a frontrunner neighbourhood plan.

The development, at Nantwich Road, Tarporley, was opposed by Cheshire West and Chester Council, but, astonishingly, Pickles invoked the 'presumption in favour of sustainable development' to overrule them. He accepted that the scheme would destroy some of the best and most versatile farmland, mostly Grade 2, contrary to national planning policy, but rejected concerns that it would harm the character and appearance of the area or its environmental quality.

In his judgement he said: 'If adequate levels of development are to be catered for, now and in the future, the planned release of greenfield land appears inevitable'. 'Sustainable development concerns other issues' – namely housing supply. 'In these circumstances he considers that housing land supply policies are out-of-date and paragraph 14 of the National Planning Policy Framework[53] is therefore engaged.' This states: 'Sustainable development should be seen as a golden thread running through both plan-making and decision-taking'. I was not the only one to read this with incredulity.

The presumption in England in favour of sustainable development is now less well defined and therefore open to abuse than it was prior to the simplification of the planning guidance by the Coalition government. Potential support for one planet living used to be found in the planning policy statements, which required planners to 'support development that delivers diverse and sustainable farming enterprises, support other countryside-based enterprises and activities which contribute to rural economies' and 'provide for the sensitive exploitation of renewable energy sources', all things that low-impact developments do. In relation to agricultural developments, planning policies should 'enable farming and farmers to become more competitive, sustainable and environmentally friendly' and 'diversify into new agricultural opportunities'.[54]

Yet heavy brakes on development were applied in determining planning applications for new development on agricultural land, where the inspector must decide whether the people who will live there really will 'engage in farming, forestry or any other rural-based enterprise ... for a reasonable period of time' and whether they really do 'require one or more of the people engaged in it to live nearby'.[55] This included a financial test.

That was bad enough. But since 2012, even more confusingly, the new English national Planning Practice Guidance, Part Two[56] calls on local authorities to take account of 'market signals', including land and house prices, rents and affordability. While the emphasis on affordability is welcome and part of sustainable development, there is a danger that 'market signals' overrides other concerns such as sustainable land use.

While this uncertain state of affairs continues, real sustainable-development applications have stringent conditions set on them. The system as it stands is unfit for purpose: it is cumbersome, riddled with contradictions and does not prepare the UK for the future. It is open to abuse at a local level, despite the introduction by the Coalition government of localism and local-development plans. Everywhere it seems that the more sustainable you try to be the more paperwork and barriers are put in your way, and the contrary is true: the less sustainable you are, the easier it is. A few examples will illustrate the general picture.

Landmatters Co-operative Ltd project near Totnes, Devon, on agricultural land, was given conditional and limited approval in July 2007 by The Planning Inspectorate, Bristol. It comprises 42 acres, of which 17 acres are semi-natural ancient woodland, 22 acres are pasture and the remainder is naturally regenerating scrub and hedgerows. Permission was given following a decision by the planning officer that there was a 'breach of planning control as … a material change of use of the land without planning permission from agriculture to a "permaculture" holding comprising a mixed use integrating agriculture, forestry, education and ancillary rural enterprises and residential use.'

The Co-op sought consent for 15 permanent dwellings. The inspector, Alan Woolnough, found the proposal to be in contravention of a whole list of regulations and plans. He was especially concerned about transport impacts, but ultimately relied on the residents' own transport plan. He accepted that the residents had 'established an ecological footprint per household far smaller than the regional average, as proved by the analysis undertaken by 4th World Ecological Design.' He also found 'there to be considerable ecological, educational and cultural benefits in further exploring permaculture'.[57]

Despite this, he granted only a three-year trial of residential occupancy with a maximum of eight dwellings. In 2010 this was extended by a further five years. Perhaps after this they will be allowed to erect permanent dwellings. Imagine living in temporary dwellings – yurts, benders and so on – yourself for so long. Meanwhile they have to submit an annual report detailing 'activities undertaken' with an update of the co-op's land management and enterprise plans and compliance with transport policy. As residents Carl and Jenny said afterwards, the problem is that 'no legislation exists for this kind of thing at the moment'.[58]

Contrast this with the decision to grant permission to build a 2,800 square foot house alongside an existing farmhouse also on agricultural land at Eglwyswrw in North Pembrokeshire. The house was built by former council leader John Davies (Cwmbetws Ltd) on his farm in 2005. The application was based on the need to house a herdsman to look after a herd of cattle that he no longer owned when the application was decided. An account of the planning decision[59] reveals that no conditions were attached and not a shred of evidence was presented in support of the application. There are many examples of this nature throughout the countryside, although in most of them the bias is not so blatantly obvious. Often, after a while, you find that the bungalow built using this planning permission is later sold for a handsome sum.

There is a further kind of inconsistency: that even when permission is granted for a sustainable development in the countryside, consistent criteria are not always applied. Kevin McCabe built a large house in Devon, the home of traditional cob construction, out of cob for over £300,000. It obtained special planning permission under Planning Policy Statement 7 (PPS7) and contains over 130 m³ of concrete and 2,000 tonnes of cob. The cob was mixed not in the traditional manner, using feet and human energy, but with a JCB. The breathability of the cob structure is completely negated by the addition of polystyrene insulation all the way round. Whilst there are thermal advantages to insulation and thermal mass, resulting in a much lower consumption of energy, it is evident that overall its environmental impact will be much greater than, say, any Lammas house. In Kevin's favour is that the concrete uses 75 per cent less cement due to the use of pulverised fly ash, a waste product from coal-fired power stations, which will reduce carbon impact. Against it is the size: 'To my mind, a house that involves digging a quarter of a mile of foundation trenches and moving 2,000 tonnes of soil to house a single family is not sustainable,' says planning consultant Michael Howlett.[60]

All three developments are in the open countryside. And, as Howlett pointed out to me:

> Lammas are monitored on an ongoing basis and face harsh financial
> penalties if they do not meet the targets set for them in terms of providing
> for their own needs. The Cwmbetws application couldn't even be justified
> when it was decided and there is no ongoing analysis. There are no targets
> for Kevin McCabe to meet either, and no monitoring.

Two arguments for not building in the open countryside built into planning guidance are: that it reduces transport impacts and the impact of installing services. Given that one planet living involves the self-provision of services such as water, sewerage and power, only the transport impacts should be a consideration in this type of planning application. And even so, this provides inconsistencies. Whilst it obviously results in a lower ecological footprint to live close to most journey destinations, such as school, employment and shops, people often live in one town and work in another, commuting every day, as pointed out by Michael Howlett.[61]

There is no test that anyone in an urban environment has to undergo relating to the distance of their dwelling from their workplace before they are permitted to live in that dwelling – and it is absurd that it should ever be so. It's just a presumption that they will require fewer or shorter journeys. Given this, it behoves planning authorities to attempt to ensure that there are plenty of employment opportunities in close proximity to all housing provision, good public transport, walkable and cycle-able cities and improved rural transport provision. This is an argument for mixed land use, not against low-impact development in rural areas.

As Howlett says, '"Conventional" houses built within development boundaries face no monitoring – nobody ever checks if the landscaping plans that are demanded by the planners have been implemented, so the majority of new houses still have barren gardens with only turf and hard surfacing, the only sop to sustainability is that they have to pass Building Regs and SAP calculations.'

A fourth kind of contradiction is to be found in the guidance to planning offices about approving planning applications in national park areas. Of course, such areas need to be protected from 'unfettered development' and visual beauty is a key consideration. However, there are large areas of national parks which are common farmland and/or hidden from public view. The guidance stipulates a requirement to 'protect and enhance the environment', but this is open to widely varying interpretations, and indeed the two terms could be seen to be contradictory. 'Protection' could mean keeping an unsustainable sheep field or monoculture forest the way it is. 'Enhancement' could mean improving biodiversity and sustainability. We also find the same phrase in the Natural Environment Framework for governance in Wales, mentioned above: 'Sustainable development is a central organising principle … by means of which natural capital will be conserved or enhanced.' Clearly some clarification is in order.

One planet living near urban areas

'The thing that drives me most insane,' says Mark Waghorn, who runs an architectural practice specialising in sustainable building, 'is the arbitrary line drawn by planners between the town and the countryside, because it doesn't allow towns or villages to grow organically in response to the needs of the communities. It doesn't allow the layering effect of permaculture: multiple uses over time.' There is an even stronger case for permitting low-impact developments within or on the edge of existing settlement boundaries.

The Land magazine has urged that there should be slightly different rules for encouraging OPDs on the edge of urban areas. Waghorn cites an example in Cwm Bran, near Newport, not far from the Severn Bridge, where a proposed project was situated on a main road surrounded by houses, with the settlement boundary bordering but outside of it, and green fields at the back. 'The planning officer decreed that it was in the open countryside. It's too either-or,' he says. 'OPD makes you do a transport assessment plan, makes you site near to a transport mode or town but you should get more credit for being near a town, schools, shops, etcetera.'

Inconsistencies in building regulations

There are similar inconsistencies in building regulations. A typical modest new house built to the Code for Sustainable Homes, which new-build homes in the UK only voluntarily have to adhere to, will emit perhaps 20 to 25 kg CO_2/m^2, perhaps 2,500 kilos of CO_2 per year. This is half that of the UK's average existing homes. A beautiful, hand-built family house (Trecnwc in Glandŵr, Pembrokeshire) applying for retrospective OPD status at the time of writing has a SAP calculation showing that it generates more energy than it uses. Net emissions are −3.39 $kgCO_2/m^2$ (kilos of carbon dioxide emitted per square metre of floor area per year), effectively removing the need to emit 243 kilos per year. The builders, a young couple known as Charlie and Meg, with a toddler, are appealing a demolition order. (Why? Because it's in the wrong place, Pembrokeshire National Park, even though it can't be seen from the road.)

Trecnwc achieves the required minimum Level 3 rating under the Code but wouldn't score much higher because the system favours volume housebuilders and major building product suppliers. It does not gain any points for using natural materials because the Building Research Establishment's 'Green Guide', referenced by the CSH, does not contain any ratings for straw-bale construction, green roofs, cordwood or lath and plaster. The Guide does, however, list 108 different variations for twin-skin concrete-block/brick-wall constructions – all rated either 'A' or 'A+', despite the enormous environmental impact of cement and concrete. Natural, sustainable materials are almost entirely absent from the lists, which are monopolised by the mainstream manufacturers who can afford to have their products tested and listed.

As there are no ratings for the natural materials used in this lovingly crafted house, the points cannot be obtained, despite the fact that using local, natural materials that lock up carbon in the structure is undoubtedly more sustainable. The other Green Guide sections concerned with materials (MAT2 and MAT3) cover chain of custody and again favour large-scale producers who can afford to have each stage of their supply chain certified and documented. Highly environmentally unsound materials can score as long as the correct documentation exists. Equally, there is no place in the Code for using recycled or waste materials. Michael Howlett comments:

> Despite being a Code for Sustainable Homes assessor, I would question its validity as a tool for assessing sustainability. It doesn't actually tell you very much about a building other than that a highly bureaucratic, rigid and inflexible process has been followed. A house built to Level 3 of the Code might have exceptionally good standards of insulation and fabric energy efficiency, provision for bicycles (that may or may not ever be used) and a detailed user manual. Then again it might have minimum levels of insulation but have 'Secured by Design' high-security windows, a rotary washing line, rainwater harvesting and some bird boxes in the garden. In addition, the Code completely ignores scale and quantity.

Although the Code is to be sidelined in the future, the system that replaces it is still likely to favour big developers. I suggest that ecological footprint analysis might be relevant here too.

Affordable housing

The 'one planet' approach can also help with affordable housing, of which the UK is in crying need. According to the housing charity Shelter:

> There are more than 1.8 million households waiting for a social home – an increase of 81 per cent since 1997.[62] Two thirds of households on the waiting list have been waiting for more than a year.[63] Nearly 41,000 households with dependent children were living in temporary accommodation at the end of December 2012.[64]

Low-impact dwellings are intrinsically cheap to build, as the Exemplary Example of Tŷ Solar towards the end of this book shows. The cost of the land and the materials minus the labour brings the overall average cost down to within, and sometimes well below, £60,000. We cannot expect most people to wish to build their own home, as some of the people within this book are doing. Far better to produce a zero-carbon kit type house, which can easily be constructed by purchasers, that is both cheap and comes pre-approved for building regulations and standard planning conditions, all other things being equal. Then aspirants to one planet living would just have to find the capital to purchase the land and such a house, financing for which could come from ethical building societies and banks such as the Ecology Building Society and Triodos Bank. To my knowledge at least two developers are pursuing such a model, and they're described in Part Four.

Reforming the planning system

The planning system undoubtedly needs to be modified in order to accommodate the changes in land use we are advocating and to remove the above inconsistencies, but that is not such a challenge as it might seem.

To be made easier, the planning requirements, and the transaction costs on both sides, need to be simplified and embedded in national legislation. After all, the transaction costs are high on the local authority side too. 'These types of applications are quite complicated, quite protracted,' the Cardiff civil servant in charge of planning told me. 'The Future Generations Bill will mandate all public bodies to take account of sustainable development in the decision-making.'

'It will be a definite step forward,' says Peter Davies, 'because at the least there will be a requirement to comply or explain why not for public sector, for example in the transition to a low-carbon economy. The focus will be on outcomes, and the measurements of progress will be sustainability indicators and the ecological footprint.'

Local planning departments will need training. The Welsh government has commissioned research on the effectiveness of planning committee decisions at the local level. This recommends that:

> Training should be mandatory, regular, and provided by a central source such as the Welsh Government. ... Training is needed for specific issues, including: affordable housing; Code for Sustainable Homes; viability; climate change; design; and SUDS. Training is especially important after an election or reshuffle – training should occur before joining the planning committee.[65]

Reforms currently in progress are addressing the fact that local authorities struggle with making certain decisions, particularly because of the political nature of their role, which can introduce bias. 'Because of their loyalty to their constituents, many councillors find it difficult to see the bigger picture. There is therefore a conflict of interest. If they can't make the decisions, then somebody else should,' said the civil servant.

Changing the conditions for granting planning permission

Conditions for granting planning permission for one-planet developments in Wales include the stipulation that either 65 per cent of all subsistence, or 30 per cent of food and 35 per cent of livelihood, must come from the land. Contrast this with a Section 106 requirement in Nottinghamshire, England, for the residents of Hockerton Housing Project in 1994, where, instead of a percentage of income, a fixed number of unpaid hours (300 per year per household) must be spent on the land and in addition 300 paid hours per year supporting the joint business which runs tours and educational events, hosts awaydays and consulting on both new and retrofit energy-efficient building. Given that a standard working year consists of 1,650 hours, this leaves 64 per cent of the working year available to do anything else.

This seems to me to be fairer, more achievable and more manageable, as well as helping to secure the planners' prime directive of preventing such developments becoming owned by people who do not want to use the land, and who will instead commute to jobs elsewhere.

On car use, the guidance in Wales says:

> Planning applications should be accompanied by an assessment of the traffic generated from the use of the site by its residents and visitors. The travel plan accompanying the planning application should clearly identify a preference for low- or zero-carbon modes of transport including walking, cycling and car sharing schemes. Where proposals are distant from larger towns and villages they should be located near public transport routes to minimise use of the private car.

Taken sensibly this should help to facilitate low-impact developments so they can be further mainstreamed. But, unless there is a concerted effort to pursue the advantages, and there are many, of low-impact development backed up by robust evidence, it's yet possible that Wales' experiment could be seen in the future as an aberrant dead end. It would be tragic were this to be the case.

The Town and Country Planning Association, a housing and planning charity, issued a year-long research project, Planning out Poverty,[66] in October 2013, which argued that planning has become 'increasingly dis-connected from peoples' lives because it no longer deals with the issues people care about'. Kate Henderson, the report's co-author and TCPA Chief Executive said: 'The reinvention of "social town planning", which has been effectively residualised for 30 years, requires a re-visioning of planning within wider social policy, rather than being left within a legislative *cul de sac*.' Dr Hugh Ellis, another co-author and TCPA Chief Planner, commented that 'no attention is being paid to the positive potential of spatial planning to provide solutions to many aspects of our most difficult public policy problems.'

Spatial planning decisions impact hugely on sustainability through the physical organisation of accessibility to land, services and key employment opportunities. Planning could play a more positive role by integrating more fully (within both local and national public policy) with sectors such as regeneration, environment, food policy, transport and health. But to do this, planners themselves must have the necessary skills and opportunity to increase their understanding of the issues: places, agroecology and organic techniques, ecological-footprint analysis and the lived experience of communities. This should be integrated in Continuing Professional Development (CPD).

All of these issues should be addressed in the National Planning Policy Framework to prioritise poverty and sustainability, and the National Planning Practice Guidance should be amended to include guidance on increasing sustainability consistently across the board, to aim towards one planet living – a global average ecological footprint for the whole of the UK – backed by new legal duties and the development of a 'new vision' for the planning profession.

I dream of a future when the number of forms you have to fill out, the amount of red tape you have to negotiate, the amount of data you have to collect and process and submit to the authorities, is proportionate to the amount of carbon you emit as an individual or as an organisation. Instead, it seems very much like it's the other way round right now. These transactional costs for low-impact development must be reduced to the bare minimum, while respecting the requirement to avoid inappropriate development on greenfield sites. We are at the very bottom of a learning curve for that paradigm shift in planning terms, but at least we have turned the corner.

Sitting inside smallholdings at Lammas, seeing the flowers, the productive land, the ducks, hens and cows, and the Wimbushes' modern house, powered by solar and hydroelectric energy with all mod-cons, I see no reason why people should have to fight so hard to be able to live like this, by a political system that is so behind the times. Anyone visiting here would feel the same. It may not be for everyone, but anyone should be able to live the One Planet Life.

The One Planet Council

It's for this reason that I and a group of very talented individuals have, during the writing of this book, set up the One Planet Council.[67] The Council is an independent voluntary body which exists to enable and promote One Planet Development and to support those who are making the transition to this more sustainable way of life by providing guidance and tools. It aims to work together with all those with an interest in One Planet Development: Local Planning Authorities, policymakers, academics, landowners, and those already living on and planning to live on OPD sites.

Conclusion

We all know that you can only deal with planning decisions on the basis of planning law and planning guidance. These are the clumsy tools that provide a common language which both sides have to speak in order to articulate their viewpoints. In one sense it doesn't matter that the view-points are sometimes poles apart. This is the common ground on which we do battle. It is a battle in some areas more than others.

But familiarity breeds acceptance, and acceptance can turn into some-thing else. I noticed when visiting many of the places described in this book, that having initially been met with opposition from locals, later the locals have become proud to have them in their midst. And in the cities where one planet living is beginning to happen – like Bristol, Brighton, Stroud, Totnes and Freiburg, Germany – people are proud to live there. They very much enjoy it.

And this is perhaps the most overwhelming argument in favour of the One Planet Life.

Notes

1   http://www.footprintnetwork.org/en/index.php/GFN/page/earth_overshoot_day. Retrieved 22.10.13.
2   *Measuring sustainability: Why the ecological footprint is bad economics and bad environmental science*, Nathan Fiala1, *Ecological Economics* Volume 67, Issue 4, 1, pp. 519–525, Elsevier, November 2008.
3   *Living Planet Report 2012: Biodiversity, biocapacity and better choices*, WWF International, Gland, Switzerland.

4   *The Ecological Wealth of Nations*, Global Footprint Network, 2010, and other information available at http://www.footprintnetwork.org. Retrieved October 2013.

5   In an article, *Admit it: we can't measure our ecological footprint,* in the *New Scientist*, issue 2944, 25 November 2013, Fred Pearce wrote of the GFN's estimate of the ecological footprint of humanity: 'If anything, it underestimates it'.

6   *One Wales: One Planet, The Sustainable Development Scheme of the Welsh Assembly Government*, May 2009.

7   He wanted to remain anonymous.

8   Technical Advice Note 6 (TAN 6): *Planning for Sustainable Rural Communities*, Welsh Assembly Government, July 2010.

9   http://wales.gov.uk/topics/planning/policy/guidanceandleaflets/oneplanet/?lang=en. Accessed 22 October 2013.

10 *Planning Policy Wales* Edition 5 November 2012. Section 9.3.12.

11 • Pembs Coast National Park (Beeview farm).
    • Pembrokeshire (Bryn yr blodau and Cornerwood – under appeal).
    • Monmouthshire (Dan and Sarah Moody): appealing.
    • Two pre-applications in process: Pembrokeshire (Rob Smith) and Pembs Coast National Park (Sue Gillooley).
    • Discussion stage with Paul Wimbush at Lammas: Powys (Kate Mobbs Morgan), Pembrokeshire (Jacqui Banks), Carmarthenshire (Salena Walker), Carmarthenshire (Bron Daioni), Pembrokeshire (Ian Ratcliffe).
    • Powys (Peter Barker).
    • Flintshire (Warren Dingle farm – resubmitting pending a great crested newt survey).

12 The term means something quite different in the United States of America, where it is to do with flood protection.

13 *Low Impact Development: Planning and People in a Sustainable Countryside,* Simon Fairlie, Jon Carpenter, 1996.

14 *One planet living*, Pooran Desai and Paul King, Alastair Sawday Publishing, 2006.

15 See http://www.oneplanetcommunities.org. Retrieved October 2013.

16 *Self-Sufficiency,* John and Sally Seymour, Faber & Faber, 1970. The latest edition is published by Dorling Kindersley as *The New Complete Book of Self-Sufficiency* (2002).

17 *Ecological footprint of British city residents,* Alan Calcott and Jamie Bull and CarbonPlan, WWF, London, 2007.

18 *Zero Carbon Britain: Rethinking the Future*, Allen, P. et al., Centre for Alternative Technology, Machynlleth, Wales, July 2013.

19 *Greenhouse Gas Emission Projections for UK Agriculture to 2030*, Economics Group, Defra, August 2011, https://www.gov.uk/government/uploads/system/uploads/attachment_data/file/69225/pb13622-ghg-emission-projections.pdf. Retrieved 22.10.2013.

20 *Public Attitudes to Food Issues*, GfK NOP survey for the Food Standards Agency, 2009 Available at: http://tna.europarchive.org/20111116080332/http://www.food.gov.uk/multimedia/pdfs/publicattitudestofood.pdf. Retrieved October 2013.

21 *Can Britain Feed Itself? The Land* Issue 4, Winter 2007–8, http://transitionculture.org/wp-content/uploads/2007/CanBritain.pdf. Accessed 28 August 2013.

22 *Can Britain Farm Itself?*, *The Land*, Issue 12, Summer 2012. http://www.thelandmagazine.org.uk/articles/can-britain-farm-itself-2. Accessed 28 August 2013.

23 *Double Yield: Jobs and Sustainable Food Production*, Vicki Hird, SAFE Alliance, 1997.

24 *Spain's communist model village, The Observer* newspaper, 20 October 2013. http://www.theguardian.com/world/2013/oct/20/marinaleda-spanish-communist-village-utopia. Accessed 22 October 13.

25 In conversation, September 2013.

26 Overton, Mark; *Agricultural Revolution in England 1500–1800*; Cambridge University Press (1996); ISBN- 978-052156859. Data after 1850 taken from British censuses.

27 Schwartz, Robert M., Railways and Rural Development in England and Wales, 1850–1914, MA, USA: Found at https://www.mtholyoke.edu/courses/rschwart/rail/railways_rural_develop.htm. Retrieved August 2013.

28 Office of National Statistics figures at http://www.ons.gov.uk/ons/rel/regional-trends/region-and-country-profiles/key-statistics-and-profiles---august-2012/key-statistics---wales--august-2012.html, retrieved August 2013.

29 *UK National Ecosystem Assessment* Technical Report. UNEP-WCMC, Cambridge, 2011. See: uknea.unep-wcmc.org.

30 *Rewilding and Food Security, The Land* magazine, Issue 14, Summer 2013, http://www.thelandmagazine.org.uk/articles/rewilding-and-food-security (retrieved October 2013).

31 The Institute of Biological, Environmental and Rural Sciences (IBERS), Aberystwyth University, Farm Business Income statistics for 2009–10: TABLE B3 Hill sheep farms. http://www.aber.ac.uk/en/media/departmental/ibers/pdf/farmbusinesssurvey/statisticalresults/outputsinputsincomes/0910/0910ly_11d.pdf. Retrieved August 2013.

32 UNEP-WCMC, Cambridge, 2011, *op. cit.*

33 *Low Impact Development – Planning Policy and Practice*, Final Report, University of the West of England, Land Use Consultants, Countryside Council for Wales, December 2002.

34 *Rewilding and Food Security, The Land* magazine, Issue 14, Summer 2013. http://www.thelandmagazine.org.uk/articles/rewilding-and-food-security (retrieved October 2013).

35 *Feral: Searching for enchantment on the frontiers of rewilding*, George Monbiot, Penguin, 2013.

36 *Mixed Vegetable Polyculture Trials*, Dr Naomi van der Velden, University of Cumbria for the Permaculture Association, 2012, available at http://www.cumbria.ac.uk/Public/SNRO/Documents/Research/NKVeldon2012MixedVegResultst.pdf Retrieved October 2013.

37 http://www.ifad.org/evaluation/public_html/eksyst/doc/thematic/organic/organic.
    htm (Retrieved 9 June 2014).

38 *Smallholder Agriculture and Food Security in the 21st Century*, Proceedings of the
    Governing Council Round Tables, IFAD, 2009.

39 H.L. Tuomistoa, I.D. Hodgeb, P. Riordana, D.W. Macdonald, *Comparing energy
    balances, greenhouse gas balances and biodiversity impacts of contrasting farming
    systems with alternative land uses*, Agricultural Systems Volume 108, April 2012,
    pp. 42–49.

40 *A Living Wales* – a new framework for our environment, our countryside and our
    seas. Consultation Document, Welsh Assembly Government, Cardiff, 15 September
    2010.

41 http://wales.gov.uk/about/cabinet/cabinetstatements/2013/
    futuregenerationsbill/?lang=en. Retrieved October 2013.

42 http://www.biosfferdyfi.org.uk/?page_id=284 and http://www.unesco.org/new/
    en/natural-sciences/environment/ecological-sciences/biosphere-reserves/main-
    characteristics. Retrieved 28 August 2013.

43 Girardet, H., *Creating Regenerative Cities*, Routledge, 2014.

44 *First European Quality of Life Survey: Urban-Rural differences*, European Foundation
    for the Improvement of Living and Working Conditions, Dublin, 2006.

45 *The UK National Ecosystem Assessment:* Technical Report. UNEP-WCMC, Cambridge,
    2011, Chapter 22, Table 22.16.

46 *Ecotherapy: The Green Agenda For Mental Health*, University of Essex and MIND
    mental health charity, October 2013, http://www.mind.org.uk/assets/0000/2138/
    ecotherapy_report.pdf. Retrieved October 2013

47 *The UK National Ecosystem Assessment:* Technical Report. UNEP-WCMC, Cambridge.
    2011, Chapter 23, p. 1154.

48 *DIY Planning Handbook*, Chapter 7, This Land Is Ours, 2013. Chapter 7 is the
    planning office of campaign group The Land Is Ours. It 'campaigns for a planning
    system which actively encourages sustainable, low impact and affordable homes'
    and dispenses planning advice to people seeking to/or already embarking upon
    living on the land, engaged in land-based livelihoods. Its website is http://www.
    tlio.org.uk/chapter7. It takes its name from Agenda 21 Chapter 7c, on Human
    Habitation Settlement. Agenda 21 is the non-binding, voluntarily implemented
    action plan of the United Nations with regard to sustainable development agreed
    by all nations at the UN Conference on Environment and Development (UNCED) in
    Rio de Janeiro, Brazil, in 1992. Chapter 7 says: 'All countries should ... strengthen
    the indigenous building materials industry, based, as much as possible, on inputs
    of locally available natural resources ... promote the increased use of energy
    efficient designs and technologies and sustainable use of natural resources ...
    promote the use of labour-intensive construction methods ... develop policies and
    practices to reach the informal sector and self-help builders ... discourage the use of
    construction materials and products that create pollution during their life cycle. All
    countries should, as appropriate, support the shelter efforts of the urban and rural

poor by adopting and/or adapting existing codes and regulations to facilitate their access to land, finance and low-cost building materials.'

49   For a detailed discussion of this process, see *Low Impact Development*, Simon Fairlie, Jon Carpenter Publishing, 1996.

50   Ben Law is one of the prime campaigners for low-impact developments. He won retrospective planning permission for a permanent dwelling for his timber house at Prickly Nut Woods in West Sussex which was voted as their favourite home by viewers of Kevin McCloud's Channel 4 *Grand Designs* TV programme. He writes regularly for *Permaculture* magazine apart and makes a living from coppicing, training apprentices and running courses on sustainable woodland management, eco-building and permaculture design. He also runs occasional open days in response to popular demand and manages a specialist eco-building company, The Roundwood Timber Framing Company Limited. He is the author of *Living in a Wood in the 21st Century* (Collins, 2013), *Roundwood Timber Framing: Building Naturally Using Local Resources* (Permanent Publications, 2010), *The Woodland Way: A Permaculture Approach to Sustainable Woodland* (Permanent Publications, 2013) and *The Woodland House* (Foreword by Kevin McCloud, Permanent Publications, 2010).

51   http://www.crofting.scotland.gov.uk. Retrieved October 2013.

52   *How To Get Planning Permission on Non-Development Land,* Chrissie Sugden, *Permaculture* magazine, July 2011. http://www.permaculture.co.uk/articles/how-get-planning-permission-non-development-land. Retrieved October 2013.

53   https://www.gov.uk/government/uploads/system/uploads/attachment_data/file/6077/2116950.pdf. Retrieved October 2013.

54   *Planning Policy Statement 7: Sustainable Development in Rural Areas*, UK Government April 2004, available at http://webarchive.nationalarchives.gov.uk/20120919132719/www.communities.gov.uk/archived/publications/planningandbuilding/pps7. Retrieved October 2013.

55   *Ibid*.

56   Available at http://planningguidance.planningportal.gov.uk. Retrieved October 2013.

57   Appeal Decisions, The Planning Inspectorate, Bristol, 23 August 2007. Available at http://landmatters.org.uk/wp-content/uploads/2013/01/Landmatters-Appeal-decision.pdf. Retrieved October 2013.

58   On Your Farm, 3 June 2012, BBC Radio 4 Programme available at http://www.bbc.co.uk/programmes/b01jg8qt. Retrieved October 2013.

59   http://freespace.virgin.net/oldgrumpy.mike/Cwmbetws%20analysis.html. Retrieved October 2013.

60   In email correspondence.

61   In conversation with the author, 16 October 2013. Michael's practice is based in Pembroke Dock, Wales.

62   The UK Government's Housing Strategy Statistical Appendix (HSSA), at http://data.gov.uk/dataset/england-hssa-housing-strategy-statistical-appendix. Retrieved October 2013.

63 Shelter analysis of English Housing Survey 2010/11 (latest available data)

64 UK Office of National Statistics figures: Statutory homelessness in England: October to December 2012, available at https://www.gov.uk/government/publications/ statutory-homelessness-in-england-october-to-december-2012. Retrieved October 2013.

65 RTPI Cymru Study into the Operation of Planning Committees in Wales, Final Report, Fortismere Associates with Arup, Cardiff, July 2013.

66 *Planning Out Poverty: The Reinvention of Social Town Planning*, The Town and Country Planning Association, October 2013, available at http://www.tcpa.org.uk/ data/files/Planning_out_Poverty.pdf. Retrieved October 2013.

67 See: www.oneplanetcouncil.org.uk.

Are you fed up with your way of life? Perhaps you want a safe and relatively affordable place to bring up your children? Do you want to be healthier and happier? Do you want to live closer to nature? Perhaps you just want to help benefit the environment and do your bit to tackle climate change.

Whatever your reason, the One Planet Life beckons to you as a way of enriching your enjoyment of every day and finding fulfilment in simple actions. The One Planet Life is not about sacrifice but enhancement. This was said by everyone whom I interviewed while researching this book. Based on their experiences, the chances are that you can find pleasure in living in a

Figure 2.1 You have an idea of your dream homestead; here's where you start to realise that dream. This sketch was made by a member of Dragonfly Housing Co-Op, of which I was a member in the 1990s.

Figure 2.2 Charlie Hague and Megan Williams' house, Pwll Broga, at Glandŵr, Pembrokeshire.
Credit: Amanda Jackson.

Figure 2.3 Hoppi and Paul Wimbush picking bilberries on their six acres at Lammas, Pembrokeshire.
Credit: Amanda Jackson.

home that emits no pollution – or even that you helped to build yourself; in generating your own energy; and in eating food that you have grown. It's likely that you'll make friends and gradually feel that you belong in a community. An improved diet gives you a greater chance of being healthier and the evidence shows that most people feel greater happiness from observing and interacting with nature more closely.

The One Planet Life uses both mental and physical skills: the whole person. It's not for everyone: it's hard work, demanding, and requires multiple skills. It must be undertaken with your eyes fully open and with no illusions about the risks and the demands that will be made upon your resources. You will need sufficient capital and sufficient commitment to take you through the demanding first years before the systems are set up, the trees you plant are of a reasonable size and the buildings are completed.

But it is rewarding. It's not self-sufficiency but it's as self-sufficient as it's possible to be in a developed country in the twenty-first century, connected world. And the crucial thing is – it's possible to measure your success. If you're wanting to step towards this goal, there are two ways of starting out:

- The first is to look for an existing project, whether already up and running or in the process of setting itself up, and discover whether it is possible to join it;
- The second is to look for land to purchase yourself.

Finding a likeminded group in the UK

Here are just a few places to start:

- **The Ecological Land Cooperative**: set up to buy land that has been, or is at risk of being, intensively managed and lease it to people that have the skills to manage it ecologically and would not otherwise be able to afford to do so: www.ecologicalland.coop;
- **The Confederation of Co-operative Housing**: promotes co-operative and tenant-controlled housing as a viable alternative form of tenure: www.cch.coop;
- **The One Planet Council**: gives support to any individual or group wishing to pursue one-planet developments: www.oneplanetcouncil.org.uk;
- **Land-Share**: Hugh Fearnley-Whittingstall's initiative connecting landowners big or small with prospective growers in need of land. Here you can find and offer land: www.landshare.net;
- **The Land Is Ours**: campaigns for access to the land for everyone and runs Chapter 7, which campaigns for a fairer planning system for low-impact development: www.tlio.org.uk;
- **One Planet Communities**: a network of some of the earth's greenest neighbourhoods managed by Pooran Desai and the BioRegional team: www.oneplanetcommunities.org;
- **The Plunkett Foundation**: helps rural communities through community ownership: www.plunkett.co.uk;
- **Radical Routes:** a network of radical co-ops whose members are committed to working for positive social change made up mainly of housing co-ops of various sizes. It has an ethical investment arm called Rootstock: www.radicalroutes.org.uk;
- **Diggers & Dreamers:** a resource of information about communal living, publisher of an online directory: www.diggersanddreamers.org.uk.

Many one-planet developments are constituted as housing co-ops or trusts. Co-ops are organisations where members democratically control and manage their homes. Some can be owned by individuals or families, others

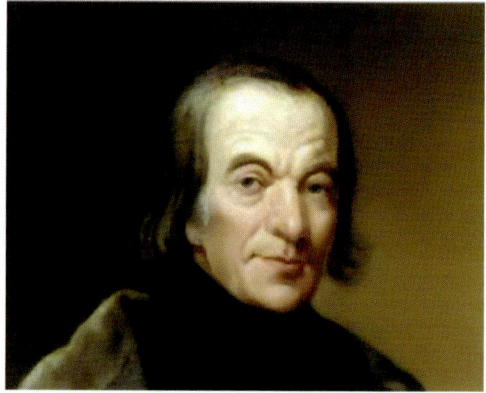

Figure 2.4 The tradition of co-operative communities in Wales goes back over 200 years. Social reformer Robert Owen (1771–1858), from Newtown in mid-Wales, is a founder of the co-operative movement and was instrumental in founding the first cooperative communities in the early nineteenth century.
Credit: (1845 portrait by John Cranch.)

collectively by all tenants. The co-operative model is a sound way of providing housing, at the same time as empowering ordinary communities. Many small community organisations are configured as co-ops and quietly sustain strong community businesses, often owning significant assets.

Most housing co-operatives are registered as Industrial and Provident Societies, a legal structure. Registration is provided by the Financial Conduct Authority.[1] Much research carried out into tenant control shows that tenants are better and more efficient at running their housing than councils and housing associations. Strong housing co-op movements exist in countries all over the world, such as Canada and Norway. There are over 600 housing co-ops in the United Kingdom. Most of them own fewer than 50 homes but some are larger. Setting one up and running it can be hard work, but the benefits do more than compensate.

The values of co-operatives include self-help and responsibility, democratic decision-making, equality, equity and solidarity, honesty and openness, and social responsibility and caring for others. They have a role in providing education and training for the members and the public. All of these are necessary qualities of sustainability; in particular the educational role is usually a requirement of planning permission for OPDs.[2]

Sample legal agreements and lots of other advice and training are available on the Land-Share website above.

Notes

1   Download the forms at http://www.fca.org.uk/firms/firm-types/mutual-societies/industrial. Retrieved November 2013.
2   Taken from *What is a Housing Co-op?* Co-op Homes 2011, published at http://www.coophomes.co.uk/Access/Download.aspx?FileID=1. Retrieved November 2013.

2 Step one towards the One Planet Life: finding land, finding finance, gaining skills

In the UK, only about 30 per cent of land coming up for sale is greenfield, the rest is land that was once or is already occupied. Sometimes it's easier as far as obtaining planning permission is concerned to find a plot that has already been developed that comes with some land. There are many different ways to find land that is up for sale:

- word of mouth – often farmers just ask around locally before contacting an estate agent;
- the Land-Share website – www.landshare.net;
- estate agents;
- land agents;
- the website woodlands.co.uk;
- auctions (usually advertised in the local press – land is often for sale as a result of bankruptcy so a bargain is possible);
- local authorities;
- government land.[1]

Figure 2.5 A proposal for a One Planet Development in the plot on the right of this picture, which is within the Pembrokeshire coastal National Park boundaries, was rejected on grounds of visual intrusion after objections by neighbours. It is well overlooked and close to a tourism destination. Restrictive planning policies may be in place within National Parks and Special Landscape Areas.

Criteria for choosing land

1 It's absolutely vital that your land has a roughly south facing aspect in order to maximise the growing potential, passive solar heating in the buildings and the potential for generating solar power.
2 As transport forms a large part of the carbon footprint of living outside of city centres you should prioritise somewhere near to a railway station and/or bus route, and not too remote from a market for your produce.
3 You might also look out for hilltops where you can generate wind power, or streams that you can tap for hydropower.
4 Also keep an eye out for land with a water supply and good drainage, as well as fertile soil and good access.
5 If the land is overlooked, there might be issues with visual appearance.
6 The idea that land should be bought at low agricultural values is principal, so this should be prioritised in your search.
7 It's nice to have land with at least a few mature trees or some woodland.

How large does your plot need to be? Paul Wimbush at Lammas argues for a minimum of three acres: one acre for woodland, one acre for the house, workshop and gardens, and one for livelihood. Four or five acres is perhaps optimal but if you want grazing for livestock then you will need at least six acres.

It's a good idea to get a surveyor to check out the land and a good solicitor will help to make sure that it can meet your needs. Land sold with outline planning permission for building is ideal because the type of property is yet to be approved so you can design your own. Once this has been granted it is valid for up to five years. Within three years a reserved matters application must be submitted, or detailed planning permission. Check the design restrictions which may prohibit you from building exactly as you would like.

Financing

Suppose you find some land, your next challenge is likely to be obtaining a loan. Even if you have little in the way of financing capital it's possible to set up a not-for-profit social enterprise or similar business structure and then use crowd-sourcing methods as a way of generating funds. You would then pay back the loans in a similar way to a mortgage.

Some banks are especially amenable to approaches from housing co-operatives, trusts and social enterprises. These include:

- The Ecology Building Society: www.ecology.co.uk;
- Triodos Bank: www.triodos.co.uk;
- Co-op Finance: www.coopfinance.coop;
- Other members of the Global Alliance for Banking on Values: www. gabv.org;
- Ethex: supports ethical businesses by matching them with ethical investors: www.ethex.org.uk;
- Funding Enlightened Agriculture: a project of the Campaign For Real Farming to support new kinds of farms – polycultural, low-input, skills intensive: info@campaignforrealfarming.org.

Advice on legal structures, marketing, financing and more is available from Social Enterprise UK, the national body for social enterprise: www.-socialenterprise.org.uk.

Gaining the skills

Many skills are required to manage your own land and live the One Planet Life, but don't worry: you can learn on the job and share the work with friends. There are several ways to gain experience and get a taste of what it's like before taking the plunge:

- You can volunteer to work on an existing project, and this is usually done via Working Weekends on Organic Farms, commonly known as WWOOFing. Search the available offers on www.wwoof. org.uk;
- Opportunities may also exist on Community Supported Agriculture projects; check the network at www.soilassociation.org/communitysupportedagriculture;
- You can join a like-minded group such as a local permaculture or Transition Towns group. You can find these listed at www. permaculture.org.uk and www.transitionnetwork.org;
- Go on a course, such as those offered by the Centre for Alternative Technology (www.cat.org.uk) or the Low Impact Living Initiative (www. lowimpact.org);

Figure 2.6 An image from the cover of *Mainstreaming Agro-ecology: Implications for Global Food and Farming Systems.*[2] It sets out how the type of food production practices intrinsic to one-planet developments can increase the food security of nations. To quote from the executive summary: 'Agro-ecological practitioners design food production systems which aim to maintain the functions that natural systems provide, both internal and external to production, and which are robust, productive and equitable. This means integrating instead of segregating, closing systems and relying on local inputs, increasing biological and genetic diversity, and regenerating instead of degrading.' A better summary of the One Planet Life would be harder to find.
Credit: Crown Copyright

- Both of these organisations also publish a wide range of valuable publications on all aspects of one planet living.

Surveying the land

A basic principle of one planet living is to work with nature, not against it. To help ensure this, a survey of the land comes in several stages. The first will tell you whether in principle it will support your requirements. Factors to consider include:

- **Aspect**: is it favourable to the movement of the sun, local wind and frost patterns? This determines how much solar and wind power you might receive, but also whether you'll need to protect your crops.

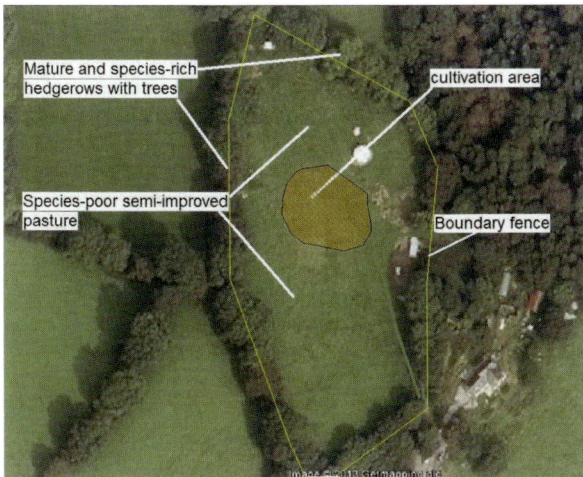

Figure 2.7 Together with walking the site, screen grabs from Google maps can be useful in identifying features. From Bryn yr Blodau's survey in Llangolman, Pembs, by consultant ecologist Paddy Jenks.
Credit: Paddy Jenks

- **Transport**: how much will travel costs add to your overall living expenses?
- **Drainage**: is there surface water? It's a good idea to visit it after heavy rain so the drainage pattern can be seen. Is there a water supply? If there is a stream, could it be exploited for hydropower?
- **Soil quality**: if possible, ask nearby growers if they can provide advice. What was the previous land use? This will determine how much organic matter and/or manure you will need to add to the soil. Is the soil deep?
- **Woodland**: are there mature trees on the site that can be used for construction or fuel? Are there younger trees that can be coppiced?
- **Building materials**: besides timber, are there sources of stone, gravel, straw bale or soil/clay suitable for cob?
- **Neighbourhood**: is there a good community nearby? Reasonable facilities? Opportunities for markets for your produce?

Assuming you go ahead and acquire the land, the next step will be the production of your management plan.

Notes

1   You can find government land to rent or buy near you at the official website https://www.gov.uk/find-government-property. Retrieved November 2013.

2 A discussion paper with a foreword by HRH the Prince of Wales: Wibbelmann,
   M., Schmutz, U., Wright, J., Udall, D., Rayns, F., Kneafsey, M., Trenchard, L., Bennett, J.
   and Lennartsson, M. (2013) *Mainstreaming Agroecology: Implications for Global Food
   and Farming Systems.* Centre for Agroecology and Food Security Discussion Paper.
   Coventry: Centre for Agroecology and Food Security. ISBN: 978-1-84600-0454.

3 Step two towards the One Planet Life: crafting a management plan

A management plan is your own routemap to the One Planet Life. It's step two in your journey. It's a detailed design document that you're advised to put together over the course of several months in response to your observations and research. It sets out your unique vision for how you can get the most out of the land you're investing in, while conserving and improving it in all possible ways and integrating with the local community.

As such it's a mixture of targets, action points and business plan. But, crucially, it's also a communications tool: it is the principal channel by which your vision will be understood by others, most importantly the planning department. Therefore it must be as crystal clear, comprehensive and well-supported as possible.

Figure 3.1 Elements of a management plan.

The contents of your Management Plan:
- land management
- energy
- water
- waste
- zero carbon buildings
- transport
- community impact

Figure 3.2 The contents of a management plan.

It's no good just making an assertion such as: 'this building will be zero carbon', or 'in five years we will have increased the food we are producing by 40 per cent'. You'll need to show to yourselves, your supporters, financers and the local planning department how you will be doing this. Unless you do, you yourself will never be certain of the effectiveness of what you are doing, let alone convincing anyone else.

The Welsh government has published Practice Guidance for both applicants and planners alongside its One Planet Development legislation.[1] Although intended as a requirement for a planning application in Wales this is useful advice for people anywhere and was written by sympathetic planning experts from elsewhere in the UK. The 77-page document covers everything from choosing a site to ecological footprint assessment and how to construct a management plan. It helps you address the main issues of land management, energy, water, waste, zero-carbon buildings, transport and community-impact assessment. Read this chapter carefully as you write your management plan to see whether you are addressing all of the points. In this chapter we go through the structure of the plan, and in the succeeding sections we look at the principal topics in more detail, together with food production.

Producing a management plan that is watertight and satisfies the planning inspector's interpretation of the Guidance is not easy. You, or your 'competent' representatives (people whose authority you and the planning department recognise) will have conducted several rigorous surveys. After you've finished you will have a good idea of:

- what you will be eating in five years' time and where it will be coming from;
- what species might be attracted to your land over the same period, despite or because of your activities;

- your water usage, domestic and other, where this will come from and how it will be treated before and after use;
- the vast majority of journeys over this period and how they will be made;
- how much energy you'll be using and where it will be coming from;
- a research-based conservative estimate of your income, and an exaggerated account of your costs.

There is no space for optimism that the planning inspector will give you the benefit of the doubt. Therefore there should be no room for doubt.

In Wales, One Planet Developments (OPDs) – whether single homes, co-operative communities or larger settlements, and located within or next to existing settlements or in the open countryside – should initially achieve an ecological footprint of 2.4 global hectares per person or less. Elsewhere in the UK the requirement is to achieve a 'low impact lifestyle' – less precise and therefore harder to establish as having been achieved.

It's important to have some objective yardstick by which to measure progress, otherwise you'll never really be sure if your hard work is truly effective. Perhaps you don't want to be, but at this stage of the global learning curve any research results that prove the effectiveness of different strategies and practices are worthwhile so they can be shared and replicated with confidence. The Permaculture Association itself admits that there is virtually no peer-reviewed hard research to prove that permaculture works any better than conventional organic agriculture.

Over the past decade the construction industry has had to go through a similar process of rigorous testing and monitoring of attempts to achieve

We must reduce our ecological footprint from this:

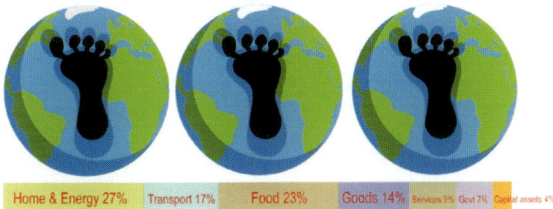

| Home & Energy 27% | Transport 17% | Food 23% | Goods 14% | Services 5% | Govt 7% | Capital assets 4% |

To this:

Figure 3.3 The average components of a UK individual's ecological footprint. This needs to reduce by one third in order to consume a fair share of the planet's resources.

zero-carbon new homes and refurbishments in order to establish what works and what doesn't. In many cases the results have been surprising and contrary to expectations. What was thought to work in theory was regularly found in practice to be implemented incorrectly and therefore ineffective. What's more, studies of how people actually live in low- or zero-carbon homes often show that they behave differently from expected and upset the intentions of the designers. That's why monitoring of actual results is really important. (I do understand that ecological footprint analysis is still a relatively blunt instrument that requires some refinement. As a tool it's in its infancy, which is why I'm considering the use of Life Cycle Analysis[2] as an alternative tool.)

If you opt to use ecological footprinting, your plan should demonstrate how you would move from the 2.44 gha baseline towards 1.88 global hectares per person over a maximum period of no more than five years from the commencement of work on the site. 1.88 was the global average availability of resources in 2003 – nowadays, to be realistic, the plan should aim to reduce this even more, perhaps to as little as 1.7 global hectares. The plan would also make plain how the dwellings will be zero-carbon in both construction and use (although exactly what this means in practice is still a subject of debate). If it's located in the open countryside, the plan would also say how the livelihood you obtain from your land would provide for the residents' minimum needs.

What are these minimum needs? They are defined as:

- 30–65 per cent of food needs;
- all clothes;
- all travel to do with your land-based livelihood;
- IT/communications;
- council tax;
- most water;
- all of the energy needed by the residents of the site (including that needed for any processing); and
- assimilation of all of the waste the site produces other than very small amounts of either non-biodegradable or hazardous wastes (such as batteries).

That's it. You *don't* have to account for any impacts as a result of any other work you do that is separate from your livelihood from the site, or for any other products or commodities you might purchase. So you can have another job or source of income (if you have time!).

> **Tip**
> Try to assess the effectiveness of how you think you will
> reduce the environmental impact of the site's occupants
> while compiling your plan by using an Ecological Footprint
> Analysis (EFA) tool.[3]

In Wales, a formal assessment of the ecological footprint of an OPD happens both at the outset, to create a baseline, and as part of annual ongoing monitoring of the implementation management plan. This means you can establish how well you're putting the plan into practice compared to your original baseline and your annual targets. Wherever you are in the world, you can still use the tool at any point, to assess, for example, where you can best achieve savings in reducing the impact of your activities: in transport, building or energy, for example. What activities will have the most impact? This tool is great for testing out in general terms the impact of your design ideas before doing them in practice.

Your management plan could (and should in Wales) include the following:

- **A Business and Improvement plan**: to identify whether there is a need to live on the site and establish the level of the inhabitants' requirements in terms of income, food energy and waste assimilation that can be obtained directly from the site;
- **An ecological footprint analysis** of how the occupants satisfy their minimum needs;
- **A carbon analysis**;
- **A biodiversity and landscape assessment**;
- **A community impact assessment**: to identify potential impacts on the host community (both positive and negative) and provide a basis to identify and implement any mitigation measures that may be necessary;
- **A transport assessment and travel plan**: to identify the transport needs of the inhabitants and propose sustainable travel solutions.

For each topic it sets out the objectives and defines the design strategy/proposals and how people will live on site. It includes:

- **how** the development will be phased;
- **when** habitation will start;
- **whether** temporary accommodation will be required to begin with;
- **plans** for any structures and land use;
- **how** livelihood requirements will be met.

It will have required a considerable amount of thought and research, particularly about the nature of the site and its potential for delivering livelihoods. It begins with site evaluation.

> **Tip**
> The plan does not need to contain your vision statement, environmental beliefs or philosophy of life. If necessary these can go in a separate document, and/or be appended to the plan if you feel the need for the planning department to see them.

Site evaluation

Evaluation of the site will include its aspect, height above sea level, the local community, transport needs, soil type, current land use, biodiversity, water flows, renewable energy resources, microclimate, and other resources such as stone, timber, existing infrastructure and cultural heritage. In particular, it must make reference to the following:

- **Geology, topography and soils** (including agricultural land classification[4]);
- **Biodiversity** as identified in a Local Biodiversity Action Plan[5] if it exists and records of important flora and fauna (species) and their abundance on the site and in the immediate vicinity;
- **Any known sites of cultural importance** including below-ground archaeological sites, earthworks and ruins, and living history, such as hedgerows marking important historic boundaries and in the immediate vicinity. Scheduled monuments, listed buildings, registered parks and gardens, registered battlefields;
- **Existing buildings and structures** on the site, their rough date (if known) and their main construction materials;
- **Landscape**: features on the site and in the immediate vicinity (such as hedgerows, scrub, woodland and shelter belts) and key views into the site from public vantage points. Is the character of the local landscape typical of the surrounding area or how does it differ? Are there important landscape, habitat and cultural features nearby? This will help understand how the site fits in its wider context and how it can contribute to broader objectives, such as the enhancement of wildlife corridors;

- **Past land use** (if known);
- **Present land use** (of each field, if more than one);
- **Statutory Designations** on the site and in the immediate vicinity:
- **Special Areas of Conservation** (SACs) and Special Protection Areas (SPAs); Sites of Special Scientific Interest (SSSIs) (all SACs and SPAs will also be SSSIs); and non-statutory Wildlife Sites identified by the Wildlife Trust or local authority. If the site lies within a national park or area of outstanding natural beauty;
- **Existing transport** generated by the site and its transport connections.

The location and extent of each of the above is best illustrated on one or more annotated maps, ideally accompanied by photographs of the features being described. A reasonable source of information initially is LANDMAP, although the website is a little unwieldy.[6] It contains, in layers, data relating to the geology, culture, biodiversity, history and visual/sensory aspects of land.

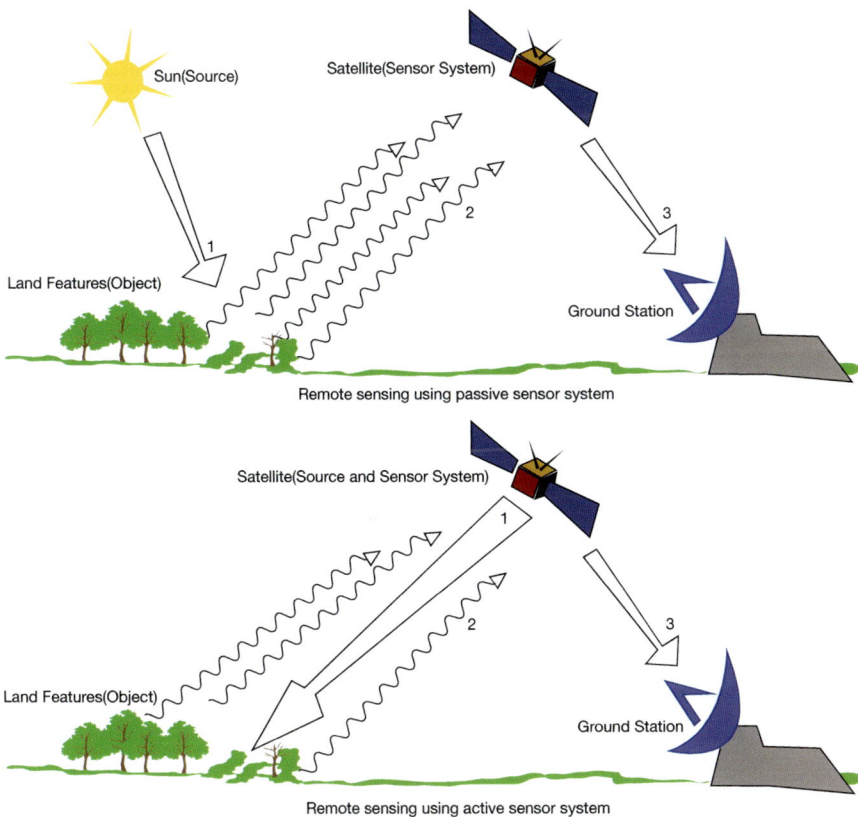

Figure 3.4 Remote sensing from satellites provides baseline data for LANDMAP.
Credit: Wikimedia Commons, Arkarjun.

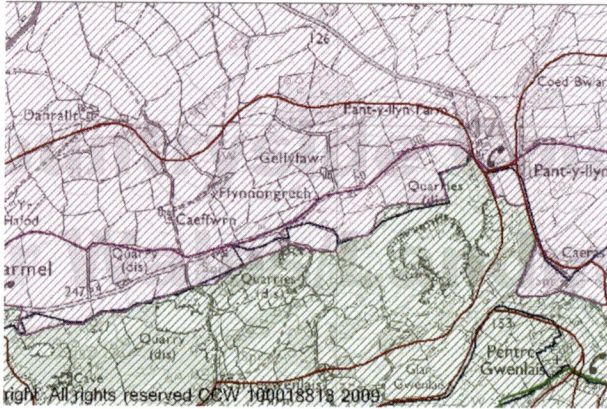

Figure 3.5 An example of LANDMAP data: an area of Carmarthenshire displaying at 1:13000 scale the 'Habitats Level 2 Classification' which by reference to the colour code key reveals that there is a Site of Special Scientific Interest in the green area.

Land-based livelihood

The land-based activities that generate an income sufficient to meet the minimum income needs of all the site's occupants may come from produce grown and/or reared on the site (including the processing of such produce). You don't include other income derived from the site or anywhere else that is unrelated to land-based activities, nor gifts. Income derived from other land-based enterprises, such as training and education courses or consultancy, would be subsidiary to the primary activity of growing and rearing produce.

Your management plan will attempt to describe how different aspects of the site can yield multiple products that will provide livelihood in an ongoing manner. This could be food, flowers, fibres, fuel and other heat or electrical energy. For example, trees may supply: nuts and fruit, fibres for basket-making, coppiced wood fuel, a growing medium for mushrooms, leaf mould, construction timber, wood for craft or furniture making, shade, wind protection, frost protection.

Inhabitants may earn other income, of course. But to justify the privilege of being able to live on agricultural land, an OPD site in Wales should be able to provide for at least 30 per cent of the food needs of all occupants, plus up to a further 35 per cent purchased or bartered using income generated from sales or surplus produce. In total, that's a minimum of 65 per cent of food needs. Your management plan should provide a simple balance sheet demonstrating how this can happen. This means that the number of occupants the land can support is directly related to the carrying capacity

Up to 65% of food needs satisfied by the land, of which...

a minimum of 30% directly

up to 35% from sales

the remaining 35% can come from elsewhere

Figure 3.6 Of all of your basic food needs, up to 65 per cent needs to be satisfied from your land, of which 30 per cent must come directly from it, in order to qualify for One Planet Development status in Wales.

of the land – including its ability to process their waste. No greater number may be permitted to live there.

Any additional produce is sold locally, which in turn reduces the community's footprint (as less needs to be imported). If there are facilities for processing produce, this can be made available to other local producers for income. Training, courses and consultancy should be offered, so as to share best practice.

To measure progress against the benchmarks you established, annual reporting contains the following data:

- the amount of food that was consumed by the household and its origin – whether off-site or on-site;
- the annual household income and costs in a balance sheet;
- the total value of the produce grown and reared on the site compared with income derived from other land-based enterprises;
- the number of occupants;
- the value of sales through each outlet;
- how much the processing facilities were used by others;
- the training and consultancy services dispensed during the year.

To work out your ecological footprint, to this would be added the number and length of delivery trips and the energy used in processing.

Tip
The management plan must only draw on livelihood derived from the land that is part of the planning application and not from any other land.

Example of Minimum Needs Calculation

Year	2012	2013	2014	2015	2016	2017
Clothes spend	£700	£700	£650	£600	£600	£600
Travel costs	£1,087	£1,087	£1,095	£1,110	£1,140	£1,160
Travel fuel	£1,500	£1,500	£1,400	£1,200	£1,100	£1,050
IT/ communications costs	£1,186	£1,086	£1,086	£1,086	£1,086	£1,086
Council tax	£728.86	£728.86	£728.86	£728.86	£728.86	£728.86
Food spend	£3,726	£3,366	£3,020	£1,660	£1,660	£1,510
Total	**£8,927.86**	**£8,467.86**	**£7979.86**	**£6,384.86**	**£6,314.86**	**£6,134.86**

This chart, from a real management plan, shows a decrease in food spend as produce increases.

Comparing needs with yields

From the same management plan, this shows that by 2016 the applicants expected to be meeting their minimum household income needs from land-based enterprises. The majority of this income derives from land-based produce and a minority derives from educational activities.

Year-	2013	2014	2015	2016	2017
Minimum household need (£)	8,467.86	7,979.86	6,384.86	6,314.86	6,134.86
Income from land-based produce (£)	2,560	3,620	3,770	4,320	5,020
Proportion met (%)	30	45	59	68	82
Income from other land-based activities (£)	330	530	1,500	2,400	3,500
Proportion met (%)	4	7	23	38	57
Total land based income (£)	2,890	4,150	5,270	6,720	8,520
Proportion met (%)	34	52	82	106	139

Appendix 1 Household Need and Plot Productivity Calculation 2012

	Plot a		Plot b		Plot c		Plot d	
	Household need	from land	Household need	from land	Household need	from land	Household d need	from land
Domestic Wood Use	500	200	105	25	270	270	150	100
Domestic Gas Use	130	0	183	0	158	0	150	0
Domestic Electricity Use	914.69	904.41	900	867	140	55	875.24	868.74
Provision of Water	410	410	410	410	215	161	254	254
Household Food (annual)	6531.2	3148.6	8046	746	6020	2012	2000	1000
Basic Household Clothing	15	0	550	0	240	0	0	0
Annual Dwelling Maintenance	750	700	0	0	0	0	0	0
Other overhead requirements: Telephone/internet	480	0	730	0	760	0	250	0
Other overhead requirements: Council Tax	600	0	616	0	600	0	452.86	0
Other overhead requirements: Service Charge, Rent plus car charge etc.	1209	0	1209	0	1209	0	1066	0
Other overhead requirements: Transport costs (including car repairs, car tax, mot , fuel etc..	140	0	3809	0	2945	0	496	0
Other overhead requirements: Insurance (household etc.)	200	0	0	0	0	0	0	0
Total	11879.89	5363.01	16558	2048	12557	2498	5694.1	2222.74
Land Based Enterprises	Details	Value Sold	Details	Value Sold	Details	Value Sold	Details	Value Sold
Produce grown or reared & sold	Eggs / Fruit & veg / Plants / Silage bales	240 / 700 / 160 / 237.50	Native edible plants to restaurants / Vegetables, salad for low impact week / Sale of Silage bales	1633 / 28.70 / 237.50	Sale of silage bales / Garlic & herbs	237.50 / 90	Silage bales / Veg. & eggs	237.50 / 484
Produce made & sold	Furniture	450	Willow baskets, domes etc.	156.15				
Income from training, courses & consultancy	Low impact course open days	500	Foraging walks for low impact & family week / Willow basket session for low impact week / Open days	50 / 30 / 90				
Grand Total	11879.89	7650.51	16558	4273.35	12557	2825.5	5694.1	2944.24

Figure 3.7 Example of a monitoring report (Tir y Gafel, Lammas, 4 of the 9 plots, 2012).

Tip

If you are intending to keep animals, identify the source of feed. Grazing can take much land and bring its own issues. A table like this might be produced:

Stock costs £	Purchase	Housing	Vets bills/year	Equipment	Imported feed/year
Ducks	45	150	0	30	0
Chickens	60	150	0	30	0
Goat	50	150	100	50	100
Horse	150	450	100	50	0
Sheep	400	250	100	30	100
Bees	0	0	0	50	0
Totals	**705**	**1,150**	**300**	**240**	**200**

You could then put a value on the outputs:

Stock	Outputs
Ducks	6 eggs per day (majority sold)
Chickens	6 eggs per day (majority sold)
Goat	1,500 litres milk per year (majority for cheese & yogurt)
Horse	Work and pleasure
Sheep	2 carcasses per year plus wool for weaving
Bees	25 kilos honey per year

Land management

The One Planet Life must respect, conserve, manage and enhance the environmental quality of the land, including biodiversity, cultural heritage and landscape. This breaks down into a number of activities. You'll describe in the plan how you will:

- use traditional management practices;
- improve soil organic matter;
- increase the populations of pollinating insects, natural predators to pests and diseases, and of once characteristic farmland birds of the local area;
- form wildlife corridors connecting to valued features that lie beyond the site boundary;
- extend areas of permanent grassland over known areas of important archaeology;
- conserve and enhance any existing flora and fauna identified in the Local Biodiversity Action Plan;
- in areas of poor existing habitat, create new habitat;
- reintroduce lost features such as traditional orchards, woodland, hedgerows, stone walls and wetlands;
- create ponds, e.g. to store (grey) water;
- grow trees for coppicing;
- use traditional woodland and shelterbelts to help protect horticultural areas and enhance carbon storage;
- help to strengthen local landscape character;

- locate dwellings and other structures, including access tracks, where they can be recessed into the landscape as part of the wider site design, so they don't stand out from public vantage points.

For the annual monitoring reports there are a number of ways in which you could measure the success of these practices, set against the baselines established in the initial surveys:

- the condition of existing semi-natural habitats such as the spread of characteristic species of that habitat;
- the decline in non-characteristic/commercial agricultural species within each habitat;
- any increase in the amount of traditional characteristic landscape features and semi-natural habitat; and the type of management they are receiving;
- the population of breeding farmland birds;
- the number of active beehives on site.

Energy and water

You will be seeking ways to minimise the amount of water and energy you will need for both domestic and work purposes. You will need to account for both of these separately even if they may overlap, by assigning a fair proportion to each. This is just the same as, if you work from home, for accounting purposes you assign a proportion of your energy and other costs to the business.

Water minimisation means the use of rainwater collection, spray taps and composting toilets, for example. Energy minimisation means using LEDs for lighting and super-efficient rated appliances. Super-insulated buildings that are highly airtight require little or no heating. Even using timber for wood-fuel heating is inefficient and polluting when other sources of heating such as passive solar are possible.

Minimisation of your water and energy needs is followed by reuse. Ideas here include using stream water for both power generation and consumption; and using grey water for irrigation. Or using the waste heat from a smithy for heating a building next door, or solar heat from greenhouse conservatories to preheat air entering dwelling or workspaces.

Meeting these reduced water and energy needs should then become easier. Usually a combination of technologies is the way forward. For example, wind and solar are common renewable electricity partners.

Rainwater harvesting, boreholes and streams or springs are the usual off-mains sources of water. The highest energy requirements are usually for cooking and washing – of clothes or bodies. Careful sizing of these systems is required, and this is discussed in the energy section. The Welsh guidelines advise that in certain situations the use of bottled LPG is permitted for cooking if the overall carbon budget can still be met. But to avoid this it's always worth looking for the most efficient means of utilising available biofuels, whether in the form of coppiced wood, biomethane, bioethanol or biodiesel, if it can be sourced sustainably.

Animal labour may be used to replace non-renewable energy. Water pumping should be renewably powered and any ponds or lakes should maximise habitat creation and should not destroy important existing habitats.

Annual monitoring will cover:

- the amount of renewable energy generated (as a percentage of energy needs);
- the amount of non-renewable fuel bought and what it was used for;
- the quantity of electricity exported to and imported from the grid;
- the proportion of water needs met from water available on site (unless there is a more sustainable alternative) and the sources and amount from each one;
- ground and surface water levels for each month;
- the amount of capital invested in renewable generation technologies.

Example

A south-facing slope of land formerly used for grazing, covering an area of five acres, includes a stream, but the soil quality is poor and your survey shows that at the moment water runs off easily. Your investigations might look at how water might be diverted to satisfy domestic or work-related water needs, then be treated in a wetland and reused for irrigation of flowers and crops and increasing biodiversity. It might enquire whether there is sufficient flow also to generate electricity and heat from a micro hydro system, or, if not, whether there is potential for wind or solar, or possibly all three. If used for irrigation, what high-value produce might be harvested, and what value might be added to that produce? For example, the growing of short-rotation coppice would soak up water, act as a windbreak to protect crops from prevailing winds, produce wood fuel for heating and raw materials for basket-making. A decision tree would be a useful tool to employ in order to examine and evaluate alternative strategies for the exploiting and development of resources on this land.

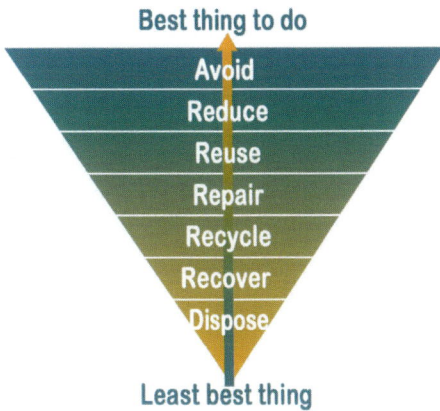

Best thing to do

Avoid
Reduce
Reuse
Repair
Recycle
Recover
Dispose

Least best thing

Figure 3.8 The waste-minimisation hierarchy.

Waste

Waste is an attitude of mind and can be seen as a resource. In nature, nothing is wasted so if you can think of a use for a given waste, so much the better. As a planet we need to move from throwing things away to a network of closed-loop systems where nothing is wasted and everything is used for something else.

All waste produced on site, other than small amounts of unavoidable non-biodegradable or hazardous waste, should be assimilated on site in an environmentally sustainable way. But that doesn't mean you have to process everything on site, such as broken hardware. A certain amount can and in fact should be taken for specialist recycling, such as batteries and refrigerators.

The strategy begins with the waste-minimisation hierarchy, seen in Figure 3.8. This is a seven-stage process:

1   The best thing to do is to avoid generating waste by not purchasing items unnecessarily, avoiding excess packaging, and repairing machinery when it breaks down or clothes when they develop holes.
2–4 The amount of 'rubbish' generated can be minimised through composting organic waste and using it for soil enrichment (or feeding it to stock), and by finding alternative uses for materials and objects.
5   Recycling for reuse involves the disassembly of a product into its constituent parts, which are then used in something new, for example crushing unwanted pottery to make mosaics or paths, plastic bottles as mini-cloches for seedlings, and processing paper to

Figure 3.9 and 3.10 Finding ways to reuse plastic is a challenge to your imagination. Here is a small insulated greenhouse made from old soda bottles sandwiched between polythene sheets held in place by strong wires found at the National Botanic Garden of Wales.

make logs or papier maché crafts. Cardboard or old carpets might be used for mulch.

6   Waste recovery means using a waste product to replace a non-waste product that would otherwise have been used. So unwanted conventional materials for recycling such as glass and metals, which could be collected by the municipal authorities, might instead be used by you for hard core beneath a track.

7   You end up with very few materials that do need to be disposed of as complete waste, such as pieces of plastic or cellophane, polystyrene packaging (which might conceivably be used for insulation if deployed properly[7]) and electronic or electrical waste, which should be taken to official WEEE recycling depots, often a nearby electrical supplier, as it contains toxic materials.

Grey water, human faeces and urine come under the category of waste. Strategies such as composting toilets, planted leach fields, reed beds or a Wetland Ecosystem Treatment (WET) system, might be designed in to complete the water-management cycle. Human urine is an efficient catalyst in

Figure 3.11 A WET system for processing grey water and black water in the foreground, with compost area.

the composting process and contains valuable nutrients. Therefore it can be collected separately and added to compost, or, following dilution by a factor of 12, can be applied directly to soil. If you are keeping animals or poultry, a safe and healthy solution for dealing with their waste products should also be designed into this system. Green waste can be fed to livestock.

All waste handling and assimilation on site must comply with Environment Agency guidelines. Your monitoring procedure will cover:

* the amount of onsite waste assimilation and offsite waste disposal;
* the amount of organic material used to improve fertility and productivity (bearing in mind that some habitats such as wildflower meadows require low soil fertility to be preserved or enhanced).

Zero-carbon buildings

There are many different approaches to building zero-carbon structures, and almost as many ways of defining what they are. Principal considerations include:

* the materials supply chain: obtaining as much as possible from on site or nearby;
* orientation, layout and location to maximise use of solar energy;
* waste minimisation during construction;
* the use of natural materials;
* reuse of materials (during construction and planning for reuse and easy disassembly at the end of life);

- structures should be 'breathable'[8] (i.e. made up predominantly of hygroscopic materials) to prevent condensation;
- structures should lock up atmospheric carbon in their fabric;
- structures should be super-insulated to approximately Passivhaus standard, therefore:
- structures should be as airtight as possible yet use passive-stack ventilation;
- life-cycle energy use and greenhouse gas emissions should be as low as possible;
- renewable energy should more than compensate over the lifetime for any carbon generated during construction or disassembly by displacing the need for the use of fossil fuels and exporting a surplus.

Attention to detail is paramount, and simplicity is a virtue in zero-carbon building. This is one case where it may be cost-effective to obtain the advice of an expert or buy something off the shelf. The effort of building a house while setting up a smallholding should not be overestimated.

Only occupied buildings need to be zero-carbon, according to the guidance, so this stipulation does not necessarily apply to workshops and polytunnels.

While it is necessary to observe building regulations where appropriate, these often don't cover the particular requirements of zero-carbon building

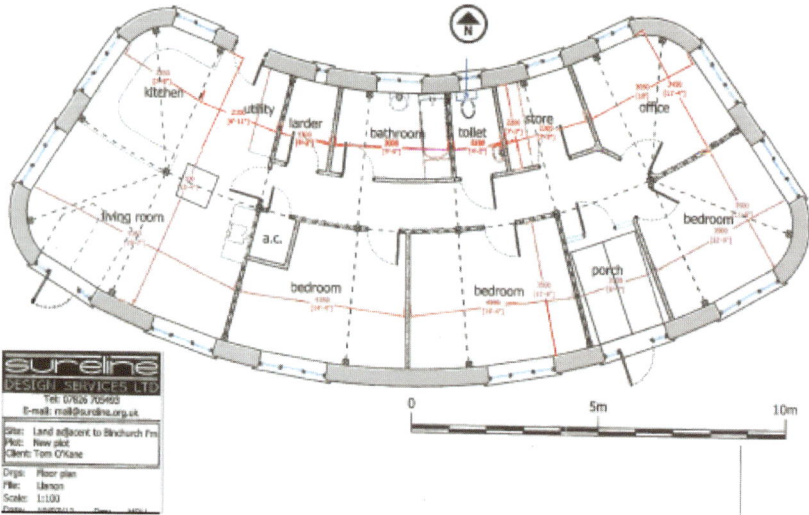

Figure 3.12 Tom O'Kane's design maximises windows facing south, with least-used rooms on the north side.
Credit: Tom O'Kane

for one planet living directly, and it's a good idea to engage in constructive dialogue with Building Control in the local authority. They often take an enthusiastic professional interest and can provide invaluable advice, but this should also be obtained from a professional organisation such as the Association for Environment Conscious Building. Reference can also be made to the Code for Sustainable Homes, which stipulates certain solutions for making homes zero-carbon; however, the points system should be treated with a certain amount of scepticism.

Windows and doors are particularly interesting, since while there are advantages to reusing old or reclaimed ones, they will generally not perform as well or last as long as double- or triple-glazed windows, properly coated and sealed and whose frames are insulated. Whilst expensive, they pay for themselves eventually. The use of passive solar for heating means that buildings should have most of their windows on the south-facing side, using conservatories to trap heat and direct it into the house. Other external doors should have porches. Continental-style shutters help to keep the heat in at night and in the winter. Conservatories can double up as greenhouses for growing tomatoes, vines, fruit and salad. All of this will minimise the need for active heating.

Attempts should be made to let the building blend in visually to its environment. Where possible the local vernacular architecture style should be imitated in some way. Whatever the construction method – lightweight timber, straw bale, earth, cob, stone and so on – the cladding or render can help with this.

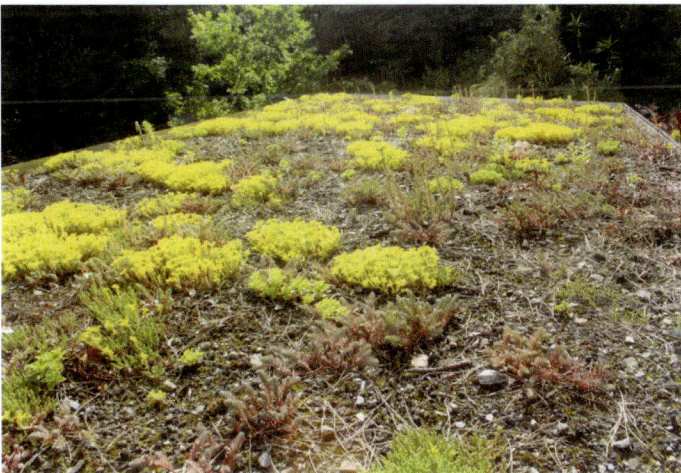

Figure 3.13 A sedum roof on my own low-impact studio after one year of planting from seed.

The use of green roofs is encouraged to an extent; sedum roofs are better for biodiversity, pollinators and flowers than turf roofs, and look neater and are easier to maintain. Bear in mind that they provide little in the way of insulation and can be heavy when snow is on the ground. South-facing roofs will most likely be prioritised for solar panels (PV and thermal).

There should also be a plan for what will happen to the building at the end of its life. It should be possible for it to be deconstructed and disposed of or moved elsewhere with minimal environmental damage, and for the land it occupied to return to a greenfield site. There is an advantage in the dwelling being easy to take apart as it could be reconstructed elsewhere. This might happen in the event that the owners are no longer willing or able to continue their land-based activities (*bearing in mind that planning permission for living on site is granted only as a condition of this continuing*). It means that the capital invested in the building would not be lost if it could be reconstructed elsewhere.

The management plan, besides containing all of the above – and architectural designs – will also detail the ecological footprint of the buildings and the capital cost of materials and construction.

Community engagement

An initial reaction of communities, upon discovering that a low-impact development is wanting to situate itself in their midst, can be negative, manifesting as a straightforward example of 'nimbyism', or fear of change. Your development is likely to be, whether you want it or not, high profile, and your powers of diplomacy will be constantly called upon. Begin by scoping the community so you know it as well as possible: its facilities, patterns of habitation, social life, and so on. Go to the local pub or church! You can then determine where the opportunities for engagement lie.

As part of this process you are well advised:

- to visit personally everybody who may be affected by your development in *a spirit of generosity and inclusion*, bearing gifts. There will always be some who will oppose you, no matter what, but in the end they will be in the minority. *Treat them all as potential friends.*
- *Ask them questions* about what they would like to see in the area, and incorporate this in your management plan as far as possible and relevant.
- Nurture a support network, but allow it to transcend 'tribal barriers' so that you *reach out to all sectors of the local population.*

- Some fears may be to do with extra traffic, visual impact or competition from traders if you are offering produce or services for sale. *See this as an opportunity to develop partnerships.*
- If situated in Wales, endeavour to *learn and speak some Welsh* at least, for this can go a long way.
- See how you can be involved in and *contribute to community events and groups*, perhaps schools, colleges (for offering training) or conservation groups.
- It is especially important to *engage with farmers*, because there will be many overlapping areas where cooperation is possible to mutual benefit, since cooperation is the backbone of farming life.
- *Have open days* to which you invite everyone.
- *Conduct a survey or questionnaire* in order to back up your assessment.

In practice you should plan to sell produce and services locally, offer training and facilities locally, and maintain hedges, fencing, footpaths and other access routes bordering or traversing your land.

From the word go you should be cultivating constructive dialogues with any significant local councillors and county councillors, keeping your potential opponents close and your friends informed. Even if people do not accept invitations, it does not mean that that they do not appreciate being invited! Often help comes from a surprising quarter.

For monitoring purposes you should keep a note of your community contacts and impacts and any mitigation measures taken to address negative impacts, as well as recording the quantity and value of local food, goods and services sold or exchanged for local consumption.

Transport

We saw at the beginning of the chapter that transport typically accounts for 17 per cent of the environmental footprint of a person in the UK. But this is an average. Part of the reason planners dislike new dwellings in the open countryside is the impact of travel. Peer-reviewed research by the US Environmental Protection Agency[9] has discovered that:

> an energy-efficient, multi-family home using fuel-efficient vehicles and located in a transit-friendly site uses 70 million BTUs [20.5 MWh) per year: less than 30 per cent of the 240 million BTUs [70.34 MWh] used by a

single-family, detached home without energy-efficient features or cars in an automobile-dependent site.

This gives a pretty high benchmark for rural dwellings on greenfield sites to reach before they can be justified in environmental terms. Ideally, living in the countryside in a zero-carbon home and growing most of your own food should compensate for the impact of travel, but this needs to be proved – and the way to do it is by quantifying it and comparing the ecological footprint.

This process begins with an assessment of the expected traffic use by the occupants of the site, and of the public transport services available. Ideally the site should be located to take maximum advantage of these. However, this is not always possible. Your mapping process for the local community will help to identify what might be the most frequent trips you or your

Appendix 2: Traffic Counter Statistics 2012

Date	Traffic Movements
18/05/2012	40
19/05/2012	46
20/05/2012	24
21/05/2012	32
22/05/2012	29
23/05/2012	46
24/05/2012	45
25/05/2012	41
26/05/2012	56
27/05/2012	66
28/05/2012	24
29/05/2012	6
30/05/2012	26
31/05/2012	65
01/06/2012	42
02/06/2012	47
03/06/2012	38
04/06/2012	32
05/06/2012	39
06/06/2012	26
07/06/2012	30
08/06/2012	24
09/06/2012	24
10/06/2012	103

Figure 3.14   Extract from Tir Y Gafel (Lammas) traffic monitoring record, where there are nine households.
Credit: Lammas

visitors are likely to undertake. The One Planet Life will try to minimise the number of journeys and trips and the impact they can have.

There are three types of trips: by residents, enterprises on the site, and visitors to the site. All should be included. There should be significant efforts made to reduce the need to travel off site or for many types of goods to be brought onto the site. Assuming trips are necessary, some ways to minimise impacts are:

- car sharing, perhaps through a carpool or community owned car;
- cycling;
- walking;
- using public transport;
- coordination of deliveries to and from the site;
- a community-owned minibus;
- combining the purposes of trips;
- electric vehicles charged from renewable energy, whether generated on site or on a renewable energy tariff;
- horses (riding or carts).

The plan therefore details all of the above and will construct a baseline of all expected trips by date, time, mode, length and purpose. It will describe a strategy, or Transport Plan, for minimising the environmental impact of journeys.

As part of the monitoring, all trips will need to be annually accounted in the same way to compare actuality to the baseline. To help in this, a traffic counter could be installed at the entrance to the site; this might be powered by a small photovoltaic panel charging an AA battery which once a day sends a text to a mobile phone with the details of daily movements (as happens at Lammas). Record-keeping will include noting:

- the cost and type of fuel purchased for transport, divided into use for domestic and business purposes;
- mileage covered by fossil-fuel-powered vehicles;
- average vehicle occupancy level;
- conversion of these figures into greenhouse gas emissions.

All of this goes towards calculating the environmental footprint.

Calculating the environmental footprint

The process of calculating the ecological footprint, while laborious, should be considered as a means of testing out the effectiveness of what you are doing. It's therefore an interesting exploration. In energy-saving circles it's a well-known maxim that what is measured gets saved. So the first thing anybody does when trying to save energy in a building or organisation is to perform an audit of existing energy use. This is for two purposes:

* to identify where savings can be made; and
* to provide a baseline so that later you can see how much energy you have saved.

The information used to calculate the ecological footprint is like this in that it includes energy usage, but it adds much more. It then divides the total by the number of people in the household. If there is more than one household, each household does it separately. This is because the final unit at the end of the whole process is the ecological impact per person, or per capita.

Ecological footprint calculators are now fairly well validated. They have been criticised but the same critics admit that if anything they underestimate the environmental impact of human activities.[10] There are a number of different ones available for use in the UK, but most of them are not detailed enough to generate meaningful results for one-planet developments. The Welsh government's specially developed spreadsheet[11] for this purpose is derived from the Stockholm Environment Institute REAP 2 tool. This was originally used to work out the average footprint of Wales in 2004. It has since been adapted to take account of lower-energy lifestyles, small-scale integrated intensive farming and other aspects of self-sufficient living. It's been validated that this results in lower ecological footprints. The results of the spreadsheet calculations are estimated to have an accuracy of ±15 per cent.

The calculation method is largely based upon expenditure, which provides a proxy measure of the use of external resources. It requires a certain level of skill or training to interpret the results. It's normal practice that business activities are separated from personal activities for ecological accounting purposes. So residents should separate their own domestic and household consumption from that of any business they operate. Care should be taken to divide them up properly so that the same things are not counted twice and nothing is missed out. Also, anything used by volunteers or guests should not be counted in the domestic figures.

The way the software checks that this is right is by trying to balance all the figures entered for expenditure against those entered for income. If there is a discrepancy, this will be picked up.

To provide a baseline, if there is one, existing household expenditure for the last 12 months is entered. Then you enter the figure for what you estimate to happen during the first year of living on site. Finally, you enter a similar figure for what you think will be the situation after five years. That's at the beginning. At the end of year three you will enter your actual household expenditure. You will do the same at the end of year five. You will then see if your predictions were correct!

The following sets of data are required to be entered:

- number of people in household;
- household income: for existing footprint and when years three and five are reached;
- energy use: electricity, heating, travel, fuels, in kWh;
- housing and infrastructure: mortgages, rents, capital investments, repairs, cleaning and mains services;
- travel and transportation: modes, costs, mileages;
- food purchased: by type, including eating out;
- food produced on site for domestic use: seeds, inputs, equipment;
- consumable goods: of all types, e.g. clothing, furniture, electrical goods;
- services: of all types, e.g. ISP, phone, insurance, professional services, accommodation;
- all other transactions: savings and spending on all fuels.

All of this is much the same as would be done in a business, which, effectively, is what you are running.

Interpreting the results

The average UK ecological footprint is 5.45 global hectares (gha).[12] To begin with a reduction of 50 per cent to 2.7gha is demanding. But the aim

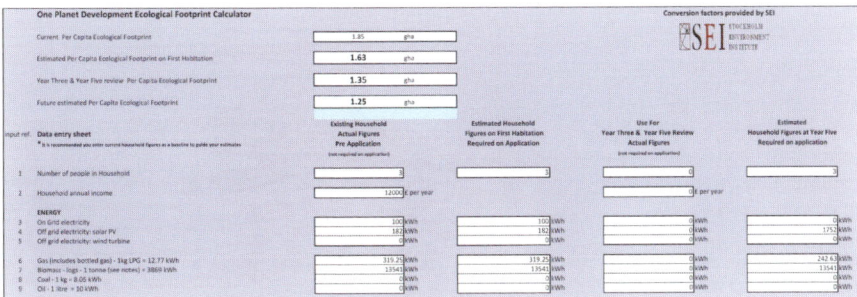

Figure 3.15 Example of part of what the EFA spreadsheet looks like when completed. Courtesy Samara Hawthorn.
Credit: Samara Hawthorn.

after five years should be to reach at least 1.88 gha, and this is extremely demanding, especially given that you will have no control over some aspects, such as the impact of government services. This is explained in the box below:

> **Out of control**
> The EFA tool used in Wales contains two parts, Capital Investments and Public Services, which are out of your control, because they are apportioned as your share of what the government does for every citizen in the country. In an attempt to be fair, the calculation therefore reduces this part by 50 per cent, assuming that a similar cut is achievable in the area of your life over which you do have control.

If this wasn't done, OPD residents would be aiming for an EF of 1.52 gha, which is 2.44 gha less 0.92 (the EF of government services in Wales). This would be very challenging at this stage.

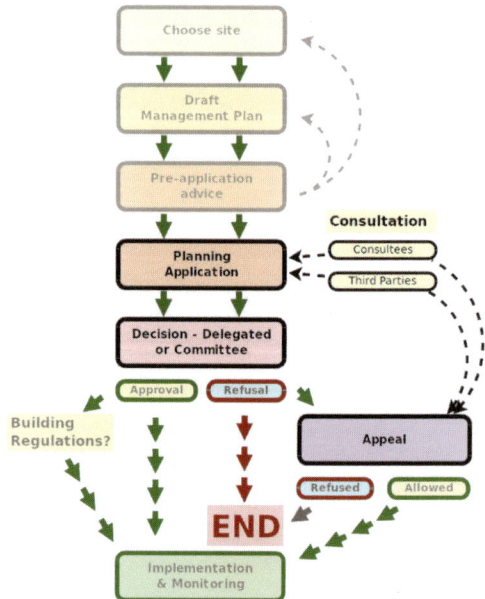

Figure 3.16 A summary of the whole planning process.

Double check

Here's some advice based on reasons actual planning appeals have been refused in the last year, despite an enormous amount of detail being submitted. Checking your plan against these will help to maximise your chances of success:

- You need 'robust' data covering the five years of the management plan relating to cropping area, anticipated yields and individual consumption patterns.
- Make allowance for soil quality, local climate, shade and other influences that might affect yield with a margin of error.
- Use substantiated market research to determine income from sale of produce.
- Agree in advance a definition of zero carbon in construction and use.
- Supply evidence to support the number of journeys estimated in transport assessments.
- Use photomontages and so on from the point of view of public vantage points to illustrate the visual impact of your proposals.
- Agree in advance the identity of the 'competent person or persons' to produce – AND evaluate on behalf of the planners – your management plan. At the time of writing the One Planet Council is in the process of reaching agreement on a pool of potential such persons.

Summary

The management plan finally decided upon from this process will quantify your chosen options in terms of both financial expenditure and income, and the relative ecological footprint derived from balancing the inputs and outputs. This is a double-sided balance sheet: financial and ecological.

Just as a business plan makes predictions for income and expenditure on a monthly basis, so will the management plan. And just as these predictions are measured against actual results on a monthly basis, so will the management plan be evaluated against actual experience. It is frequently the case that plans made at the beginning, even though approved by all concerned, in practice turn out to be impractical for one reason or another; for example, inclement and unpredictable weather may cause a crop to fail, or illness may necessitate lengthening a timescale or more journeys.

> **Tip**
> If in doubt, get a consultant who is approved and agreed as competent by yourself and the authority to whom you are submitting the application, to validate your plan and check your figures prior to submission.

Paul Wimbush believes that planning applications provide an opportunity for applicants to do their research and write a really good management plan that is robust and reliable so that when 'you hit the ground, you hit the ground running, because when you suddenly have to get things in the ground you are not going to have time to look at things like root stocks and soil types. You're not going to have time to research planting spaces. You're going to want to have done all your homework, knowing the gradient of the land.' What's more, the requirement to obtain livelihood at a minimum level from the land creates a sense of responsibility in the mind of the OPD practitioner which might not be there otherwise, say those practicing it now, such as the Acting Secretary of the One Planet Council, Stefan Cartwright.

At Lammas there are people with experience of building but not growing and growing but not building, and everyone is learning all the time. Everyone has their own level of experience, 'but experience does not necessarily translate into success, because there is the issue of overconfidence,' says Paul. 'Planning and preparation to create a really good management plan is the way to get around this. It's not just about designing how you are going to produce, say, globe artichokes, but whether you can actually see yourself doing this day after day, for a living and maintaining the same degree of passion and enthusiasm for it. Many potential applicants do not even make it as far as the management plan because they realise when they look at it closely that this kind of lifestyle is not for them.'

Personally, I am in awe of all of the individuals going through the One Planet Development process because of the sheer amount of hard work entailed. No one should underestimate this. There will be frustrations, setbacks and bitter disappointments as mistakes are made and hard lessons learnt. But the rewards are tremendous.

Equally, living this closely with nature makes it obvious that you, yourself, are part of the systems you engage with. Your energy levels, your stamina, your commitments, your skills and talents, as well as your weaknesses, foibles and blind spots will all become part of the processes. When looking at whatever projects you are hoping to create and maintain, it is critical, then, to choose ones which chime with your passions and commitment but are not arrested or inhibited by any deficiencies you may have that you are not prepared to challenge.

Notes

1 At http://wales.gov.uk/topics/planning/policy/guidanceandleaflets/oneplanet/?lang=en. Accessed March 2014.
2 Using ISO 14040 Environmental management – Life cycle assessment – Principles and framework. See http://www.iso.org/iso/catalogue_detail?csnumber=37456. Accessed March 2014.
3 Available at http://wales.gov.uk/topics/planning/policy/guidanceandleaflets/oneplanet/?lang=en. Accessed November 2013.
4 See *Natural England Technical Information Note TIN049: Agricultural Land Classification: protecting the best and most versatile agricultural land* at http://bit.ly/Lx6B25.
5 Seek the advice of the local authority, Biological Records Centre or the Wildlife Trust.
6 Available at the website of the single environmental watchdog and agency for Wales, Natural Resources Wales, at http://naturalresourceswales.gov.uk/out-and-about/maps/LANDMAP/?lang=en#.UsbdFWRdUZB.
7 I.e. there must be no gaps between the insulation, otherwise it is worthless.
8 Breathable constructions are composed of hygroscopic materials, such as wood, stone, brick, adobe, earth, straw bale, lime, hemcrete and organic sheet materials. Lime and insulating plasters are very good at absorbing and releasing unwanted moisture in problem areas. Materials which prevent air from passing through include: metal, non-permeable plastic sheeting, and polystyrene-type slab insulation, with the partial exception of expanded polystyrene.
9 Location Efficiency and Housing Type, Jonathan Rose Companies, EPA, February 2011, http://www.epa.gov/smartgrowth/location_efficiency_BTU.htm. Retrieved November 2013.
10 Pearce, Fred, *Putting Our Foot In It*, *New Scientist*, 23 November 2013.
11 Available at http://wales.gov.uk/topics/planning/policy/guidanceandleaflets/oneplanet/?lang=en. Retrieved November 2013.
12 Global Footprint Network's 2010 Data Tables: http://www.footprintnetwork.org/en/index.php/GFN/page/footprint_for_nations. Retrieved March 2014.

Part Three
Practical guidance

4 Land management

Your strategy for land management will demonstrate how you are respecting the needs of the environment and enhancing it for future generations. It will also help you to sustain yourselves and, possibly, others – but we look at this in more detail in the chapter on Food.

How you choose to develop the land will be based on an iterative design process derived from your observations of how the land performs throughout a calendar year or more. It may be that the existing infrastructure for land use can simply be improved, but sometimes you'll want to make bigger changes. A given plot of land contains interacting complex systems that need to be understood in order to take advantage of them. Surveys at different times of the day and year will indicate how much sunshine, wind, rainfall, shade and so on is received by different areas. Several types of survey are possible and we will look at these one by one:

Figure 4.1 You start with the land as you find it. But what will you make of it?

- A Phase 1 Habitat Survey[1] will refer to any nearby Sites of Special Scientific Interest and Special Areas of Conservation, to Local Biodiversity Action Plans, LANDMAP information and registered parks and gardens in the vicinity. The impact of human presence on biodiversity should be properly assessed.
- A soil survey will document the soil types found.
- A gradient survey will look at water flows through the land and can involve the use of surveying equipment.
- A renewable-energy resource survey will, over a year, measure any of the wind, solar or hydro resources of which you think you might be able to take advantage. *See the section on renewable energy.*
- A temperature survey will measure the temperature at different times in the year. This will help you work out ways to protect your plants and so on.
- Surveys of elevation, moisture levels, rainfall patterns, topography, geology, previous land use, shade and wind shelter can all be used to generate gradient maps showing how these vary through the site.

Using these surveys will help you determine where the main tracks will go for access to different areas; and where the main dwellings and workshops ought best to be situated. Be prepared to revise your ideas depending on what you find out later.

> **Units of area**
> 1 hectare (ha) = 100 m × 100 m or 0.01 sq km (100ha to the sq km)
> 1 ha = approx. 2.407 acres (or the size of Trafalgar Square)
> 1 acre = approx. 0.407ha. 4,840 square yards, 4,047 square metres or a square of sides 69.57 yards.

Your site evaluation will describe the existing state of affairs. This will form a baseline against which your activities will be measured. Your aim is to improve quality, biodiversity and productivity, as well as to preserve any historic or culturally significant features and buildings that might lie within your boundaries. Also look for the effects of the microclimate:

- Where do frost pockets occur?
- Where will you need to build shelter banks to protect against wind?
- Is the soil acid or alkaline and what is the proportional organic content?
- How does water travel through the landscape?

Figure 4.2 Example of an Ordnance Survey map coloured according to the colour key advocated in the Phase 1 habitat survey guidelines.
Source: Defra

What will be the carbon balance of your activities? This will quantify the different carbon impacts of different activities on part of the land.

Habitat survey

The Phase 1 habitat classification and associated field survey technique is an approved method for conducting an environmental audit. It provides a relatively rapid way to record semi-natural vegetation and other wildlife habitats. Each habitat type/feature is defined by way of a brief description and is allocated a specific name, an alphanumeric code, and unique mapping colour. Species are also allocated codes. The system has been widely used and continues to act as the standard 'phase 1' technique for habitat survey across the UK, so planners understand it.

This biodiversity survey will document and map the main species, of plant, insects, birds, invertebrates, reptiles and mammals found. Different species will thrive in different zones and at staged times of the year. You will end up with a colourful, annotated map.

The carbon cycle and climate change

Together with the nitrogen cycle, the carbon cycle and the water cycle comprise the three great processes that help to sustain life on Earth. Your humble plot of land plays a part in these. Water, nitrogen and carbon

Components of the Global Carbon Cycle

Atmospheric Carbon Net Annual Increase

GtC/y: Gigatons of carbon/year

Plant photosynthesis. Plants convert atmospheric CO_2 into organic compounds used to build plant biomass.

Carbon flow in plants. Regulatory networks and biochemical pathways control how much organic matter is released as CO_2 from respiration and how much accumulates belowground in roots and aboveground in leaves and stems.

Net terrestrial uptake 3

Microbial respiration and decomposition

Soil carbon

Soil (2300)

Fossil pool (10,000)

Phytoplankton photosynthesis. Algae and photosynthetic bacteria form the base of the marine food chain by converting dissolved CO_2 into energy-rich organic compounds that make up living cells.

Consumption and respiration of sea life. Carbon in phytoplankton is consumed by higher life forms that respire CO_2.

Surface ocean (1000)

Phytoplankton photosynthesis

Respiration and decomposition

Net ocean uptake 2

Deep ocean (37,000)

Reactive sediments (6000)

Zooplankton

Root-microbe interactions. Chemical exchanges among plant roots, soil microbes, and fungi influence nutrient and water flows, plant productivity, and soil carbon content.

Microbes
Root
Soil particle
Fungal hyphae
Soil particle
Soil particle

Microbial respiration and decomposition. Bacteria and fungi decompose plant litter (remnants of roots, leaves, and animal litter into organic compounds, inorganic nutrients (nitrogen, phosphorus), and CO_2.

Plant litter
Nutrients
Soil microbes
Organic compounds

Soil organic matter formation. Enzymes released from microbes transform plant litter into diverse soil organic compounds that have different structures and residence times in soils.

Enzymes
Soil organic matter

Decomposition and deposition in ocean depths. Microbes decompose dead organisms to form CO_2 and dissolved nutrients used by other marine life forms. A small fraction of organic matter remnants of dead organisms, coccolithophore shells, fecal pellets) forms small, degradation-resistant clumps (marine snow) that sink to the sea floor.

Microbes
Coccolithophore
CO_2 Nitrogen Phosphorus
Marine snow

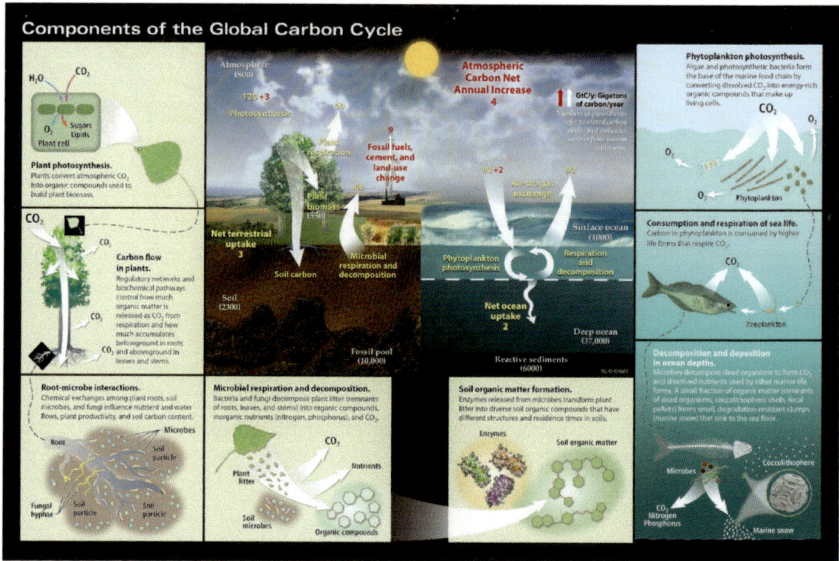

Figure 4.3 Components of the Global Carbon Cycle. Values in parentheses are estimates of the main carbon reservoirs in gigatons (GT). The natural flux between the terrestrial biosphere and the atmosphere is about 120 GT of carbon per year, and that between the oceans and atmosphere is about 90 GT per year (IPCC 2007). Human activities (primarily fossil-fuel use) emit about 9 GT of carbon each year. About 4 GT of this remain in the atmosphere; 3 GT are taken up by natural terrestrial processes, and another 2 GT are removed by the ocean (Canadell et al. 2007). The boxes round the sides describe some of the biological processes (photosynthesis, partitioning, respiration, and organic-matter formation) that play key roles in regulating the flow of carbon in and out of terrestrial and ocean ecosystems.
Source: Office of Biological and Environmental Research of the US Department of Energy Office of Science.[2]

flow through the land, miraculously changing their form as they do so. Depending on conditions, you might want to store water for use in the dry season; or you'll have too much of it and want to drain it away. The peril of climate change means that it's beneficial to take carbon dioxide from the atmosphere, so you should look for ways to store it.

We can help sequester (lock away) carbon by incorporating plant products like timber or straw in our buildings, fencing, furnishings and so on. Plants use the power of sunshine to take carbon from carbon dioxide in the air, returning oxygen back to the air for us to breathe, and in the process combining the carbon with water to grow fibres. If the plant is a tree we can harvest the wood and build with it or make goods to sell, thereby keeping that carbon out of the atmosphere and doing our bit to fight global warming. If we burn wood as fuel we return that carbon back to the atmosphere. This is why for heating it's better to use solar energy or ground source heat pumps powered by renewable electricity and make

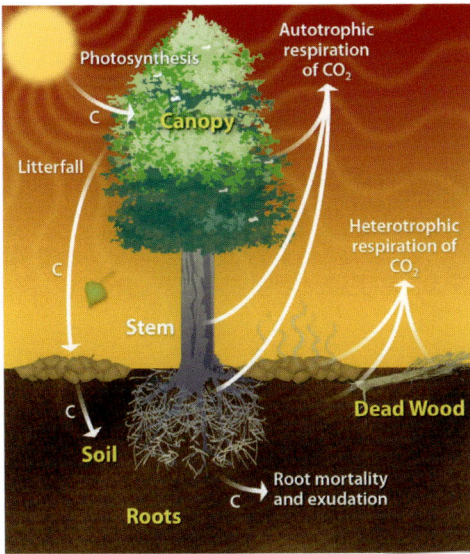

Figure 4.4 Terrestrial Photosynthetic Carbon Cycle. Courtesy of N. Scott and M. Ernst, Woods Hole Research Center, whrc.org.[3]

buildings superinsulated, and burn less wood, even though burning wood is supposed to be 'carbon neutral'.

Land use is vital to reducing carbon emissions. It's more important than insulation or using renewable energy. We're only just beginning to realise this. According the US Department of Energy:

> The amount of carbon exchanged between the biosphere and atmosphere each year is many times greater than the carbon emitted by human activities. Thus, even minor changes in the rate and magnitude of biological carbon cycling can have immense impacts on whether ecosystems will capture, store, or release carbon.[4]

If carbon saving were to be the only measure for determining land use, then leaving land as dwarf shrub heath would provide the best carbon storage. Arable agriculture or horticulture reduces the carbon-storage capacity of the soil by almost two thirds, as seen in Table 4.1 But local cultivation and consumption must of course be balanced against the carbon savings of not having to import food onto the site, and not needing the fossil-fuel-based inputs used to grow this food.

Making healthy soil

You can examine the soil by digging it, feeling it, smelling it. It's a sensual activity. Good soil is a living thing. Whereas chemically treated arable soil may

Table 4.1 Carbon stock (tonnes per hectare) in the top 0–15 cm of soil in different habitats by year. Acid grassland is more than twice as good at storing carbon than arable land. Grazed land is just under twice as good. Cultivating land, paradoxically, is the worst, but minimising ploughing or digging is beneficial. Use this table to calculate the baseline carbon balance of your land as it is at the start. You can then compare it to what will happen when you change the land use of different areas of your plot. Source: National Sustainable Development Indicators for Wales[5]

Measure	2007
Dwarf shrub heath	88
Acid grassland	75
Broad leaved mixed and yew wood land	71
All broad habitats	65
Neutral grassland	63
Improved grassland	62
Coniferous woodland	61
Arable	33

have as little as 1 per cent organic content, healthy soil can have as much as 10 per cent. If soil is waterlogged, it means that there is less air present: the atmosphere needs to penetrate the top few centimetres of the soil in order for the bacteria and other creatures which promote fertility to do their job. If the soil is compacted it performs less well. It can become impermeable.

Try performing this activity in the different areas of your site where you notice that different types of plants are growing, so that you can compare the difference in the soil at these points and see how it affects what grows there. As Bill Mollison,[6] one of the founders of Permaculture, has observed, different types of soil are necessary to preserve biodiversity. Your survey will show how your site can be zoned to take maximum advantage of what is already there. It's no good trying to work against nature, you have to work with it. That way you will get the most out of your efforts.

Warm, moist, well-aerated soil is the most beneficial to high yields (but emits the most greenhouse gases). It aids the process of nitrification, which is the process of extracting nitrogen from the atmosphere that plants need to grow. Bacteria in the soil and on the roots of plants fix this nitrogen. They need the oxygen-rich atmosphere that aerated compost and organic matter in the soil can give them. This is why it's important to add compost to soil.

The nitrogen cycle

Nitrogen is an essential building block of amino and nucleic acids, which form all life on Earth. It forms about 80 per cent of the Earth's atmosphere.

We cannot use it directly nor can any plants or animals; it must first be converted to a reduced (or 'fixed') state. Most fixed nitrogen reaches the soil surface as nitrate, where it is assimilated by plant roots.

This happens with the help of specific bacteria. These possess enzymes that can fix atmospheric nitrogen into a form that is chemically useful, in a process that requires a large amount of energy and anoxic (oxygen-free) conditions. They normally live in a symbiotic relationship with the root nodules of leguminous plants (e.g. clover, *Trifolium*, or soybean plant, *Glycine max*) and fertilizer trees. They form proteins and other molecules in exchange for sugars the plants give to the bacteria.

Plants can also assimilate nitrogen directly in the form of nitrates that may be present in soil from natural mineral deposits, artificial fertilizers, animal waste, or organic decay (as the product of bacteria, but not bacteria specifically associated with the plant).

The use of artificial fertilisers to add nitrogen is one of the main causes of eutrophication, or pollution, of watercourses. It deprives organisms in the water of oxygen, killing them. This is why it's better to practice organic methods of improving soil fertility. This involves deploying well-rotted

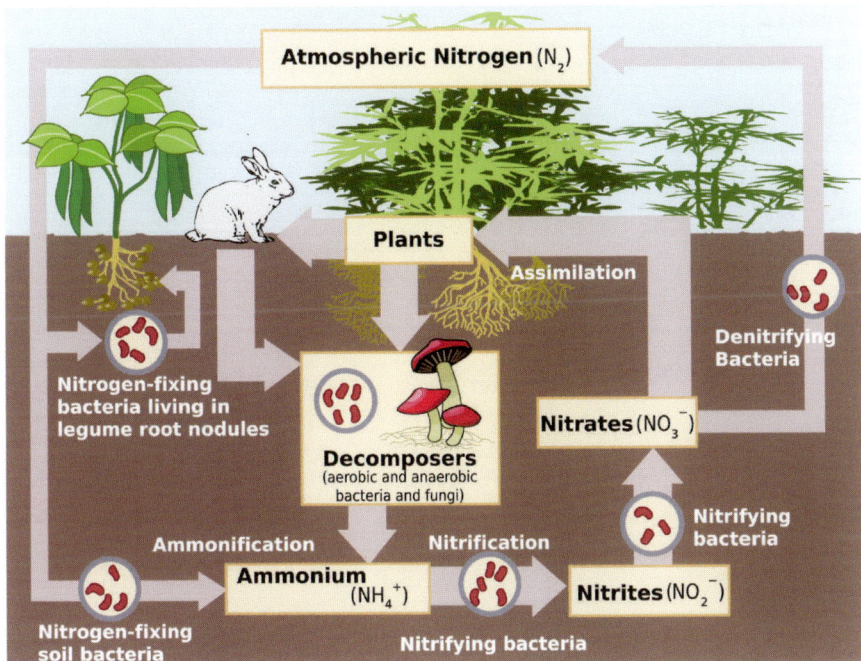

Figure 4.5 The Nitrogen Cycle.
Source: Johann Dréo, Wikipedia.

animal manure with straw or hay, compost, and situating nitrogen-fixing plants whose roots support the bacteria that fix atmospheric nitrogen amongst your crops (see box).

Some nitrogen-fixing plants

These include cover crops / green manures and members of the legume family:

- beans, lupins, alfalfa and so on;
- hairy vetch;
- clovers;
- comfrey;
- alders;
- broom (*Cytisus scoparius*);
- oleasters (*Elaeagnus* spp);
- fenugreek.

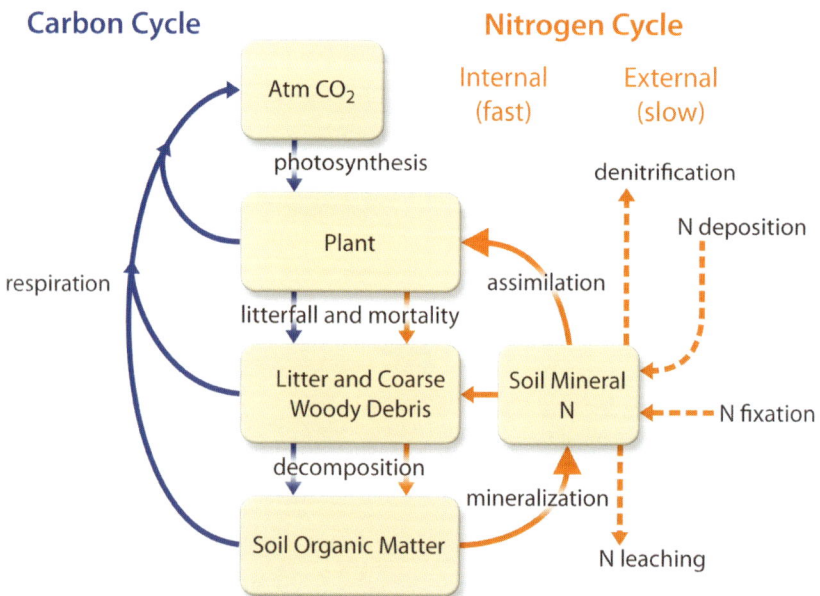

Figure 4.6 The Coupling of the Carbon and Nitrogen Cycles showing how decomposition of organic matter during the nitrogen cycle releases carbon back into the atmosphere.
Source: Office of Biological and Environmental Research of the US Department of Energy Office of Science.[7]

The pH value of soil

Fertile soil also needs to have the right pH value. This is a measure of its acidity or alkalinity on a scale of zero to nine, where nine is the most alkaline. You can cheaply buy a device to test the pH of your soil at a garden centre or purchase some litmus paper, which you dip into a mixture of your soil with water. Your target should be organic soils of pH 5.5 or mineral soils of pH 6.5. High acidity will result in a toxic amount of aluminium and magnesium in the soil. If the land is former pasture you will be able to tell if it's acidic because there will be a lot of purple moor grass and rush.

• If you find that your soil is too alkaline add powdered gypsum for calcium sulphate.
• If you find it is too acid, add lime, although this gives no permanent change in pH.

Figure 4.7 Chart showing the variation of colour of universal indicator paper with pH.
Source: Wikimedia Commons, from Bordercolliez.

Figure 4.8 Waterlogged acid soil is identified by lots of rushes. If the land is to be grazed these should be mowed once or twice a year to give the grass a chance as most species (except, for example, Belted Galloway cattle, which are less productive) can't eat rushes. The land on this organic farm on the right of this picture has been deliberately left unmowed to show the difference.

Waterlogged soil removes nitrogen. This is why it's important to have a drainage plan for your land. This is covered more in the section on Food.

Woodland survey

Hopefully your proposed site will contain trees already. Your survey should determine what types of woodland are present on the site and the area allocated to each. The main types of woodland are:

- **ancient woodland:** has been around for at least 400 years and contains trees of many different ages;
- **shelter belts:** narrow strips of woodland to protect fields from prevailing winds;
- **plantations**: trees planted for the eventual harvesting of planks and poles for construction purposes in regular grid formation. Their presence is a great asset since you may be able to use some trees for construction. The trees may be uniform or not and of any type, e.g.:
  - **broadleaf plantations:** densely planted;
  - **coniferous plantations:** also densely planted;
  - **mixed plantations;** of broadleaf and coniferous trees;
- **orchards**: lucky you! But some may have been neglected and be in need of loving care;
- **coppice:** areas which have been used for coppicing in the past or still are being used. Many branches, sometimes quite high if the coppicing has been neglected, might be growing out of stools (the word for stumps). Sometimes they are interspersed with standards, typically oak, ash and hazel;
- **Short-rotation coppice:** on a four-year rotation, meaning that the oldest branches will be four years old, after which they are cut back;

Figure 4.10 A young (15-year old) woodland consisting mostly of birch with some beech, ash, conifer and hazel, that has grown up on what was a grazing field. Cornerwood, Ceredigion.

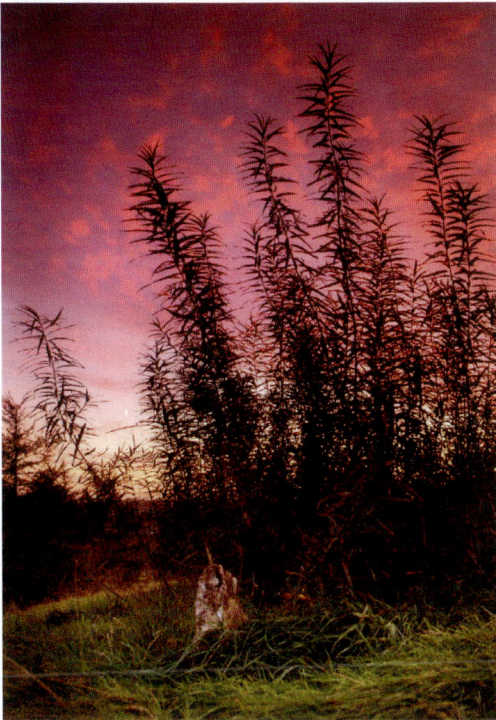

Figure 4.11 Short Rotation Coppice willow in Lammas (Simon and Jasmine's plot).
Credit: Jasmine Dale

usually consisting of willow, but in some places poplar, alder and even sweet chestnut; typically these are used for crafts or kindling;

- **pollarded**: where broadleaf trees have been cut back at a height of at least 6 feet or 1.8 m above the ground;
- **wood pasture:** an area planted with trees that are undergrazed;
- **hedgerows**: can be a good source of firewood and providing livestock corridors.

You will want to determine how you will manage the resources you currently have and whether you'll be planting more areas of trees and for

Figure 4.12 Plums on a 10-year-old tree at Hockerton Housing Co-op.

Figure 4.13 Orchard at Hockerton Housing Co-op.

what purpose. Trees can provide beauty, wind shelter, nuts, berries, fruit, wildlife habitats, construction and craft materials, firewood, charcoal and fungi. It will also be important to provide continuous wildlife corridors across your site.

For each area or type of woodland a separate management plan could be drafted. This would describe the trees, their age and condition; the management objectives, e.g. biodiversity enhancement, removal of certain species and brambles, thinning, employment, production of timber prod-ucts and charcoal, and so on. For example, you might find that you have trees which are ideal for the production of fencing you could sell.

It takes a practiced eye to look at different trees and ascertain the use that can be made of their timber. For example, straight poles are not the only useful parts of trees: graceful curves can also be used to make rustic

Figure 4.14 A shelter belt of trees planted 10 years ago also for coppicing; they have only just reached the required size for harvesting for firewood.

Figure 4.15 Oak slabs stacked for seasoning. The spacers allow the air to move between the slabs to dry. Picture taken at Hockerton, Notts.

furniture. Forks in branches have multiple uses, such as when making rustic chairs. Twigs may make kindling or pea climbers. Ben Law is an acknowledged expert on woodlands and obtaining the most benefit and even finds ways to utilise the sap from certain trees.

It is essential to receive proper training in many woodland crafts and practices, not least because there are legal aspects to what is permissible. Skills

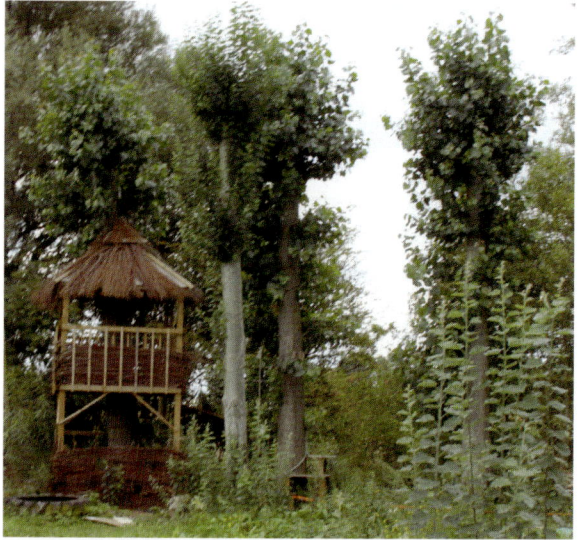

Figure 4.16 Pollarded trees next to a playhouse at Hockerton Housing Co-op.

Figure 4.17 A new orchard planted out with many different species and cultivars. Phil Corbet's land, Notts. (See Exemplary Examples.)

such as safe cutting, extraction and milling need to be taught, and knowing how to, for example, use green wood, practise bodging or joinery are generally learnt by attending courses or volunteering on existing projects.

Crop rotation

Much of your land will be productive for food. For vegetable and livestock fodder production, growing different crops in the same plots in rotation on four or five-year cycle has many benefits:

- Plants needing nitrogen are planted the year after nitrogen-fixing plants;

- Helps prevent the build-up of pathogens and pests in the soil;
- Can improve soil structure and the yield;
- Can help combat soil erosion and weeds;
- Allows the land to be more productive.

Plants within the same taxonomic family tend to have the same pests and pathogens, for example potato blight, clubroot in brassicas and onion white rot. By practising crop rotation, by the time the potatoes are planted in the same plot the blight has disappeared.

The exact choice and sequence of rotation crops depends on the nature of the soil, the climate and rainfall levels, as well as what crops are desired all the year round. Intercropping and companion planting introduces some complexity into the picture, but this is a common practice with Permaculture as a way of pest control and improving yield. Different plants' roots extend to different depths in the soil, and so will not be in competition with each other. Similarly, they grow to different heights and the same can apply. For example, carrots might be shaded by tomatoes and loosen the soil beneath them.

Double cropping is practised where two crops are grown sequentially within the same growing season. For example, winter rye and barley may be sown after oats and harvested before the next crop of oats is planted.

A common simple rotation system includes the following groups of crops:

- **Legumes**: Pea, broad beans (French and runner beans suffer from fewer soil problems and can be grown wherever convenient);
- **Brassicas**: Brussels sprouts, cabbage, cauliflower, kale, kohlrabi, oriental greens, radish, swede and turnips;
- **Potato family**: Potato, tomato, (pepper and aubergine suffer from fewer problems and can be grown anywhere in the rotation);
- **Onions**: Onion, garlic, shallot, leek;
- **Roots**: Beetroot, carrot, celeriac, celery, Florence fennel, parsley, parsnip and all other root crops, except swedes and turnips, which are brassicas.

Legumes, onions and roots can also be grown in the same bed.

Exceptions to crop rotation are perennial vegetables (such as rhubarb and asparagus) and certain annual crops such as cucurbits (courgettes, pumpkins, squashes, marrows and cucumbers), French and runner beans, salads (endive, lettuce and chicory) and sweetcorn. These can be grown wherever convenient, as long as you avoid growing them too often in the same place.

Bed/year	1	2	3	4
1	Potatoes	Onions & roots	Legumes	Brassicas
2	Brassicas	Potatoes	Onions & roots	Legumes
3	Legumes	Brassicas	Potatoes	Onions & roots
4	Onions & roots	Legumes	Brassicas	Potatoes

Figure 4.18 A four-year crop rotation plan. Years are horizontal.

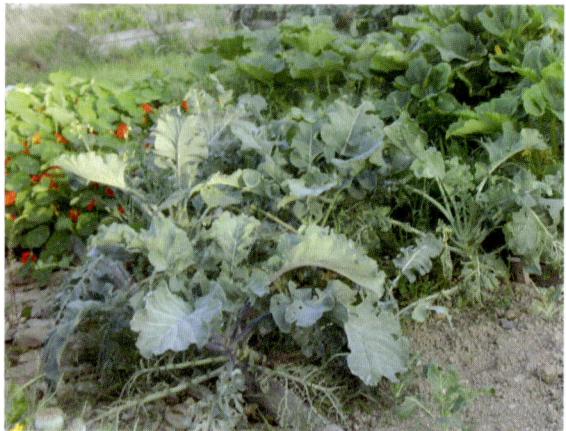

Figure 4.19 Companion planting of nasturtiums next to brassicas (kale).

Companion planting

Companion planting is the planting of different crops near to each other. The advantages include:

- pest control;
- improved pollination;
- providing habitats for beneficial creatures (biodiversity);
- maximising the use of space;
- increasing crop productivity;
- providing shelter for crops.

Figure 4.20 Preparing for alley cropping. Phil Corbet has laid out his orchard in diagonal rows on this south-facing slope to maximise the use of sunlight on each tree, and so that in the future when the plastic has killed off the weeds below he can make holes in it into which he will plant vegetables between the rows.

Flowers are typically planted amongst vegetables. Examples include:

* Nasturtium (*Tropaeolum majus*), to divert caterpillars from brassicas;
* Marigolds to deter aphids from feeding on neighbouring crops and attract nectar-feeding adult hoverflies, whose larvae eat aphids.

Many other beneficial companionships exist and lists of them can be easily found.

Intercropping

This is the practice of planting crops in between other crops, again to produce greater yield and improve biodiversity:

* Alley or row cropping is where vegetable crops are grown in between rows of trees in an orchard.
* Fast-growing crops may be planted alongside slow-growing ones and harvested before the slow growing ones have reached a certain height.
* Relay cropping involves delaying the planting of a second row until the first has grown to a certain extent, such as the fruiting stage, so that the first planting is harvested to leave room for the second planting to mature.

Figure 4.21 Conversion of an orchard to a forest garden in mid-process. Vegetables (pumpkins and others) are being intercropped, and when the weeds are killed off other beneficial plants will be installed. Source: John Hargraves' OPD site.

Figure 4.22 An edible hedge in our garden. It contains raspberries, hazelnuts, fuchsia, blackberries, blackcurrants (in the front row), rosehips, blackthorn, hawthorn, plums and cherries. Gooseberries are planted in front and bamboo at the right for stakes.

Forest gardens

Forest gardens are claimed to require less maintenance for a similar amount of yield of certain produce. The main products are fruit, nuts and green leafy vegetables. This approach utilises a form of intercropping with plants of up to seven different heights. From the ground upwards, these are:

- a layer of plants grown for their roots and tubers;
- a ground-cover layer of edible plants that restricts weed growth;
- a herbaceous layer of perennial vegetables and herbs;
- a shrub layer of soft fruit such as berries and currants;
- a low tree layer of smaller nut and top fruit trees such as dwarf apples, pears and almonds – which may be coppiced to keep them smaller;
- a canopy layer of taller mature fruit and nut trees such as cherry, mulberries, plums, quinces, hawthorn, hazelnut, large apple trees and horse chestnuts;

- a vertical layer of vines and climbers, including nasturtiums, grapes, clematis and honeysuckle.

Edible hedges

Hedges provide:

- habitat for biodiversity, including acting as wildlife corridors between wooded areas;
- windbreaks and frost protection;
- another opportunity to provide food.

Initially, fast-growing species such as willow and bamboo may be planted so that wind protection can be quickly provided. Bamboo can be harvested for plant support. Any trees to be planted thereafter which may be slower growing or provide less wind cover might as well be useful and, preferably, edible – if not for humans then for other species. Some of my favourite varieties include:

- *Corylus avellana* (hazelnut);
- *Akebia trifoliata, Akebia x pentaphylla* or *Akebia quinata*: deciduous climber growing to 12 m (39ft 4in) at a fast rate. Fruit has a delicate flavour and a soft, juicy texture;
- *Fuchsia splendens*: moist soil, shade. A juicy berry, it is tart with a peppery aftertaste;
- *Humulus lupulus* (the hop): a perennial climber growing to 6 m; leaves can be eaten in salads;
- *Prunus cerasus austere* (Morello Cherry): growing to 9 m;
- *Prunus insititia* (damson): growing to 6 m;
- *Ribes nigrum* (blackcurrant): growing to 1.8 m;
- *Ribes rubrum* (redcurrant): growing to 1.8 m;
- *Rubus deliciosus* (Rocky Mountain raspberry): growing to 3 m
- *Sambucus nigra* (elderberry).

When choosing species keep in mind that:

- deciduous trees, losing their leaves in winter, will provide less wind protection when most needed, so evergreens such as spruce, firs, holly and ivy should also be included for this purpose.

- Plant one or two each of many different varieties of the same tree, such as apple, to start with, and observe which ones thrive in your particular habitat and climate. This will save a lot of grief in the long run.

Productive ground cover

Ground cover keeps weeds down; it might as well be edible also. Again, here are a handful of my favourite varieties to start you off:

- *Reichardia picroides* (French Scorzonera): perennial, growing to 0.5 m, Leaves may be eaten raw in salads or cooked;
- *Barbarea verna* (Land Cress): spicy watercress flavour; grows best in a moist well-drained soil and usually attains a height of around 30 cm;
- *Barbarea vulgaris* (Yellow Rocket);
- *Umbilicus rupestris* (Pennywort): the leaves can be eaten raw or cooked in the winter and early spring;
- *Viola odorata* (sweet violet): flowers produced late winter and early spring have a sweet scent and can be eaten in salads.

Mapping example

Hopefully I've given you an overview of the possibilities for zoning. Let's now put our knowledge into practice. Here is an example of a hypothetical piece of land, showing some of the above principles in operation using three maps.

Power comes from the combination of solar thermal, solar PV and hydropower. Following in-depth surveys of the resource, and consultation with the Environment Agency, it was found that an average of 1.5 kW of continuous electricity could be obtained by putting a Pelton wheel in a shed fed by a constructed leat. This outputs into a pond in which aquaculture could be practised before water is returned to the watercourse. Carp could be reared in the pond for food. This nicely complements the solar power since it is available all the time. When not required, surplus electricity can be directed to provide heat to either the dwellings or a polytunnel. This will greatly extend the growing period.

It was decided at first only to put solar panels on the dwelling roof, not the workshop roof. Most of this roof slopes south at an angle optimum for collecting solar power.

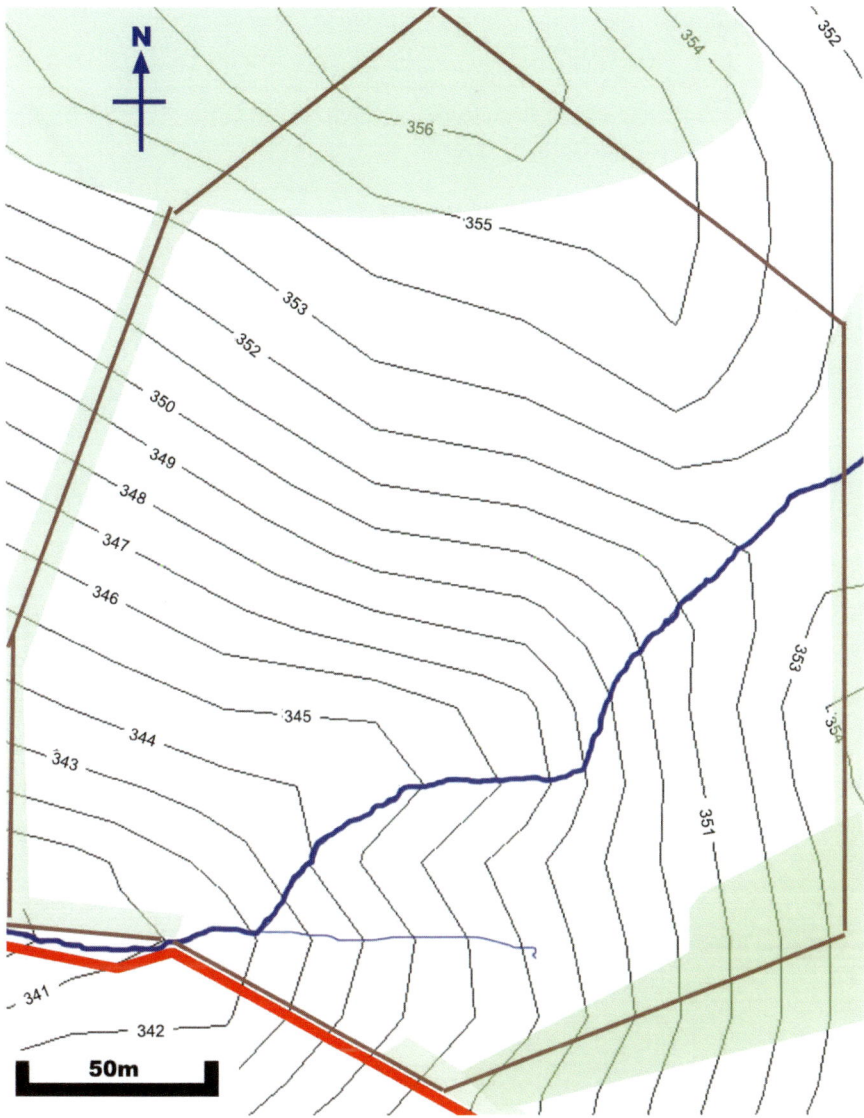

Figure 4.23 The initial survey shows that the land broadly slopes from the northeast to the southwest. The aspect is good, facing more or less south-southwest. The prevailing wind also comes from the northeast. The border of the land is shown by the brown line. The contours are at five-metre intervals. Drainage is reasonable to good. There is a small river and a stream coming from a spring. The western side of the land is less well irrigated. Hedges form the perimeter on two sides, and woodland to the north and the southeast. Additionally, not shown on the map, there is an SSSI (site of special scientific interest) towards the south-east. There is a main road (red line) to the southwest for access.

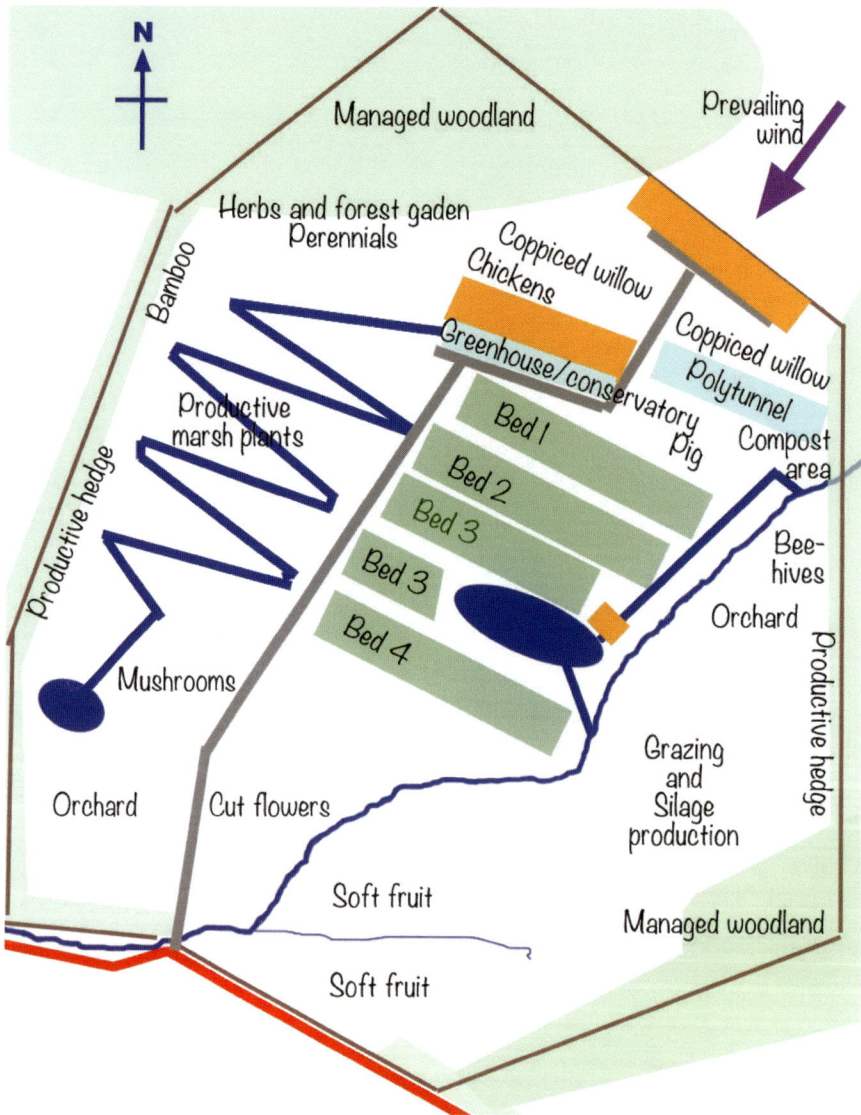

N

Managed woodland

Prevailing wind

Herbs and forest gaden
Perennials

Coppiced willow
Chickens

Bamboo

Coppiced willow
Polytunnel

Greenhouse/conservatory

Compost area

Productive
marsh plants

Bed 1

Pig

Productive hedge

Bed 2

Bed 3

Bee-hives

Bed 3

Orchard

Bed 4

Productive hedge

Mushrooms

Grazing
and
Silage
production

Orchard

Cut flowers

Soft fruit

Managed woodland

Soft fruit

Figure 4.24 This map shows a sketch of how power, water, buildings and access were envisaged upon the land. To the northeast a long structure for workshops, storage and so on would form a windbreak against the prevailing wind along the perimeter. Beneath this, and in a commanding, central position, another long building for the main dwelling house would be in a prime position to take maximum advantage of solar gain. It would harvest rainwater, and a wetland ecological treatment system on the west side of the site would help to irrigate that side, with bunds constructed along contours, cleaning the greywater from the dwelling to the extent that it is fit to flow into a duck pond. This area will be planted with a variety of species to maximise biodiversity and productivity. The access road is constructed to occupy as little as possible of the productive land area.

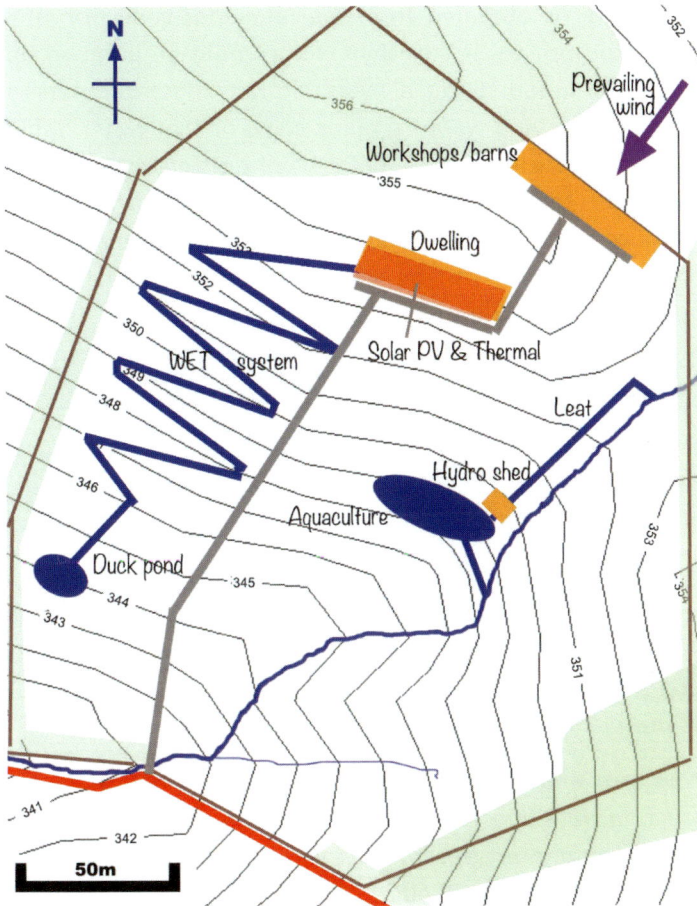

Figure 4.25 This map explains how the land will be used. The neglected woodland at the top will be managed for conservation and productivity, yielding firewood, wood for crafts and food. The perimeter becomes part of a layered forest garden, descending into ground cover and herbs for the kitchen nearby. Willow is planted on the northeast edge to be coppiced for fuel and craft materials, as well as providing a windbreak and frost protection. Chickens are kept behind the house and a pig to the right. The pig is fed scraps of food over four months of the latter end of the year before being slaughtered for food. It can also be used for breaking up the land for cultivation. The front of the dwelling has a long greenhouse/conservatory to grow exotic foods such as tomatoes, grapes and figs. It also pre-heats air going into the dwelling, reducing the need for artificial heating to almost zero, since the building is extremely well insulated. Directly in front of the building are four beds for crop rotation. A productive or edible hedge goes along the west and east sides. More managed woodland is in the southeast. The area beneath the vegetable beds is used for growing cut flowers for sale and soft fruit for sale, including strawberries, raspberries, blackcurrants and so on, as this will be a very attractive introductory sight for visitors. To the left of the access drive is an orchard. There could be another orchard on the east side. It was thought that some fruit could be eaten, some sold, and some used to make cider. Beehives will be kept in that orchard. Near the duckpond it was hypothesised that at some point there could be a facility for growing shiitake mushrooms on dead wood, a potentially profitable activity. It was thought that either a cow or a goat could be kept, and this would be in a field to the southeast of the river. This contains three paddocks, only one of which is occupied at any time in order to provide silage for the winter. One could be planted with beet.

Drinking water is obtained from the rainwater collection. If in practice this is found not to be sufficient, some could be pumped up to the house from the stream using a hydraulic ram. Hydraulic rams use the power in the descending water to pump some of that water uphill. This is necessary because there is a two-metre height difference between where the stream enters the property and the position of the dwelling.

For the purpose of the management plan, a further map would detail the existing biodiversity on the site, and another how this would be enhanced over time. If there were any existing significant archaeological or historical or cultural features on the landscape they would be noted on the first map.

Frost protection

One thing not noted in the maps is where the potential frost pockets lie and what should be done to protect them. This can only be done by observation in the winter. Bear in mind that cold air flows downhill and particularly from watercourses and bodies of water. There are several ways to protect your precious plants from frost:

- planting trees and bushes to act as shelter;
- constructing walls (if on four sides you're making a walled garden but this is labour intensive) from stone or cob to act as thermal mass (warmed by the sun) and shelter;
- burying organic matter – *Hugelkultur*.

Hugelkultur

Hugelkultur is about burying organic matter such as branches and logs just beneath the surface. The principle is very simple and the advantages are many. A pioneer in this practice is the Austrian Josef 'Sepp' Holzer,[8] who has managed to cultivate hundreds of productive fruit trees above the traditionally assumed treeline in the Austrian Alps. The material can be buried either in trenches or in long, parallel mounds. Either are then covered with topsoil and, optionally, mulch. As the buried organic matter decomposes it:

- generates heat, increasing growing time;
- creates soil fertility or humus;

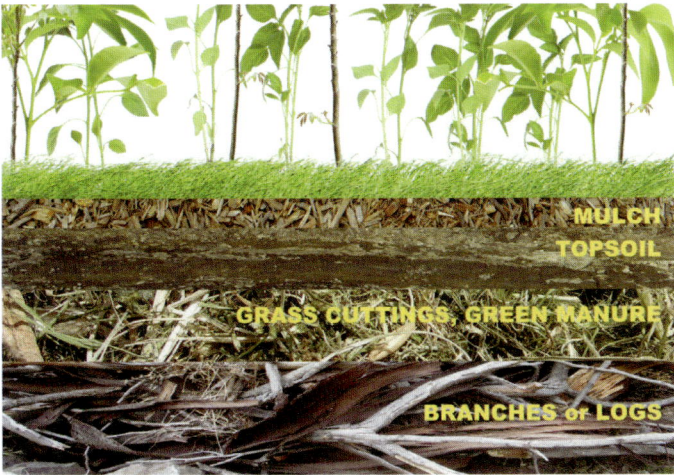

Figure 4.26 Cross-section of a Hugelkultur trench.

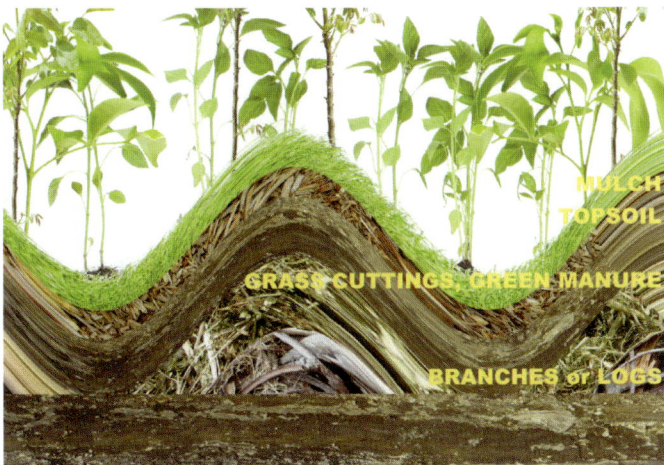

Figure 4.27 Cross-section of Hugelkultur mounds.

- retains water;
- if used in mounds as in Fig. 4.27 it increases the surface area that can be cultivated (the long sides and the top of the mound).

The amount of heat generated can be imagined by comparing it with that which would be generated if the wood was burnt, except that it is released over a period of years. Adding green manure (e.g. leaves, grass cuttings) to the branches before burial introduces nitrogen to the carbon, which produces better quality soil. This is an excellent way of dealing with branches from woodland clearance, hedge cutting, and so on. Sepp Holzer

Figure 4.28 A demonstration Hugelkultur bed at the National Botanic Garden of Wales' Get Growing plot. This bed fed 100 people for lunch one day, following which it was still packed with produce.

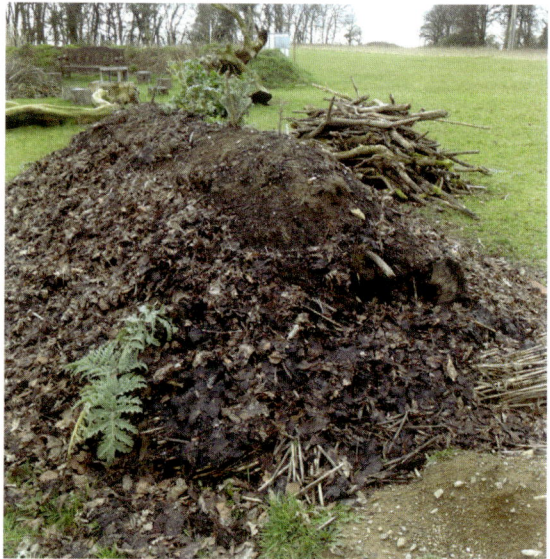

Figure 4.29. The same bed in winter, revealing the underlying structure: note the branches visible at this end.

recommends steep-sided beds to avoid compaction over time. With more surface area to grow plants, doubling or tripling productivity, the height also makes for easy harvesting. Strawberries and squashes, beans and salads may be grown out of the traditional season.

Table 4.2 Example of land-use allocation. This would be attached to a plan of the land.

Activity	Acreage needed
Vegetable & seed production	1.5
Field scale cereal & seed crops	1.5
Livestock grazing	2
Livestock fodder	0.75
Native woodland planting	2
Short rotation coppice	0.5
Buildings, parking & other infrastructure	0.5
Orchard & soft fruit	1.5
Agroforestry crops	0.5
Wildlife reserve in addition to native woodland plant	1

Bryn yr blodau   Site Layout 1   1:1000

Parc y ty   Drawing 1·3

Figure 4.30 An actual hand-drawn rough site plan from Bryn yr Blodau in Pembrokeshire.

Land allocation

You're now ready to begin to think about how your own plot of land might be managed. The next sections home in on further details of other aspects of your One Planet Life.

Further reading

1 Whitefield, Patrick, *The Earth Care Manual: A Permaculture Handbook for Britain and Other Temperate Countries*, Permanent Publications, 2011.
2 Holmgren, David, *Permaculture Principles & Pathways Beyond Sustainability*, Permanent Publications, 2011.
3 Seymour, John, *The New Complete Book of Self-Sufficiency*, Dorling Kindersley, 2009.
4 *Permaculture Design*, Aranya, Permanent, 2012.
5 Crawford, Martin, *How to Grow Perennial Vegetables: Low-maintenance, Low-impact Vegetable Gardening*, Green Books, 2012.
6 Crawford, Martin, *Creating a Forest Garden: Working with nature to grow edible crops*, Green Books, 2010.
7 Holzer, Sepp, *Sepp Holzer's Permaculture*, Permanent Publications, 2010.
8 Fern, Ken, *Plants for a Future: Edible and Useful Plants for a Healthier World*, Permanent, 2011.
9 *How to Grow Winter Vegetables*, Green Books, Charles Dowding, 2011.
10 Law, Ben, *The Woodland Year*, Permanent Publications, 2008.
11 If you plan to manage woodland or keep livestock such as poultry, cattle, sheep, goats, pigs or bees, seek out some of the many manuals on the subject.

Notes

1 Defra provides a free handbook for how to conduct a Phase 1 Habitat Survey at http://jncc.defra.gov.uk/page-2468.
2 US DOE, 2008. *Carbon Cycling and Biosequestration: Report from the March 2008 Workshop*, DOE/SC-108, US Department of Energy Office of Science (pp. 2–3).

Prepared by the Biological and Environmental Research Information System, Oak Ridge National Laboratory, genomicscience.energy.gov.

3 US DOE, 2008. *Carbon Cycling and Biosequestration: Report from the March 2008 Workshop*, DOE/SC-108, US Department of Energy Office of Science (p. 28). Prepared by the Biological and Environmental Research Information System, Oak Ridge National Laboratory, genomics.energy.gov.

4 *Revealing the Role of Microbial Communities in Carbon Cycling*, Joseph Graber, Genomic Science Program, Biological Systems Science Division, Office of Biological and Environmental Research at the US Department of Energy Office of Science, July 2011, available at http://genomicscience.energy.gov/carboncycle/BSSDCarbonCycleFlyer_sm.pdf. Accessed December 2013.

5 From https://statswales.wales.gov.uk/v/lsN, referencing http://wales.gov.uk/docs/statistics/2012/statswalessustainablecontents.html. Accessed November 2013.

6 Mollison, Bill, *Permaculture, A Designer's Manual*, Tagari, 1988.

7 US DOE, 2008. *Carbon Cycling and Biosequestration: Report from the March 2008 Workshop*, DOE/SC-108, US Department of Energy Office of Science (p. 65). Prepared by the Biological and Environmental Research Information System, Oak Ridge National Laboratory, genomics.energy.gov.

8 Sepp Holzer, *The Rebel Farmer*, Sepp Holzer, Stocker Leopold Verlag, 2004.

5 Water

Water has so many aspects: we need it to live, we need to collect it, drink it, wash in it, cook with it, dispose of it, irrigate with it and reuse it. Sometimes there is too much and sometimes there is too little. Overall, throughout the world, there is an increasing shortage of clean water. Water uses energy when we heat or pump it. All of these are reasons why we consider water as a complete topic – from the moment it enters your land to the moment it leaves.

Figure 5.1 and 5.2 The same place in normal times and drought: in our volatile climate, sometimes there's too much and sometimes too little rainfall. If our livelihood depends upon it we need to plan for all eventualities.

In the section on land management we mentioned the water cycle and the need to survey the land to see which soils are waterlogged and which are drier. Depending on the result of the survey you may need to introduce drainage or irrigation, hopefully being able to combine both in one system. If you don't have water piped on site you will need to tap a stream or a spring, should you be lucky enough to have one of these on or near your land. Failing that you will either have to drill a borehole or engage in rooftop collection and storage.

Conceiving the system as a whole also means treating your sewage as a resource, both for irrigation and as a source of plant nutrients. By the time it leaves your land, water should be as pure as when it entered it. This section is divided into three parts: sourcing water, minimising water needs and dealing with sewage. It even shows you an example of a swimming pool!

Sourcing it

Surveying the resource

A survey of the land should reveal where the bodies of water and watercourses lie, as well as where the drier and wetter areas are. But you probably won't be able to tell if water lies beneath your land unless it's just

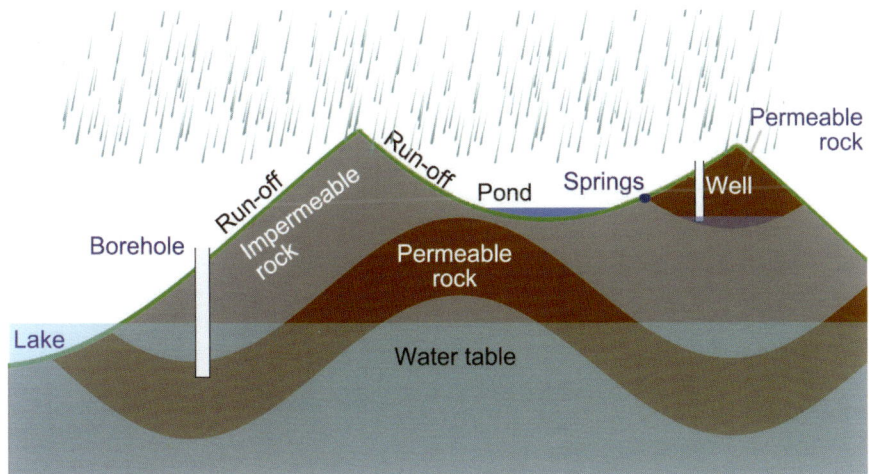

Figure 5.3 Possible sources of water. From the left: a lake that is filled from the level of the water table and run-off; a borehole reaching down into the water table; run-off from rainfall might be collectable; a pond might collect water from run-off when the rock below is impermeable to water; a well might reach down to an aquifer (underground water channel), but this may only be filled some of the time and may be depletable.

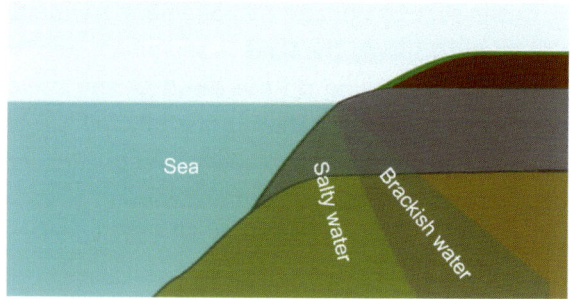

Figure 5.4 If your plot is close to the sea, sinking a well might tap into brackish water.

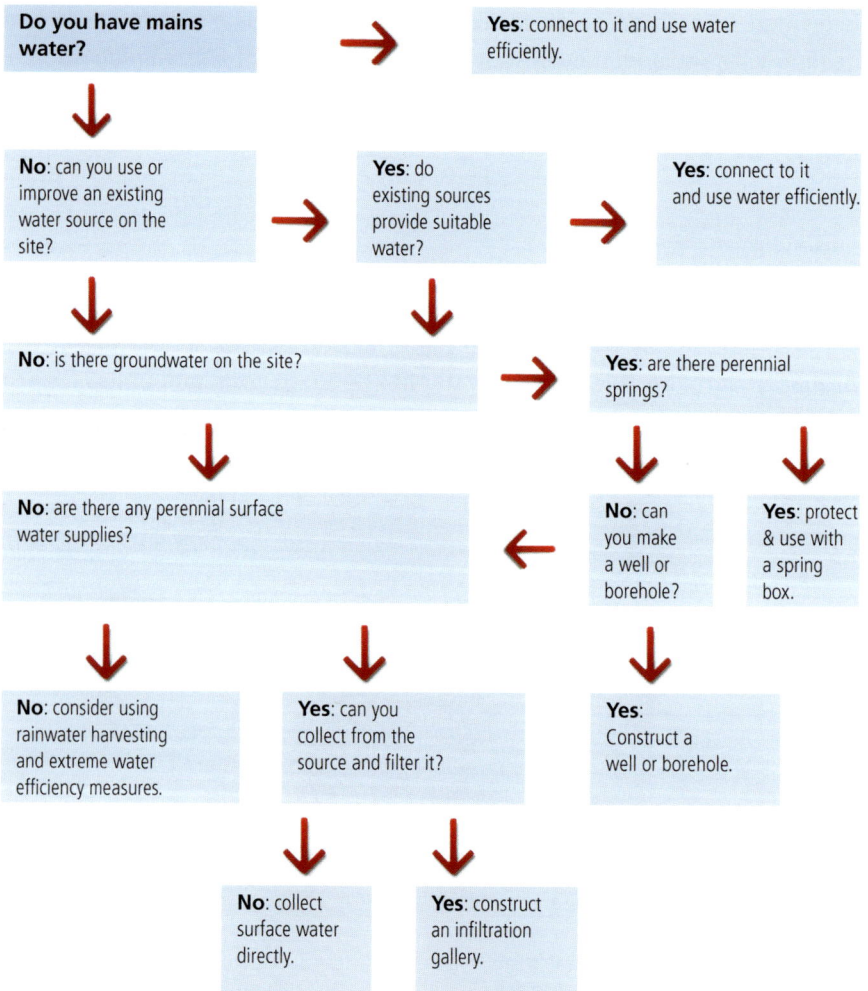

Do you have mains water? → **Yes**: connect to it and use water efficiently.

↓

No: can you use or improve an existing water source on the site? → **Yes**: do existing sources provide suitable water? → **Yes**: connect to it and use water efficiently.

↓

No: is there groundwater on the site? → **Yes**: are there perennial springs?

↓

No: are there any perennial surface water supplies? ← **No**: can you make a well or borehole?   **Yes**: protect & use with a spring box.

↓

No: consider using rainwater harvesting and extreme water efficiency measures.   **Yes**: can you collect from the source and filter it?   **Yes**: Construct a well or borehole.

↓

No: collect surface water directly.   **Yes**: construct an infiltration gallery.

Figure 5.5 To identify your optimum water supply it's helpful to use this decision tree. Adapted from *The Water Book* by Judith Thornton.

below and its presence is betrayed by ferns, sedges, rushes and reeds. The survey, together with other information, should allow you to figure out where your water supply will come from, how to irrigate or drain your land if necessary and the best location for your sewage treatment area.

If you don't have mains water supply or any other existing supply and it is not obvious where this will come from, then you will want to ask your neighbours what they know about groundwater in the area, as well as consulting hydrological maps, usually available from the Institute of Hydrology and the Meteorological Office. Nearby farmers will probably be able to tell you how rainfall and soil conditions alter throughout the seasons and where the level of the water table rises and falls accordingly. It's also necessary to talk to the local representative of the Environment Agency, as there are legal aspects concerning water abstraction.

Sometimes there is no available water supply. But even in water-scarce areas of the UK a reasonably sized home can provide sufficient water by collecting the rain to last through dry spells if there is sufficient storage provision. I have seen this myself in Brenda and Robert Vale's self-sufficient home in Southwell, Nottinghamshire, during a summer of drought when a hosepipe ban was in force and all other properties in the county had restrictions upon use. Their supply was only one third used up. It requires a large cellar to hold the tanks (in their case 20 1,500-litre re-used orange-juice-importing containers, one of which contains sand-filtered water, the rest unfiltered rainwater) and a pumped system. They also use a Clivus Multrum composting toilet. If you don't fancy going to this much trouble or don't fancy a composting toilet, ask the local water company to connect the property to the mains. It's likely that the environmental footprint of pursuing each option will be about the same because of the economies of scale of mains water production, unless you're miles from a supply.

Tapping springs and streams

If you have a reliable spring on your land you can build a springbox (see Fig. 5.6), which lets water in on the uphill side and withholds it. A pipe then feeds by gravity the water down to the filtration tank or other collection point.

If you have a stream, then you can divert some of the water to a treatment chamber or infiltration gallery. If there is a chance that the stream may not provide sufficient water throughout the year, divert it to a holding pond first.

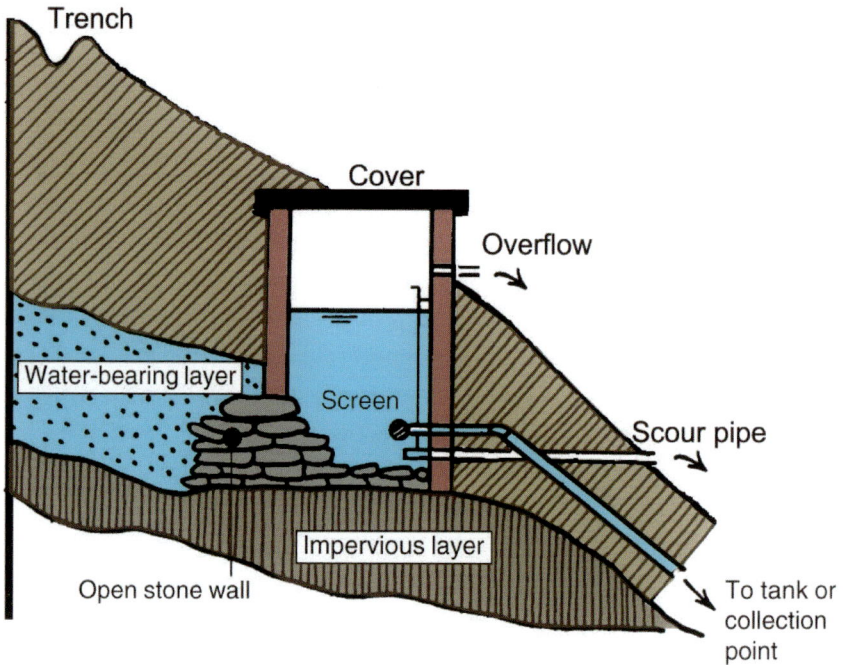

Figure 5.6 Cross section of a springbox for collecting springwater.

Wells and boreholes

If you need to have a well or borehole constructed you will have to bring in professionals. You may also need to have the water pumped and this will require energy that you will have to supply. It could be supplied from a separate solar panel, wind turbine or from your general circuit depending on how close the well is to the house.

Collecting run-off and rainfall

Rainfall and run-off may be collected in a reservoir, an artificial hole dug in the ground. It should be situated as far up the site as possible so that it may be fed by gravity to where it is needed.

Treatment of water

Water treatment begins with testing: this would involve sending a sample either to the environmental health officer in the local authority or to your local water utility. When you have the results, you will know what

Figure 5.7 A reservoir constructed to collect water for five households. It is possible to drain it for maintenance. It's on the highest point of land at Hockerton Housing Project: the turf roofs of the houses may be seen down the slope in the background.

Figure 5.8 A collection tank and sand filter for the same system, fed by gravity. The bank of the reservoir is in the background (with a lifebelt provided for safety). The ball valve may be seen, which shuts off the supply when the tank is full. The insulation in the lid may be seen, which prevents it freezing.
Sourcing the water is only the first stage. The second is making it safe to drink.

contaminants you will need to remove to make it safe. Most contaminants can be removed by using a sand filter and UV (ultraviolet light) treatment in a two-stage process, but there may be others peculiar to your location.

Rainwater harvesting

Rainwater may be collected, stored and used for toilets, washing machines, gardening and other purposes. It will need filtering, using a sand and gravel filter. If used for drinking, it will need further treatment, such as ultraviolet light exposure, or passing through an ion-exchanger. Larger roofs are more cost-effective to utilise.

In order to calculate the amount you could collect you need to know the annual rainfall for the location, together with the roof collection area. (That's the aerial view footprint area, not the roof's surface area.) This is

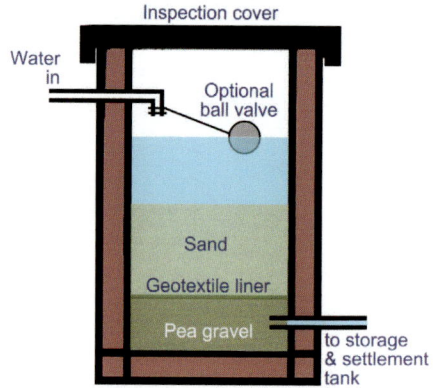

Figure 5.9 Cross section of a gravity-fed sand filter. It's about 1.5 m tall. The sand and layer of micro-organisms that builds up on the geo-textile layer help to remove some bacteria and suspended solids. The water should then flow down a slope in the pipe to a settlement tank. This will need an overflow pipe (fly and rodent proof), and, ideally, UV strip lights inside the lid which will kill most pathogens. Water is then drawn off to the dwelling for consumption.

Figure 5.10 An above-ground collection tank from a single gutter. Water is pumped inside.

then multiplied by a drainage factor, which is dependent on the roof type. The higher the roof factor, the greater the proportion of rain falling on the roof will reach the gutter and be collected. Since rainfall is sporadic, storage tanks, for example, reused large fruit-juice containers which can be obtained from importers, will be needed in a quantity sufficient to hold about 14 days' worth of demand, or 5 per cent of annual roof yield, whichever is the lowest.

Figure 5.11 and 5.12 Watering plants in polytunnels using rainwater harvesting from the covers. Two polytunnels are joined together in this instance, creating a gully between them.
Water is collected on the outside and brought in to feed four large containers. A hosepipe and series of overhead sprinklers powered by a small pump can irrigate the plants. After a prolonged downpour the tanks can overflow and so an overflow pipe is required. John Hargraves' One Planet Development plant nursery.

Table 5.1 Approximate annual yield of rainwater in cubic metres per year for a range of roof sizes with varying rainfall.

Plan roof area (m²)		50	75	100	125	150
mm rain	500	15	22.5	30	37.5	45
	1000	30	45	60	75	90
	1500	45	67.5	90	112.5	135
per year	2000	60	90	120	150	180
Plan roof area (yd²)		59.8	89.71	119.60	149.5	179.40
inches rain	20	17.94	26.91	35.88	44.85	53.82
	40	35.88	53.82	71.76	89.71	107.64
per year	60	53.82	80.73	107.64	134.55	161.46
	80	71.76	107.64	143.52	179.40	215.28

Table 5.2 Drainage factors for different roof types.

Roof type	Drainage factor
Pitched roof tiles	0.75–0.9
Flat roof smooth tiles	0.5
Flat roof with gravel layer	0.4–0.5

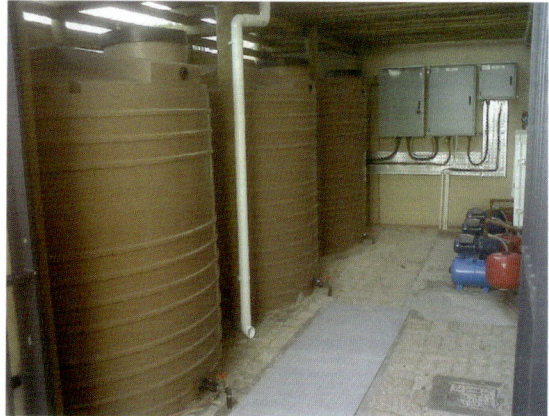

Figure 5.13 Three (5,000 litre or 22,730 gallon) rainwater harvesting tanks supplying the False Bay Ecology Park centre in South Africa with all its fresh water needs. From the tanks the water is pumped into the building with the pumps on the right.
Source: Cape Water Solutions.

Example: A roof has an area of 530 m² (633.87 yd²). It receives 1,500 mm (60 inches) of rain per year. The maximum collectable volume is therefore 90 × 5.3 = 477 m³ (624 yd³). It is a flat roof so this is multiplied by 0.5, yielding a total of 238 m³ (311.29 yd³).

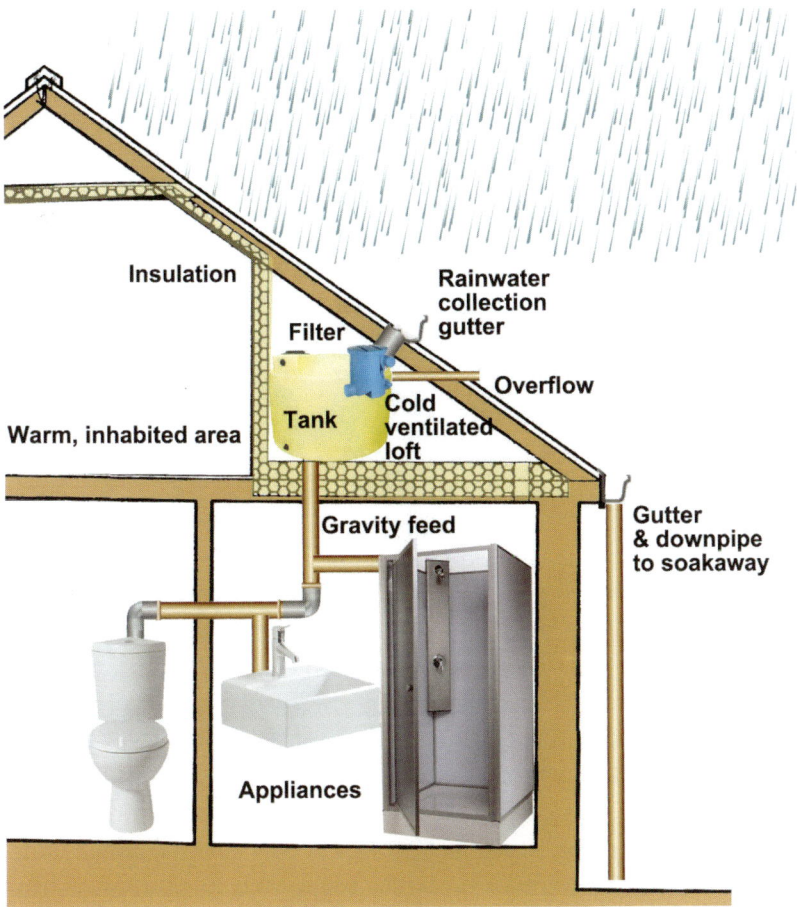

Figure 5.14 A schematic layout for rainwater harvesting off part of a roof to enable storage in the loft space so that the water can be distributed by gravity, removing the need for a pump.

To calculate the tank size, multiply this figure by the filter efficiency (90 per cent) and by the 5 per cent storage factor. This results in 10.73 m³ (14 yd³).
A minimal system will involve:

- reliable guttering (ideally steel or copper, which are anti-bacterial);
- downpipes;
- accessible filtration;
- frost-protected storage away from sunlight at a temperature which prevents bacterial growth;
- a floating intake to draw water from the top of the water so sediment at the bottom is not collected (new water comes into the tank near the bottom);
- a rat-proof overflow.

Treatment

Bird and animal faeces and leaf litter on roofs or guttering can pose a health risk if they are washed into the system. Gutters should be cleared regularly. Sophisticated rainwater-harvesting systems can be bought that divert the first intake of water – the most contaminated – to prevent it from fouling the rest.

A filter is the next thing the water should encounter. This prevents solid debris and leaves from entering the storage tank. It then enters the tank via a calmed inlet designed to avoid splashing. This helps to avoid stagnation at the bottom and maintains the quality of the water. You don't really need any further treatment if the water is to be used for toilet flushing and garden watering but there are some things you could install to maintain the quality:

- overflow siphons to allow floating material to be removed;
- a rodent barrier such as a mesh on the holding tank overflow pipe;
- a floating extraction pipe with an extra filter. This allows water to be taken from just below the surface where it's cleanest.

The size of the tank can vary, from a small tank on the side of a house to large underground tanks that can contain thousands of litres of water. In the UK, larger tanks are generally constructed from glass-reinforced plastic, polyethylene or, outside, concrete. You should seek advice from a reputable rainwater harvesting supplier on which material is most appropriate for your needs. Further treatment for drinking water would involve sterilisation with UV lighting, just as for boreholes and wells (above). The tank needs to be able to overflow to a soakaway or storm drain, which must be adequate to cope with the rate of flow to avoid contaminated water back-flowing into the storage tank.

Distributing rainwater

Appliances can be supplied with rainwater in two ways:

- Gravity-fed (header tank) systems – these involve rainwater being collected and piped to a header storage tank, usually in the loft, which then delivers the rainwater to appliances using gravity. This is the simplest method, but the tank will generally be smaller than if outside. Water is heavy and the structure will need to be able to support it and the tank should be located outside of the insulated area of the house in the ventilated loft so that it is less likely to get warm, which can promote the breeding of bacteria;

- Direct pumped systems – rainwater is collected and held in a storage tank at the side of the building, or even buried underground (which has a financial and carbon cost) and then pumped directly to the point of use as and when required.

The solution depends on the layout in your instance. The highest embodied carbon is in the storage tanks, but they tend to be long lasting. Pumps, if used, are usually the second-largest contributor to embodied carbon and require energy to run. They will need replacing from time to time.

Minimising the amount of water needed

Check for leaks

Checking for leaks should be done regularly. One way to do this is to have a water meter and to take a meter reading last thing at night and again first thing in the morning, in other words when it is not expected that any water should be used. If the reading has changed you may have a leak! Reading the water meter regularly and working out how much average water is used for each individual can create a benchmark from which to improve.

The AECB has a Water Standard applicable to new homes, the refurbishment of existing dwellings and to non-domestic buildings, to complement its CarbonLite system. The Water Standard, aimed at architects, designers, house builders and specifiers, is aimed at reducing hot-water use and water use during drought and is free from the AECB.[1]

Toilets

Toilet flushing is usually the largest single water use in a home. Flushing not only wastes water but any carbon emissions involved in its supply. Traditional toilets can flush away up to 9–11 litres each time. If you have a water-using toilet, then the most efficient flushing option is a flush siphon. It is better than a dual-flush (the valve will eventually leak, and this is hard to detect; the seals can also leak or break, especially in hard water areas). There is an interruptible-flush version which means that the user presses a lever and when they release it, it stops flushing. So as soon as they see that the waste in the bowl has gone they release the handle and no more water is used. For existing toilets there are conversion kits.

Table 5.3 Dead leg volumes

Pipe diameter	10 mm plastic	15 mm plastic	15 mm copper	22 mm plastic	22 mm copper
Litres per 10 m pipe run	0.6	1.1	1.5	2.4	3.1
Max length for 1.5 litre dead leg (m)	25.0	13.0	10.0	6.0	5.0
Max length for 0.85 litre dead leg (m) and for 30 second wait with 1.7 litres per minute spray fitting (m)	14.0	8.0	6.0	3.5	3.0

Figure 5.15 A low-flush water-efficient toilet in Tŷ Solar (see Exemplary Examples).

Minimise dead legs

Dead legs are the length of pipe between the hot-water source and the tap. Taps should be as close to the heat source as possible to minimise both heat losses along the way and water losses while people run the taps waiting for the hot water to arrive. Use smaller bore pipes to minimize the volume in the pipe: try to aim for no more than 0.85 litres. The table above will help to work out the maximum such length for the type of pipe used.

Make sure all hot-water pipes are properly insulated and sited above cold-water pipes to reduce heat transfer. A radial layout for pipes to outlets from the tank will also help keep heat losses down.

Figure 5.16 Spray taps fitted in a bathroom basin.

Taps

Spray taps can save about 80 per cent of the water used in normal taps. Some users complain that washing-up bowls or sinks don't fill up quickly enough, in which case a 'Tapmagic' insert can be fitted to most taps with a round outlet or standard metric thread. At low flows, this device delivers a spray suitable for washing hands and rinsing toothbrushes. As the flow is increased it opens to allow full flow. Water-saving cartridges for single-lever mixer taps can also be installed. These operate on a similar principle. An aerator or laminar flow device can prevent splashing.

Basin taps should be limited to four to six litres per minute and sink taps should be limited to six to eight litres per minute. All mixers should have a clear indication of hot and cold. The convention is to situate the hot tap or lever position to the left.

Tips for taps

- A running tap can waste over six litres per minute. Turn them off when they're not being used, for example during tooth brushing;
- When using hot water, don't let it disappear straight down the plughole, but fill a bowl or the sink with a tight-fitting plug in;
- Replace washers in dripping taps immediately. They can waste at least 5,500 litres of water a year.

Figure 5.17 A low-flow shower-head.

Showers

Showers and baths can account for up to 45 per cent of the water used at home. Showers can save water compared to baths, but people tend to take more of them. Showers should ideally take no longer than five minutes. Power showers and mains pressure systems are out of bounds!

Is the water for the shower coming from water that is already heated in an insulated tank, or is it heated on demand? Most modern fitted showers now use electric on-demand heaters. Unless this comes from a renewable source, these should be avoided in preference to tank-fed showers. If the dwelling uses solar water heating, a heat pump with a buffer tank, and/or a biomass stove, then the water feeding the shower should come from the tank, using either a gravity feed or a small pump because these sources of heat are renewable and save electricity.

Water-saver showerheads work by creating finer drops or by incorporating air into the flow. This requires a pressure of at least one bar – fine with mains supply and pumped systems but not usually with gravity-fed systems. They operate at a flow rate of between four and nine litres per minute. Flow rates can go as low as 3.2 litres per minute without users feeling robbed of a good shower experience. A mixer shower (with pump if the existing head from a gravity system isn't sufficient) with flow regulation provides an effective solution.

A three-minute shower with the flow adjusted to a comfortable 5 litres per minute uses only 15 litres of water, while ten minutes at 15 litres per minute will use 10 times as much water and energy without getting you any cleaner! So with good design you can achieve efficiency savings and better showering by fitting:

- small bore pipes (10 mm is the smallest available);
- regulated aerators;
- low water-use shower heads with an on-demand pump fitted if needed;
- pressure and flow regulators.

Washing machines

Most new washing machines now use less than 50 litres per 6 kg wash, with some using as little as 35 litres. Most now have only a cold-water inlet and heat the water themselves using electricity. This is unfortunate unless the electricity source is renewable, since it's better to use water that has already been heated by solar thermal panels, biomass or gas. They used to be available with hot- and cold-water inputs and combined them to the right temperature. Avoid driers – if it's raining dry clothes in the polytunnels/conservatory. Models which use mains water to condense moisture can increase water consumption to 100–170 litres per wash.

- Choose a machine that is A++ rated and with a low water consumption;
- most washes produce a good result at 30 °C;
- use only with a full load – most can take 6 kg nowadays;
- where possible, dry clothes in the air.

Avoid dishwashers if at all possible; washing water-wisely will save water and energy!

Outside use

Features of water-efficient land management include:

- The use of drought-tolerant plants, e.g. thyme, oregano, crocus, tulips, sedums, grasses, geraniums, poppies, cyclamen, daffodils, lavender, juniper;
- mulches on the soil, e.g. bark, gravel;
- organic matter regularly added to the soil that can retain water, such as compost, grass cuttings and manure;

Figure 5.18 Roof water collection leading to a water butt with an overflow into a trough at Lammas.

Figure 5.19 Another water butt with a tap.

- watering plants only in the evening or early morning to avoid wastage by evaporation;
- watering using rainwater collected in butts from downpipes from the roof guttering;
- using cooled wastewater from the kitchen, baths and showers (grey water);
- on slopes, using a system of earth banks to retain and direct water along key- or contour-lines;
- if using a hosepipe, using a lance or trigger device to control the flow and direct the water gently to where needed, frequently but lightly and not directly on the soil.

Keyline design

Keyline design is potentially useful for large sites, particularly where they are conversions from traditional farmland such as grazing. It is a system of water-flow management and spatial planning developed in Australia, but applicable elsewhere in regions of low or variable rainfall, or even high rainfall to spread the run-off. Based on observation of the locations of water channels and contour lines on your land the idea is to seek the optimal water storage areas, irrigation and drainage channels, and let access tracks follow contour lines. Some areas of the land will be dryer than others. Drainage channels can follow contours to lead water from the wetter areas through the dryer ones. According to practitioner Darren Doherty:

> The Keyline of a landscape refers to the contour that runs through the change in slope in a primary valley known as the 'Keypoint'. Running parallel with this line, any plowlines or tree lines encourages water movement (both run-off and run-through) towards the adjacent primary ridges, thereby increasing whole slope hydration and consequently improving production.[2]

Swales (troughs in the landscape) are dug along an elevation contour line to slow and capture run-off and spread it horizontally across the land. This helps to spread the run-off infiltration into the soil and irrigate crops or divert water from some areas where there is too much. The soil from the swale is mounted on the downhill side of the ditch to create a berm or raised barrier. This also helps prevent soil erosion. Building on this principle, biologist Jay Andrews has developed the powerful Whole Site Water

Figure 5.20 Run-off ponds collecting drained water.
Source: Wikimedia Commons: Vmenkov.

Figure 5.21 This 'scrape' is one of a row of pools 'scraped out' at the bottom of a field to collect run-off and provide a habitat to encourage biodiversity.

Reticulation System. This harvests and manages water flows (rainwater, any water courses/springs and wastewater) over a whole site, incorporating keylines. The site-specific system is designed, then earthworks are created, planted up, and then the system is managed as an integrated resource recovery and production system; it would often include a Wetland Ecosystem Treatment (WET) System as a component to purify the water within the overall whole site system (see below and the WET System Exemplary Example).

Dealing with sewage

The world is gradually coming back to the idea – common in the past – that sewage is a resource. In a high-energy lifestyle sewage is flushed away and treated expensively, wasting the nutrients contained in it. But the One Planet Life means getting used to not feeling disgust at the idea of using it somewhere on your land; if handled properly it is valuable and useful.

There is a distinction between grey water and other waste (known as black water). The latter comes from the toilet, while the former comes from everywhere else: sinks, basins, showers and washing machines. The grey water is collected separately and treated biologically using a living system that irrigates the land, while the solid human waste is composted in a composting toilet with the valuable result applied to the land as fertiliser.

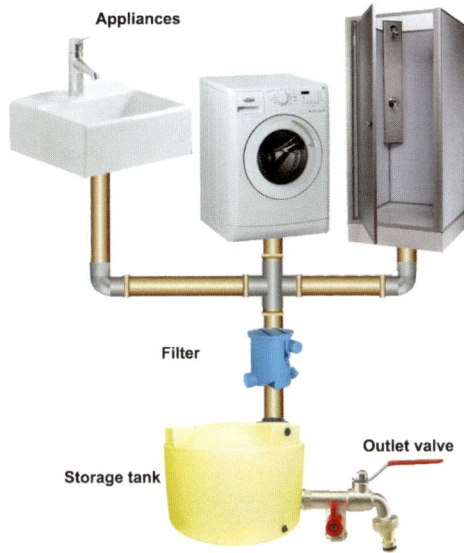

Figure 5.22 Grey-water collection systems collect and filter used water from all water-using appliances except a toilet. The filter may be very simple, including straw. Its purpose is to trap hairs and grease and must be cleaned frequently.

Using grey water on the land

The outlets from showers, washbasins, the kitchen, laundry, baths and so on would be connected to this system. The water goes through a filter, a storage tank and out through a pipe distribution system onto the land. Grey water may not be stored for longer than 24 hours before use as it becomes unhealthy and smelly. You would need to check that the amount of land you have available is sufficient to beneficially absorb the amount of grey water that you will create. To do this add up the weekly volume in litres per week from each of the outlets you have. Good soil can accommodate about 25 litres of water per square meter each week, but water moves more slowly through clay soil than through sandy soil, so make allowance for this. The amount of land area you will need to process your greywater is therefore:

Land area (m^2) = grey water generated per week (litres) / 25

The purpose of the filter is to remove fats, and so on, that could block the pipes when they cool and set. The purpose of the tank is to allow the water to cool; to prevent surges into the land that could create pooling; and to allow appliances in the house to drain quickly. The filter can be a

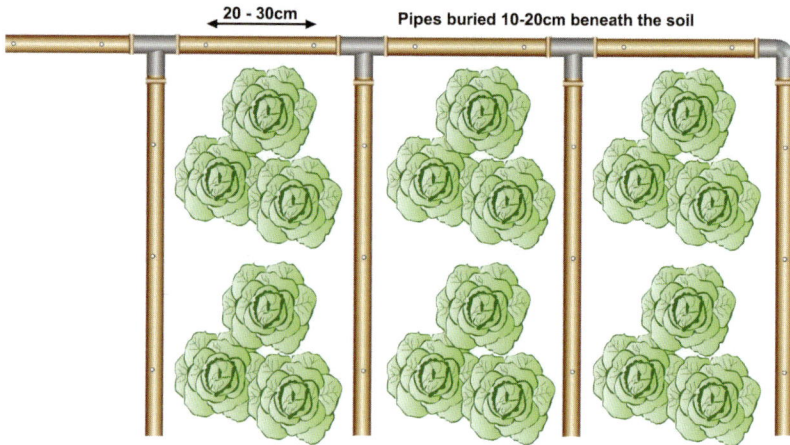

Figure 5.23 A branching system for grey-water distribution in a vegetable patch.

conventional mesh which will need cleaning every now and then, or a straw bale which will need removing for compost and replacing every month. A tank or water butt the size of a bath should suffice for normal purposes. A valve controls the rate of drainage from the tank. The water then disperses through a network of pipes pierced with holes. It's possible to buy entire grey-water systems quite cheaply, or you can make your own. Whether or not you need a pump will depend upon whether the leach field is downhill of the storage butt or tank.

You should avoid using non-ecological detergents and cleaners, which are often high in phosphorus and sodium salts, chlorine-containing bleaches, greases, oils and corrosive chemicals.

It is **extremely important** to label in a very obvious way any plumbing used for this system so that it is distinguishable from that used for potable water as any error will result in serious diseases such as gastroenteritis. Also, different coloured piping should be used.

As for the pipe layout into the ground, it's best to use a branching system because otherwise the points furthest away would receive much less water. The pipes can be 32 or 40 mm in diameter and the holes can be anything over 3 mm in diameter and anything over 20 cm apart. The Centre for Alternative Technology in Wales has trialled a system that irrigates a vegetable patch. Here, the pipes are buried in woodchip-mulch-filled trenches up 20 cm below the ground between the rows of vegetables. It's very important that the water does not come into direct contact with leaves but is directed towards the roots of the plants.

Figure 5.24 to 5.26 A WET system that had recently been installed by Jay Andrews, so the plants are not yet quite established. It services up to 1,000 people at peak demand and covers one acre at Coddington Court, Herefordshire.

Reed beds and wetlands

An alternative is to create a natural wetland in a leach field. In the past it was assumed that reed beds were best for this purpose, but we now know that many other plants may be used. How do they work? Plants such as reeds thrive in waterlogged conditions by transferring oxygen to their roots. This allows naturally occurring bacteria to remove and process organic matter. Wastewater is passed through the soil in which these plants are growing. The bacteria, fed by oxygen from the reeds and nutrients from the wastewater, process the waste and create something beautiful and useful, a haven for wildlife that will be indistinguishable from a naturally occurring wetland habitat.

Suitable plants include: rushes, reeds, sedges, meadowseet, cranesbill, marsh marigold, yellow flag, water mint, bogbean, lilies, comfrey, colts-foot and spearwort. The treatment area should be lined with clay or pond liner. Trees such as willow that thrive in waterlogged conditions can be planted for coppicing at the bottom end of this bed and will benefit from the nutrients in the water.

Figure 5.27 and 5.28 Two views of a small grey-water-processing WET system for use by a two-person household. Also in the pictures is a compost container made of old tyres.

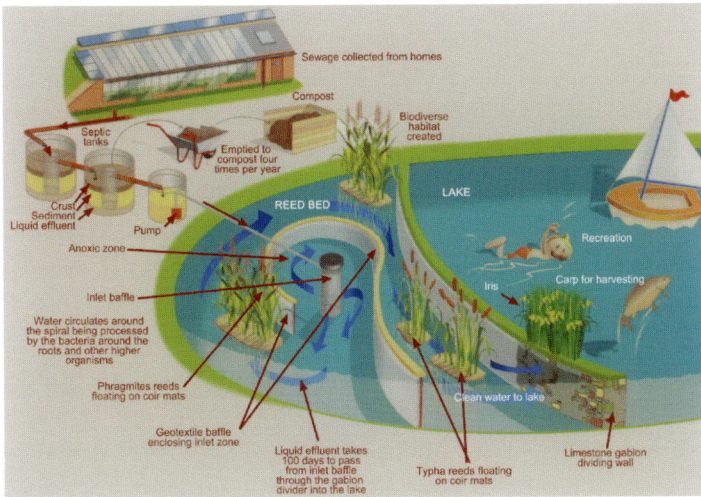

Figure 5.29 The reed-bed system at Hockerton Housing Project, Nottinghamshire, which processes the sewage from five households, produces compost, a richly biodiverse wetland and outputs into a lake where carp are raised for harvesting.
Credit: Hockerton Housing Project

Figure 5.30 The lake at Hockerton, with the homes in the background and the reed bed on the left.

With both rainwater and grey-water reuse, the carbon cost of creating and installing the system, plus running any pumps, should be taken into account before a decision is taken. Any pumps used should be of the minimum power specification for the job and not oversized. If possible, gravity-fed systems should be deployed to remove the need for a pump. In both cases as well, using the water for irrigation purposes is the simplest end use.

Composting toilets

The one-planet way of life doesn't have to incorporate a compost toilet, of course, and even if you do opt for one, there are compact models available off the shelf, that look almost like the toilets we are used to using; an example is pictured in Figure 5.31 (although avoid models which use electricity to heat the poo to accelerate decomposition!). Having a composting toilet means you don't have to use water to flush the waste away. Instead, the waste is composted and later used as a fertiliser. These are the two reasons why composting toilets are the most ecological.

The alternative to buying a compost loo is to build one yourself. The most common design is the 'twin vault'. This has two adjacent chambers, each with a door for access and a hole above. A movable seat fits over one hole while the other is covered. When the compost from one side of the twin vault has been harvested, you move the seat over the now empty vault, while the compost on the other side matures. The reason for this is that human manure needs two years to compost (seven years in countries where *Ascaris* exists) and this can take up a lot of space. To compost a year's manure from a single individual, two chambers 1.2 m × 1.2 m × 0.9 m are required. Multiply this by the number of people expected to be using it to arrive at a suitable volume. There can be either a single joint vent or separate vents for each chamber. Vents remove smells and heat and draw in air from below to help aerate the process.

Since human manure is nitrogen rich it needs to be mixed with a source of carbon to produce good soil at the end of the process. So, instead of

Figure 5.31 A Sun-Mar Excel compact composting toilet with urinal, as installed at Hockerton Housing Project.

Figure 5.32 and 5.33 The interior and rear view of a small single-vault composting toilet just outside a house. Inside can be seen a red container of 'soak' – sawdust in this case – to add when the toilet is used. At the back outside, is the access hatch to remove the compost. It is composted separately, with hay, sawdust or leaves. Twin vaults remove the need to handle the sewage before it has decomposed and is safe.

flushing the toilet before leaving a user would throw a handful of sawdust, fine woodshavings, leaves or chopped straw down the hole instead. This creates the correct ratio of about 1:30 of nitrogen and carbon. The carbon material is dubbed 'soak' and also helps aerate the result so it doesn't smell and soaks up liquid.

A DIY toilet could be located within a home if there's space for a composting chamber in a basement or undercroft. Or it could be in an extension beside the house as in Fig. 5.33; or in a free-standing shed away from the dwelling, as in Fig. 5.34. The foundation of the chamber is usually a poured concrete slab, sloped and grooved for drainage, or provided with a drain-pipe that can be rodded to remove blockages. The drainpipe transports liquid into a reed bed or wetland treatment area, or it can be collected and, when diluted 10:1, used as a liquid fertiliser as it is high in nitrogen.

When it's ready for use, the compost will not smell, and will look just like peaty soil, with no trace of what it once was. It's advised not to use it directly on vegetables, but to apply it to the soil in an 8 cm thick layer. According to biologist Peter Harper at the Centre for Alternative Technology, it makes a good weed-suppressing nutrient mulch, can be used as potting compost, around fruit bushes and trees, and there is no need to dig it in.

Why not have a swimming pool?

The One Planet Life should be fun as well as eco, so why not make yourself a swimming pool? Cassie and Nigel, who live at Lammas in Pembrokeshire, Wales, are doing so and Figure 5.37 shows the pool half made. When finished it will have a border of marshland plants and be lined. The pool

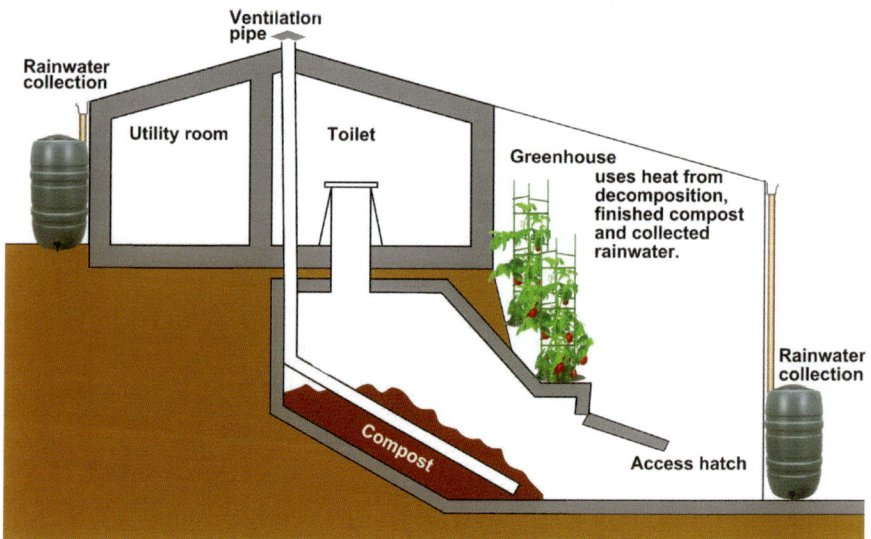

Figure 5.34 Schematic cross-section for a combined outside composting toilet and greenhouse with optional utility room and rainwater collection. The ventilation chimney uses rising heat to draw off odours. This is a twin vault, but only one vault is visible. The greenhouse is optional but would benefit from the heat from decomposition, the finished compost (used carefully), plus collected water from the roofs. The design requires sloping ground. The slope of the composting chamber allows the compost to turn and be aerated, and makes collection easier. The doors are at one end.

Figure 5.35 and 5.36 Self-built composting twin-vault composting toilet at Lammas. Two chambers are installed beneath two seats, accessible via steps. When one chamber is full, it is left to compost and the seat moved to above the other chamber. In this instance a plastic tank also collects the liquid separately.

Figure 5.37 A hole dug for a swimming pool with surrounding planted marshland for bulrushes and other marsh plants to improve biodiversity.

could be lined with clay if some is available, or with damp-proof membrane as used around the base or roof of a building. This pool is situated near the bottom of their sloping plot, which gets plenty of rainfall. It will take water from a stream that is behind the hedge.

Figure 5.38 A sculpture by a pool inside a polytunnel at Lammas.

Swimming pools are relatively easy to construct for the pleasure they give. People sometimes install them inside a conservatory area, where they will absorb and store solar heat, which also helps to keep the house warm. Simple homemade solar water-heating panels can also be used to heat the water,[3] which should then be covered up when not in use to keep the heat in. Such a luxury need not be the province of the rich!

Further reading

The Water Book, Judith Thornton, CAT Publications, 2005.
Rainwater Harvesting Workshop Manual, The UK Rainwater Harvesting Association, 2012. http://www.ukrha.org/wp-content/uploads/2012/04/Guide-5-Training-Manual.pdf.
Fertile Waste, Harper and Thorpe, CAT Publications, 1996.
AECB Water Standard – see below.

Notes

1 At www.aecb.net/publications/aecbs-water-standards-design-for-sustainable-water-systems-is-less-complicated-than-you-may-expect. Retrieved November 2013.
2 http://carbonfarmingcourse.com/workshops/keyline-farming. Retrieved November 2013.
3 See my book *Solar Technology,* Earthscan 2012.

6 Energy

The first rule of energy in the One Planet Life is to try to minimise the need for it. The second rule is to supply your remaining needs as far as possible from renewable sources. Having minimised energy use, we then have to use renewable energy. This all begins with our sun.

Figure 6.1 All energy comes from the sun and this house uses all three kinds of solar power: passive solar space heating with the large south-facing windows; solar water-heating panels; and solar photovoltaic panels for electricity.

The energy power-down

The One Planet Life has to use energy much more efficiently than before.

1 In **buildings** the energy power-down means superinsulating and protecting from draughts.
2 With **lighting, appliances and gadgets** it means trying to do without them first and then buying only the most efficient ones possible.
3 With **transportation** it means prioritising walking, bicycles, public transport, car sharing and so on, and not flying.
4 It means trying to use **fewer power tools** and greater ingenuity.

Some 'low-carbon' homes attempt to proclaim themselves as environmentally sound by bolting on a renewable energy feature like a wind turbine or photovoltaic panels to a fairly conventional structure. This is not an elegant solution. Taking account of energy use throughout the whole life cycle of a product, service, activity or building is the proper way to compare different strategies or products.

Solar energy

Free energy is abundant. It comes from the centre of the solar system across around 93,000,000 miles (150,000,000 km) of space and reaches us in eight and a half seconds. With it you can:

- heat and cool your buildings and polytunnels or greenhouses;
- capture its heat with solar water-heating panels to heat the water you wash in;
- use its light to make electricity with photovoltaic modules;
- use it to make plants grow by photosynthesis and then take advantage of the energy stored in the plants as food or fuel;
- take the heat from the ground and water that has been absorbed from the sunshine using a heat pump to heat buildings;
- possibly even use energy from wind and water power, both of which depend upon the sun heating the atmosphere, if you are lucky enough to have a windy hill or a reliable stream on your land. This energy could be mechanical or electrical.

Solar energy and climate change

On average:

- about 30 per cent of the sun's energy reaching the edge of our atmosphere is reflected back into space;
- about 22 per cent is absorbed in the gases of the atmosphere on the way down;
- along the way 1 per cent creates the wind;
- 23 per cent evaporates water, which will fall as rain and make streams and rivers;
- only 48 per cent reaches the surface, on average – about 340 watts per square metre. In the UK it tends to be less;
- 0.023 per cent is used by plants for photosynthesis, taking carbon dioxide from the atmosphere and turning it into plant cellulose – stored carbon.

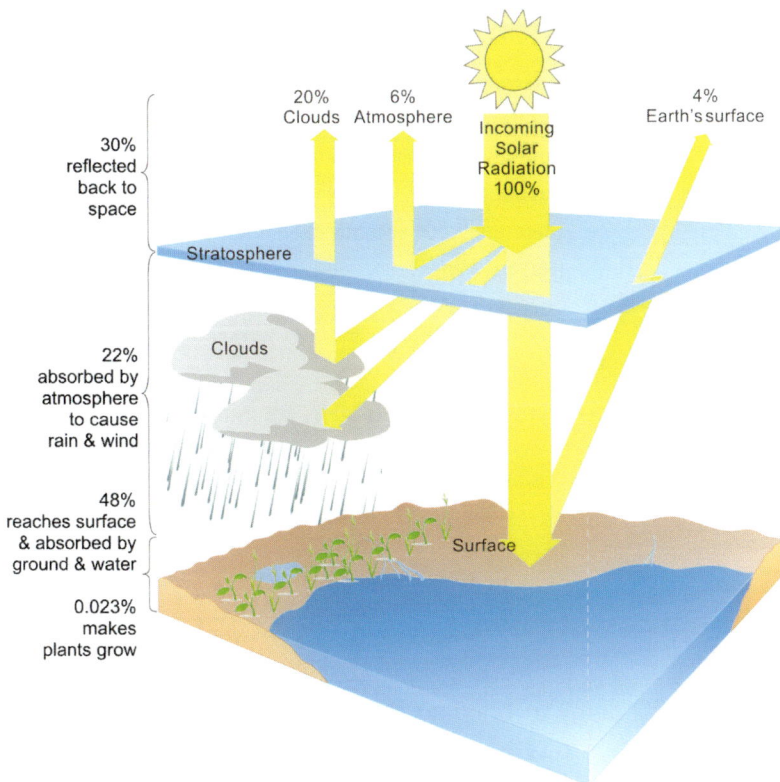

Figure 6.2 What happens to solar energy.

In the prehistoric past much of this solar-energy-plus-carbon that was stored in plants became coal, oil and natural gas. It is the burning of these 'fossil' fuels that is returning that carbon to the atmosphere today and causing climate change.

> **Power and energy**
> **Power** is the rate at which energy is produced by a generator or consumed by an appliance.
> *Unit*: the watt (W). 1000 watts is a kilowatt (kW).
> Volts × amps = watts (V × A=W)
> **Energy** is the amount of power produced by a generator or consumed by an appliance over a period of time.
> To find it you multiply the power by the number of hours the appliance is used for. This gives watt-hours.
>
> *Unit*: the watt-hour (Wh). A kilowatt used for one hour = 1 kilowatt-hour (kWh), or one unit of electricity that appears on electricity bills.
>
> *Alternate unit*: the joule (J). Watt-hours can be used to describe heat energy as well as electrical energy, but joules are also used for heat. 3,600 Joules = 1 Wh. Put another way, a joule is one watt per second, since there are 3,600 seconds in an hour; or 3.6 megajoules (MJ) = 1 kWh.

Examples:
One photovoltaic solar panel producing 80 W for two hours, or two panels producing 80 W for one hour would produce 2 × 80 = 160 Wh.
Three panels producing 90 W each for five hours will produce 3 × 90 × 5 = 1350 Wh or 1.35 kWh.

The energy powerdown

Ways of saving energy in building design are covered in the section on building. Other ways to save energy are:

- to find other ways to meet the need – or avoid it;
- to choose the least power-consuming devices.

Figure 6.3 A sample EU energy label – for a washing machine. It has the highest rating: A+++, but this alone doesn't enable you to compare it with other machines. That's why you need to look at the kilowatt-hours per annum, the water use and even the noise level when comparing with other models.

For example, drying clothes outside or in the polytunnel means that you don't need to use a tumble dryer or spin them in the washing machine for too long. Using daylight to maximum effect reduces the need for lighting.

To choose a low-power device, look at the label to find its power requirements: the more volts, amps or watts it says, the more power it needs. The label usually gives the wattage, but sometimes just the current, in which case multiply that by the voltage to get the watts. Multiplying the watts by the number of hours of use will give the energy consumption in watt-hours. Divide that by 1,000 to get the number of kilowatt-hours. The larger the appliance, such as a fridge, the more electricity it will consume even if it has the same AA energy-rated label.

Example: a 500 W appliance is on for 3 hours.
500 W × 3 hours = 1500 Wh = 1.5 kWh.

What gets monitored gets saved

Seeing what is being used enables everyone to observe the effect of their use of electricity. This is done with smart meters, which come in two parts: one

Table 6.1 Some typical appliance energy requirements.

Appliance	Average watts
CFC lightbulb	15
Kettle	2,000
Microwave	600–1,000
Toaster	800–1,500
Refrigerator	35
Washing machine	700 (2,000 heat, 500 spin, 250 wash)
Clock radio	15
Vacuum cleaner	300–1,100
Laptop	50–75
PC	120
LCD monitor	75
Modem	15
TV with LCD	115
DVD player	20
MP3 player charging	5
Mobile phone	1–5
Game console	25–200
Hover mower	1000–2,000
Strimmer	300
Jigsaw	300
Electric drill	500–1,000

part clips onto a cable where the electricity enters the building and the other goes into a socket in a convenient place. They can save up to 20 per cent depending on user attitudes. The best way of saving energy is to turn things off when they are not being used. This includes items with standby lights.

Hot water

All existing hot-water pipes should be well insulated and the most efficient showerheads, taps and washing machines installed to minimize the hot-water requirement. Use the lowest bore pipes that will still deliver the right amount of water. Design the layout to minimise 'dead legs' (the distance between tank and tap). See the Water section for more info.

Figure 6.4 A smart meter display.

Figure 6.5 A bayonet-fitting LED bulb.

Lighting

Wherever possible, artificial lighting should be supplied by LEDs (light-emitting diodes). LED lamps nowadays come in a huge variety of colour temperatures, sizes and fittings to suit every purpose. They are preferable and far more cost-effective compared to compact fluorescent lights because they last longer: up to 80,000 hours.

Cooking

A diet that is high in raw food such as salads and fruit is not only more nutritious but saves energy. Nevertheless, cooking is necessary. Cookers can

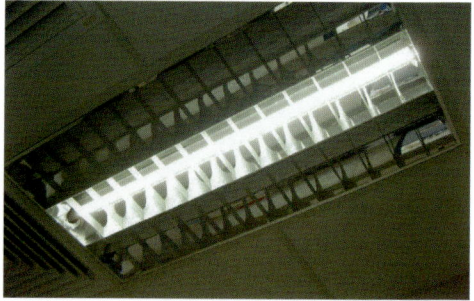

Figure 6.6 An LED T5 fluorescent strip light.

be fuelled either by biomass, gas or electricity. The priority from a carbon-reduction angle for cookers is as follows, with the best choice at the top:

1 Induction hobs, electric cooker using renewable electricity. They use up to 90 per cent of the energy produced compared to 55 per cent for gas hobs;
2 Ordinary electric cookers using renewable electricity;
3 A range heated by your home-grown well-seasoned wood;
4 LPG gas cooker.

This assumes that mains gas is not available. Ovens should always be extremely well insulated. The disadvantage of wood-fuelled cookers or ranges is that they can overheat a superinsulated or summertime house and take a long time to warm up, therefore they are not terribly efficient. It is possible to buy flat-bottomed kettles that work on hobs or wood stoves – get one with a whistle.

Renewable energy for heat

The really great thing about renewable energy is that the fuel source is free and using this energy will not contribute to global warming. The following forms of renewable energy are available on a small scale:

Heating

For **space heating** it is more efficient to use passive heating wherever possible. This is because you don't have to buy any extra equipment. Passive heating is covered in the section on building. But passive heating may not be available when you most need it on those dark winter nights, therefore some kind of active heating system is required. Let's take an overview of

Table 6.2 Applications of renewable energy.

	Passive heating	Active heating	Electricity	Mechanical power
Solar	✓	✓	✓	
Water		✓	✓	✓
Wind			✓	✓
Heat pumps		✓		
Wood fuel		✓		

Figure 6.7 A good-sized well-insulated heat store and pipes. It can be fed by solar, electrical immersion heater, wood fuel and/or heat pump.

the four options for both space (with the optimum outputs) and domestic hot water:

• **Solar water heating** requires solar collectors in a permanently unshaded position linked to a (preferably large) well-insulated storage tank. The tank can also take input from an electrical element and a wood-fuelled boiler.

The output is water-based radiators or underfloor heating and hot water.

- **Hydropower** heating requires a reliable nearby stream or river. Since it usually never stops generating, electricity is used for heating when not required for anything else.

  The heat output is electric heaters or electric underfloor heating and hot water

- **Heat pumps** require coils to collect the heat, being either buried underground or immersed in a watercourse or lake. A pump, powered by renewable electricity you would have to supply, takes the heat to a heat exchanger.

  The output is water-based underfloor heating and hot water.

- **Wood fuel** requires a reliable source of seasoned timber, regular labour and a chimney. When not in use the open chimney can remove warm air from the building. Burning wood does cause air pollution and carbon emissions. The carbon will not be reclaimed from the atmosphere for several years.

  The output is a boiler or stove or underfloor heating with a heat store and hot water.

Renewable heat is eligible for premium payments in the UK, like feed-in tariffs for renewable electricity, even if you consume it yourself. This helps finance the installation.

Underfloor heating

If you're installing a new floor, underfloor heating is a great idea. This is because it is so much more efficient, as the delivery temperature is a lot lower (18–20 °C) and the comfort levels are higher since the heating is evenly distributed. It can be inserted beneath tiles or timber, but timber gives a faster response. If timber, store it in the same room as the heating for several weeks before laying to avoid it warping. Beneath the pipes or wiring install a layer of thermal mass (such as Hemcrete, concrete or clay) to store the heat. Surround this with a good amount of insulation. The heating source can be water in pipes or electrical wiring.

Traditional installations for water-based systems consist of flexible piping connected to the heat source fastened on to the thermal mass in a spiral or snaking pattern, with usually about 30 cm gaps between the lines. Rooms or sections are divided into zones with separate thermostats and valves.

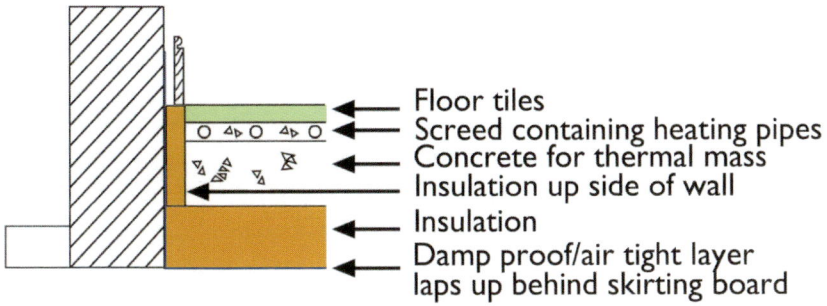

Floor tiles
Screed containing heating pipes
Concrete for thermal mass
Insulation up side of wall
Insulation
Damp proof/air tight layer
laps up behind skirting board

Figure 6.8 Example of how to install underfloor heating on the ground floor.

Figure 6.9 An underfloor heating pipe layout, in this instance laid upon a damp-proof layer and metal grid before concrete is poured for thermal mass.

Water-based underfloor heating can be used with any of the above forms of active heating.

Electric underfloor heating is very simple to install, consisting of a snaking pattern of insulated wires with a predetermined amount of resistance. Usually these are bought off-the-shelf.

Solar water heating

Some basic kind of solar water heating can be installed by anyone with basic plumbing and carpentry skills. Left in the sun, the water in a tube or

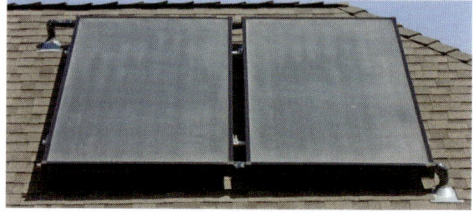

Figure 6.10 Flat plate panels on a roof.

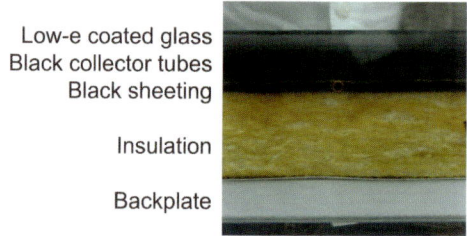

Low-e coated glass
Black collector tubes
Black sheeting

Insulation

Backplate

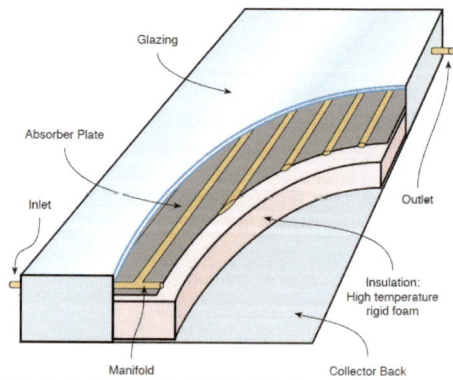

Glazing

Absorber Plate

Inlet

Outlet

Insulation:
High temperature
rigid foam

Manifold

Collector Back

Figure 6.11 and 6.12 Cross sections
through a flat-plate solar panel.
Credit: F. Jackson (top) and the Energy Saving
Trust.

old radiator heats dramatically. The heat is hindered from escaping by glass
at the front. A black matt backing surface will absorb more of the thermal
radiation than a shiny white one. Insulation stops the heat leaving. So any
liquid passed through narrow black pipes beneath glass pointed at the sun
will quickly heat up.

There are two types of heat collector (panel): cheaper, less efficient flat
ones and dearer evacuated tubes. Several can be linked together, either in
series or in parallel. They come in grades of sophistication, the most basic of
which are DIY and either an old central heating radiator, or a snaking pipe/
hosepipe, that has been painted black, covered in glass and put in an insulated box. These are the least efficient, though, meaning they take longer
to heat up and produce less hot water. The latest flat panels on the market

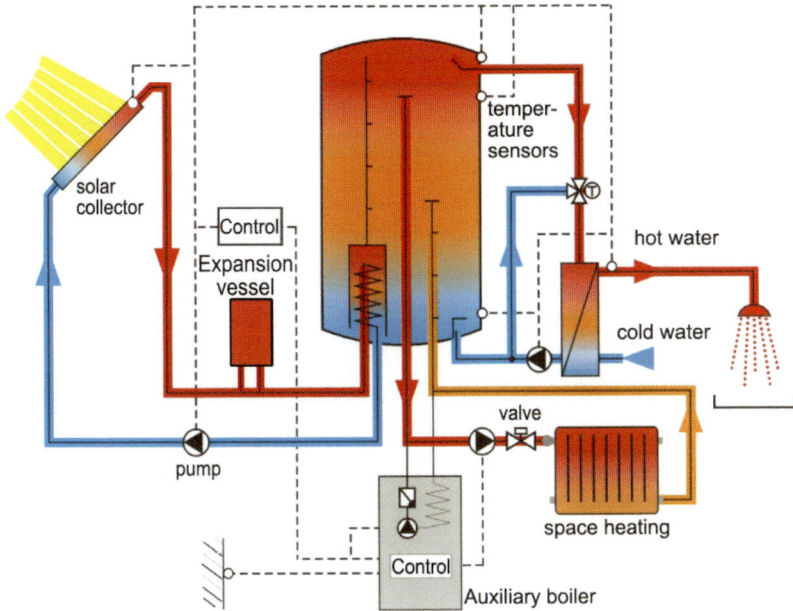

Figure 6.13 Diagram of a basic closed-loop solar water-heating system. A pipe loop conveys heat from the collectors to the storage cylinder, where a heat exchanger transfers the heat to the water in the tank, and the liquid in the loop returns to be reheated. A second coil higher up in the tank, or an immersion heater, can top up the temperature if required using another heat source such as a wood stove. Water is then drawn off at the top for consumption or space heating. Pumps, controls and wiring are shown.
Source: Energy Saving Trust.

Figure 6.14 Evacuated tube solar collectors on the roof of an organic farmhouse in Carmarthenshire.

are very efficient and the tube types even more so because they will work over more of the year/time of day.

Collectors need to be facing directly at the sun, preferably at the position it will be in the sky at midday during the middle of the winter to be most effective at that period, when the heat is most precious. They should never be shaded.

The heat-collecting fluid is circulated into the building and through a coil in the bottom of a hot-water storage tank. The heat is conducted to the water in the tank. The hot water now rises by convection to the top of the tank, ready to be drawn off for use. The cooled fluid returns back to the roof to start the process all over again.

A pump is used to push the fluid around. This may use as little as 10 watts and can be powered directly by a 10-watt PV module. A controller with a temperature sensor lets the pump only work when the collector is hotter than the tank, to stop the heat leaving the tank at night. But if the whole of the panel can be situated below the tank so that the liquid in the closed loop circulates by convection (called thermosiphoning) then you don't need a pump. An expansion tank is needed in this circuit because, when hot, liquid occupies more space. The pipework may undulate as long as air can be released at high points and fluid drained at low points. An isolation valve is essential to shut off the collector from the tank for maintenance, while allowing any back-up water heater to continue to supply hot water.

How many panels?

In latitudes between 50° and 60° (as in the UK), allow 2.5–3 m² of collector area per person. A four-person household uses slightly less than 5000 kWh per year of hot water. In the UK's climate a normal flat-plate collector could produce around 400 kWh per square metre per year in a well-maintained system. Therefore up to ten square meters is required for four people if this is a principal heat source. An estimate of the available energy at a site and therefore the size of collector area and storage volume can be derived from inputting the latitude and longitude, angle of incidence of the slope of the roof and the orientation of the roof towards the sun, into freely available software.[1]

Storing the heat

Usually, 300 litres (80 gallons) of hot-water storage is sufficient for four people. Typically, for every square metre of solar panel about 50–100 l (15–25 gallons) of storage volume is appropriate. So, for example, a system with 5 m² of solar panel might need a tank capable of storing around 300–375 l. The tank should be thoroughly insulated. They can be coupled to work with a biomass stove with a back boiler, which would have its own indirect closed loop entering and leaving the tank.

Figure 6.15 A ground source collector for a heat pump.
Credit: John Cantor.

Heat pumps

Heat pumps can take heat from the ground, air or a nearby body of water if it's available. All of them basically work like a fridge, except backwards. In a fridge, heat is extracted from a small space inside and pumped out into the world. With a heat pump it is pumped from a large space outside and concentrated into a small space: your building.

Heat pumps are judged by their coefficient of performance (CoP). This is the ratio of the amount of heat produced divided by the electricity consumption of the pump. So, for example, a heat pump with a CoP of 3 (or 3:1) will produce three times as much heat energy as the electrical energy it consumes. The higher the CoP, the better the performance. You can maximize the CoP by choosing a heating distribution system requiring a lower water temperature – underfloor heating rather than domestic hot water and radiators – and by choosing a heat source with a high average temperature (e.g. the ground or water rather than air). Air-source heat pumps are not always terribly efficient so we will ignore them. If any type is used for domestic hot water then the efficiency will be significantly lower.

Ground-source heat pumps require a hole to be dug at least 1.5 m deep and the collecting coil to be buried – usually a closed-circuit loop of 20–40 mm high-density polyethylene piping filled with a mixture of water and glycol antifreeze. The commonest hole is a series of horizontal trenches (wet ground is better than dry). A couple of organic farmers I know have put them in fields at the back of their farmhouses. The system also includes a heat exchanger, pump and delivery pipes passing under an exterior wall to the destination. Water-source coils are laid on the bed of the lake or river.

The coil needs to have good contact with the ground. Sizing is complex and specialized software is required, available, amongst other places, via the website of The International Ground Source Heat Pump Association (IGSHPA). They have a long life expectancy.

Heat pump manufacturers' own estimates of their CoPs should be treated with caution because real operating conditions will not necessarily reflect the test conditions. If the heated water is for radiators, they should be larger than the usual kind, with no TRVs and large bore pipes. A buffer

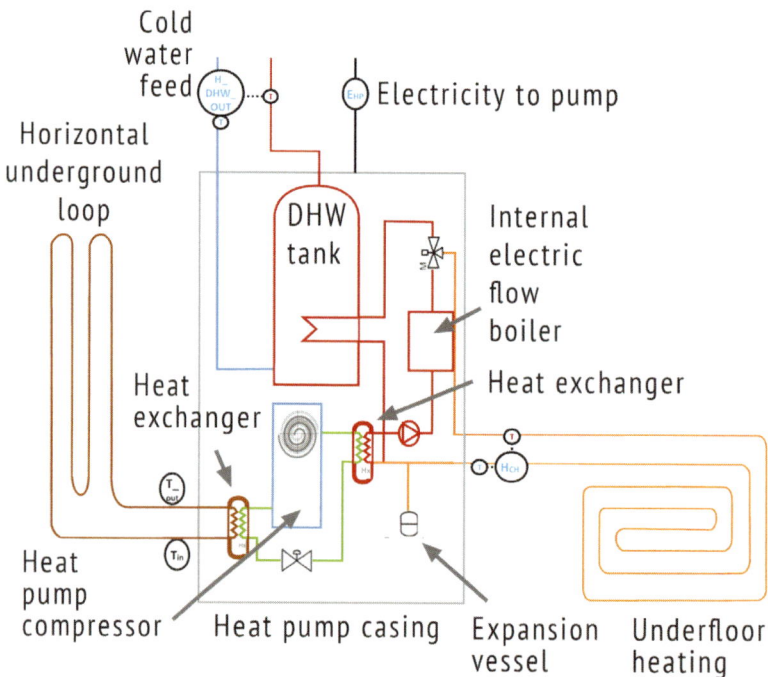

Figure 6.16 Diagram of a heat pump to hot-water tank and underfloor heating system.

Figure 6.17 A storage tank with an expansion vessel on the top connected to a heat pump and auxiliary heating from a back boiler from a woodstove.

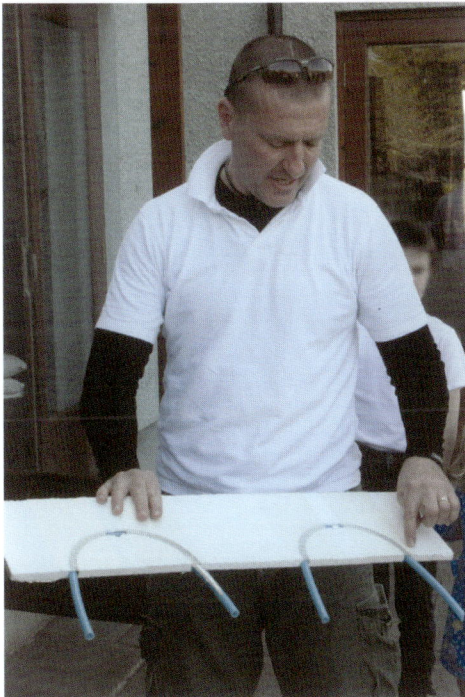

Figure 6.18 An organic farmer demonstrates on his rear patio how his underfloor heating pipes fit into the insulation in the farmhouse behind. The heat-pump collector coils are in a field twenty metres to his left. The tank in Fig. 6.16 is in a room to his right.

tank is recommended, so that, say, a wood stove or solar can provide backup. A coil much larger than normal in a DHW tank would be used in the tank to give the heat a chance to transfer.

Biomass

A biomass heating system can be incorporated into any central heating or hot-water system, but is especially suited to less airtight homes. Stoves, like boilers, may have back burners to heat water for space heating and hot water. Avoid traditional open fires as 80 per cent of the heat disappears up the chimney.

A large storage tank makes an ideal companion. Wood fuel (biomass) comes as logs, woodchips or pellets. Pellets are expensive. Logs may be burnt in stoves, and all three may be burnt in boilers. When burnt it should have as low a moisture content as possible – 20–30 per cent – to produce the best heat and least smoke/pollution. Hardwood is denser and burns for longer.

It's important to note the potential health-reducing impact of biomass-burning boilers. They can emit pollutants such as nitrogen dioxide (NO_2), particulates (PM) and sulphur dioxide (SO_2), depending on the boiler and fuel quality. Even a well-maintained biomass boiler will pollute more than a similar gas system.

Figure 6.19 A modern stove, with high thermal mass so it absorbs lots of heat and sends it out for ages after the fire has gone out. The alcove in the top can be used for slow cooking.

Stoves

Modern stoves have efficiencies of up to 90 per cent, meaning that only 10 per cent of the heat in the fuel is lost. They contain sophisticated systems to achieve the optimum burn and recycle combustion gases. Larger versions have back boilers to supply hot water, in which case expect a maximum efficiency of 80 per cent. A caution: stoves can easily be oversized, despite the fact that modern stoves come with temperature controls, because the burn must occur within a limited range (around 650 °C/1,200 °F) to be efficient and avoid wasted fuel and toxic by-products such as carbon monoxide. So don't buy one with a heat output in kW bigger than you need.

Ceramic, cob and masonry stoves

These stoves are the most efficient because the ceramic, cob or masonry (brick) material absorbs the heat of a properly combusted 'burn' to release it slowly, for up to 24 hours, after the fuel has disappeared. They're heavy,

Figure 6.20 A cob oven situated outside.

dense, heat-absorbing materials so we say they have 'high thermal mass'. Superinsulated, airtight small-to-medium sized homes can be heated with one of these in cold weather with the equivalent of only three or four logs a day. The burn must be efficient so that flue gas temperatures remain sufficiently high to prevent tar and acid building up. Controlled ventilation must be supplied to replace incoming air and draw the heated air through the other rooms.

While ceramic stoves are more expensive they can pay for themselves in the fuel saved. But you can build your own masonry or cob stove to your own design. They should be situated right in the middle of the house so their heat radiates everywhere. They may also be used for cooking by incorporating ovens and hobs in the designs, which could remove the need for a separate cooking appliance. (Cob or mud and straw building is covered in the chapter on Building.)

Figure 6.21 This large log boiler (left) is in a barn adjoining a farmhouse and connected to a large, well-insulated heat store (right). It will usually, in winter, need just one firing a day of a barrow-full of logs to supply the house and workshop with sufficient heat and hot water.

Ranges

Ranges are another form of stove primarily designed for cooking. Wood-burning models are available. Some have back boilers for space and water heating, drastically increasing the fuel demand. Although it may seem attractive to use the same appliance for cooking, space and water heating, it will not make efficient use of the fuel in all but the smallest of non-airtight homes.

Log boilers

These produce space and water heating for large buildings and workshops. They are loaded by hand, on average once a day. They are usually put in a dedicated boiler/utility room and are available in versions of 5–50 kW.

The best options for heating

If you have hydropower potential (see below) – install that and use the waste energy as heat. Everywhere else, install solar water heating for the

Figure 6.22 A temporary house at Lammas. The greenhouse-conservatory on the south-facing side preheats much of the air for the interior. This reduces the amount of heat required to keep the occupants warm. A flue can be seen coming through the wall from a wood stove that supplies the remaining heat requirement. Picture credit: Jasmine.

hot-water supply. But as the sun alone will not provide sufficient heat for water all year round, use a large superbly insulated tank containing heat exchangers from both the panels' circuit and either an LPG gas boiler or a cob/brick/ceramic biomass stove/boiler. You might opt for an electric immersion backup if you have sufficient renewable electricity available (e.g. hydro, wind or PV). A heat pump with underfloor heating is also a great idea, again if you have sufficient renewable electricity available for the pump.

A typical tank will have the bottom coil connected to the solar system and the top coil to the back-up heating source. When there isn't enough solar energy the back-up boiler is used to top up the heat demand. An extra buffer tank could store the sun-heated water until needed and/or to contribute to space heating.

Growing biomass for fuel

Burning wood produces carbon dioxide, which will not be replaced until the trees regrow. It also emits dioxins and persistent organic pollutants such as PAHs and PCBs, as well as particulates such as DM10, all of which are dangerous. Their level is at its highest just after lighting, until it reaches its optimum operating temperature of 200 °C, when pollution is still only reduced by about 50 per cent. Unseasoned wood produces even more pollution as freshly cut wood can contain up to 80 per cent moisture; useful energy is therefore wasted boiling off this water. Seasoning, which lets this water

Figure 6.23 Willow being grown on short-rotation coppice at Lammas for wood fuel. Successive plantings are at different heights.
Credit: Jasmine.

Table 6.3 Calorific values of different biomass fuels; this varies according to their moisture content and their energy density, as well as the volume they take up.

Fuel	Net CV1 MJ/kg	CV kWh/ kg	Bulk density kg/m³		Energy density by volume MJ/m³		Energy density by volume kWh/m³	
			Lower	Upper	Lower	Upper	Lower	Upper
Woodchips @ 30%	12.5	3.5	200	250	2,500	3,125	694	868
Log wood (stacked – air dried: 20% MC)	14.6	4.1	350	500	5,110	7,300	1,419	2,028
Wood – solid oven dried	18.6	5.2	400	600	7,440	11,160	2,067	3,100
Wood pellets	17	4.7	600	700	10,200	11,900	2,833	3,306
Miscanthus (bale – 25%MC)	12.1	3.4	140	180	1,694	2,178	471	605

Source: Gastec at CRE Ltd. and Annex A, Digest of UK Energy Statistics 2007.

evaporate naturally, takes at least a year and requires a well-ventilated, dry fuel store. Even at 30 per cent moisture, it has one third the calorific value of completely dry fuel.

Don't underestimate the amount of labour, time and land you need to supply firewood. This all has a cost relative to the rest of your livelihood. This is why it's important to minimise the amount of firewood required to insulation, airtightness of the building, and use alternative sources of heat energy.

How much land will you need?

Estimates vary as to how much land would be required to service a home if it were to be heated completely using biomass. It depends on the soil, climate and tree varieties. These are rough figures from what was the Forestry Commission: to produce 20,000 kwh per year (20 kW heat demand), sufficient for a reasonable sized house that is relatively uninsulated and a bit draughty, you would need 2 ha of broadleaf and/or conifer or mixed species coppice with or without standards. which would yield 12 m³ of timber per year.

Mixed coppice/standards are generally a reliable option, positioning species to best advantage: willow and alder on the wettest areas, tall standards (sycamore, eucalyptus) at the north end where they do not provide shade. A permanent belt of well-spaced standards might go around the perimeter for wind protection, including coppiced hazel.

Coppicing

Short rotation coppice (SRC) is the most common energy crop in the UK but is used mostly for woodchip (after four years); willow is the preferred species, although poplar is increasingly being used. In fact any native broadleafs can be used. From initial planting, all tree species take at least five years to begin to provide a usable crop. For obtaining reasonably sized logs it takes longer – up to ten years, depending on the climate.

A suggested strategy is to plant 600 trees in a grid with each tree 2 m or 8 feet apart. After three years cut the 120 trees closest to the south. This wood will be about 2" in diameter, good for kindling or bundles for a ceramic or brick stove. This will let sunlight through to the trees behind. In year 4 cut the next 120 trees behind them. Year 5 the next 120. These trees will be about 4 to 5 inches in diameter. By year 6 there will be only 120 original trees left, of about 6 inches in diameter. Cut and use them. This is the earliest year by which you could get enough fuel to satisfy your winter demand. After this, return to coppicing the first coup. The amount of growth depends on the species, the local climate conditions and whether it is matched to the underlying soil type.

Fuel figures

The amount of fuel you use is equal to the delivered heat divided by the delivered heat per unit mass of fuel, ie:

$$\text{tonnes/year} = \frac{(\text{kWh/year})}{(\text{kWh/tonne})}$$

So based on how much water you need and how much space heating you need per year added together you know how many kilowatt-hours per year of delivered heat you will need:

Delivered heat [kWh/year] = boiler peak-rated capacity [kWth] × 8,760
(the number of hours in a year) × estimated capacity factor (the number of
hours that you will be using it in a year)

The heat you get from your wood fuel depends on the boiler efficiency
and the fuel's calorific value (CV). It can be calculated using the following
equation:

Delivered heat per unit mass of fuel [kWh/tonne] = Net CV of fuel [MJ/kg] ×
boiler efficiency × 0.2778 (the conversion factor for MJ to kWh) × 1,000 (to
convert kg to tonnes)

The calorific value of dry biomass fuel is its energy content assuming no
moisture. This will vary between different types/species but a typical value
is 18.9 MJ/kg (or see Table 6.2). To calculate the CV of your wood fuel per
tonne, use the following formula:

Net CV [MJ/kg] = (18.9 − 2.442) × % moisture content

You can purchase meters which read the moisture content of timber.
    Volume and weight (based on a 50 per cent unit of softwood and
hardwood chips):

- 1 m³ of solid content of woodchips takes up approx. 2.8 m³ In
  other words 1 m³ of woodchips contains approximately 0.35 m³ of
  solid content. It weighs approximately 250 kg (0.25 tonnes) and yields
  2.53 GJ or 702.2 kWh (based on softwood at 40 per cent MC).
- 1 tonne of woodchips fills approximately 4.0 m³ and contains approx.
  1.4 m³ of solid content and yields 11.2 GJ or 3,121 kWh.
- For comparison (say you're moving and you use gas now) 1,000 m³
  of natural gas yields 10,948 kWh and is equivalent to 3.5 tonnes or
  15.6 m³ of woodchip.

Much more detailed information is available from the Biomass Energy
Centre at http://bit.ly/19vakWN.

Figure 6.24 Two turbines, not visible from the roads around, can be seen sticking their blades above the surrounding trees on the land belonging to Brithdir Mawr, a pioneering low-impact development in North Pembrokeshire which contains several smallholdings.

Renewable electricity

Choosing a technology

The first stage is to survey the site, and if possible quantify which renewable technology is appropriate. Questions to ask would include:

- Is there a stream or river nearby that could be used for a hydroelectric scheme?
- Is there an accessible, equator-facing site which is not shaded?
- Is the site windy for much of the year? Is there no turbulence nearby?

General design advice

The following advice comes from experience of many systems:

- Keep it simple: increased complexity reduces reliability and increases costs, especially for maintenance;
- Plan for periodic maintenance: renewable energy systems have a good reputation for unsupervised operation but all require some degree of monitoring and care;
- Be realistic when estimating loads: including a large safety factor can increase costs substantially;
- Repeatedly check weather data in the case of wind and solar power: errors in estimating the resource can cause disappointment;
- Different hardware with different characteristics have different costs. Investigate thoroughly all options before deciding on the optimum combination;
- Ensure the system is installed carefully: each connection must be made to last 30 years, because it can if installed properly. Use the correct tools and techniques. Reliability is no higher than the weakest connection;
- Be rigorous about safety during installation and in operation.

In any renewable electricity system it's not the generator but the 'balance of system costs' – control technology, batteries, and so on – that make up most of the total cost. Therefore there are advantages in scale – a larger system. This makes collective projects with neighbours worthwhile. That

Figure 6.25 A mobile array of solar photovoltaic panels serving a house belonging to Paul and Hoppi Wimbush at Lammas. The house is on the right, the milking shed and henhouse on the left.

said, solar and wind power are modular: you can always add more wind turbines or photovoltaic modules or solar collectors, providing there is space on a suitable site when more funds are available.

Renewable generators have little impact on the environment. Planning permission will be required in most cases. Intermittency is an issue except for micro-hydro (unless there is a drought). Consequently, either backup or storage may be required. If a grid connection is possible then electricity not required at the time of generation can be exported for sale and feed-in tariffs.

How much electricity do you need?

There are several ways of working out the power requirements of a renewable electricity system:

- list all your planned appliances and gadgets, how many watts they use and how many hours a week they will be used and multiply this by 52 to get the annual requirements;
- look at your existing electricity bills for the whole year, as long as the bills reflect the savings made from following efficiency recommendations and how you will be living.

This gives the annual electricity requirement in kilowatt-hours. If the home is connected to the grid, it can supply the extra electricity needed above what is being generated at the time. When more is being generated than is being used, that is sold to the grid. To do this requires a 'net metering arrangement' with the utility company. You should also calculate the maximum amount of power you may need at one time to estimate the size of your system.

AC or DC?

To work out how much power will be available at the sockets you need to factor in the efficiency of the generator plus other equipment such as controls. Renewable electricity is often, but not always, generated as 12-volt direct current (DC). There is a decision to be made whether to use a 12-volt DC system or a 240-volt alternating current (AC) system like the mains. Many appliances can be bought in 12-volt versions, as these are frequently used on boats and caravans. Modern digital gadgets are happy with these. This is more efficient than using 240 volts since you would have to purchase an inverter, which converts DC into AC, losing some energy in the process.

Often systems are bought in as turnkey 'plug and play' installations, which inevitably costs more but saves time and headaches. Several estimates

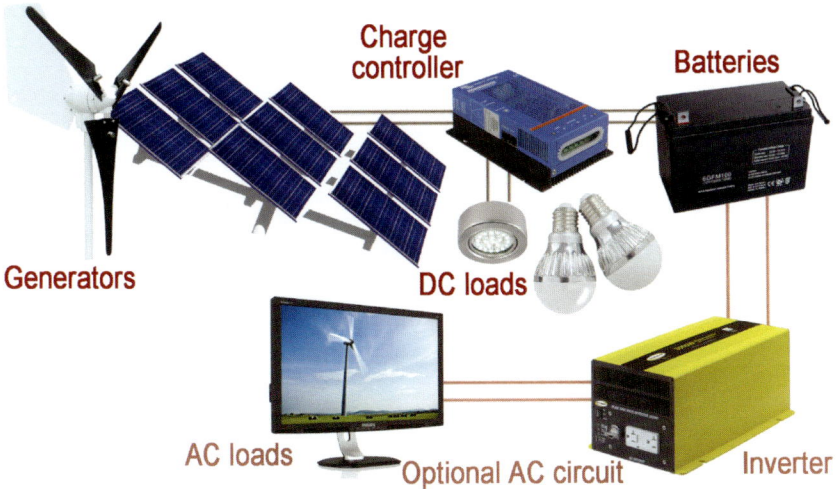

Figure 6.26 A generic circuit diagram for a DC system with optional AC circuit.

should be sought from different suppliers. You can build your own system, which is cheaper, but if you want to take advantage of feed-in tariffs to get a regular income from generating your electricity (even if you use it all yourself) you would need a mains connection and to use a certified installer.

Hydroelectric power

Hydroelectric power requires a consistent flow of water, together with a drop in level sufficient to provide the force required to turn a turbine. In such a case it is highly reliable and cost-effective. A system, once installed, can last for up to 100 years.

The greater the volume of water flow, and the greater the head – vertical distance – it drops, the more electricity can be generated. The more power that can be generated, the more cost-effective it is. A small flow will not produce much power. Therefore the power in the stream must be measured first.

To do this, for small streams the flow is diverted into a receptacle of known volume, and the time taken to fill it is measured. From this, a flow rate in litres per second, or gallons per minute, can be calculated. To get a rough idea in the case of larger watercourses, the area of a cross section is calculated using the width and the depth, then the average speed between two points 10 metres or yards apart is measured. From this the flow rate can be deduced. A more accurate idea is obtained by utilising hydrological

Figure 6.27 and 6.28 A micro-hydro system on an organic farm. 500 metres up from the turbine on a small stream is the intake, where a proportion of the stream is diverted into a six-inch pipe. In the turbine shed at the bottom of the property the flow is split into four, which suits this particular type of 'impulse' turbine, a Turgo.

maps and flowmeters or stream-gauges, which take readings of the flow at 15- or 30-minute time intervals. From the flow rate, the expected electrical output of the turbine can be calculated by using the formula:

Power out (in kilowatts) = the flow (Q) × the head (in yards or metres) (H) × the specific weight of water (Y, or 13.81 kilonewtons/m²)

For example, a scheme with a flow rate of 0.5 m²/second over a 12-metre head, would in theory produce an output of 0.5 × 12 × 13.81 = 58.86 kW. In reality, efficiency losses usually account for around half of this output, making it more like just under 30 kW. Multiplying this by the length of time in hours over which the generator would be expected to operate in a given year or month can give you the number of kilowatt-hours for that period. Different turbines are efficient for different heads and flow rates, and specialist help should be sought in choosing the right type.

Planning permission must be sought and a licence obtained from the Environment Agency or Natural Resources Wales.

The components of a micro-hydropower system are:

- A water conveyance, which is a channel, leat, pipeline, or pressurized pipeline (penstock) that delivers the water;

- A turbine, pump, or waterwheel, which transforms the energy of flowing water into rotational energy;
- An alternator or generator, which transforms the rotational energy into electricity;
- A regulator, which controls the generator.

There may be an inverter to convert the low-voltage DC electricity produced by the system into 120 or 240 V of AC electricity. Optionally, a dam may be constructed as a holding bay for the water for times when rainfall is low, but these are very unusual in micro-hydro projects.

Wind power

In general, horizontal-axis wind turbines only have a chance of working at maximum efficiency in open, exposed spaces. Turbulence caused by any nearby buildings or trees means that the wind speed of 5 m/s (11 mph) required to operate efficiently is rarely reached. Vertical-axis wind turbines have a lower cut-in speed and can operate in more turbulent conditions as they don't have to turn to face the wind every time the direction of the wind changes. However they are more expensive.

Substantial monitoring of installed horizontal-axis micro-wind turbines,[2] published in July 2009 by the UK Energy Saving Trust found that to operate efficiently turbines require a tower (10–25 metres high) and exposed sites with no obstructions in the direction of the prevailing wind. This report says:

Figure 6.29 A 5 kW Proven wind turbine (erected in 2002) and a 5 kW Iskra wind turbine (2005) at Hockerton Housing Project. Both turbines are 26 m high. Data on their output is published on their website. The first received much local opposition, but was eventually passed. When locals realised it wasn't as bad as they'd thought, there was no opposition to the second turbine.

'a properly sited and positioned 6 kW rated free-standing pole mounted turbine ... would be expected to generate approximately 18,000 kWh per annum'. This represents a very quick payback.

Turbines come in many sizes and power ratings, from 50 W upwards. A 5–15 kW, domestic machine has rotors 8 to 25 feet in diameter, would be 30 feet (10 metres) tall and could supply the needs of a small community. A typical small wind generator has a rotor that is directly coupled to the generator, which produces electricity either at variable frequency 120/240 volt alternating current, or at 12/24 volt direct current (DC) for battery charging. Control equipment and, if needed, inverters that convert the DC electricity to mains-quality AC are necessary. It is possible to buy versions of most appliances, however, that run on DC. Conversion of DC to AC entails power losses.

Small turbines are often used in combination with photovoltaic modules in off-grid situations. They make a good pairing because the sun is often shining when the wind is not, and vice versa. They may be supplied as a kit, complete with battery storage for up to three days' backup.

Wind resources are characterised by wind-power density classes, ranging from class 1 (the lowest) to class 7 (the highest). Good wind resources (class 3 and above), which have an average annual wind speed of at least 6 m/s (13 mph) are found in many locations.

Calculating the power

The annual average wind speed needs to be greater than 5 m/s (11–13 mph). Wind resource maps are available on the National Renewable Energy Laboratory website, and the Google Application Google Earth, or in the UK, the RENSmart website – www.rensmart.com/Weather/BERR. A proposed site should be monitored with an anemometer for 12 months.

Once the average wind speed is known, then a glance at manufacturers' brochures will reveal power/energy curves like the one illustrated, from which can be read off the level of power it might be possible to generate from a given wind speed.

The larger the diameter of the turbine, the greater the swept area and the more power is collected. This helps to explain how the power output increases with the cube of the wind speed, so a doubling of wind speed would result in eight times more power. The longer the high wind speeds last, the more energy will be generated. The proportion of energy in the wind that can be converted to electricity is the 'power coefficient' (C_p) of a turbine and is within the range 35–45 per cent. Once losses in the system are

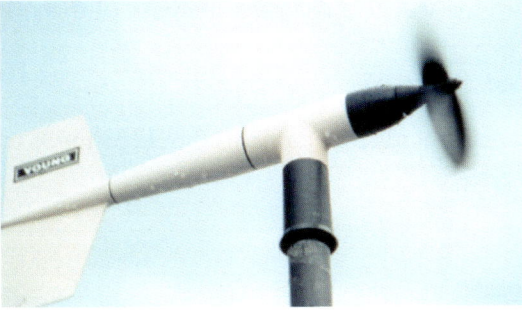

Figure 6.30 An anemometer being used to measure the wind speed.
Credit: Wikimedia Commons (NOAA Photo Library, NOAA Central Library; OAR/ERL/National Severe Storms Laboratory (NSSL)).

Typical 'Power curve'

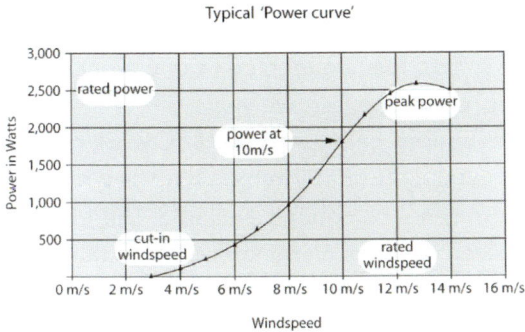

Figure 6.31 A power curve for a 2.5 kW turbine with a cut-in speed of 3 m/s, showing how much energy it will generate at different wind speeds according to its rating.
Credit: the Centre for Alternative Technology, Wales

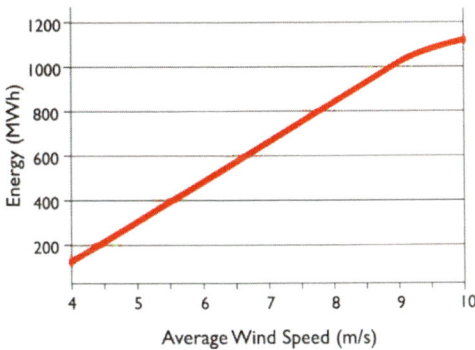

Figure 6.32 A graph showing, for different wind speeds, the expected output of a wind turbine. Manufacturers often supply graphs of this nature for each wind turbine they produce.

taken into account, only 10–30 per cent of the power of the wind is actually made into usable electricity.

There are various important wind speeds to consider:

- Start-up wind speed: that will turn an unloaded rotor;
- Cut-in wind speed: at which the rotor can be loaded;
- Rated wind speed: at which the machine is designed to run (the optimum tip-speed ratio);

- Furling wind speed: at which the machine will be turned out of the wind to prevent damage;
- Maximum design wind speed.

A careful matching of the electrical energy requirements should be made to maximise the use of the wind power.

Solar power

Solar photovoltaic (PV) electricity has the advantages of being low-maintenance, due to the absence of moving parts; durable, lasting up to 30 years; modular, so a system can be expanded later; and quick to install, as a medium-sized roof-mounted system may be erected in one week. Prices have come down by over 50 per cent in the last two years.

But there are disadvantages: besides being intermittent, working only when the sun is shining, it is seasonal, particularly in high latitudes, so when electricity is needed most, there may not be enough available. Therefore PV systems must be appropriately sized to provide enough power in the depth of winter, or supplemented with other sources of electricity. In 99 per cent of cases this will be the grid, but off-grid it is usually wind. Module output also declines gradually, producing possibly 95 per cent of rated output for the first 10 years, 90 per cent for the next 10 years, and so on, depending on the type of cell. The site must have no shading falling upon it at any time of day throughout the year.

Figure 6.33 The solar roof at the Centre for Alternative Technology, Wales.

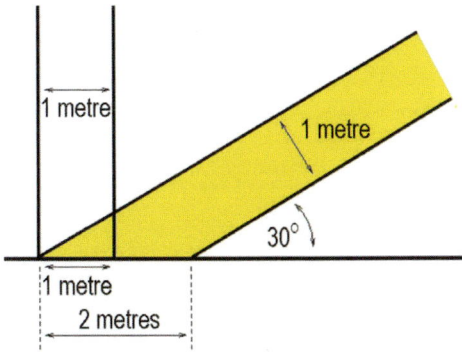

Figure 6.34 The angle at which the light hits a silicon module is important. Ideally, it needs to do so straight on. At 30 degrees, for example, the same amount of light will be spread over double the area of the module, halving its effectiveness.

Figure 6.35 An example of poor siting: there needs to be no shading on the module, as this will prevent it from generating electricity. Even a small shade can reduce output disproportionately.

Table 6.4 The effect of tilt and orientation on a solar module's performance at latitude 52° (Birmingham, UK). The table shows that the efficiency of a PV array is compromised by 17 per cent when placed vertically on a building façade, and that east- or west-facing arrays suffer a 50 per cent loss.

Orientation	Tilt	Generation (kWh/m2/ day)	Difference from optimum
South	35°	3.00	optimum
South	Vertical	2.18	17%
South	Horizontal	2.63	12%
East/West	35°	2.46	18%
East/West	Vertical	1.63	47%
East/West	Horizontal	2.63	12%

Source: BRE.

The amount of power produced by a solar cell depends on its efficiency and how much light is hitting it. A c-Si (silicon) cell will produce most power when pointed directly at the overhead summer sun on a bright, clear day. To enable them to be compared, modules are characterised by 'peak power'

Figure 6.36 A field of solar panels generating electricity for feed in tariffs in Pembrokeshire. The income has financed the research and development for an affordable self-sufficient home, Tŷ Solar, discussed in the Exemplary Examples section.

(watts-peak or Wp) output. It does not mean that they will always produce this amount of power. Peak power, as measured under internationally agreed Standard Test Conditions (STC), is what is produced when they are exposed to 1 kW per square metre of light at 25 °C in an atmospheric air mass of 1.5.

A typical system includes: the modules, an inverter, if AC electricity is required, controllers, disconnects, meters and fuses.

Calculating output

The annual energy that can be produced depends mostly upon the peak power of the module and the insolation data (amount of sunshine) for the location. Public sources of insolation data at most locations are available from PVGIS or the US NREL. This will give the average amount of energy available per square metre for that location – in kWh/m^2 – for the whole year. To calculate the estimated output per year per PV module, use the following formula:

Module rated output (peak watts) × peak sunshine hours (per year) × 0.75 (performance ratio) = energy generated (kilowatt-hours/year)

For example:

1500 W × 900 peak hours per year × 0.75 = 1,012,5005 watt-hours (Wh) or 1102 kilowatt-hours (kWh) (approximately)

Other factors to be taken into account include:

- The orientation (azimuth) (–90° is east, 0° is equator-facing and 90° is west);
- The tilt angle of the modules from the horizontal plane;
- The energy conversion efficiency of the modules;
- The extent to which their efficiency is affected by temperature;
- Factors to do with the clarity of the atmosphere and the path of the sun;
- Possible shading at any time of day and year;
- System efficiencies, such as those of the chosen inverter and the wiring;
- The type of mounting structure: fixed or tracking (tracking increases output).

Estimating CO_2 emissions saved

To calculate the CO_2 emissions saved by using renewable energy, you use the emissions factor for the grid electricity you're avoiding using. This will

Figure 6.37 A communal solar PV system for five terraced homes on the earth-covered roofs at Hockerton Housing Project. The rear of the roof is covered in turf and insulation and the front is glazed to capture solar energy. See the case study in the Exemplary Examples section of the book.

depend on the location and the make-up of this electricity. The figure is available from the Carbon Trust's website.[3] Multiply the total number of kWh generated in a year by this factor to determine the number of kilograms of carbon dioxide saved.

Off-grid systems

Solar and wind-powered renewable electricity systems not connected to the grid will need to use batteries and charge controllers. A typical, small off-grid or standalone system will include the following components:

- a photovoltaic module or array;
- a battery charge controller;
- batteries;
- safety disconnects and fuses;
- a grounding circuit;
- cables;
- an inverter or power-control unit, if it is necessary to convert direct to alternating current (DC to AC) in larger systems;
- loads: e.g. LED lamps (usually DC) rated from 1 W to 5 W.

Figure 6.38 This photovoltaic panel is simply charging a small battery that powers an electric fence to keep the pigs and hens in and foxes out at Lammas.

PV modules are commonly rated at 20 to 80 Wp, with 50 Wp the most popular size. An 80 Wp system can power four 8 W lamps and a small television set.

Batteries

Batteries ensure a supply of electricity when the sun isn't shining and the wind isn't blowing. Batteries that are not properly looked after can severely reduce the efficiency of the entire system. Over the lifetime of the system, they may even have the highest cost, as they need replacing now and then. Some batteries are sealed and require less maintenance, but all wear out and all need to get a full charge regularly.

Battery sizes are defined by their capacity in ampere-hours: the amount of energy that can be drawn from the battery before it is completely discharged.

The choice is typically lead-acid batteries. These fall into two types: 'deep discharge' and 'shallow discharge'. The former are preferred because they can be almost completely drained without too much damage. Avoid auto batteries because they are of the shallow-disharge type and need much more attention. Lead-acid batteries are heavy. Other types, such as nickel-metal-hydride, nickel-cadmium and lithium-ion batteries, are sometimes used as they are lighter, require less maintenance, have a longer life and are more flexible in use; but they are more expensive. Lithium-ion batteries suitable for RE systems can now be leased.

The size of the battery bank is according to the maximum amount of storage time required for a given amount of electricity to be used during that period. This is usually a reasonable number of cloudy/windless days when the batteries can't be charged. Two or three days is usual. The more days you allow for, the more expensive it gets. Once calculated, this figure is used to purchase the batteries.

For example, if the requirement is for 506 Wh for three days, divide by the voltage of the system (usually 12V) and multiply by the number of days (3):

$$506/12 \times 3 = 42 \times 3 = 126 \text{ Ah}$$

To store 126 Ah, three deep-cycle batteries of 56 Ah capacity each would therefore be required – extra capacity is always needed as batteries should never be completely discharged. Suppliers usually recommend the particular type of batteries that work best with their PV modules or wind turbines, since not all batteries are the same. Expert advice should always be sought.

> **Measuring charge**
>
> An ampere-hour or amp-hour (Ah) is a unit of electric charge. One ampere-hour is the electric charge transferred by a steady current of one ampere for one hour.

For example: 100 Ah can deliver 1 A for 100 hours, or 2 A for 50 hours, and so on (though in practice it will be less because amp-hour capacity is dependent on discharge rate).

Warning: lead-acid batteries give off explosive hydrogen gas when charging, so must be housed in a well-ventilated space away from the other electrical-system components and living spaces.

Charge controllers

Charge controllers adjust the charge going from the modules into the batteries to ensure optimal performance. They include a low-voltage

Figure 6.39 An inverter, leased lithium-ion batteries and controllers for the PV panels on Tŷ Solar demonstration house (see the Exemplary Examples section).

disconnect that prevents overdischarging, which can permanently damage the batteries. The best charge controllers also include maximum power-point tracking (MPPT), which optimizes the PV array's output, increasing the energy it produces. The choice of controller depends on the size of the PV system and the system voltage.

Inverters

If you are using an AC system you will need an inverter. This box will come after the batteries and before the AC loads in the circuitry. The inverter will be of the self-commutating or 'standalone' type. Inverters vary according to the voltage and current they can accept and the frequency and power of the output. Therefore choose one according to the peak load it will have to meet; they range at the domestic scale from 100 W to 10 kW.

Further information:

Renewable Energy Systems: The Earthscan Expert Guide, Dilwyn Jenkins, Routledge, 2012.
Solar Technology: The Earthscan Expert Guide to Using Solar Energy for Heating, Cooling and Electricity, David Thorpe, Routledge, 2011.
Stand-alone Solar Electric Systems: The Earthscan Expert Handbook for Planning, Design and Installation, Mark Hankins, Routledge, 2011.
Solar Domestic Water Heating: The Earthscan Expert Handbook for Planning, Design and Installation, Chris Laughton, Routledge, 2011.
Wind & Solar Electricity, Andy Reynolds, Low impact Living Initiative, 2009.
Heating with Wood, Andy Reynolds, Low-impact Living Initiative, 2010.
The Home Energy Handbook: A Guide to Saving and Generating Energy in Your Home and Community, Allan Shepherd, Paul Allen, Peter Harper, Centre for Alternative Technology Publications, 2012.

Notes

1   The EC-funded project MESoR (Management and Exploitation of Solar Resource Knowledge) is a comprehensive portal giving user-friendly access to several free sources of solar energy data using a map-based graphical user interface (GUI). The sources include NASA, PVGIS, SoDa, HelioClim, NCEP, SWERA, METEONORM and

MeteoTest, plus others. Users input their locations and the output format can be chosen. Map layers can be shown in Google Earth.

2   'Location, location, location: The Energy Saving Trust's Field Trial Report on Domestic Wind Turbines', EST, 2009, London.

3   http://www.carbontrust.com/resources/guides/carbon-footprinting-and-reporting/ conversion-factors. Accessed January 2014.

Everyone has their own idea of a dream house. From a pole roundhouse to a straw-bale mansion, from a cob cottage to a Passivhaus terrace, there are any number of possible styles and construction methods. Then there are workshops and outbuildings to construct…

The One Planet Life doesn't prescribe what your buildings should look like or how they should be built. You can design them however you like as long as they meet building regulations and are zero carbon over their lifetime; it's not about appearance but performance. This is mainly to do with:

- how comfortable and healthy it is to live in;
- how eco-friendly it is; and
- how much energy it uses in its materials, construction, lifetime and eventual demolition.

If you take care of these aspects, you can render or clad it to look how you like.

So this chapter spends a lot of time looking at the principles of zero-carbon building so you can apply them however you like. For example, Tŷ Solar (see Exemplary Examples) could have been rendered with lime or hemcrete in any colour you want (like The Lime House – see the end of the chapter). 'Affordable' passive houses are being built that can look so much like a 'normal' house as to be virtually indistinguishable. Or you can eschew right angles completely and go for a 'hobbit house', but there is, as yet, no guarantee that it will pass building regulations (no pole roundhouse has yet done so to my knowledge). Some, like Tony Wrench's roundhouse at Brithdir Mawr, have been given retrospective planning permission but really only because much media fuss was created – not a very repeatable tactic.

Figure 7.1 Straw-bale house rendered in lime
Credit: Rachel Shiamh.

Figure 7.2 Timber-frame house clad
with boards and with corrugated iron roof
(Paul and Hoppi Wimbush's temporary
home, Lammas).

Figure 7.3 Roundwood pole construction rendered in lime and with turf roof
Credit: Simon Dale.

Figure 7.4 Passive house timber-frame construction rendered in lime with sedum roof (my own studio).

Figure 7.5 Passive house timber-frame construction clad with larch (Tŷ Solar affordable home).

Figure 7.6 Passive house concrete construction with earth roof and large conservatory facing the sun (Hockerton Housing Co-Op).

Figure 7.7 Tony Wrench outside his roundhouse at Brithdir Mawr admiring the recent lime rendering work.

You can still disguise the right angles or build with eccentric angles with cut lengths of timber frame and achieve a high level of airtightness and pass Building Regulations, but it's vital to appreciate at the outset that this will significantly increase the time taken to build – and the cost.

Self-build or buy?

At this stage in the growth of one-planet developments many pioneers are building their own houses. But this is hard work. It's a lot to expect of people to be providing for their sustenance and livelihood at the same time as building a house while living in temporary accommodation. On the other hand, designing and building houses can be fun, and construction is often a community-based collaboration, an opportunity for people to come together and learn. But if one-planet developments are to become more popular I expect to see types of housing that are affordable, zero-carbon and meet building regulations being made available 'off-the-peg'.

The purpose of this chapter is to enable you to either design your own building or understand the principles so you can talk to suppliers, contractors and architects and project manage the process. Let's discuss first the general principles then move on to summarise some techniques, before talking briefly about finishes and decoration.

Principles of zero-carbon building

Buildings should be at least zero-carbon on balance, when totalling the impacts of materials, construction, use and demolition. Features of this are to:

- minimise the use of fossil-fuel energy during the supply chain and process of construction;
- encourage the use of materials which store atmospheric carbon in the fabric of the building;
- encourage the generation and even export of renewable energy by the building;
- construct and manage it in such a way that it minimises the emission of greenhouse gases during its lifetime and eventual demolition.

Such a building could, over its lifetime, become zero-carbon, or even negative carbon by generating enough power to more than make up for the fossil fuels it has used.[1] To achieve this, the following features are needed:[2]

- favouring the use of 'natural' and cellulose-based materials (timber, straw, cob, hemp-line, and so on);
- making the structure very airtight;
- making the structure breathable;
- making it durable, fire- and weather-resistant;
- incorporating a large amount of insulation;
- taking advantage of free, renewable energy.

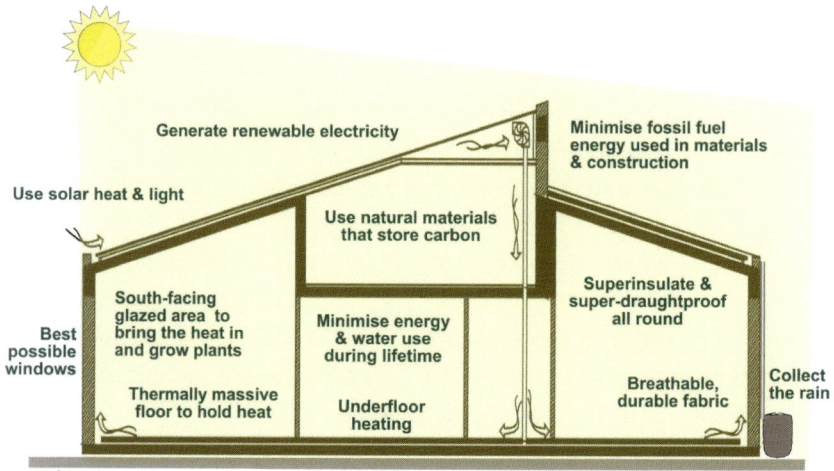

Figure 7.8 The ideal features of zero-carbon homes.

Existing techniques and approaches shared by most low-impact buildings

- siting the building in a sheltered spot that is south-facing to make the most of the sun's free energy;
- passive solar design to capture and hold the sun's heat;
- high levels of insulation, with a preference for organic, natural materials;
- management of ventilation and shading to prevent unwanted heat losses or gains;
- the use of locally sourced timber and other materials that lock up carbon in the building;
- low-tech construction techniques that do not require highly skilled labour;
- using volunteer, training workshop and community labour;
- the re-use of existing materials, for example windows and doors;
- green roofs, whether of grass, moss or sedum (which replace the greenness displaced by the building);
- solar electric and solar water-heating panels on the roof.

First choice: light or heavy?

Do you want a heavy building made of light materials or heavy ones, or some combination of the two? A thermally light building is made from materials like timber and straw, a heavy one from dense materials like stone and rammed earth. This is an important design choice right from the start, because on the answer depends how much energy you will need to supply to keep warm.

All building materials have three essential thermal properties:

1 **Thermal conductivity**: how well it conducts heat energy;
2 **Thermal mass** or thermal capacity: how much heat energy is required to raise its temperature;
3 **Thermal inertia** or diffusivity resistance: how quickly it responds to temperature changes.

It's the combination of these properties that dictates how a material performs in real buildings with changing temperatures. Most, but by no means all, low-impact buildings are thermally 'light', but this tends to be because of cost rather than performance.

In a 'light' building you are predominantly heating the air and the building will cool down quicker – particularly if the air is allowed to leave easily. Although more heating is required to keep the temperature constant it will warm up more quickly from cold. This might be good if the house isn't occupied during the day.

A 'heavy' building takes longer to warm up but stays warm for longer. This is because the more dense a material, the more heat it will hold. Traditional materials like stone, adobe, cob, brick or rammed earth, and modern ones like concrete and hemcrete (made from hemp and lime) absorb heat and take several days to release it slowly as they cool down. They also help prevent overheating. They will need insulating on the outside to stop the heat escaping. The degree of success is more dependent on big temperature variations between day and night. How to choose?

Applying this to passive solar design

All zero-carbon homes use a passive solar design. This means harnessing as much of the sun's free energy as possible – its light and heat. With a passive solar design, in cooler climates like the UK's, sunlight is allowed to fall

Figure 7.9 and 7.10 Turf-covered building with greenhouse on the timber-framed thermally 'light' front to capture heat, with a thermally 'heavy' earth-covered rear and grass roof.
Credit: Simon and Jasmine's temporary first house at Lammas.

Figure 7.11 and 7.12 South-facing room on The Hub timber-frame community building at Lammas, which collects solar heat and light and directs it inside.

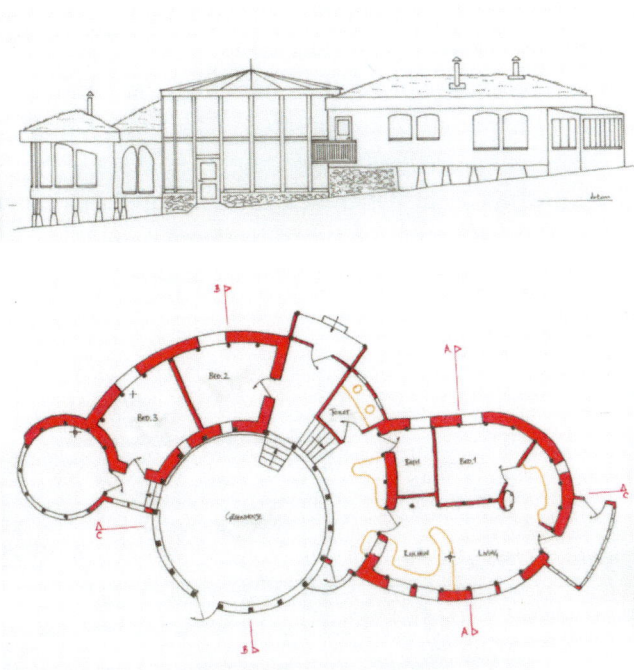

Figure 7.13. and 7.14 Plan and profile view of the as-yet unbuilt permanent dwelling for Paul and Hoppi Wimbush at Lammas. The core of the building is the south-facing circular greenhouse that will be tall enough to grow Mediterranean fruit trees as well as lots of other food, and capture heat that will be sent into the rest of the dwelling. The uphill, north-facing side is well insulated and contains few windows.
Credit: Paul and Hoppi Wimbush at Lammas.

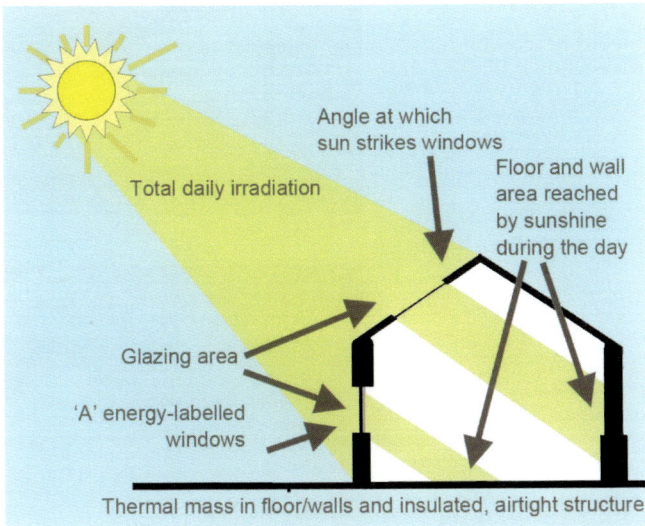

Figure 7.15 Principles of passive solar design.

through high standard glazing (see below) onto thermally massive materials (like ceramic tiles above concrete/hemcrete), warming them up in the day. During the night they release their heat into the internal space overnight, moderating extremes of temperature. The floor is insulated below and at the sides.

In the cooler British winters when heating is needed, thermal mass helps to hold heat and carry it to areas not directly heated. The thermal mass

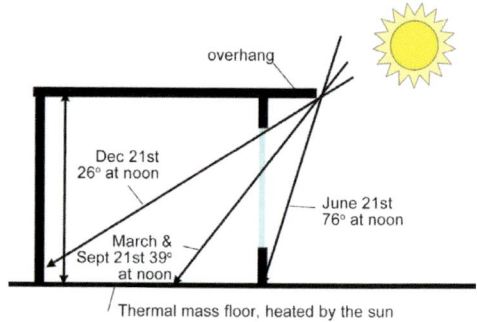

Figure 7.16 Overhangs or pergolas above windows help to prevent overheating in summer but let the sun in during the winter. They should be sized relative to the latitude, location and window size.

overhang

Dec 21st
26° at noon

June 21st
76° at noon

March &
Sept 21st 39°
at noon

Thermal mass floor, heated by the sun

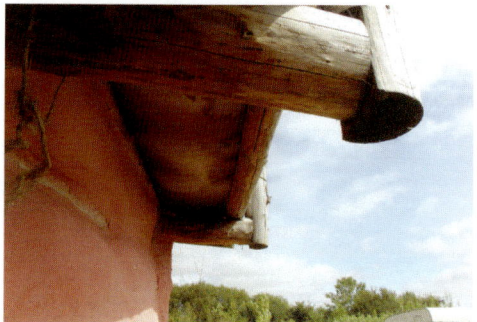

Figure 7.17 and 7.18 Overhangs on (above) Paul and Hoppi's timber-frame home and Cassie and Nigel's cob home (right) with a reciprocal frame roof.

should not be too thick (much over 100 mm for masonry) and should be insulated on the outside to prevent the heat escaping.

The ideal then is for sunshine coming through the glazing to fall onto exposed ceramic tiles or similar. Timber floors or floors covered with rugs and carpets will not help. A rule of thumb is a floor surface-to-glazing area ratio of 6:1.

Materials compared

Scientifically speaking, thermal mass is the product of the specific heat capacity of the material and its total mass and conductivity, and can be worked out precisely. Higher thermal mass is indicated by higher thermal admittance values. This is another term for the heat-transfer coefficient, a way of quantifying a material's ability to absorb and release heat from a space as the indoor temperature changes over time. Admittance is measured in W/m²K (watts per square metre Kelvin) as follows:

$$h = \Delta Q / A \times \Delta T$$

Where:

h = heat transfer coefficient, W/m²K

ΔQ = heat input or heat lost, in watts

A = heat transfer surface, in m²

ΔT = difference in temperature between the solid surface and the adjacent air space.

Examples are given in Tables 7.1 and 7.2.

Table 7.1 Examples of the admittance values of different wall types.

External wall	Internal finish	Admittance value
Timber frame (brick outer leaf)	Plasterboard	1.0
	Wet plaster	
Masonry cavity wall (100 mm aircrete block)	Plasterboard	1.85
	Wet plaster	2.65
Masonry cavity wall (100 mm dense aggregate block)	Plasterboard	2.65
	Wet plaster	5.04

Table 7.2 Examples of the conductivity and heat capacity of different materials.

Material	Specific heat capacity (Joules per Kg.Kelvin)	Thermal conductivity λ (W/mK)	Density (Kg/m³)	Effectiveness
Stone	1,000	1.8	2,300	high
Brick	800	0.73	1,700	high
Concrete	1,000	1.13	2,000	high
Hemcrete	1,500–1,700	0.06	275	medium
Timber	1,200	0.14	650	low
Mineral fibre insulation	1,000	0.035	25	low
Wood fibre batt insulation	2,100	0.038	45–55	low

What happens in practice?

- A straw-bale or timber-frame building insulated with wool, recycled cellulose or wood-fibre batts and with timber floors is thermally 'light' and will cool down relatively quickly.
- A building with at least some of the floors and walls made of stone, concrete or rammed earth will be thermally 'heavier' and store the heat that is introduced into it for longer.
- An ideal compromise for the British climate is to have 100–150 mm of thermal mass in the floor (surrounded below and on the sides with insulation) and in a wall in the centre of the building or in the rear (north-facing) wall and a lot of insulation on the outside of the building, plus special attention to airtightness.

Eco-alternatives to concrete

Stone and rammed earth are traditional materials, while concrete has high carbon emissions associated with the use of Portland cement: one tonne of the stuff results in the emission of about the same amount of CO_2. This is a major blow to the otherwise exemplary environmental credibility of many 'low-carbon' buildings such as Hockerton Housing Project in Nottinghamshire.

But there are exciting alternatives to Portland cement which actually store carbon. Some use the waste material fly ash, others use magnesium

Figure 7.19 The BaleHaus at Bath University, built using 'ModCell' – prefabricated panels consisting of a timber structural frame infilled with straw bales or hemp and rendered with a breathable lime-based system. A research team studied its performance over two years. It withstood hurricane force winds up to 120 mph, was as fire resistant as houses built of conventional building materials, protected against over 100dB of white noise, and they established that it maintains heat through very cold winters and stays dry.
Credit: NHBC

silicate. These materials react, like hydraulic lime, with the carbon dioxide in the air, absorbing it as it hardens. Hemcrete, a mixture of lime and hemp, also stores carbon (but is not as structurally strong as concrete). There are also: Calix calcined products, alumina silicate-based Blue World Crete, Eco-Cement, a blended cement with reactive magnesia, and Canada's CarbonCure Technologies' low-carbon concrete masonry. But all of these alternatives are comparatively expensive as yet.

Cellulose-based materials

'Natural', 'green', 'bio' or 'renewable' building materials can be classed together as 'cellulose-based'.[3] Cob, straw bale and thatch are included in this, as are hemp-lime (Hemcrete) and recycled newsprint. Amongst their benefits are that they:

Figure 7.20 Hemcrete wall at CAT heated by south-facing windows.

- lock up atmospheric carbon in the building;[4]
- have varying degrees of insulation ability;
- are easy to work with;
- make structures that are breathable.

Choosing insulation

Insulation comes in many forms. How to choose? The effectiveness of a material at insulating is measured by its k or lamda value: the smaller the number the better the insulation value, so the less thickness you need to reach the same level of insulation. Its unit of measurement is W/mK, meaning the amount of energy (in watts) that can move through the material (in metres) for a given temperature difference of 1 °C or 1 °Kelvin.

The external walls, ceilings and floors, doors and windows (including frames) are made of a number of different materials of different depths. Each material provides a level of insulation, and should be chosen so this level can be maximised. The level of insulation is given by its U-value, which is the k-value of the materials used multiplied by their depth in metres.

Table 7.3 Cellulose-based materials currently used in construction.[5]

Material	Application
Flax	Roofing insulation
Hemp fibres	Insulation
	Medium-density fibre board
	Oriented strand board
Hemp shiv	Monolithic construction of walls, floors and roofs
	Insulation
	Panel construction
Jute	Carpet
	Plastering mesh
	Scrim
Paper	Recycled and shredded for insulation
	Mixed with cement to form blocks
Reed	Thatching
Reed mats	Plastering base (like laths)
Sisal	Carpet (mixed with reinforced cement in some countries)
Straw	Bales as building blocks
	Wall panels
	Thatching

Table 7.4 Approximate U-values needed to achieve Passivhaus or Code for Sustainable Homes level 5 or 6.

Building element	Typical heat loss	U-value W/m^{2}K
External fabric (walls)	35%	0.14
Roof	25%	0.12
Floor	15%	0.15
Windows and doors	15%	<1.2

Again, the smaller the number of the U-value, the better it is. Doubling the thickness of an insulating layer doubles its thermal resistance. U-value is described in watts per square metre Kelvin (W/m^{2}K) – the amount of energy lost in watts per square metre of material for a given temperature difference of 1 °C or 1 °Kelvin from one side of the material to the other.

The U-value of a given element like a wall is calculated by totalling the U-values of each of the component elements. For the whole structure, you total all four elements and multiply the total by the net internal area of each surface. (The total wall area is the net area of the walls after subtracting the area of windows and doors – the same for the roof. If you have a party wall, it's assumed that it is heated to the same amount and so is disregarded.) In each case, measurements are taken on site and then reference is made to information tables[6] for the purpose of the calculation.

Insulation materials

The general priorities for selecting insulation materials are:

• k-value and the level of depth you can install;
• cost;
• ease of installation;

Figure 7.21 Installing Warmcel recycled cellulose (newsprint) insulation in a loft using a blower. Source: Warmcel.

Figure 7.22 Hemp-cotton batts being used for internal wall insulation between studs.

Figure 7.23 Wood-fibre batts being squeezed in between rafters to ensure there are no gaps.

- longevity and durability;
- environmental issues.

Sheets, rolls and batts are perfect for large areas, where the distances between joists or studs are standard sizes or where shapes are rectangular. Loose-fill cellulose (e.g. Warmcel) can easily be blown or sifted into a horizontal space and unusual shapes.

Cost should be compared on the basis of total installed cost per unit of volume, per unit of U-value, bearing in mind that different thicknesses will be required for different materials to achieve the same value. Costs should also include:

- transport cost: the compressible types of insulant are generally cheaper to deliver than rigid forms (except foils);
- installation cost: the loose-fill insulants are cheap and easy to install.

Material which is loose and comes in rolls, like cellulose and glass wool, is used predominantly in lofts and flat areas. Batts and slabs can be used both in these places and vertically on the inside or outside. Rockwool is commonly used on the outside, but wood fibre can also work. A render or cladding over the top of the insulation material protects it from the weather. The preferred renders from an environmental point of view are lime or hemcrete, since they are breathable.[7]

I did a quick market survey, attempting to calculate for common materials the equivalent price per cubic metre. The results are in Table 7.5 below. It's nice to know that the most environmentally sound is by far the cheapest: Warmcel – everybody should use it in their lofts. It's so easy to buy and apply. It's also nice to know that woodwool and sheep's wool are relatively cheap, as are Rockwool and other mineral wool.

Table 7.6 shows the depth of insulation required to reach a U-value of 0.15 W/m^{2}K for some common or sustainable materials. If space is limited and the depth of insulation is a consideration, use this table as a guide. In general, expanded polyurethane, XPS and some other materials derived from fossil fuels take up less space.

Table 7.5 Approx. cost per cubic metre from cheapest upwards.

Material/product	Price £ (2013 prices)
Recycled loose cellulose (Warmcel)	11.67
Expanded Polystyrene Board (Jabfloor 70)	13.56
Woodwool (NOVOLIT)	33.33
Black Mountain sheep's wool	46.66
Rockwool quilt	53.81
Mineral wool slabs	56.91
Woodwool (HERAKLITH)	59.33
EPS Jablite Polystyrene Sheet	75.52
Cork sheet	80.00
Hemp Steico Canaflex	81.28
Woodfibre batts (Steico Flex)	106.89
PIR (Celotex XR4000)	117.93
Woodfibre batts (NaturePro)	127.74
PUR (Kingspan Thermawall TW50)	151.54
Woodfibre Board (Steico Therm)	176.66
Hemp batts (Black Mt)	317.98
Woodwool KOMBIVOL	330.00

Table 7.6 Depth of insulation required to reach a U-value of 0.15 W/m²K.

Material	Depth
Expanded polyurethane	130 mm
Unfaced polyurethane	160 mm
Rockwool (60–100 kg/m³)	195 mm
Glassfibre slab	205 mm
Expanded polystyrene	215 mm
Mineral wool	225 mm
Flax	230 mm
Cork board	240 mm
Glass fibre quilt	240 mm
Cork slab (160 kg/m³)	250 mm
Woodwool board	250 mm
Cellular sheet glass	280 mm
Foam glass (140 kg/m³)	305 mm
Cork slab (140 kg/m³)	325 mm
Foam glass (130 kg/m³)	330 mm

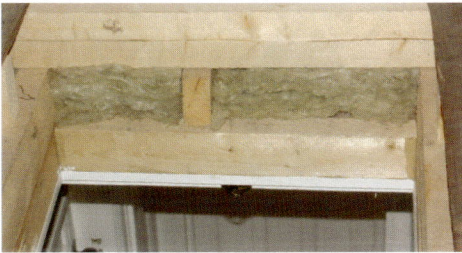

Figure 7.24 Mineral wool used as loft insulation (between floors).

Finally, Table 7.7 (below) summarises the properties of different insulation materials. Completely unsustainable ones are ignored. I've categorised them by their source, with the organic, natural, more sustainable ones first, followed by other relatively environmentally friendly ones made from natural materials, and lastly the category of materials derived from fossil fuels. In each case the ones with the lowest k-value, i.e. the most insulating, are listed first. Within each category, the best insulating materials are at the top and the worst performers are nearer the bottom (based on K-value).

Table 7.7 Summary comparison of different insulation materials.

Type	Material	K-value (W/mK)	Notes
Organic sources	These have absorbed carbon from the atmosphere and so are more climate-friendly.		
	Sheep's wool batts and rolls	0.038–0.043	Can absorb some moisture whilst remaining efficient
	Wood-fibre batts	0.038–0.043	Good for most walls, ceilings, roofs, timber joisted floors.
	Cotton-based batts and rolls	0.038–0.043	Best for horizontal surfaces.
	Cellulose (loose, batt or board, e.g. Warmcel, Homatherm)	0.038–0.040	Recyclable, renewable, made from finely shredded newspaper, easy to install, best for horizontal surfaces.
	Flax batts, slabs and rolls	approx 0.042	Hard to obtain and expensive.
	Hemp batts	0.043	Relatively expensive.
	Cork board (e.g. Korktherm, Westco)	0.042–0.050	Commonly used as under-lay under hardwood and ceramic floors.
	Wood-fibre board	0.080	The rigid insulation has a higher (worse) U-value than the batt form. Some products are made from recycled cellulose. Good for wall and pitched-roof construction.
	Hempcrete (e.g. Hemcrete, Canobiote, Canosmose and Isochanvre)	0.12–0.13	Made of hemp shiv with a lime matrix. High elasticity and vapour permeability. Used for external wall insulation. Typical compressive strength 20 times lower than low-grade concrete. Density: 15 per cent of traditional concrete.
Naturally occurring minerals	Usually environmentally ok but some have high embodied energy.		

Type	Material	K-value (W/mK)	Notes
	Fibreglass mineral wool batts and rolls (BSI kitemarked available) (e.g. British-Gypsum Isover, Knauf, Superglass) or Fibreglass board (e.g. Isowool, Dritherm)	0.033–0.040	Made from molten glass, sometimes with 20 to 30 per cent recycled content. The most common residential insulant. Usually applied as batts, pressed between studs. Most include a formaldehyde-based binder – exceptions are beginning to appear.
	Mineral (rock & slag) wool batts and rolls (BSI kitemarked available) e.g. Rockwool	0.033–0.040	Used for loft and external wall insulation.
	Perlite	0.045–0.05	Naturally occurring volcanic glass that greatly expands and becomes porous when heated sufficiently. Must be installed in sealed spaces.
	Exfoliated vermiculite	0.063	Clay-based, otherwise like perlite
Fossil fuels	These have emitted carbon to the atmosphere during manufacture. Avoid unless you don't have the space or budget for natural products. All manufactured at high temperatures, derived from fossil fuels. Extremely high embodied energy. Non-breathable (except EPS), so may cause damp problems.		
	Phenolic foam board (e.g. Kingspan Kooltherm)	0.020–0.25	For roofing, cavity board, external wall board, plasterboard dry linings systems, floor insulation and as sarking board.
	Expanded polystyrene board and beads (EPS)	0.032–0.040	Beads are used primarily in masonry cavities. Is more breathable than the other boards. Recommended for external wall insulation where there is high rainfall.

Table 7.7 (Continued)

Type	Material	K-value (W/mK)	Notes
	Extruded Polystyrene board (XPS) e.g. Kingspan Styrozone	0.028–0.036	Very high compressive strength.
	(e.g. Kingspan Therma)	0.02–0.033	Foam or rigid board. Foam is sprayed in at high temperatures; within seconds it will expand by over 30 times, giving a seamless rigid covering. Good for plugging gaps or leaks. High compressive strength.
	Eco-wool (e.g. non-itch) – batts	0.039–0.042	Alternative to glass wool, made from 85 per cent recycled plastic. Comes in rolls or slabs. Suitable for loft and stud walls.

Figure 7.25 Where possible choose interlocking cladding or insulation like these wood-fibre slabs to help prevent draughts through bad installation.

Summary

The bottom line for insulation then is:

- Use as much insulation as you can afford and you have space for;
- Use insulation from natural materials wherever possible;
- Avoid the use of foams wherever possible (improperly used these can expand and cause structural damage);
- For horizontal spaces use Warmcel recycled cellulose;
- Install with great care to absolutely eliminate draughts;
- For exterior insulation use EPS with a render; or wood fibreboard with wood-fibre tongue and groove cladding and lime render; or Woodwool/Rockwool with lime render.

Thermal bridging

Zero-carbon buildings must eliminate thermal bridging. It severely compromises the value of the work and can lead to cold spots and condensation. It occurs when a relatively conductive material passes through the building

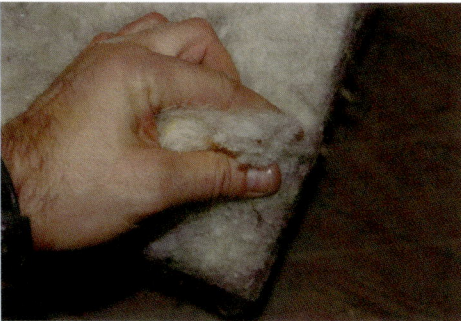

Figure 7.26 Sheep's wool batts.

Figure 7.27 Sheep's wool insulation (loose) in bags.

Figure 7.28 Installing tongue-and-groove wood-fibre slabs, which are impregnated with wax to make them waterproof, as cladding all around the outside of my studio. This prevents thermal bridging of the timber frame, which can be seen behind it, and which has wood-fibre batts stuffed between the studs. The slabs were later lime rendered (see Exemplary Example).

envelope from the interior to the exterior. This may be a single-paned window or a lintel in a windowsill, any fixings, window or door frames, joists, services. Sometimes the floor slab or a joist is extended through the building envelope. To 'break' a thermal bridge, insulation is added on the inside or outside, or in between. In a superinsulated building, even timber can form a thermal bridge and must be insulated to prevent it going from the inside to the outside.

Airtightness and breathability

Introducing airtightness and superinsulation will maximize your opportunities for control over the energy cost. Airtightness is achieved by creating a continuous airtight layer around the building 'envelope' to completely surround it. The idea is to prevent unwanted draughts through often invisible or inaccessible holes in the building fabric. Examples are: underneath floors or where mortar has not been applied consistently in between blockwork, or where joists enter the exterior walls. There should be no breaks in the barrier, for example: tears, gaps or nail punctures. Professional long-lasting tape must be used to seal joins so they last for many years. It must be able to withstand pressures created by wind or stack-effect drafts.

air barrier lapped to
plaster stop bead

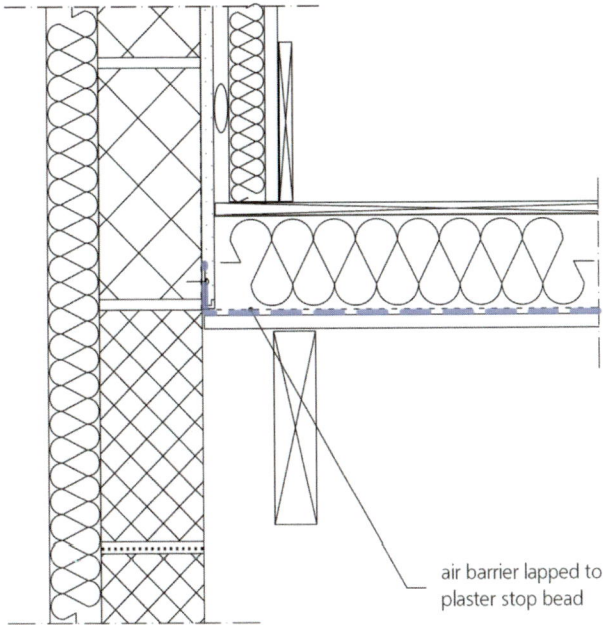

Figure 7.29 A detail (architects' drawing) of a suspended floor, showing (with the blue line) where an airtightness membrane should be located beneath the insulation, then lapping up the side around it and behind the plasterboard, where it should join the plasterboard. (Plaster itself will continue the airtightness layer.) This drawing is part of the free set of details available from the Energy Saving Trust (see below).

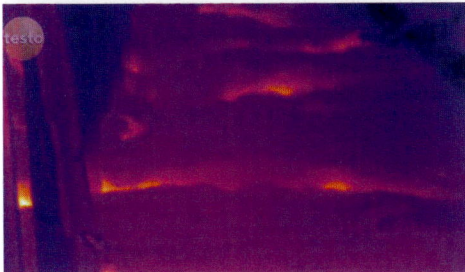

Figure 7.30 Leaving even the slightest gap between materials in the building envelope can ruin the intention, undoing the rest of your hard work. This picture shows poorly installed insulation in a loft and a thermographic image of the same view revealing how hot air is being sucked through the gaps in a funnel-like way. Lack of attention to detail during construction is the most common reason low-carbon homes often don't perform as well in practice as predicted in theory. I can't stress this point enough! In this case a breathable windproof layer should have been laid over the top and taped securely all round.

> **What can the airtightness barrier consist of?**
> Any of the following in combination will be joined
> seamlessly together to completely surround the building:
> *Vapour permeable (and hygroscopic) materials:*
> Vapour permeable membranes, intelligent membranes,
> lime, concrete, timber, hemcrete, bricks, stone, plaster.
> *Non-permeable materials:*
> PVA and vinyl paint, when used as a coating on plaster,
> metal, glass, PVC, plastic, plastic foams.

Regardless of the utmost efforts, a building is never completely airtight, nor should it be. Building regulations specify the number of air changes per hour permitted for safety (especially if you have a live fire indoors). The introduction of fresh air is managed with controlled ventilation. The level of airtightness can be tested by professional pressure-testing devices, called blower doors. The standard of airtightness for Passivhaus certification (see below for more information) is that a new building must not leak more air than 0.6 times the building volume per hour at 50 Pa pressure. This standard is around four times better than most building regulations.

Figure 7.31 Where services enter the building they penetrate the airtightness layer and any potential gaps must be eliminated.

Airtightness and breathability

Problems with damp and condensation are to be expected in our climate. The best way to deal with this is to let buildings 'breathe', i.e. absorb and release moisture, without doing any damage. Therefore moist air must be able to pass through the airtightness layer. This is not possible with non-permeable materials. So the materials used in the wall and roof should be hygroscopic (able to absorb moisture) and vapour permeable (except, obviously, for glazing). Hygroscopic materials include: wood, stone, brick, adobe, earth, straw bale, lime, hemcrete and organic sheet materials. Lime and insulating plasters are also very good at absorbing and releasing unwanted moisture in problem areas. By contrast, materials which prevent air from passing through them are the non-permeable ones listed in the box above.

Airtightness is different from breathability. A building can be airtight and still 'breathe' if the airtightness layer is permeable and these hygroscopic materials are used. If you are not going to use natural hygroscopic materials like lime plaster then you should use intelligent membranes.[8] The permeability of these membranes is dependent upon differences of air pressure, humidity and temperature between the outside and the inside.

Windows and doors

Modern windows and doors are beautiful, highly technical constructions. I believe it's worth shelling out for the best that you can possibly buy. Windows' size, position, shading and coatings can be used to capture the right amount of solar energy depending on the times of the year and day. This section explains how.

The amount of solar energy transmitted through a window is quantified by a coefficient called the 'G-value'. G-values range from 0 to 1 (with a higher value indicating more solar gain). It is specified on the energy label of a new window. For south-facing windows in temperate or cooler climates like the UK's, a G-value of 0.76 or greater is recommended. For large west-facing windows a G-value below 0.6 will prevent overheating.

Windows come with energy labels so choose windows with the highest possible rating of 'A'. 'C' is the minimum level for an eco-home (which the Energy Saving Trust says has a payback of five or six years).

Triple glazing is the best, if you can afford it, for long-term energy saving, and is necessary to achieve an 'A' rating. These are the sort used in Passivhaus standard housing. If possible choose windows with an inert gas (argon, krypton or xenon) sealed between the panes – they are better than

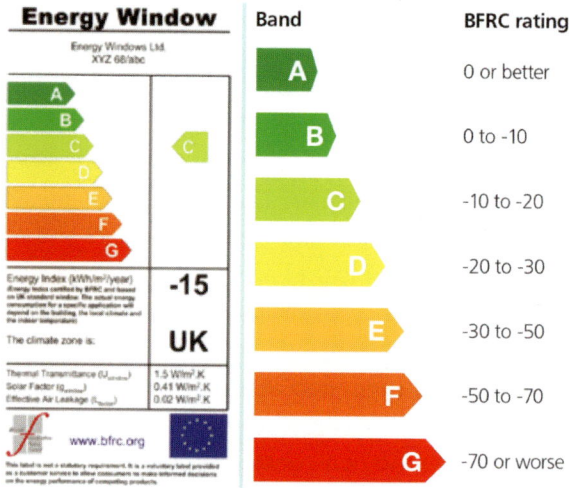

Figure 7.32 Energy Label for windows. The label displays the following information:

- *the rating level: C*
- *the energy rating: −14 kWh/(m²K)/yr (= a loss of three kilowatt hours per square metre per year)*
- *the U-value (a measure of the insulation value of the window): 1.7 W/(m²K)*
- *the effective heat loss due to air penetration as L: 0.10 W/(m²K)*
- *the G value: 0.5.*

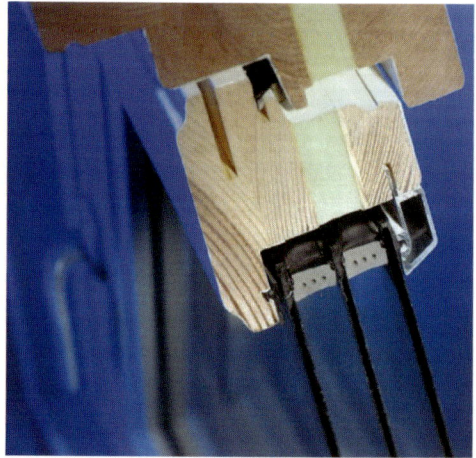

Figure 7.33 A triple-glazed window: note the insulation within the frame to break the thermal bridge.

air at minimising heat conduction back outside; xenon is the most effective but argon is cheapest. Ideally, the gap between the panes should be 16 mm or more if they contain no gas, but can be less if filled with gas.

It goes without saying that you should ensure that the seals are perfect. It is possible to specify windows made with up to 33 per cent of recycled glass.

Figure 7.34 A low-E coating on the inside of the inner pane of this triple-glazed French window in my studio helps reflect heat back into the building, while triple seals prevent draughts.

Low-E coatings

A special coating – called 'low-E' (for low emissivity) – that reflects infrared radiation should be specified for the interior, innermost surface of one pane. A huge range of further coatings is available: e.g. that let only a fixed amount of light into the building, and self-cleaning coatings. Panes designed for eco-homes in higher latitudes have extra-clear outer layers, letting up to 80 per cent of light and 71 per cent of the sun's heat in.

Frames

Frames for windows and doors should ideally be made of sustainably sourced timber, preferably hardwood or treated soft wood. There should be insulation between the inner and outer frames (see Fig. 7.33) to avoid thermal bridging. It's hard to find a local carpenter who can make this type of window and they are usually sourced from specialist suppliers.

The amount of the window opening taken up by the frame should be minimised to maximise the amount of light admittance. For example, avoid the use of grids or muntins if at all possible. Avoid sash windows because of the large area taken up by the frames, and the difficulty of draughtproofing. Glazing can be positioned nearer to the inside or outside edge of the frame; the ideal is to have it centred when seen in cross-section.

You wouldn't think it, but research by energy specialist Bronwyn Barry has also shown that positioning windows in the centre of a wall in a room can reduce heat demand by up to 22 per cent. In south-facing walls, there's an optimum ratio for energy efficiency (heat gain versus heat loss) of window glazing to wall area that is 0.3 (with no shading) to 0.45 (with an overhang). You can reduce the cost by reducing the number of openings and mullions and by keeping the windows to a standard size. A taller, more narrow window with a single opening, which fills the whole window, will be cheaper and perform better than one, for example, with a transom at the top and split into two panes below. It will also have a lower U-value.

Shutters and curtains

I would like to see more use in Britain of shutters, as they are used on the continent (and were in the past in the UK). They are a great idea, both inside and out, and together with curtains can be used both to keep heat within a building and to prevent drafts, and, if closed in the daytime, prevent overheating in the summer. Blinds or curtains on the inside also prevent overheating in summer and keep in warmth in winter.

Figure 7.35 Shutters can be a beautiful addition to a building – and save energy. Credit: Luke McKernan.

Figure 7.36 An angled reveal in this skylight maximises the spread of light from it, as does the white paint.

Using natural light

A zero-carbon home will try to minimise the use of artificial lighting by making the most of natural light. There are several tricks that can help to reduce lighting costs by 30–50 per cent while avoiding the risk of overheating, such as:

- by painting the reveal, lintel, windowsill and opposite walls a light colour to reflect more light;
- it may be possible to slant the sides of reveal to increase the amount of light entering the room (see Fig. 7.36);
- by positioning mirrors in the reveal and opposite the window to reflect more light into the room;
- by adding light shelves to reflect more light deeper into the room.

Fitting windows and doors

Correct fitting is vital to preserve airtightness and prevent thermal bridging. If the building uses external insulation, this should overlap slightly the outside of the window frames. If it uses internal insulation, the insulation in the reveal should meet up with the wall insulation. If there are gaps around the window frame you can fill them with insulation. Lintels and sills, if they cross from the interior to the exterior, must be insulated on the inside or outside to prevent thermal bridging.

More on passive solar techniques

Besides lots of south-facing glazing, superinsulation and the use of thermal mass to retain heat, passive solar building design uses a few other tricks. The 'stack effect' helps to circulate heat and moderate the internal temperature and climate. Warm air rises by convection to exit at the top through open windows, vents, chimneys or leaks, drawing in colder air through any openings near the bottom. Good passive solar design takes advantage of this principle.

Here are some valuable lessons learned from the last 10 years of various developers' and builders' attempts to build zero-carbon homes:

- involve a qualified architect or Code Assessor right from the start;
- solve all your problems at the design stage and you will save a great deal of time and money later;
- keep the structure dry during construction;
- use already proven detailing;
- know where your airtightness barrier is all the way round;
- every single part of the construction requires great attention to detail to achieve the promised levels of performance. This means especially leaving absolutely no gaps in the structure, no thermal bridging and the use of reliable, durable materials.

The Passivhaus Standard

The Passivhaus Standard (see www.passiv.de) is the safest method for achieving low- and zero-carbon buildings. It's a method of analysing all of the heat gains and losses within a building, and modelling improvements through the use of software to achieve the optimum result cost efficiently. The standard is defined in terms of the energy used by the building and requires that:

- the space heat requirement should not exceed 15 kWh/(m²/a);
- total primary energy use (of all appliances, lighting, ventilation, pumps, hot water) must also not exceed 120 kWh/(m²/a);

- building fabric U-values must be less than 0.15 W/m²K;
- U-values for windows and doors U-values less than 0.8 W/m²K (for both the frame and glazing) with solar heat gain coefficients around 50 per cent;
- an airtightness level of 0.6 times the building volume per hour at 50 Pa (N/m²).

We've already discussed the strategies that can be deployed. In addition you can use the following tricks:

- Passive preheating of fresh air: brought in through conservatories or greenhouses on the south-facing side, or underground ducts that exchange heat with the ground to reach above 5 °C (41 °F), even on cold winter days;
- Hot water supplied using renewable energy;
- Energy-saving appliances: ultra-low energy lighting, refrigerators, stoves, freezers, washers, dryers and so on.

MVHR (Mechanical Ventilation with Heat Recovery from the expelled air transferred to the incoming air) is often used, but this has been eschewed by Tŷ Solar (see Exemplary Examples) on grounds of simplicity (occupants often don't use it correctly), and I would tend to agree with this.

Passivhaus designs are modelled using the Passivhaus Planning Package (PHPP) software, which may be purchased from the Passivhaus website. Usually it's better to get your architect to sort this out if you are using one. Otherwise do your best with the above guidance and try to aim for the standard (or buy a pre-approved packaged house if you can

Figure 7.37 These homes at Hockerton Housing Project, Nottinghamshire, use a long, glazed conservatory to trap solar heat, plus a lot of thermal mass to retain it. See Exemplary Examples.

afford it) rather than prove you have achieved it, which can add consider-able costs.

Enhanced construction details

With building design and construction the devil is always in the details. 'Detail' is the name given to an architectural drawing which prescribes how builders should deal with part of the construction. Instead of paying an architect to make these drawings, you can download free detail drawings for many situations from a couple of websites which are useful depending on what type of construction you are using:

1 Enhanced construction details (ECDs) that focus on heat losses that occur at the junctions between building elements (walls, ceilings, floors) and around openings are freely available from the Energy Saving Trust. See http://bit.ly/Qsbs2r.
2 A manufacturer, St Gobain, offers free details that can be applied even if you don't use their Isover products. Register to view them at: www.isover-construction.com.

That's all about principles. Now we can take a quick look at some construc-tion techniques.

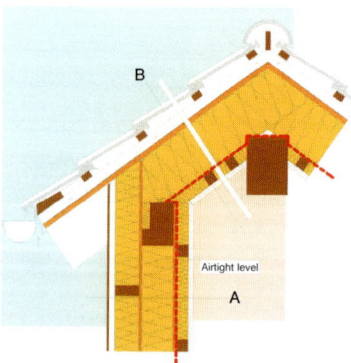

Build-up A in cm
2,5 Rigips Rigidur H double layer, each layer 12.5mm
6,0 ISOVER Integra UKF 1-032 (wood 6/6 e=40cm, 13% wp)
      ISOVER VARIO KM Duplex UV
1,5 OSB board or chipboard
16,0 ISOVER Integra ZKF 1-032 (wood 6/16 e=62.5cm, 14%wp)
1,5 OSB board or chipboard
12,0 Kontur FSP 1-032 Easy Fix 120 (wood 6/12 e=60cm, 12%wp)
3,0 Rear ventilation
1,0 Exterior cladding (e.g. wood, metal, plastic, stone)

Build-up B in cm
      Roof covering
3,0 Roof lathing
5,0 Counter battens 5/8
      ISOVER Integra ZUB underlay sheeting
2,4 Solid timber panelling
24,0 ISOVER Integra ZKF 1-032 (wood 6/24 e=70cm, 8% wp)
      ISOVER VARIO KM Duplex UV
6,0 ISOVER Intergra UKF 1-032 (wood 6/6 e=50cm, 11% wp)
2,5 Rigips Rigidur H double layer, each layer 12.5 m

Figure 7.38 An example of the free details available from St Gobain (Isover) – you don't have to use their products. A sample of the EST's Enhanced Construction Details can be found in Figure 7.29. Credit: St Gobain

Types of construction

Thermally light construction

Examples include:

* Pole houses with cellulose insulation;
* Straw bale;
* Timber frame with cellulose insulation.

All of these lock up in the building the atmospheric carbon absorbed by the plants while they were growing. They are also biodegradable and may support local agroforestry. Pole houses and timber-frame buildings do not need foundations: the posts sit on pads, stones or rammed earth-filled tyres. For straw bale a stone base equivalent to the width of the bales is required. In all cases, building regulations will need to be followed.[9]

With some of these building techniques there is a risk that they can decompose or pests can get inside and infest the building material. Great care must be taken to prevent the risk of moisture getting into the cellulose-based materials such as straw. There are regulations covering this, and it applies not just to great care over construction, but a proper attitude to maintenance. Damp-course detailing should focus on preventing rising damp. Roof overhangs help prevent water getting in through the tops of walls. Detailing must make sure that water can't get around the frames of openings in the walls or any interfaces between different building elements.

Pole houses

Pole houses are the ones most commonly associated with low-impact developments because they often use locally felled, pollarded or coppiced trees when they are in ready supply. The advantage of pollarding or coppicing is that the trees regrow. The advantage of using round as opposed to squared wood is that it avoids an industrial process and resulting emissions. The process lends itself to DIY. Roundwood is also stronger than similar sized squared timber, so the diameter does not need to be so great to support the same load. Erecting the roof section of a round house is a great communal activity. They can be made using hand tools to fashion the mortice and tenon joints: a slot into which the tenon fits. After this, a hole is drilled through the joint for a peg to secure them together. Typically these are tapered or wedged in.

They may be used for non-essential buildings, not dwellings, as building regulations are tough to meet for this type of construction. The guidelines for airtightness and insulation remain as above but are more difficult to obtain unless the infill for the walls actually surrounds the posts, as with conventional timber frame (below) or hemp-lime.

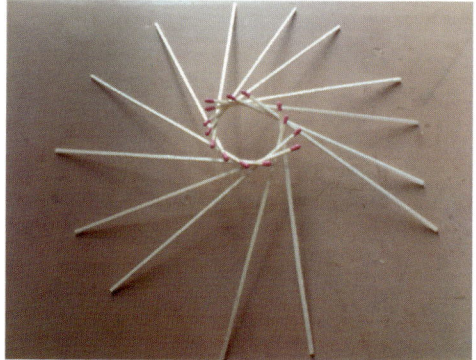

Figure 7.39 A model reciprocal frame made from matches. Try it yourself!

Figure 7.40 and 7.41 A reciprocal frame roof that has just been completed and with cross-members in place. The ladder is just for access and will be removed after construction is completed.

Reciprocal frame roofs

Pole houses or roundhouses often have reciprocal frame roofs. These are self-supporting structures made of three or more beams which require no centre support. They are used particularly for modern roundhouses. Try making one out of long matches, as in the picture. Supports are used while the logs are put in place and removed after the last one is inserted. Such roofs may also be used on load-bearing cob-walls.

Figure 7.42 (left). Detail of a reciprocal roof support (Tony Wrench's roundhouse at Brithdir Mawr).

Figure 7.43 A roundhouse at Brithdir Mawr.

Figure 7.44. and 7.45 This round-house uses cut sections of logs placed lengthways and infilled with hemp-lime. It is a good technique for a non-residential building.

Figure 7.46 Green oak pegs are often used as easy ways to joint timbers together. This one is in The Hub, Lammas.

Straw bale

Straw is an agricultural waste-product; when bound into bales, it makes a building material which is easy to handle, cheap and sustainable, with a low embodied energy. Bales can be bought direct from farmers. They must be tight, well strung and kept absolutely dry. A 500 mm-thick structural straw wall with finishes has good insulation: a U-value of around 0.15 W/m^{2}K.

Figure 7.47, 7.48 and 7.49 Different roundwood timber frame styles of roofing (The Hub, Lammas).

However, the building will cool more quickly than with materials with good thermal mass, like stone.

With good weathering details and regular maintenance, a straw house can last decades. Foundations and roofs can be made conventionally; they need a roof overhang of at least half a metre and a good foundation to keep the bales away from splashes. Lime render is added because it is flexible and can yield in case of compression of the bales, reducing cracking. As long as

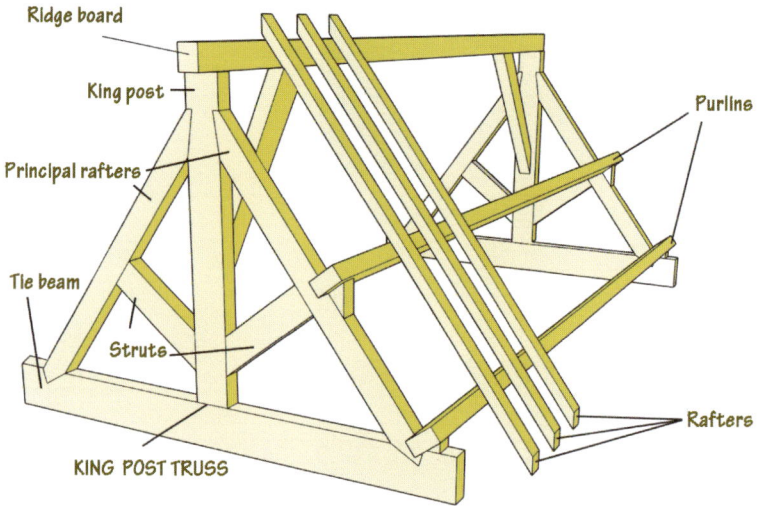

Figure 7.50 Typical construction for a King Post truss roof.

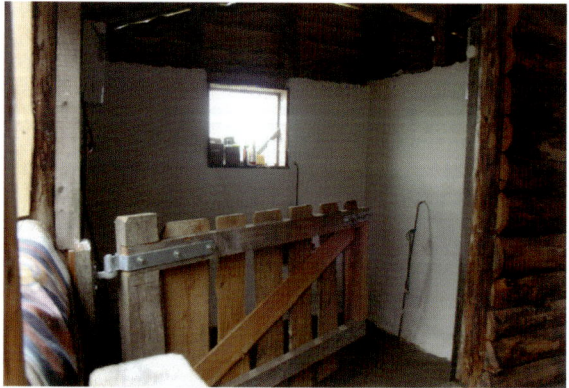

Figure 7.51 and 7.52 Rough timber used for a cowshed (Paul and Hoppi Wimbush).

Rafters, usually 225 mm x 38 mm to allow for enough insulation

Wallplate 150 mm x 50 mm (6" x 2") placed vertically with 18 mm SmartPly glued and nailed

Internal hazel pins 1¹/₂" (38 mm) diameter x 3'3" (1 m) long

Wallplate incorporating floor joists

Insulation eg tightly packed straw

Two or three coats of lime plaster/ render averaging 30 mm thick

Internal hazel pins, two per bale, fourth and every second course thereafter

Overhang 18" (450 mm)

Bales

Hazel stub

Base plate

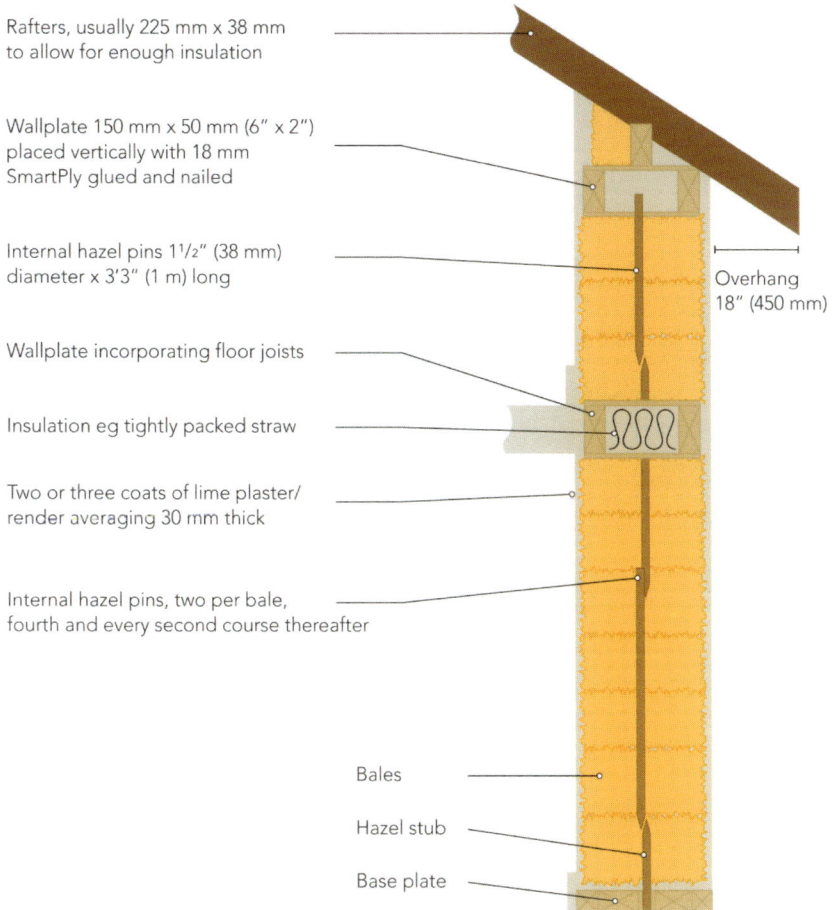

Figure 7.53 Section through a Nebraska System (frameless), straw-bale wall.
Credit: NHBC and Jones.[10]

bales are allowed to dry out, no decomposition will occur. Another concern is that they will attract rodents and bugs, but there is no documented experience of this. Surprisingly, they are also fireproof.

Building solid foundations is very important. Bales are laid on in rows and pinned together with stakes. The finished walls are compressed and wall plates are placed on the top of them before plastering. The wall plate spreads the roof loads over the wall and gives a level surface. A plate that goes over a wide window or door opening must be strong enough to carry the roof. The depth of this beam should be around one twelfth of the span; i.e. a 10 cm depth will span a 120 cm opening.

Figure 7.54 Stone plinth created for straw-bale walls. Plinths should rise up to 45 cm above the ground. Note the damp-proof layer and the stakes poking out from the stones ready to impale the bales.

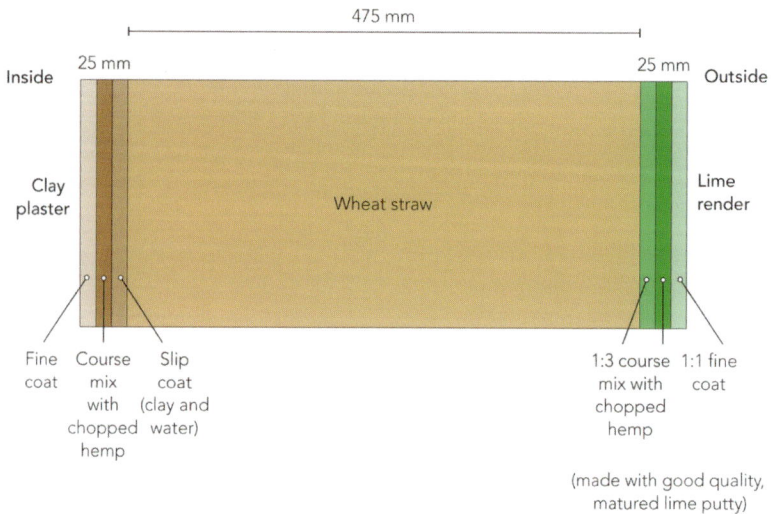

Figure 7.55 Cross-section through a typical completed straw-bale wall.
Credit: NHBC from Atkinson.[11]

Figure 7.56, 7.57 and 7.58 A straw-bale workshop: the completed workshop, footings for the base, and a side view of an opening showing the rendered bales, the airtightness layer and the timber cladding.

Doors and window spaces are created during building by making simple wooden frames of four planks joined together. Conventional roofs are used; either an assembly of cut rafters and ceiling joists or industrially made pre-fabricated trusses. The easiest is a mono-pitch roof, which has a single slope on one side, made up of ceiling joists running between the wall plates.

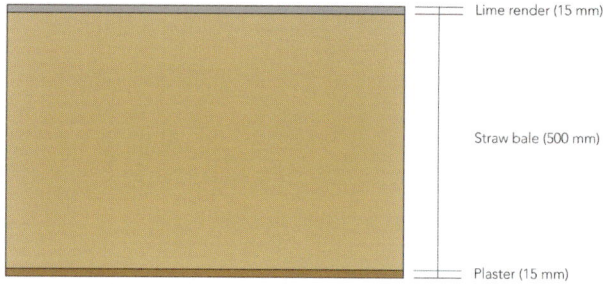

Lime render (15 mm)

Straw bale (500 mm)

Plaster (15 mm)

Figure 7.59 Plan view of a simple straw-bale wall from outside (top) to inside (bottom). Credit: NHBC.

Straw-bale buildings can be built with or without timber frames. The Nebraska Method is the name given to the method which does not use frames, after the techniques used in the Midwestern US. It is the simplest and cheapest option and was used to build Rachel Shiamh's straw-bale home (see Exemplary Examples). The roof is triangulated to minimise the lateral loading applied to the tops of the walls. There's a school of thought which advocates this approach since, if the bales compress over time, this doesn't create gaps below beams.

Load-bearing straw-bale square buildings are stronger with short walls; long walls will need buttressing. Never place windows or doors directly next to corners; have at least one whole bale between the frame and the corner. Openings for windows and doors should not occupy more than half the wall space. Window openings must co-ordinate with bale heights so that window frames can be placed on full bales. Make sure that the loads are distributed as evenly as possible to avoid the creation of any point loadings.

If the building does have a timber frame then the spacing of frame supports will be dependent on the size and type of timber used. The straw bale acts as an infill and insulation. The advantage is that a roof can be constructed before the walls are infilled, providing protection from rain. The roof is initially positioned about 100 mm above what will be the finished level of the straw walls once the roof plate is added. When the walls are built up, the roof's bracing is removed and the roof is lowered onto the bales, compressing them.

Prefabricated load-bearing wooden frames can be bought that are filled with manufactured compressed straw-bale panels.

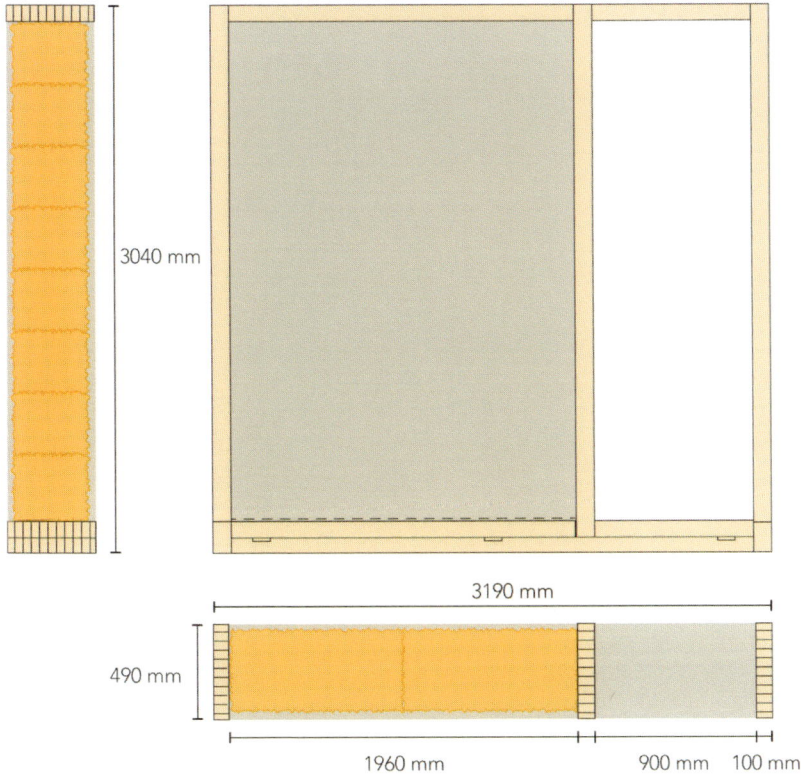

Figure 7.60 Straw is used in a panellised system as well, as this diagram explains (system manufactured by ModCell). As with the hembuild system it works with a timber frame.
Credit: NHBC.

Making lime plaster

In a large plastic bucket mix:

- two parts sand;
- one part aggregate (graded up to 1/6" or 4 mm);
- one part lime putty (see materials).

Empty onto a 1 m square board and chop the mixture together with a shovel until consistent and workable. Apply lime render conventionally with a plastering trowel and hawk in three coats of 10 mm to minimise cracking. Wet the surface first. Allow a day or so between layers. To maintain a good surface, apply coats of limewash every year or two. Limewash is made by adding water to a quarter of a given volume of lime putty until it is milky.

Figure 7.61 The nice thing about lime and hemcrete renders is that you can have fun with them: Cassie and Nigel's house at Lammas.

Figure 7.62 The 'hub' community building at Lammas is constructed using local materials, which as far as possible were natural and/or recycled (whilst complying with stringent building control requirements). It was built by residents, local tradesmen and volunteers. The Douglas-Fir timber frame supports a massive turfed roof. Straw bales provide insulation in the walls and roof, and heating is supplied by a combination of hydro power, underfloor heating, passive solar gain and biomass (masonry stove).

Figure 7.63 The ecological Walter Segal house at the Centre for Alternative Technology, Wales.
Credit: Lindy Zubairy.

Adding linseed oil (at a rate of one small spoonful per five litres of limewash) will improve durability.

Timber frame

Easy-build planed-wood timber frame is characterised by the approach pioneered by the architect Walter Segal. He took traditional timber-frame principles but calculated the dimensions to avoid waste and to make it easier to alter and enlarge. By doing this he wanted to eliminate or reduce the 'wet trades' of concreting, bricklaying and plastering, to reduce the weight of the building and to use cladding, insulating and lining materials in the sizes you buy them to minimise cutting and labour. Segal even wanted to remove the need to make joints: cross pieces rest upon each other, a hole is drilled through them and they are bolted together, so you don't need to be a skilled carpenter; the disadvantage is that you need more land space.

The Pattern Language method was pioneered by the architect Christopher Alexander.[12] Patterning is a good design tool you can use to map out your building, as explored in *Out of the Woods*, by Cindy Harris and Pat Borer,[13] who updated the Segal Method for eco-building at the Centre for Alternative Technology, Wales, by adding some of the features talked about in this chapter. Cindy wrote:

> The first step in making a plan is to use a grid. The dimensions of the grid's unit squares match those of commonly available building materials, [plus the width of the timber posts] therefore minimising the amount of cutting to fit. Your plan sits on this grid and superimposed on the grid lines are the

doors, windows and walls. The dimensions of these are multiples of the unit lengths. You can therefore use squared paper to design the layout. Vertical dimensions are similarly determined by the dimensions of the materials used.

I took this principle to design my own studio (see Exemplary Examples), with further refinements from more recent research in sustainable building.

Thermally heavier construction

Hemp-lime

Hemp-lime, otherwise known as hempcrete, is a mixture of hemp shiv (the tougher parts of stalks) and lime. It is marketed under names like Hemcrete and Isochanvre. (Some formulated lime mixtures contain Portland cement, but not hydraulic lime.) Hemp-lime walls must be used together with a timber frame to support the vertical load of the building. Like other plant

Figure 7.64 The Renewable House at BRE built in 2009. A social-housing demonstration project test house, it uses a timber-frame and hemp-lime-based wall form and meets Level 4 of the Code for Sustainable Homes.
Credit: NHBC.

Figure 7.65 Private house in Lincolnshire built using a system comprising hemp shiv panels (called Hembuild), a timber frame and cladding. Claimed to have a U-value of 0.15 W/m² k. Credit: NHBC.

products, the hemp absorbs carbon from the atmosphere as it grows. 165 kg of carbon can be theoretically absorbed and locked up by 1 m³ of hemp-lime wall over many decades. Hemp-lime can either be applied by hand or sprayed on in layers, allowing previous layers to dry out. It is vital to get the lime–shiv ratio right otherwise there will be problems with drying out. If less binder (lime) is added the density decreases and the insulation U-value improves, and vice versa.

Care must be taken if you are mixing hemp-lime yourself to follow the manufacturer's instructions, otherwise it may not dry correctly. Hemp-lime shrinks as it dries, so care needs to be taken with external finishes and the detailing of the roof and the openings to eradicate gaps that might arise. Once dry it resists the weather, including frost, but if it gets extremely wet, as in a flood, a new coat of render should be applied.

Hemp-lime can also be mixed with an aggregate for floor slabs and screeds, and at low density for roof insulation, renders and plasters. Factory-produced panels are also available. They may either provide a cladding panel for a structural frame or be structural panels that support the building. The hemp-lime is fully dried before delivery. Panels can include hemp-fibre insulation if required.

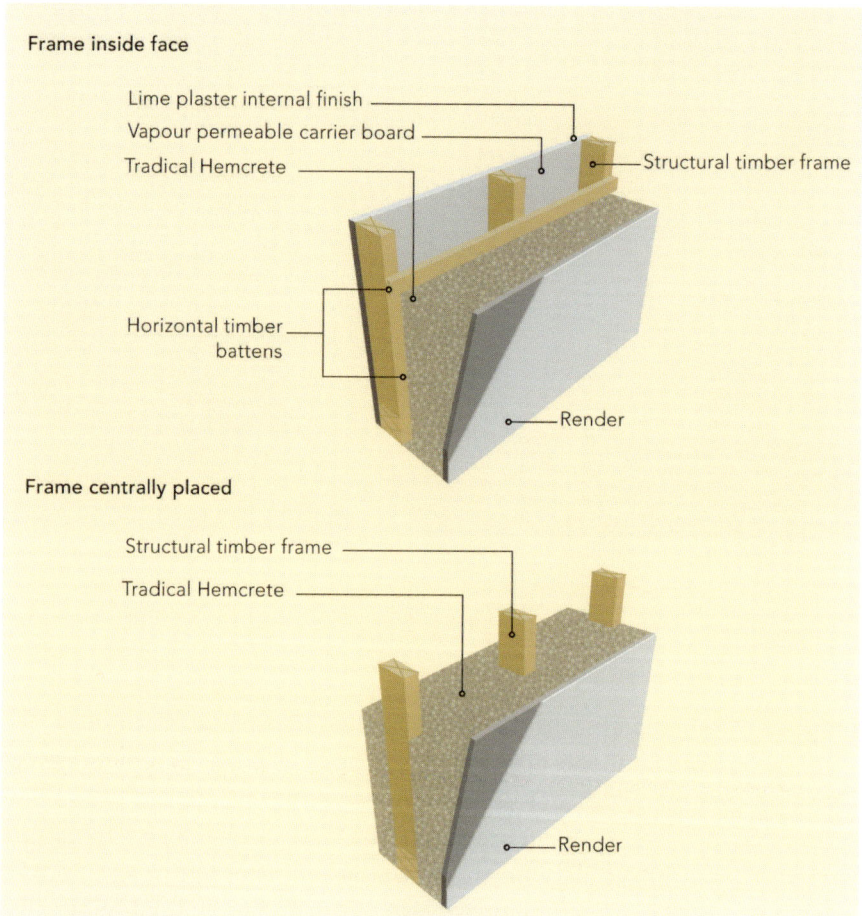

Figure 7.66 Two ways of building with hemp-lime, either: a lightweight timber frame with the frame being placed centrally within the hemp-lime; or, the timber frame separate from, and inside, the hemp-lime wall.
Source: NHBC (© BBA, certificate 10/4726 (redrawn from an image © Lhoist UK).

Cob

Cob is a mixture of a straw and clay that has a long tradition as a building material, especially in the south west of England and south Wales. It's not hugely insulating (hemp-lime is more so). A 900 mm-thick cob wall, comprising 860 mm of cob and 20 mm thick layers of lime-based render and plaster on each face, will achieve a U-value of about 0.45 W/m²K.[14]

Making cob is laborious but fun – and definitely a communal activity. You mix (perhaps with your bare feet!) subsoil containing equal proportions of clay and silt, sand and fine gravel with water and straw to a fairly stiff

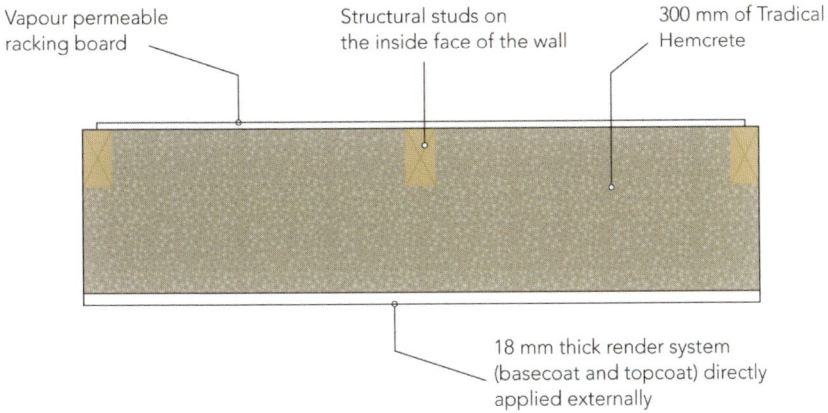

Figure 7.67 Plan view of a frame on the inside of a face hempcrete wall, U-value 0.25 W/m²K
Source: NHBC

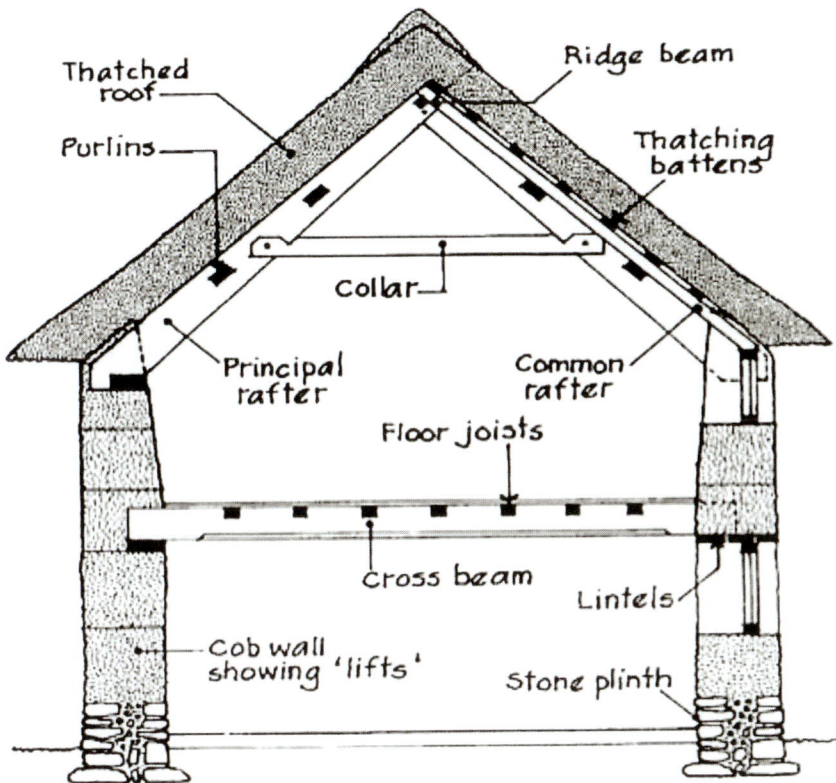

Figure 7.68 Traditional cob construction.
Source: NHBC.

Figure 7.69 Nigel at Lammas inspects the interior of his and Cassie's cob-walled greenhouse.

Figure 7.70 The outside of the greenhouse. The thermal mass of the cob helps to store the heat from the daytime so the plants within don't get frost at night, but also don't overheat on summer days due to an over-abundance of glazing.

but malleable consistency. Then you build a wall up off a masonry plinth in successive layers, each about 600 mm high, allowing each one to dry out before adding the next one. It dries, hardens, and can then be rendered with lime or plaster and a clay wash or clay paint, as you wish. It gives a lovely, soft, rounded feel to walls. A damp-proof layer beneath the base of the walls and floors is required (as with all buildings) to protect from rising damp. Frames for the doors and windows are prepared and worked into the walls during construction. Make sure the openings are both secure and well-sealed.

Figure 7.71 and 72 A cob wall under construction as part of a walled garden to protect plants from frost. All four pictures taken at Lammas.

Rammed earth

Rammed earth is cob without the straw. Loose, damp (rather than wet) soil is either rammed hard into formwork moulds in layers 100 to 150 mm deep, using either manual or pneumatically powered rammers. The shuttering is removed straight away. It can also be crammed into bags which are then piled up and secured.

Figure 7.73 Cob can be moulded into any shape.
Credit: Solargilly.

Figure 7.74 Bagged clay wall being infilled with cob.
Credit: Solargilly.

It's a quicker way of building a wall than traditional cob, but only if mechanical tamping is used. Stability is an issue. The soil must be suitable, with a fair degree of clay. Sometimes a stabiliser is added. The thickness of walls can be between 300 and 450 mm.

Finishes

Natural floor coverings are available, such as linoleum made completely from natural ingredients without Volatile Organic Compounds (VOCs) or

Figure 7.75 and 7.76 Jasmine and Simon's second, permanent house, at Lammas, will have a floor area of 180 m². It is a semi-earth sheltered construction using rammed earth, a straw-bale thermal envelope with lime render and predominantly round timber sourced from close by. 'Everything that is being dug out of the hole will go back in but in a different order,' says Jasmine. It will be largely passively heated through a combination of high thermal mass and 250 m² of greenhouse on the south-facing side that will both pre-heat the incoming air and be a growing space. As part of the construction process using rammed earth, soil is dug out of the hillside to create a flat area suitable for foundations. After the large stones have been removed manually the remaining clay is stuffed into plastic bags made of recycled plastic which are then stacked up in double rows along the back of the plot against the exposed earth to act as a retaining wall on the north-facing side. Water management for this and other buildings is handled across the whole plot. There are three water sources. Greywater mostly goes into the greenhouses and into the reedbeds, and we're catching water off the roof. The whole plot is on a south-facing downward slope so the process is gravity-fed. Water off the workshop roof also irrigates the greenhouses.

other toxic chemicals. It may be installed with solvent-free adhesives. Wool, flax, sisal and other hard-wearing natural substances are available in many types of carpet, rug and floor covering. Use vitrified clay pipes for drains and steel or copper for gutters and downpipes rather than PVC.

When the building is finished it's time to paint it. I have found that clay paints, despite the high price, cover well and are cost-effective. They give a lovely soft and breathable finish. For wood surfaces, natural oils such as linseed are perfect. The main thing is to avoid vinyl and gloss paints if possible, as these are not breathable. They will attract condensation in wet rooms.

Summary

Low- and zero-carbon buildings are not low- or zero-carbon just because they claim to be, or because they use 'natural' materials. If you only remember two things from this chapter they should be:

Figure 7.77 The Lime House – a prototype affordable passive house in Ebbw Vale intended for housing associations, designed by Bere Architects, and monitored, has performed very well.[15]
Credit: FW

Figure 7.78 Tigh Na Cladach affordable housing project in Dunoon, Scotland. Passive house design but substandard services installation led to higher than expected heating bills.
Credit: NHBC.

- Make every effort to keep the building airtight and superinsulated, double-checking every detail of jointing and construction as you build and removing thermal breaks;
- Make sure that occupants and users understand how the building works so they don't compromise the effects of all the hard work.

These rules apply whatever construction method you use and are the result of recent post-occupancy checks on existing buildings. For example, a report on a Scottish passive house development built as affordable housing in 2011 and announced to great fanfare at the time found that there were 'significant issues with its servicing systems and these appeared to have a knock-on effect with low internal temperatures and high energy bills'.[16] And Kevin McCloud's hemp-lime affordable housing project also suffered from poor construction leading to damp (see the case study).

We're learning all the time. The second generation of zero-carbon buildings are being built now, and you are lucky: you can learn from the successes and mistakes made while building the first.

Reading list

Dadeby, A, and Cotterell, J, *The Passivhaus Handbook: A Practical Guide to Constructing and Retrofitting Buildings for Ultra-low-energy Performance*, Green Books, 2012.

Nunan, J., and Hart, K. (Foreword), *The Complete Guide to Alternative Home Building Materials & Methods: Including Sod, Compressed Earth, Plaster, Straw, Beer Cans, Bottles, Cordwood, and Many Other Low Cost Materials*, Atlantic Publishing Group (FL), 2009.

Bevan, R. and Woolley, T., *Hemp lime construction: A guide to building with hemp lime composites*. Bracknell, IHS BRE Press, 2008.

Bouwens, D., *Earth buildings and their repair*. Tisbury, Cathedral Publications. www.buildingconservation. com/articles/earth/earth.htm.

Law, Ben, *Roundwood Timber Framing: Building Naturally Using Local Resources*, Permanent Publications, 2010.

Burch, M., *Complete Guide to Building Log Homes*, Babcock & Wilcox Company, 1984.

Jones, Barbara, *Building with Straw Bales: A Practical Guide for the UK and Ireland* Green Books, 2010.

Bingham, W. J., and Smith, C. F., *Strawbale Home Plans*, Gibbs Smith Publishers, 2007.

McRaven, C., *Building with Stone*, Storey Books, 1989.

Walker, P., Keable, R. and Marton, J., *Rammed Earth: Design and Construction Guidelines*, IHS BRE Press, 2005.

Notes

1 On average the carbon impact of the construction of conventional buildings is between 10 and 20 per cent of their use during their lifetime.

2 In Wales, One Planet Developments, according to TAN 6, 'should be exemplars of the Welsh Assembly Government's zero carbon aspiration and achieve zero carbon status in terms of the construction and use of the development', in line with Technical Advice Note (TAN) 22 – Sustainable Buildings.

3 See *Cellulose-based building materials,* NHBC Foundation, January 2014.

4 An average new house made with conventional materials contains the equivalent of 50 tonnes of CO_2 as 'embodied carbon' that could be reduced to 38 tonnes with greater use of timber and modern methods of construction, or even to approximately 25 tonnes by using cellulose-based materials, such as hempcrete. See: Monahan, J., and Powell J. C., *An embodied carbon and energy analysis of modern methods of construction in housing: A case study using a lifecycle assessment framework. Energy and Buildings* 2011, 43: 179–188.

5 Yates, T., *The use of non-food crops in the UK construction industry. Case studies. Journal of the Science of Food and Agriculture*, 86: 1709–1796. Chichester, Wiley Interscience, 2006.

6 The Engineering Toolbox has the thermal conductivity values of everything! See http://www.engineeringtoolbox.com/thermal-conductivity-d_429.html. Accessed January 2014.

7 My personal favourite system for this is called Steico Protect, which is easy to apply and is available, like many of my favourite products, from Ecomerchant, a trading style of Burdens Ltd.

8 Intelligent membranes adjust the breathability of a wall as follows: at low temperature and humidity, the molecules in the membrane close up and work as an effective water vapour retardant. At higher temperatures and humidity the molecules move apart, allowing trapped moisture to pass through. They also function as an airtightness barrier.

9 Explained in: Yates, T., Ferguson, A., Binns, B. and Hartless, R. *Cellulose-based building materials: Use, performance and risk*, NHBC Foundation, November 2013, ISBN 978-1-84806-355-6.

10 Jones, B., *Building with straw bales (revised and updated): A practical guide for the UK and Ireland.* Totnes, Green Books, 2009.

11 Atkinson, C., *Energy Assessment of a straw bale building*. MSc thesis. 2008. www.homegrownhome.co.uk/pdfs/Energyassessmentofastrawbalebuilding.pdf.

12 http://www.patternlanguage.com/ whose most beautiful and inspirational book is *The Timeless Way of Building*, OUP, USA, April 1980.

13 Centre for Alternative Technology Publications, May 1998, unfortunately out of print.

14 Devon Earth Building Association. Website FAQ: www.devonearthbuilding.com/faq.htm. Accessed January 2014.

15 See this report: http://bit.ly/1iqJWCq. Accessed January 2014.

16 Report on Tigh Na Cladach, an affordable Passive House in Dunoon, Scotland. Murphy, G.B., and Tuohy, P., ESRU, *Monitoring and Modelling the First Passive House in Scotland*, Department of Mechanical and Aerospace Engineering, University of Strathclyde, Glasgow, available at www.ibpsa.org/proceedings/BS2013/p_991.pdf. Retrieved January 2014.

What do you fancy to eat?

To supply much of your own food all year round, as well as a surplus to sell or barter, is extremely rewarding. Organically produced fresh ingredients straight from your own land even taste better, never mind being uber-sustainable. The choice of produce is wide, embracing not just vegetables, salads and herbs, but also soft and top fruit, nuts, meat, eggs, cheese, yoghurt, honey and so on.

It is way beyond the scope of this chapter to cover this topic in great detail. But to start you off I do touch on the principles of organic growing and the role of animals, if any, within the ecosystem you create. We'll look

Figure 8.1 A variety of freshly harvested vegetables. Yum!

at soil requirements, a suggested year planner, crop rotation and the needs of different crops, ways of dealing organically with some pests and diseases, fruit and nut trees and bushes and some animal and fowl husbandry. As you work, you should get to know your plot's preferences by trying out different types of cultivation, and experimenting with different crops, with different varieties, perhaps with different animals. Over time, you'll see how your efforts are also rewarded by an increase in the biodiversity of your site.

Diligence and constant care are required when you are relying on your own land and efforts for your own sustenance. You need to be alert to changes in the weather and to early signs of pests and diseases.

Planning the garden

If you've read the Land Management chapter you may already have sketched out your plot and located the orchards, fruit bushes, hen runs, polytunnels, duck pond, vegetable beds, and so on. You will have decided where the paths go to the vegetable beds, for ease of access and so you don't have to transport materials like compost for too far. Making raised beds for the vegetable plots is common; they make it easier to apply compost, to weed, and they help with drainage.

Figure 8.2 Make sure your paths provide easy access for wheelbarrows. Do you think this one does?

Figure 8.3 A well-organised plot in early March, ready for planting out. Note the use of bark chippings as mulch. This remote, low impact development is inhabited by a single woman in her late sixties.

For the garden area, use Table 8.1 to work out space allocation that will supply food all the year round. For each crop type you wish to grow, work backwards from the quantity you are likely to need, both for own consumption and for exchange, and the time(s) of year at which you will be harvesting. Allow an extra 10–20% for wastage, but on the other hand don't be too enthusiastic: a single tomato plant can yield 40 tomatoes. Some crops planted at the same time ripen all at once (such as some varieties of tomatoes and some salad leaves), some can be harvested over a period of time (such as courgettes and squashes). Some plants require much space (e.g. sweetcorn). Green salads can be planted at weekly intervals so you will have a constant supply, but only if you plan for the allowable space. Cut-and-come-again plants (perpetual spinach, purple sprouting broccoli) can be harvested for perhaps half of the year; they will just keep producing.

Seed catalogues are great for helping you choose what varieties to plant. Hardy salads and oriental greens might include: mizuna, mibuna, mustard, greens, pak choi, mispooona, komatsuna, and winter varieties of lettuce or land cress. Summer salads might include: lettuces, endive, cress, rocket, radish. Your area might also have seed swaps at crucial times of the year where you will pick up invaluable advice with your seeds. Of course, you collect your own seeds! Make sure they are dried well. One seed supplier, Real Seeds, tells you how to collect and dry seeds for each plant on their website: www.realseeds.co.uk.

Table 8.1 The grower's year

Crop	Jan	Feb	Mar	Apr	May	Jun	Jul	Aug	Sep	Oct	Nov	Dec
Solanium (potato family)												
Aubergine		Inside	Inside	Inside	Outside			Harvest	Harvest	Harvest		
Pepper			Inside	Inside	Outside	Harvest	Harvest	Harvest	Harvest	Harvest	Harvest	Harvest
Potato, main crop			Outside	Outside	Outside	Harvest						
Tomato			Inside	Inside	Plant Out	Harvest	Harvest	Harvest	Harvest	Harvest	Harvest	
Allium (onion family)												
Garlic	Outside	Outside					Harvest	Harvest	Harvest	Outside		
Leek		Outside	Outside/Inside	Harvest					Harvest	Harvest	Harvest	Harvest
Onion, from seed			Inside		Plant Out		Harvest	Harvest	Harvest	Harvest		
Onion, from sets			Outside	Outside			Harvest	Harvest				
Onion, autumn sown					Outside	Outside		Outside	Outside	Outside		
Onion, spring				Outside	Outside	Harvest	Harvest	Harvest				
Shallot			Plant Out									

(Continued)

Table 8.1 (*Continued*)

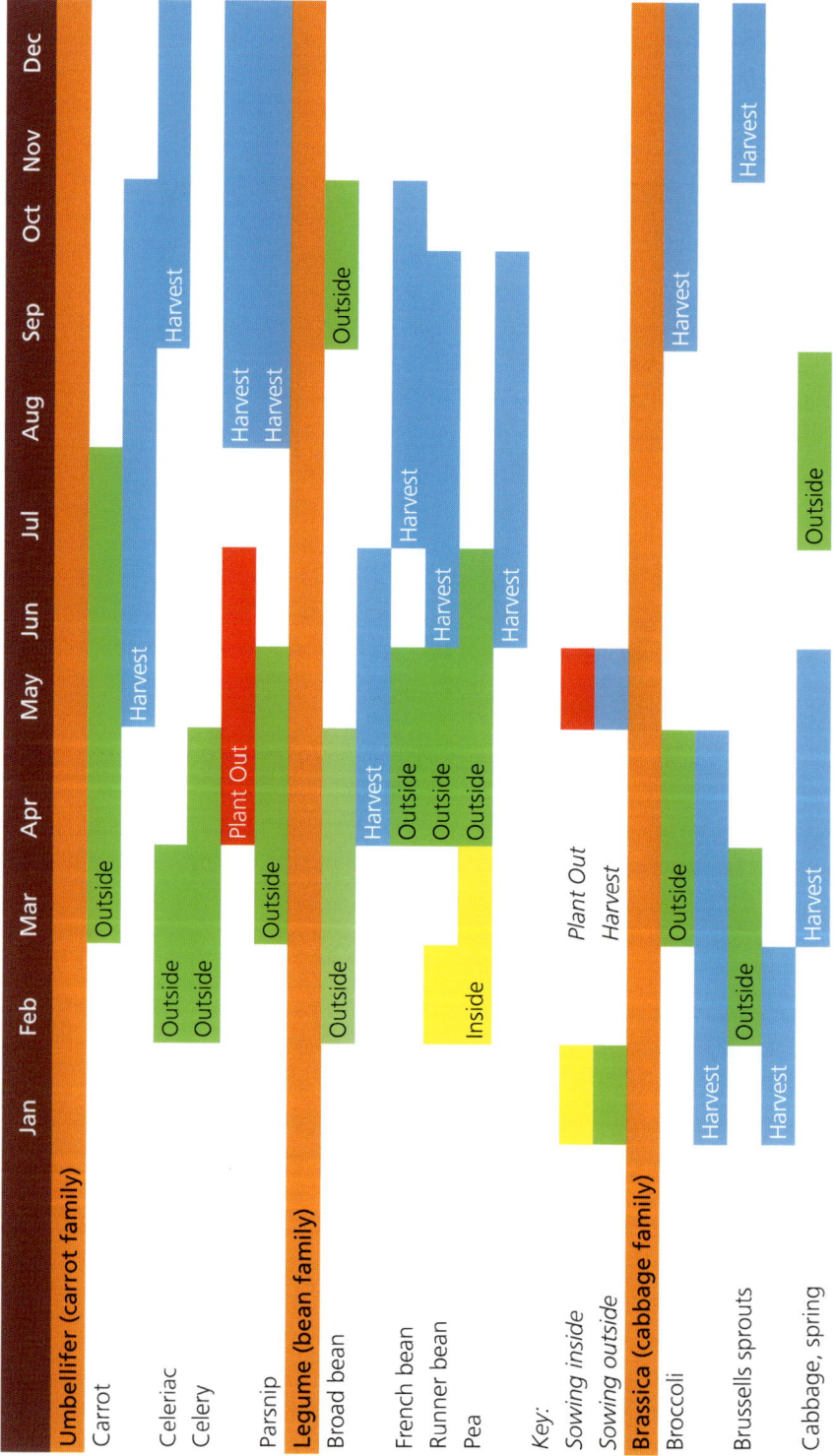

	Jan	Feb	Mar	Apr	May	Jun	Jul	Aug	Sep	Oct	Nov	Dec
Umbellifer (carrot family)												
Carrot		Outside	Outside		Harvest	Harvest	Harvest	Harvest	Harvest	Harvest		
Celeriac		Outside	Outside									
Celery		Outside	Outside					Harvest	Harvest	Harvest	Harvest	Harvest
Parsnip			Outside	Outside	Outside			Harvest	Harvest	Harvest	Harvest	Harvest
Legume (bean family)												
Broad bean		Outside	Outside	Harvest	Harvest	Harvest	Harvest	Harvest	Outside			
French bean				Outside	Outside	Outside	Harvest	Harvest	Harvest	Harvest		
Runner bean				Outside	Outside	Outside	Harvest	Harvest	Harvest	Harvest		
Pea	Inside	Inside	Inside	Outside	Outside	Outside	Harvest	Harvest	Harvest			
Key:												
Sowing inside					*Plant Out*							
Sowing outside					*Harvest*							
Brassica (cabbage family)												
Broccoli	Harvest		Outside	Outside	Plant Out				Harvest	Harvest	Harvest	Harvest
Brussells sprouts	Harvest	Outside	Outside	Outside					Harvest	Harvest	Harvest	
Cabbage, spring	Harvest	Harvest	Harvest	Harvest	Harvest		Outside	Outside				

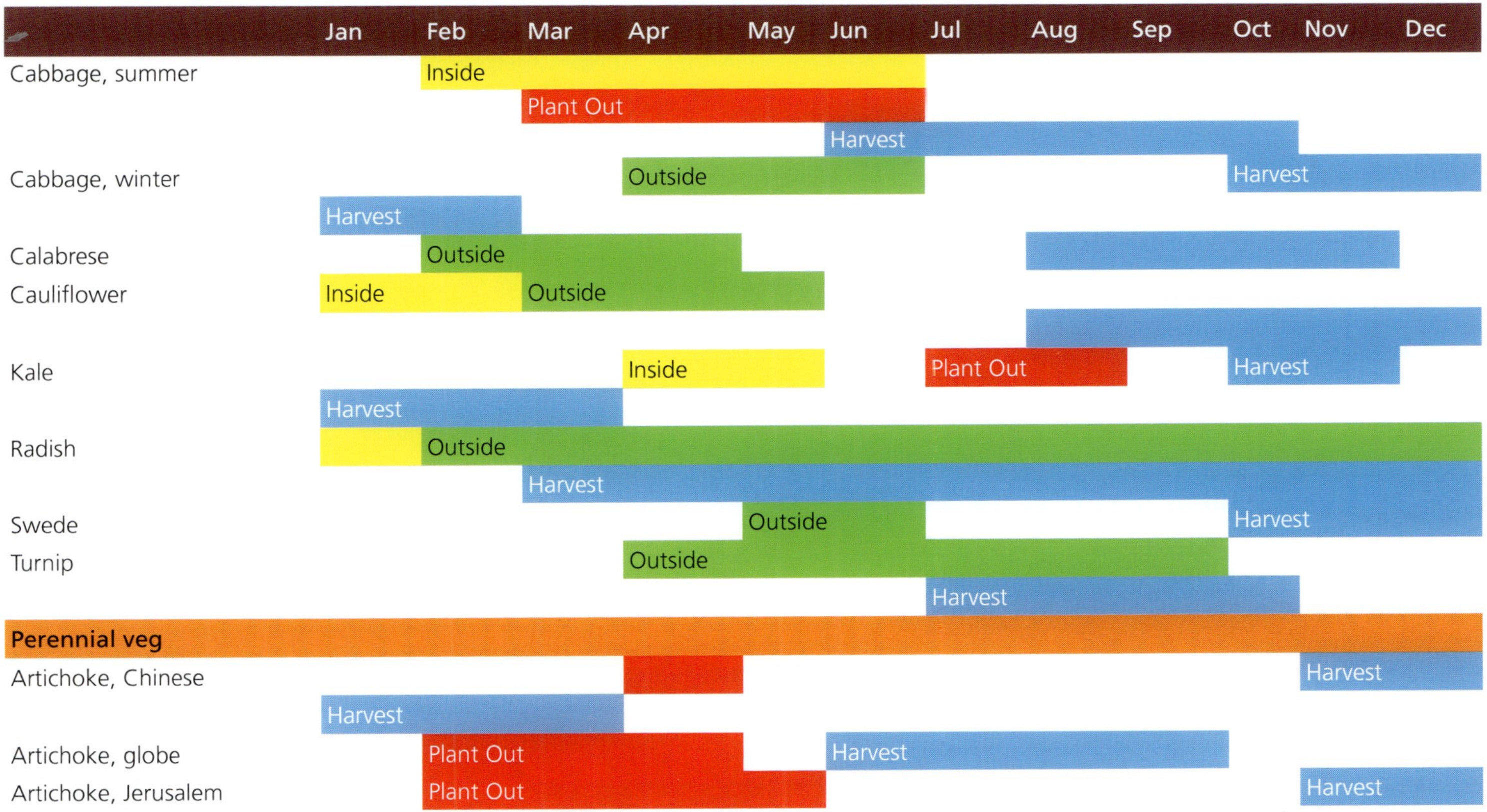
Jan
Feb
Mar
Apr
May
Jun
Jul
Aug
Sep
Oct
Nov
Dec
Cabbage, summer
Inside
Plant Out
Harvest
Cabbage, winter
Outside
Harvest
Harvest
Calabrese
Outside
Cauliflower
Inside
Outside
Kale
Inside
Plant Out
Harvest
Harvest
Radish
Outside
Harvest
Swede
Outside
Harvest
Turnip
Outside
Harvest
Perennial veg
Artichoke, Chinese
Harvest
Harvest
Artichoke, globe
Plant Out
Harvest
Artichoke, Jerusalem
Plant Out
Harvest

(*Continued*)

Table 8.1 (Continued)

Crop	Jan	Feb	Mar	Apr	May	Jun	Jul	Aug	Sep	Oct	Nov	Dec
Asparagus			Plant Out	Harvest	Harvest	Harvest						
Perpetual spinach			Harvest	Harvest	Harvest	Harvest						
Sea kale		Harvest	Harvest	Harvest	Harvest							
Summer crops												
Sweetcorn				Inside	Outside		Harvest	Harvest	Harvest	Harvest		
Summer salads & greens			Inside	Inside	Outside	Outside	Harvest	Harvest	Harvest	Harvest	Harvest	
Hardy salads, oriental greens	Inside	Inside	Outside	Outside	Outside	Harvest	Harvest	Harvest	Harvest	Harvest	Harvest	Harvest
Marrow & courgette				Inside	Plant Out		Harvest	Harvest	Harvest	Harvest		
Pumpkin & squash				Inside	Plant Out		Harvest	Harvest	Harvest	Harvest		

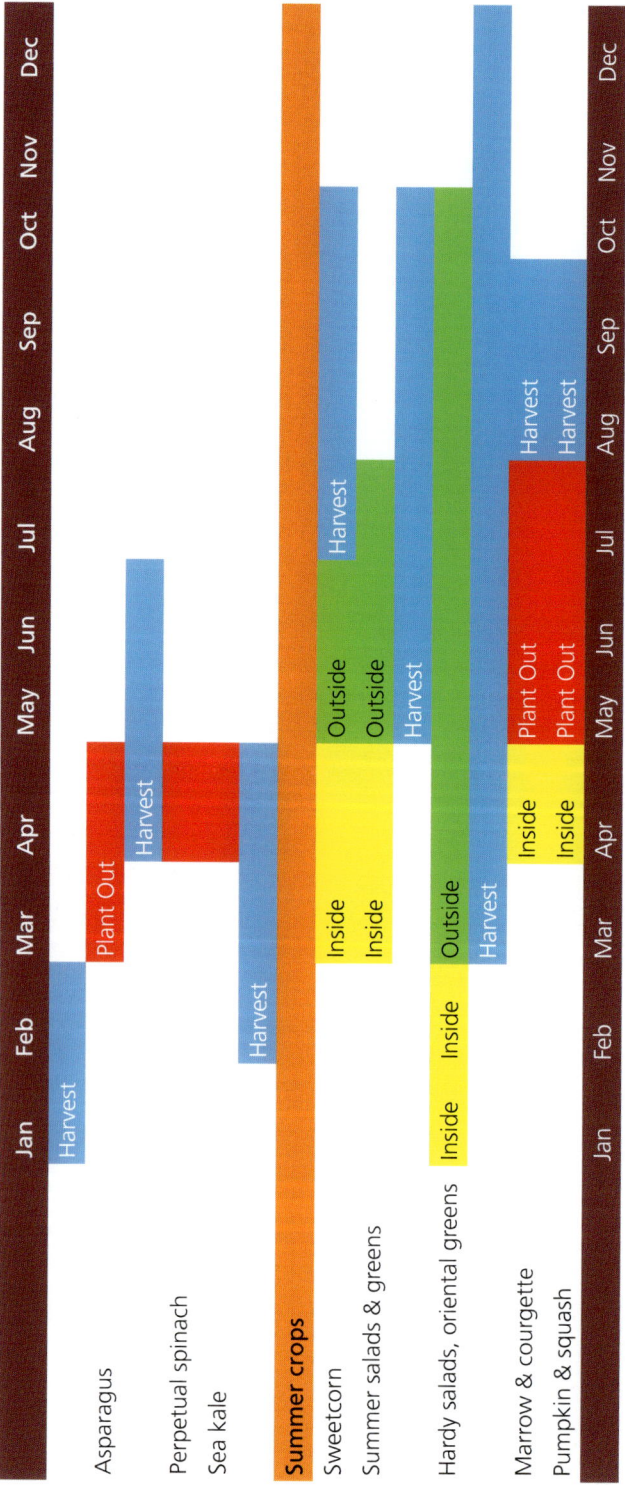

Hardy salads and oriental greens might include: mizuna, mibuna, mustard greens, pak choi, mispoona, komatsuna, winter varieties of lettuce, land cress

Summer salads might include: lettuces, endive, cress, rocket, radish

Collect the seeds! Make sure they are dried well. My favourite seed supplier (because local) is Real Seeds and they tell you how on their website: www.realseeds.co.uk.

Figure 8.4 Asparagus being grown as a cash crop by Andy and Jane at Lammas. It's a smart idea because it fetches a good price.

An early decision is to allocate the proportion of time and land area you are going to devote to cultivating staple foods such as potatoes, which can be cheaper to buy, versus high-value foodstuffs such as asparagus and artichoke. Then there is the prospect of adding value to your produce for resale, for example by producing cured meat, home-made preserves, or yoghurt and cheese. You might think that grains are the crop least likely to be grown as they require mechanical help for harvesting and processing into flour, but why not consider trying out some unusual crops such as quinoa?

What do plants need?

Part of the planning process involves thinking about the soil. What chemicals do plants need in order to grow, and where do they get them? Plants need:

- the six major elements: oxygen, hydrogen, carbon, nitrogen, phosphorous and potassium;
- calcium, sulphur and magnesium;
- traces of elements such as iron, boron, zinc, copper and molybdenum.

Of these elements, carbon, hydrogen and oxygen are supplied by the air. The remainder have to be obtained from the soil and are absorbed in

Figure 8.5 A cold frame can be made out of reclaimed windows and used to warm the soil and give seedlings an early start or keep some vegetables going through the winter.

soluble form through tiny root hairs. On unmanaged land, soil fertility is maintained by a permanent coverage of living or decaying vegetation that produces small but appropriate quantities of the soluble plant nutrients. But on managed plots, your challenge is to supply what plants need artificially, using organic methods.

Feeding the soil

Organic horticulture is practised in the One Planet Life because the production of manufactured fertilisers such as nitrates uses large amounts of fossil fuel energy; because some phosphate fertilisers aren't good for organisms that live in healthy soil; and because fertilisers may leach into and pollute water supplies (for example producing algal blooms that can effectively suffocate other water-dwelling organisms).

Organic growers instead enhance fertility by adding organic matter to the soil. This could take the form of manure, leaf mould, peat, garden compost, seaweed, composted straw, spent hops and mushroom compost. In certain circumstances they might also apply: shoddy (wool and cotton waste), waste paper or cardboard, composted human manure, worm compost and so on. There are also some specific 'organic fertilisers' such as bone meal and 'hoof and horn', but many growers try to build up sufficient organic matter in the soil to make their use unnecessary.

These materials are processed by organisms living in the soil, causing the nutrients to be released slowly during and after a growing season. There are slight disadvantages to using organic matter: the nutrient value

Table 8.2 Estimate of the nitrogen (N) phosphorus (P) and potassium (K) content of various organic fertilisers.

Organic Fertiliser	Content			Appropriate use
	N%	P%	K%	
Compost	1.5	2	0.5	Before planting any crop except some roots
Horse manure	0.7	0.2	0.5	Use on the potato area. If well rotted bury,
Cow/Farm manure	0.6	0.2	1.0	otherwise use as a mulch.
Sheep droppings	0.7	0.3	0.9	Use in a liquid manure
Poultry droppings	1.5	1.0	0.5	Usually in small amounts. Add to compost heap
Leafmould	0.5	0.25	0.25	Use in seed compost
Peat	0.75	tiny	tiny	Avoid or use in seed compost only
Seaweed	0.25	0.25	0.5	Use with potatoes, tomatoes or in compost
Shoddy	10	tiny	tiny	Slow to break down. Use under potato or legume area
Mushroom compost	0.5	0.25	0.5	Contains lime. Use to improve soil structure but keep away from the potatoes
Woodash	0	0	5–10	Use around fruit or tomatoes. Remember fresh ash is alkaline. Store in a dry place and use under potatoes.
Bonemeal	4	22	0	Use under permanent plants. E.g. Fruit trees

is imprecise and if improperly handled it may also cause water pollution. To prevent soil nutrients from leaching out, keep the soil covered with crops, plastic or mulch and plant cover green manure crops.

Organic fertilisers

Compost

Because different materials compost at different rates, it's a good idea to have different compost bins for each type. For example, one for leafy material (leaf mould, grass cuttings), and another for more woody material that takes longer to decompose. Kitchen waste can be mixed with the former. Include paper (wastepaper and tissues) and cardboard (especially corrugated) with this pile, but it should be scrunched up or in some other way contain air pockets. Do not include flat papers (newspapers, magazines and so on); these will not decompose, just become a soggy mess. Composting paper and cardboard in the presence of air (aerobically) with leafy materials

Figure 8.6 Compost bins made from reclaimed wood for different types of material.

will give your final compost the correct carbon-to-nitrogen ratio and help to prevent it from becoming smelly.

Compost can be produced continuously or in batches. A continuous system needs to have an easy way of extracting the finished compost from the bottom of the pile. A batch system needs two piles or containers, one of which is maturing and readying for harvest and the other of which is being compiled. Both should be able to drain.

Compost matures more rapidly in the presence of brandling worms and heat. The little reddish worms can be obtained from a friend's compost heap – they will reproduce rapidly in their new environment. Heat is naturally produced by the decomposing process and can be kept in by having a thick, insulating cover over the compost such as old carpet.

Compost is ready to be spread onto or dug into the soil when the original ingredients are not recognisable. If it is soggy, don't use it but turn it and mix in more material that has air within it. It should be quite crumbly. The worms will be in the relatively unprocessed part at the top. Use this to start a new heap. If you need them, more information, containers and brandling worms can be obtained from Wiggly Wigglers.[1]

Green manures

Green manures are grown when a plot is not being productive. This helps to retain soil fertility, restrict weed growth and protect soil structure. They include legumes (e.g. clover, field beans, alfalfa, mustard, winter tares and trefoil) which help to harvest nitrogen from the air. Many, such as *phacelia*, lupin and red clover, look attractive if you allow a few plants to flower and set seed. Some have deep root systems that draw up nutrients leached into the subsoil.

Table 8.3 Green manures[2]

Name	Sowing	In soil	Conditions	Legume	Sowing g, per square mile
Alfalfa	April-July	1 year	Avoid acid and wet soil	Yes	2
Field beans	Sept-Nov	overwinter	Heavy soil	Yes	20
Buckwheat	April- Aug	1–3 months	Likes poor soil	No	6
Clover	March-Aug	2–3 months	Sandy soils	Yes	3
Fenugreek	March-Aug	2–3 months	Well drained	Fixes some N	5
Lupin	March-June	2–4 months	Sandy soils	Yes	10
Mustard	March- Sept	1–2 months	Fertile soils	No (brassica)	5
Phacelia	March-Sept	1–3 months	Most	No	2
Hungarian or Grazing Rye	August- Nov	overwinter	Most	No	16
Winter Tares	March-Sept	2–3 months	Avoid acid and dry soil	Yes	16
Trefoil	March-Aug	3 months	Light dry soils	Yes	3

Figure 8.7 Comfrey being grown for its nitrogen-fixing benefits.

Sow green manure seed over a smooth growing area. Rake the soil containing the seeds lightly. Before the green manure plants flower, cut the foliage just above the surface of the soil. In winter you can leave this as mulch. At other times dig it into the top six to eight inches of soil. Let the soil organisms ingest the material and plant your crops a few weeks later.

Figure 8.8 A polytunnel makes it easier to manage diseases and weeds but must be kept watered. This one, which I worked in at George Monbiot's place, Machynlleth, has a sprinkler system using rainwater collected from the roof of an adjacent workshop.

If club root (see below) is a problem you might want to avoid planting mustard. *Phacelia* has advantages over several other crops as it is not related to any of the common vegetable plants and can fit anywhere in the rotation. You can use a surplus of leafy crops, such as rhubarb and celery, as a surface mulch of green manure, and dig in temporary grass or weeds.

A liquid manure recipe

1   Soak some organic matter (comfrey, grass cuttings, nettles and/or manure) in a barrel of water; add urine to water in a ratio of 1:10.
2   At the end of two weeks (depending on the time of year) you will have some evil smelling liquid.
3   Dilute it 8:1. Apply with a watering can.

Comfrey liquid is rich in potash whilst liquid animal manure is rich in nitrates. Nettles provide a more balanced feed. All are great for giving plants a growth boost when pests and diseases may be lurking.

To rotate or not?

We looked at crop rotation in Chapter 4 and Figure 4.17. You don't have to rotate crops. You can instead let different crops occupy a different space as an opportunity occurs. For example, winter salad crops or leeks could go in the space left by the harvested potatoes. Several growing systems were trialled

Figure 8.9 Growing in old tyres makes efficient use of compost and helps contain roots and water. This one is at Cornerwood.

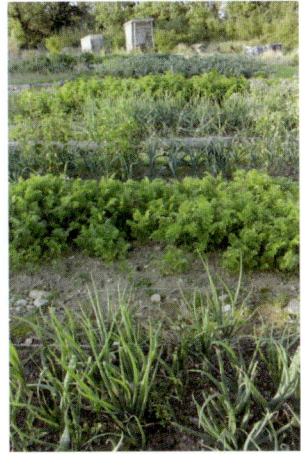

Figure 8.10 and 8.11 Two other crop rotation systems, in Simon and Jasmine's plot (left), and Andy and Jane's (right), Lammas.

in the Get Growing course at the National Botanic Garden of Wales in 2013; the bed which was the most productive was planted directly with seeds as follows: the plants were all mixed up; the larger seeds such as legumes were pushed into the earth first, then medium-sized seeds were scattered, and finally smaller seeds were scattered. Plants grew up crowded together and were harvested as they grew to make room for the remaining ones.

But one advantage of rotation for beginners is that it helps them to understand the predilections of different species and utilise other organic growing principles described in the Land Management Chapter (Chapter 4), such as:

• *Intercropping:* Growing two crops side by side which germinate and mature at different rates, e.g. radish and parsnip.

- *Catch cropping:* While the brassica plot is weed free and empty, waiting to be planted, you can grow a quick crop of *green manure* to maintain the fertility of the soil, and bury this crop to feed the cabbages when they are planted.
- *Companion Planting:* e.g., planting carrot and spring onions together, since the smell of the onions deters a pest (carrot fly).

Vegetable tips

So for convenience, we'll look in turn at each of the 'families' in a four bed rotation.

Legumes

Broad beans, peas, French beans and runner beans are the most widely grown in the UK. Broad beans are the hardiest and can be planted even when frosts are expected; some varieties can be planted in autumn. Peas are slightly less hardy; early varieties can be planted from late March onwards. Main crop peas can be planted in May and June. French beans can be planted in April if protected with fleece or cloches. Don't plant runner beans outside until the last chance of a late frost has gone.

Legumes seem to grow better in a less acidic soil, so add lime or green manures if the pH is too low. Their growing roots, together with a soil bacterium (*Rhizobium*), convert nitrogen in the air into nodules of fertiliser

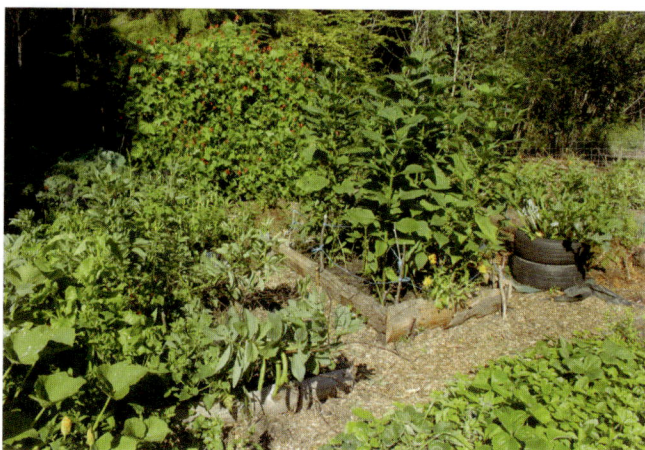

Figure 8.12. Legume beds (Cornerwood).

attached to the root, which the plant partially feeds on. If the roots are left in the soil after harvest, the fertiliser remaining can benefit the following crop. Mulch around legumes with grass clippings, compost, cardboard and so on when the soil is wet to reduce evaporation and keep the roots moist.

Pests

- *Black fly* can attack broad beans. Look out for the aphids on the growing tips just before harvest. Ants are often found with them, feeding on the sap the aphids have exposed. If pods are forming remove the growing tips of all the plants to deprive the aphids of food. If the pods have not formed, spray the creatures off with a jet of cold water.
- *Slugs* affect young French and runner beans. Start the plants off in a protected environment and plant out when about to produce a vigorous vine. Once the plant tips are 20 cm. above the ground they are usually safe from slugs. Grow a few spares just in case.
- *Mice* sometimes eat seeds and young plants: to protect, cover seeds with fleece to speed up growth and restrict access.

Brassicas

Brassicas (the cabbage family) include Brussels sprouts, cabbage, cauli-flower, broccoli and kale but also swede, turnip and kohlrabi. The latter are sometimes grown in a 'root area' in a rotation; if so, do not follow another brassica. Among green manures, mustard is a member.

Figure 8.13 Kale varieties being kept for seed (Andy and Jane, Lammas).

It's relatively easy to grow all brassicas from seeds. F1 Hybrid seeds are derived from two sets of plants that have been self-pollinated for eight to twelve generations to produce a guaranteed uniform crop. They may have been bred for vigour, pest resistance, size or hardiness but are usually more expensive. Sow in seed compost in a separate bed or containers, under protection, well away from pests. When the seedlings have four leaves, transplant into modules or separate small pots. Bury roots and stem up to their lowest leaf.

I plant brassicas after the legumes, leaving the roots of these as nitrogen fertiliser. The ground may have been limed if I think it is necessary. They're fed with liquid manure as soon as they are established in the plot.

Pests and diseases

- *Club root* is caused by the fungus *Plasmodiophora brassicae.* It's a tough old spore that lives for years in the soil once established. You can recognise it by swollen roots with 'finger and thumb' projections. The plants wilt, appear stunted and go grey/blue. Infected roots rot, discharging spores into the soil. Making the soil more alkaline with lime, crushed egg- or seashells should prevent it. Club-root-resistant varieties are available. Improving drainage (e.g. raised beds) helps too.
- *Slugs.* Crushed eggshells, bran, sharp sand and prickly twigs are all meant to keep slugs away for the first few days after transplanting

Figure 8.14 Romanesque calabrese, an amazing brassica to cultivate.

the crop. From then onwards, regular hoeing will help. The secret of growing brassicas is to grow them faster than the pests can eat them and use companion planting (see below).

- *Cabbage root fly:* Spreading carpet between seedlings and putting a piece of rhubarb leaf in the transplanting hole stops this pest laying its eggs and discourages the larvae, which bores into roots and stems.
- *Aphids and caterpillars* can be sprayed off with a powerful jet of water.
- *Cabbage white butterflies:* companion-planting aromatic flowers like marigolds should help distract them and encourage parasitic insects, such as the ichneumon fly. Caterpillar-decimated plants can be left in the ground as they usually recover by winter.

Alliums

This family includes: onion, onion sets, spring onions, pickling onions, leeks, shallots and garlic. They prefer highly fertile, phosphate-rich soil. Growing onions alongside carrots is beneficial.

For a summer crop, after brassicas in the rotation have been harvested in autumn, spread compost on the soil. Fork it in over the winter. Add wood ash in the spring, then rake the surface smooth. Onions may be grown from seed in potting compost under protection in February/March. In April plant them out about 1 cm deep, 10 cm apart, in rows 20 cm apart. Don't let the leaf tips touch the soil or they may rot. August-sown Japanese onions should be planted in the same way.

Onion sets are seedlings whose growth has been stopped the previous autumn. For these, cover the soil with agricultural fleece in February to warm it. After two weeks plant the sets about 10–15 cm apart in rows about

Figure 8.15 Leeks, with a broad beans bed in the background (Cornerwood).

Figure 8.16 'Red Baron' onions and leeks ready for harvest (Melissa, Lammas).

Figure 8.17 'Conqueror' onions pulled and left for three days before removal.

15 cm apart. If you want large onions increase the spacing. Cover with fleece for two more weeks to protect from birds. As bulbs develop help them along with liquid feed.

Spring onions and pickling onions can be grown in succession from spring onwards. Sow directly in the soil in rows 10 cm apart. Thin to 2 cm apart, eating the thinnings! Harvest as needed. They can also be sown in August and overwintered.

Pests and diseases

- *Onion fly maggots* affect onions grown from seed. Pick or spray off with jets of water.
- *Bolting.* Should onions bolt and go to seed very quickly, snap off the flower stem and pick early. If this happens a lot it may mean that the

soil is too nitrate rich and lacks potassium, so add wood ash to the following year's onion plot.
- *Onion white rot* is a fluffy fungal mould at the base and roots followed by black spots on the onion skin. Destroy infected onions by burning or in a hot compost heap. Keep infected onions away from the store or it will spread.

Storing onions

Harvest on a dry sunny day. Remove all soil but do not wash. Store in a warm, dry airy place until the foliage is brittle. Snap it off. When the roots and remaining stem are really brittle put the onions in string bags and suspend them in a cool, dry airy place. Check regularly for fungal attacks.

Leeks

Grow the first crop under glass in February or start the previous autumn. The second crop can be planted in a seed bed in May and can be used as a catch crop after early potatoes. Plant out when as thick as a pencil in soil treated as for onions. Large leeks don't taste so good so plant them 10–15 cm apart in rows 20 cm apart and harvest before too large. With a dibber, make a hole 10 cm deep for each one, and wash soil onto the roots, which helps to blanch the stem. After six weeks give them a weekly liquid feed. The blanching can be increased by piling earth around the stems. Harvest as you need them. Those that go to seed are inedible.

Problems

Sometimes you see a brown fungal infection called 'rust'. Fertile soil and liquid feed are the best defence. Pull up any affected leeks and hot compost or burn them. A certain moth lays eggs near leeks; its caterpillars can burrow into the plants. Disturbing the soil in winter and encouraging bird predators can provide a defence.

Shallots

Shallots are grown from bulbs. They have a milder flavour than onions. Treat the soil as for onions. Plant out in early spring about 15 cm apart with the bulb tips just below the soil. In early summer brush soil away from the bulbs to help them ripen. Lift when the foliage dies back, dry as onions, and store. Keep some for the next crop.

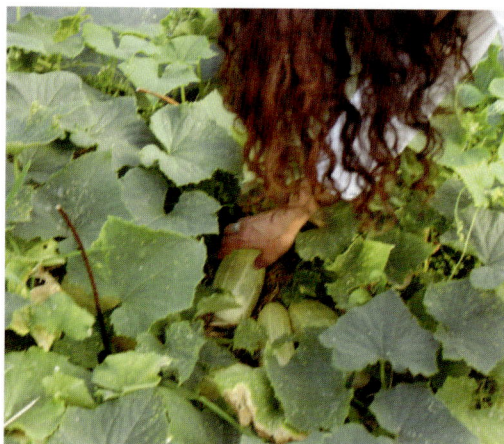

Figure 8.18 Cucumbers sit outside of a rotation system and can be grown wherever there's a suitable space in a polytunnels. These are being grown for seed, by Melissa, at Lammas, seen here picking one.

Figure 8.19 Celery growing at Cornerwood (see Exemplary Examples).

Garlic

Garlic is easy to grow. Treat the soil as for onions. Plant cloves 15 cm apart in early spring. Keep the soil weed free and harvest like other onions.

Root crops

The main root crops in the UK are potato, celery/celeriac, carrots, parsnips, turnips, swedes and beetroot. In a rotation they follow brassicas and are planted near the onion family, which can deter pests, and intercropped with quickly maturing salad crops inserted from April into spaces between the slower developing roots.

Carrots, parsnips and beetroots

They like a fine, firm seed bed, a sunny spot where humus was added for the previous crop, since they don't like fresh compost or manure. Any stones in the soil will cause the crop to fork. Prior to seeding, suspend some bird feeders above the growing area to encourage predators to seek out pests lurking in the soil. Water the soil copiously before you sow and then cover the seeds lightly.

Carrots

It's difficult to transplant carrots, so sow seeds *in situ* in fortnightly succession from March until August, or from when the soil temperature reaches at least 10 °C. Either plant in rows 15–30 cm apart or in a broad strip about 30 cm wide. After germination thin to between 5 and 15 cm apart. The soil must be kept moist (but not soggy) and warm. Fleece can help.

Pests

Slugs and carrot root fly, which causes yellowing foliage, wilting plants or harvested crops like veined blue cheese.

Parsnips

Parsnips are slow to germinate. Warm the soil with fleece and sow in February or March. Sow in clusters 15 cm apart in rows 20–30 cm apart. Thin out all but the best. You can interplant with radishes. When weeding, take care not to damage the root, which can lead to infection.

Beetroot

Sow later than parsnips, April to June, in pairs 10 cm apart in rows 20 cm apart. Remove the weakest seedlings. Harvest and eat alternate plants when they reach golf-ball size, allowing space for other plants to mature. Harvest the entire crop before the first frost. If you notice small white tunnels in the leaves, these are caused by Leaf Miners. Remove the affected leaves and hot compost them.

Turnips and swedes

These are brassicas so take precautions against club root. See above for how to deal with it. Turnips grow faster than swedes and the roots above. Use as a catch crop after early potatoes but not winter cabbage. Wait until

Table 8.4 Green leaf salads.

Variety	Brassica?	Hardy?	Requirements	Notes
Lettuce	No	Not very	Moist fertile soil. Prefers cool germination. Will not germinate above 20 °C.	Many varieties.
Chicory and endive	No	Yes, more than lettuce.	Unfussy. Sow in cool conditions, in modules and transplant. Avoid very humid conditions.	Hot weather is said to cause bitterness.
Kale	Yes	Yes	Rugged plants that will survive when others fail. Fertile well-drained soil is best. Sow in trays and transplant.	Use younger more tender leaves.
Chinese cabbage and Komatsuna	Yes	Some are very hardy.	Need much water. Do not transplant well, so grow in modules.	Mild flavour.
Mustard cabbage: Mizuna and Mibuna	Yes	*Mizuna* yes. *Mibuna* less so.	*Mizuna* is a forgiving, attractive plant that you can cut and come again at most growth stages. *Mibuna* is less productive but adds a pretty dimension to salads. Modules or direct sowing.	Mild mustard flavour.
Mustard cabbage. 'Green in snow' and red and purple leaved mustards	Yes	Yes	Not as vigorous as *Mizuna*. Cut and come again sparingly. Modules or direct sowing.	Hot flavour.
Leaf beet including Swiss chard	No	Yes	Fertile, moist soil required. Red varieties are more slug resistant… you might be able to sow directly into the soil. Otherwise use modules.	Use small leaves and thinnings in salad.

Variety	Brassica?	Hardy?	Requirements	Notes
Alfalfa	No	Yes	Used as a green manure. Legume which does not like wet soils.	Eat young leaves.
Winter purslane, 'Miner's Lettuce'	No	Yes with protection.	Sow in situ or in modules. Adaptable but likes well-drained soil. Cut and come again.	Eat leaves and succulent stems.
Summer purslane	No	No	Needs warmth and well-drained soil. Sow in situ or in modules. Keep well watered.	Pick single leaves only.
Corn salad 'Lambs Lettuce'	No	Yes	Robust, forgiving plant but doesn't like hot dry conditions. Can be transplanted.	Eat single leaves and use quickly. Mild taste.
Land cress	No	Yes	Needs moist humus rich soil. Grows well between taller plants.	Pick single leaves. Strong flavour.
Rocket	No	Fairly	Most varieties grow very quickly. Grow in situ or in modules.	Leaves and flowers are edible.

late April before sowing either. Grow in rows about 20 cm apart. Gradually, selecting the best, thin the seedlings to about 10 cm apart for turnips and 20 cm apart for swedes.

Radish

These tolerate a wide range of soil conditions, so grow as a catch crop or as space becomes available. Sow small amounts in succession in rows 15 cm apart.

Pests

The flea beetle; this eats holes in the leaves. Best deterred by rapid growth in rich soil or give a sharp spray with water.

Storing

Most root crops can be stored in the ground until November or later. Then, all root crops can be stored above ground if in perfect condition. Avoid letting them touch each other and layer them in dry sand, compost, bark, sawdust or woodchips in a cool, frost and mouse-proof spot.

Leaf salads

What a choice there is!

Brassica salad crops

The leaves of all the common brassica plants can be eaten raw in salads. Kale can be grown in several varieties. Many are very resistant to pests and red varieties seem to discourage slugs. Some of the brassica salad crops, like *Mizuna*, can be grown through out the year and look fine as well as spicing up a salad. All need fertile, well-drained soil. The pH needs to be neutral or slightly alkaline as a defence against club root, so lime should ideally be applied to the legume plot a year prior to planting and compost a few months prior. Soil fertility is maintained with green manures.

Hardy salad leaf crops

Many of these can provide winter harvest, so sow kale, *Mizuna* and corn salad from July to September. Protection with a cloche, cold frame or greenhouse can help. Because seedlings will be ruined by slugs, some have fragile roots, and some may not germinate in high temperatures, start them off in a safe place, protected from temperature extremes, and in modules; plant out without disturbing the roots.

Figure 8.20 Salad leaves being grown for sale by Melissa of Lammas.

Figure 8.21 Squash being kept protected from rot by a sheet of plastic (Cornerwood).

Sweetcorn

Needs a long sunny growing season. Start off in March/April indoors in modules or small pots. Keep moist and warm. Harden off after the last frost and plant outside on a mound of compost, at least 20 cm apart but together in a group as they are wind pollinated. Male flowers are high up on the plant; females are lower down between the stem and a leaf. Harvest the cobs when the tassel has begun to wither and turn brown. You can plant sweetcorn with French beans so that they will climb up the sweetcorn and fertilise the soil, and with pumpkin or squash plants, which will help keep the soil damp.

Tomatoes, peppers, chillies and potatoes

Plant **tomato** and **pepper** seeds in March, six to eight weeks before they will be transplanted outdoors after the last frost, unless they will spend their entire lives in a greenhouse or polytunnel, in which case you can start them earlier. They germinate in five to ten days. When 8 cm tall move into individual pots. When night time temperatures remain above 10 °C begin to harden them off. Plant out in well rotted compost on an overcast day in sheltered, sunny areas. Stake and keep tied up. Feed and water regularly and check daily for blight.

Potatoes are easy to grow but a low-value crop. Nevertheless there is huge variation to choose from both for taste and usefulness, and to see which is most suitable for your soil. They are planted at different times depending on whether they are earlies (planted from mid March to late May, harvested three months later), second earlies (mid March to late April) or maincrop (ditto, harvested three to four months later). You can also

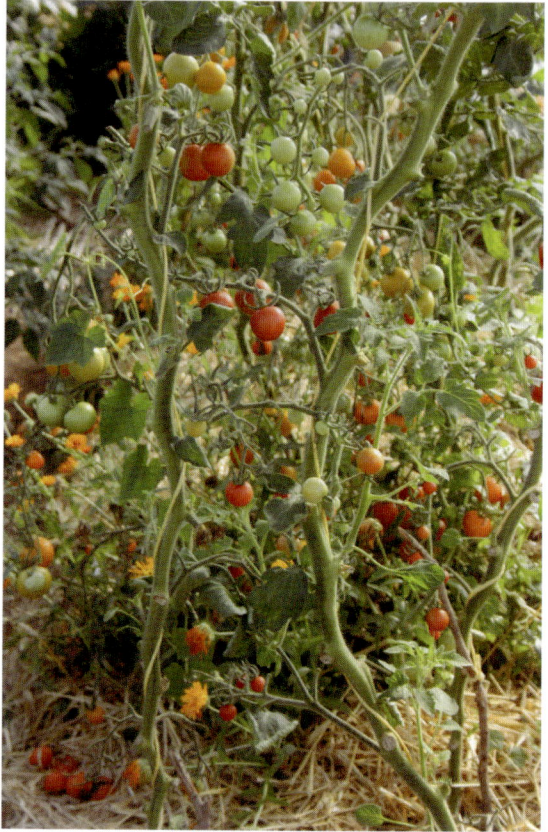

Figure 8.22 Tomatoes being grown for sale by Melissa of Lammas.

Figure 8.23 Chilli tomatoes being grown by Andy and Jane, Lammas.

plant 'new potatoes' in August for harvest at Christmas. Soil should have well-rotted manure or homemade compost dug in in spring.

Any potatoes kept as seed potatoes from the previous year can be 'chitted' (allowed to grow tubers) at the beginning of the year. For planting, soil temperature should be over 6 °C. The seed potatoes are planted with the roots facing downwards, 15 cm deep, spaced at 30 cm, in rows 60–75 cm apart. Soil or compost is heaped above them, continuing to build this heap as they grow. If potatoes show leaf dieback this is a sign of blight. Cut the stems back to ground level. After the frost has come, protect them with fleece or straw. Do not grow potatoes in the same bed until the fourth year following as a precaution against blight. Store potatoes in paper sacks after they have been dried.

Pests and diseases

Blight is an airborne fungal infection that can ruin crops on humid days, especially in July and August. It affects all members of the potato family. Crops harvested before July are not affected and those grown in polytunnels and greenhouses seem less susceptible. If tomatoes are planted, keep them away from potatoes and encourage air flow around each plant, avoiding stagnant, humid conditions where blight thrives.

Attract pollinators for your plants!

It's a good idea to plant a few species and varieties that butterflies, bees and other pollinators love, to make sure your plants are pollinated. Some of these creatures will also devour pests like aphids.

Figure 8.24 Chillies ready for harvest to be taken to market. Another high-value product.

Table 8.5 Plants that attract bees and other pollinators.

Perennials	Herbs	Shrubs	Climbers
Salvia	Lavender	Corylus	Lonicera
Borage	Melissa officinalis	Viburnum	pericleum
Alcea rosea	Foeniculum vulgare	Ribes sanguineum	
Verbena bonariensis	Savia		
Papaver	Centranthus		
Digitalis	Echinacea purpurea		
Lathyrus	Allium		
Achillea fillipendulina	Mentha		
Eupatorium			
cannabinum			
Sedum			
Scabiosa			
Eryngium borgattii			
Dipsacus follonum			
Circium rivulare			

Figure 8.25 A cabbage white butterfly distracted by sedums!

Watch the temperature!

Temperature affects plant growth. Growth rates increase up to an optimum rate at 70 °F or 21 °C. Photosynthesis starts at about 6 °C. Germination temperatures vary but usually begin at 6 °C.

Plants can often tolerate a slow reduction in temperature but cannot stand sudden fluctuations. Wind chill and excessive wet weather can also impair plant growth. For vegetables the last frost is a significant time after which tomatoes, cucumbers and so on can be planted outside and potatoes can survive without protection. The first frost signals the end of runner beans and squashes and alerts you to protect tender plants.

Troubleshooting

Dealing with pests

Techniques for keeping out pests include:

* barriers and traps for larger animals;
* introducing or attracting natural predators like birds for insects;
* the removal of infected material in the case of infested leaves and plants;
* the use of vigorous growing plants capable of withstanding attack;
* intercropping and companion planting (see Table 8.6);
* the use of resistant cultivars.

Certain organic chemical controls are allowed by the Soil Association:

* *Advanced slug killer* pellets are based on ferrous phosphate that will break down to iron and phosphate nutrients as part of garden soil. They kill only slugs and snails and are safe for children and pets, birds, hedgehogs and other wildlife. They last for several weeks.
* *Soft soap* is intended to deal with aphids, but they can equally well be sprayed with used washing-up water or a fierce jet of water.

Table 8.6 Common companion plants and their advantages.

Plant	Good with	Repels
Alliums (onion, leek family)	chrysanthemums, carrots, cabbages, sunflowers and tomatoes	slugs, aphids, carrot fly, cabbage worms
Asparagus	tomatoes	nematodes
Basil	asparagus	asparagus beetle, mosquitoes and flies
Borage	all	multiple pests
Carrots	leeks	onion fly
Chervil	lettuce	aphids
Chives	cabbage, carrots	cabbage worms, carrot fly, aphids

Table 8.6 (Continued)

Plant	Good with	Repels
Coriander	green leafs	aphids
Dill	cabbage, carrots	aphids, spider mites, squash bugs, cabbage looper
Garlic	roses	aphids, cabbage looper, ants, rabbits, cabbage maggot
Geraniums	many	leafhoppers, Japanese beetles
Hyssop	cabbage	cabbage moth larvae, cabbage butterflies
Leeks	carrots	carrot fly
Marigold	many	(produce a pesticidal chemical from their roots) nematodes, beet leaf hoppers, many other pests incl. greenfly and blackfly
Nasturtium	cabbage	caterpillars
Oregano	cabbage, lettuce	aphids
Peppermint	cabbage	cabbage fly, ants, cabbage looper
Petunia	many	leafhoppers, Japanese beetles, aphids, asparagus beetle
Sage	carrots, cabbages	cabbage flies, carrot fly, black flea beetle, cabbage looper, cabbage maggot
Spearmint	cabbage	ants, aphids
Sunflower	lettuce	aphids
Tansy	many	flying insects (*Ichneumonid* wasps), Japanese beetles, striped cucumber beetles, squash bugs and sugar ants
Tomatoes	asparagus	asparagus beetle
Yarrow	many	attracts many pollinators and ladybirds

- *Sulphur*, mixed with water (it doesn't dissolve) can be sprayed on fungal infections.

Dealing with slugs

Slugs can be discovered sheltering in dark, damp hideouts during daytime, venturing out to feed at night. They are most active in spring or early summer, and are particularly fond of delphiniums, French marigolds, young brassicas, lettuces and potato tubers. Once they have found a good food

Figure 8.26 Companion planting in a polytunnel.

Figure 8.27 Slugs can be beautiful – except when they're devouring your cabbages!

source, on successive days they will follow their slime trail back to the same site. Other slugs can join this trail to target particular 'victim' plants or garden patches, favouring young shoots or slightly vulnerable leaves. This means decoys can be set and the slugs harvested after three or four days when a good crowd has got the message. Good decoys include:

- piles of leaves of the above plants and comfrey leaves;
- animal bones with some meat left on;
- a shallow container of beer with a 'ramp' for the creatures to crawl into and drown.

These can be placed near vulnerable plots or in a plot before planting, with the slugs being harvested over a few subsequent nights (days in the case of beer traps).

In the daytime you can hunt for the blighters under traps such as stones or lengths of slabwood placed between crop rows, but inspect the traps regularly. Slugs can be thrown in the compost bin where they help to break down paper and cardboard, and their eggs will be consumed by predators. Or they can be fed to ducks.

If you keep ducks, allow them to roam around the vegetable garden. They will root out and eat the slugs as a delicacy. Do not do this with hens as they will scratch up your plants! Other predators include ground beetles, hedgehogs, blackbirds, song thrushes, frogs, toads and newts. Encouraging these things into your growing area makes good sense.

Biological control is also possible by purchasing tiny worms called nematodes, which kill the slugs. They only last about six weeks, however. Apply when the soil temperature is over 5 °C (40 °F) but the soil must not be waterlogged or they will drown. For vulnerable potatoes apply six to seven weeks prior to harvest. As they may harm innocent water snails, keep them away from ponds.

Dealing with diseases

General advice for protecting crops from diseases:

- Plant sensibly;
- Swap and buy from people you trust;
- Maintain hygiene on tools, clothes, flower pots and so on;
- Create a healthy living soil with appropriate additions of compost;
- Avoid too much nitrogen and not enough potassium;
- Rotate crops.

An organic non-chemical treatment for dealing with diseases once they have arrived is to compost the offending material at 80 °C, at which point most weeds, pathogens and pests will be destroyed but the nitrifying bacteria will survive. This is done by covering a good mass material to keep it warm. It will generate its own heat and self combust. Specific diseases and pests are mentioned above, and others are:

- *Black spot* affects the rose family in the summer. Spots grow on the leaf until it dies and falls off. Remove and hot compost diseased leaves. Black spot is a symptom of infertile soil, so mulch with compost in spring.
- *Blight,* a fungus affecting potatoes and tomatoes, is identified by grey/brown patches on leaves. It spreads in damp, warm conditions. Hot

compost affected foliage quickly. If the outbreak is widespread, remove all foliage but keep it off the ground. Leave potatoes in the soil for a couple of weeks and harvest.

- *Canker* is a general term for an infected area of trees and shrubs sparked by careless damage to the bark. Cut out and burn the area. Paint the remaining exposed wood with copper sulphate solution.
- *Club root* is described above. There is no cure, but crop rotation and liming before the brassicas is the best defence.
- *Coral spot* occurs on fruit tree and bush branches, such as redcurrants. This fungal infection may be caused by an overdose of nitrates in fresh manure. Cut affected parts with clean secateurs and burn.
- *Damping off* is often found in greenhouses and polytunnels, attacking seedlings just above the soil and causing routes and stems to rot. It is usually caused by growing seedlings too close together in wet, poorly ventilated conditions. Improve ventilation and keep plants well spaced.
- *Fire blight* infects trees and shrubs and is spread by pollinating insects. Identified by withering leaves and flowers; twigs exude a slime. Cut off and burn affected parts.
- *Gall* is a lumpy abnormal growth on a root, stem or leaf. Not a problem unless it's on brassicas, in which case it could be club root. See above.
- *Grey mould,* or *botrytis,* is a fungus that affects strawberries, lettuce, tomato and cucumbers. It can be caused by cold, wet weather, overcrowding and the rough handling of seedlings. Alter the conditions and compost affected plants as above.
- *Honey fungus* kills trees and is identified by a fan of white fungal growth below the bark near the ground. There is no choice but to dig up the tree and burn it.
- *Powdery mildew* tends to occur in dry spells on many different kinds of plants. Mulching the soil after watering may help.
- *Rust* is rust-coloured spots on the underside of leaves which can spread to flowers and stems, often a sign of potash deficiency. Comfrey liquid, seaweed or wood ash will protect the following year's plants.
- *Scab* affects the leaves of apples and pears and vegetables such as potato, beetroot and radish. Cut out affected areas each year. It is caused by the soil being too alkaline. Add compost thoroughly to the plot where they are to be grown next year.

- *Viral infections* are usually spread by insects such as aphids that are hard to identify. In general, remove and destroy all infected material.

When all else fails you can phone and send samples to the HDRA Garden Organic Centre at www.gardenorganic.org.uk.

Fruits and nuts

If you're going to have plants in your garden they might as well be edible in one sense or another, and so shrubs, hedges, bushes and trees as well as other groundcover could produce fruit and nuts. This again is a potentially huge subject so I will just mention a few ideas and tips.

Rhubarb is officially a vegetable but of course everybody uses it as a fruit. I love its unique taste. It can be planted at any time between November and March, in well-manured ground. As soon as growth is spotted you can 'force' it by covering it with a bucket or plant pot with a hole in the top which makes the stems grow long. The soil must be kept moist. Pick from April onwards. Do not harvest during the first year to give the plant time to establish.

Delicious **strawberries** come in many varieties that will ripen at different times of the season and are extremely good ground cover for keeping weeds down. They should ideally be planted in a warm, south-facing slope and encouraged to spread, which they will willingly do almost anywhere.

Figure 8.28 Copper sulphate solution (blue-green) painted on an apple tree to treat canker. (John Hargreaves' OPD.)

Figure 8.29 A newly established fruit area. A south-facing slope has been constructed on at the back with strawberries beginning to spread across from the left. Blackcurrant and gooseberry bushes planted in the foreground on the right, and in the background some young apple varieties. All the soil has been covered in a mulch of woodchip or bark. (George Monbiot's place, Machynlleth.)

Planting and pruning bushes and trees

Siting

Freedom from frost during the budding and blossoming period is the prime consideration in choosing a site. Fruit has high value and so deserves priority in the allocation of space. A site nearer the dwelling will also mean birds might be less likely to pinch your harvest, but vulnerable trees and shrubs will need to be protected with netting. Hazelnuts, too, from cheeky squirrels. Fruit needs shelter from wind and plenty of sunshine to ripen.

There is a small controversy about the relative advantages of using your own rootstock or grafted dwarf tree rootstock. The latter are what are commonly sold commercially, because they will start to bear fruit sooner. But the former can be coaxed, and have the advantage that you know what you are going to get in terms of the complete properties of the tree, and particularly if you ever have to cut the tree back, which provides a way of producing more trees. For more on this see the Exemplary Example of Phil Corbett.

Plums, cherries, peaches, nectarines, apricots and almonds are all part of the genus *Prunus*. Not all will grow in the UK without help, but plums themselves come in around 40 varieties, including gages and damsons. There are nearly 30 cultivars of cherry too. Yet there are a hundred times more varieties of pear, a huge number that itself is dwarfed by the number of known cultivars of apple, of which there are over 7,500! Perhaps around 1,500 are recorded as having been grown in the UK. It's an astonishing variety, given how few are commercially grown and supplied to shops.

You would be doing yourself, your taste buds, biodiversity and future generations a favour by experimenting with different varieties. If you're moving onto land and plan on growing an orchard, you would do well to

Figure 8.30 A young walnut tree fruiting. (Phil Corbett's nursery – see Exemplary Examples.)

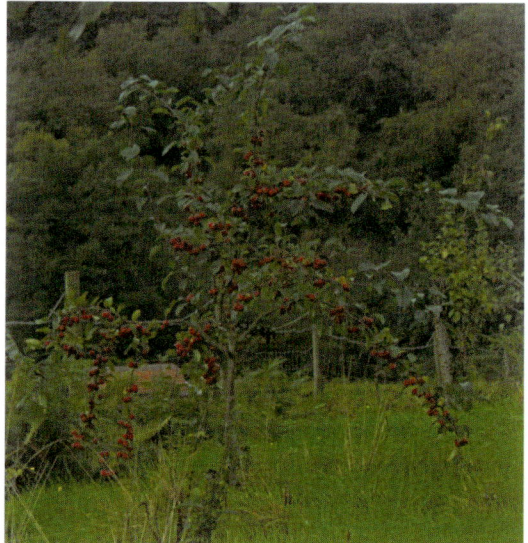

Figure 8.31 A crab-apple tree on a dwarf rootstock. The apples' redness makes a brilliant contrast amidst the green landscape. The fruit is good for making jelly – Dan and Sarah Moody, on whose land this sits, like to make jelly flavoured with mint and rosemary. They also add it to the cider they produce, to provide tannin, and make wine with them.

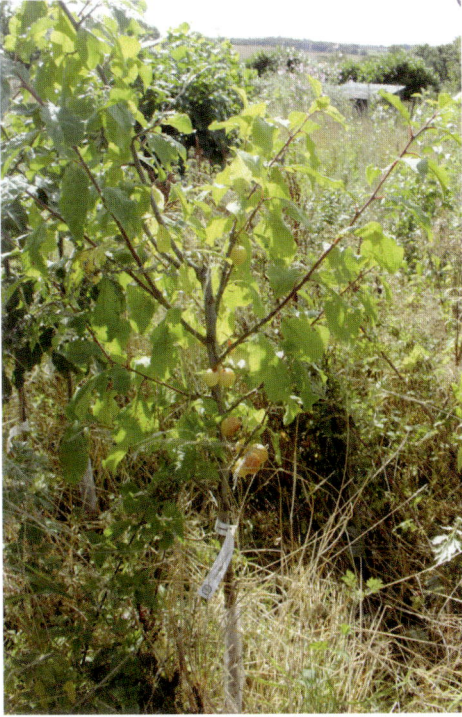

Figure 8.32 A young Victoria plum tree fruiting. (Phil Corbett's nursery – see Exemplary Examples).

Figure 8.33 'Red Devil' apple variety (Phil Corbett's nursery – see Exemplary Examples).

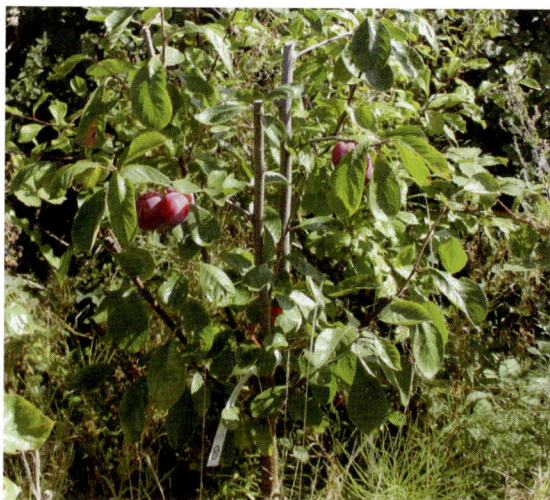

Figure 8.34 (left) 'Scrumptious' apple variety (Phil Corbett's nursery – see Exemplary Examples).

plant at least 30 varieties of apple and perhaps 10–15 of pear to evaluate over a few years which ones thrive under the local conditions and which ones, of these, you like.

Most bushes and trees are ideally planted in the late autumn to early spring. This is also when pruning should mostly be done (Jan–Feb), except for top fruit containing stones, which are pruned mid-May–August. For soft fruit members of the *Rubus* genus, such as raspberries, blackberries, their crossbreed loganberries, and dewberries, the general pruning principle is to cut down to ground level the branches which fruited this year, leaving other branches to produce fruit the following year. For fruit bush members of the genus *Ribes*, such as blackcurrants, redcurrants and gooseberries, you only really need to cut off old dead branches and make room for new shoots. For 'top fruit' *Prunus* and nut trees, such as cherries, apples, pears, almonds and plums, which are not being trained, cut off any deadwood, leave space in the centre for growth, and prevent branches from crossing too near to each other. Hazelnuts and walnut trees can either be left or, if in a productive hedge, trimmed in line.

Hothousing

Our Victorian estate-owning ancestors competed amongst themselves to grow exotic fruit using energy-intensive methods to compensate for the poor climate. Pineapples and oranges, peaches and grapes were grown in hothouses heated by ingenious methods from an array of chimneys in the rear wall fed by a row of coal fires, and underground boilers and

Figure 8.35 A mature orchard at Hockerton (see Exemplary Examples).

Figure 8.36 Grapes and a peach tree in a polytunnel in Pembrokeshire. (John Hargraves' OPD – see Exemplary Examples)

pipe systems, to fresh manure, laboriously changed every three days when the initial heat of decomposition had died down. Fortunately, these days there are solutions that don't involve such labour or fossil fuels. These are, principally:

- better draughtproofing of the polytunnel or greenhouse;
- improved glazing and insulation to retain infra-red heat; and

- additional energy sources: heat pumps powered by wind or PV and a hydropower heat dump if you're fortunate enough to have a stream nearby;
- siting the greenhouse on the south facing side of the dwelling for heat retention.

Espaliering

It's a nice idea if you have a south-facing wall or fence to train trees by espaliering them. This saves space and helps protect them. It involves stapling wires to the surface of the wall, either fanning out from near the base of the tree, and/or horizontally along the wall. They may also be espaliered without the use of a wall, in rows. Branches are encouraged to spread horizontally where they emerge from the vertical trunk by being attached to the wires. Any branches which do not conform to this pattern are strictly removed!

Pests and diseases

Some of the same diseases, such as leaf curl, that affect vegetables can also affect fruit and nut trees. The remedy is the same: if caused by aphids, spray with a hard jet of water; if necessary remove affected parts and heat compost. Some parasites – such as midges – that affect the buds can cause

Figure 8.37 Espaliered apple tree (Gaasbeek, Belgium).
Credit: KVDP.

Figure 8.38 Chickens kept in an orchard. (Andy and Jane's plot, Lammas).

Figure 8.39 Phil Corbett demonstrates how young saplings need to be protected from rabbits, where they are a pest, with a guard.

the flowers or young fruit to drop off. They have a lifecycle that involves a larval stage in the soil below the tree. Besides removing all affected parts, the larvae should ideally be removed. A nice method of doing so in an orchard is to keep hens or ducks and let them roam around. You shouldn't keep more than 60 birds in one acre of orchard or they will cause damage such as over-nitrification of the soil.

Unusual plants

It's also fun to experiment with unusual or neglected species. The chocolate vine is one; originally from eastern Asia, it grows to 10 metres or more in height and the flowers smell of chocolate, with three or four sepals. The fruits are sausage-shaped pods which contain a sweet, edible pulp. The rind is used as vegetable and the vines are traditionally used for basket-weaving.

Another is the tree mallow (*Lavatera arborea*), a profusely growing annual or perennial shrub which traditionally is used for animal fodder. The seeds are also edible by humans and known as 'cheeses', having a subtle nutty flavour.

A third is sea buckthorn (*Hippophae rhamnoides*), a great nitrogen fixer for the surrounding soil – its roots spread a fair distance. The female of the species produces orange berry-like fruit the size of large blackcurrants that are soft, juicy and rich in oils. The fruit is harvested by breaking off the branch, freezing it, then shaking the berries off. This also 'bletts' them, making them less bitter and quite palatable. If pressed, they produce a

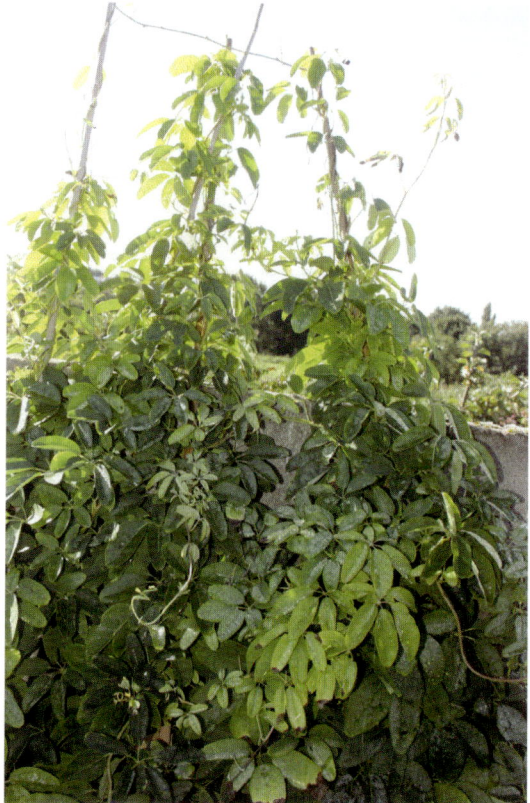

Figure 8.40 Akebia quinata or Chocolate Vine / Five-leaf Akebia (Phil Corbett's nursery – see Exemplary Examples).

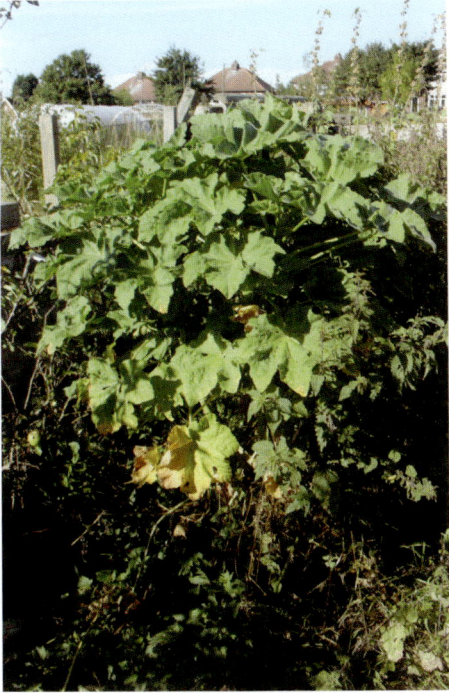

Figure 8.41 A young tree mallow. (Phil Corbett's nursery.)

cream that is useful for beneficial cosmetic purposes, and a syrup that is used to make pies and a conserve jelly with a high level of vitamin C and other beneficial compounds. The plant itself is dense, so good for barrier hedges.

Bees

The orchard is the best place (but not the only one) to keep honey bees, if you plan to do so. Beekeeping is a rewarding activity that can produce a reasonable income. With pollinators on the decline due to intensive agriculture and bees populations threatened by colony collapse disorder there is an additional environmental motivation for becoming an apiarist (as beekeepers are known)! Bee-sides the honey, you'll get beeswax, which can be used to make candles, soap and polish, for added value. And all your plants will benefit from their avid activity as pollinators. Every area has a Beekeepers' Association whose members will help you obtain the necessary equipment and a swarm or two. Check the British Beekeepers' Association website, bbka.org.uk; the Welsh Beekeepers' Association, wbka.com; or the Scottish Beekeepers Association, www.scottishbeekeepers.org.uk.

Figure 8.42 Sea buckthorn: female on the left, male on the right. Needless to say, you need both to produce fruit. (Phil Corbett's nursery.)

Figure 8.43 Making preserves is a great way to save produce for the winter or create an income.

Figure 8.44 Bee-keeping skills can be learnt at your local Beekeepers' Association – this one is in East Carmarthen.
Picture: Chris Jones.

Beehives should be carefully sited in a sheltered but ventilated sunny spot away from places where people will walk, and from frost pockets. But if you have to move them, remember the rule is 'less than three feet or more than three miles' otherwise they may get confused and lost. It costs a little to set up, with the equipment, but after the first year or two, providing you get over 70 lbs of honey per hive, you should be breaking even. Three to five hives can provide the beginning of an income, but the real money comes with over 40 hives, which are likely to be in different locations. May to June is the busiest time: that is when bees swarm, and then August when the honey is harvested. You need to check they have enough to see them through the winter; if not, you feed them a sugar solution.

Chickens, ducks and geese

In a one-planet growing ecosystem, animals fulfil a variety of valuable roles. They can process organic waste into manure; keep some pests at bay by eating them; provide edible produce; and in some cases remove or keep weeds down, preparing land for growing. All livestock must be kept humanely and treated with respect for their needs, which will enable them to thrive. These are encoded in the Five Freedoms for Animal Welfare (see box).

The Five Freedoms for Animal Welfare

1 Freedom from hunger and thirst;
2 Freedom from discomfort and pain;
3 Freedom from disease and injury;
4 Freedom from fear and distress;
5 Freedom to express their normal behaviour.

Figure 8.45 Ducks by a pond at Cassie and Nigel's plot. Lammas.

Poultry are no exception: besides the eggs, of which you can sell any surplus, they produce meat and feathers. Eggs of unusual species fetch more at market: quail, guinea-fowl and rare chicken breeds. They are easy to keep, provided you keep the foxes away. You can keep up to 50 birds before you have to register with the Department for Environment, Food and Rural Affairs (Defra). Ducks need a pond, but will eat your slugs and snails. Hens love to scratch up everything so can be used to keep weeds down and remove pests in an orchard. Geese will roam a lot, requiring a density of 15 birds per acre, and graze on grass, keeping it down. You can even keep pheasant, partridges and turkeys if you want to. In all cases a moveable, solar-battery-powered electric fence is an asset to control their range and contain their labour where you want it. The same applies to pigs (see below).

The source of food is an issue. While chickens will obtain some nutrition from household non-protein scraps, they do need properly balanced mash and grain to thrive and produce a good supply of eggs. A local, organic supply will need to be sourced. Young 'point of lay' birds can be bought from another commercial keeper.

Figure 8.46 and 8.47 Happy hens and a cockerel at Hockerton, with their house (below).

Hens need a constant water supply. They will roost at night in a house, but will need to be put in and let out in the morning. A hen house is easy to fabricate. It needs private nest boxes, a roosting shelf and hay at one end for them to lay, with a small door to extract the eggs. They should be cleaned regularly, because red mite can take hold. This is a tiny parasite which causes discomfort to the birds. Scrupulous and weekly cleaning is the way to tackle an infestation.

Livestock

Keeping stock is a huge responsibility, and, however much you may enjoy working with animals, involves you with significant rules, paperwork, fees for vets and later, of course, abattoirs. Before undertaking it you must have worked with animals before and/or undergone some level of training. You must obtain a holding number from the Rural Payments Agency in Newcastle. Animals must be registered in multiple places. If producing milk you can expect random visits from Food Standards Agency inspectors, who will be looking to count faecal coliforms and the like. The regulations can be off-putting, but are there to prevent the spread of disease. They differ slightly according to the animal species; for example, cattle must be registered with Defra, must be identified by a unique herd mark from your local Animal Health and Veterinary Laboratories Agency (AHVLA), and by a unique County Parish Holding (CPH) number for the pasture that is their home, before you even get them, not to mention have a passport. Their ears will be adorned with two tags bearing this data. It's similar for sheep, deer, pigs and goats, but the ID method is different: pigs are tattooed while sheep are dye-branded and given electronic tags. All this is described on the government website www.gov.uk. Before any animal can be transported it must have a General Licence for Movement.

Stock-proof boundaries are essential. Most young animals need suitable accommodation, with attention being paid to ventilation and hygiene. For milking and dairy work, a clean area and storage suitable for food production is required. You'll need to consider provision for winter feed for some grazing animals: fodder/forage crops for silage or winter grazing (depending on the crop and conditions) include high-protein plants such as: sugar beet, kale, stubble turnip, forage rape, swede, maize, rye, forage peas, lucerne, chicory. So your land-management plan will include fields set aside for growing such crops as well as grazing land, all proportionate to the number of animals you can keep. How much pasture do you need for grazing different animals? The answer is sometimes calculated using livestock units (LSU), where a cow = 1 LSU and a sheep = 0.15 LSU. But other proportions are also used as 'rules of thumb', e.g. 1 pony = 2.5 to 3 cattle = 5 sheep. It really depends on the land type.

It's likely you'll be friendly with your neighbouring farmers, and able to gain advice, contacts and share some equipment. Farmers generally are happy to help each other out, so if you are moving to an area, get to know everyone and offer help in turn, as this is a great way to gain local knowledge. Most important is the relationship with your veterinary practice, who, incidentally, should be transparent with their scale of fees; these could be a significant factor in your business plan, affecting your profit margin.

If you've got the space and if the land isn't suitable for growing crops, then the choice is grazing or woodland, and sometimes both, intermingled (e.g. deer, goats, or pigs can be used to clear or prevent undergrowth in woodland). You don't have to own the animals – you can rent it out to another farmer for grazing, and this might be a good way to learn. If you're going to keep them yourself, it's important to choose breeds that suit your purpose and your land. There are breeder directories online, and breeders are happy to introduce you to the characteristics of particular breeds.

Genetic diversity is declining among livestock as well as farmed plant species. Shockingly, over 90 per cent of crop varieties have disappeared from farmers' fields since 1990 and over 30 per cent of livestock breeds are at risk of extinction. Six breeds are apparently lost every month, an unbelievable statistic.[3] All of this makes humanity vulnerable, since greater variety means greater resilience to disease, parasites and changes in climate and conditions. One of the main causes of depleted livestock variety is the

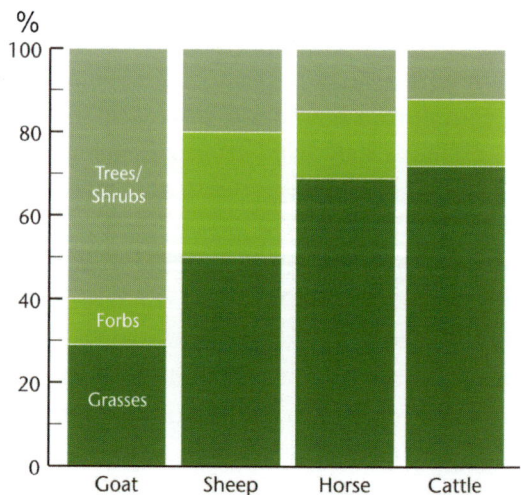

Figure 8.48 The proportion of different dietary requirements of four main grazing animals.[4]

replacement of local varieties by 'improved' or 'exotic' varieties and species. This is a profound reason to choose rare breeds.

The choice of animal might also be determined by the need to use what's called 'targeted grazing[5]' to tackle the problem of unwanted or invasive plant species. This is the use of carefully controlled grazing for improving land health by performing weed control and aiding in habitat restoration. Chief amongst the animals chosen for this task are the goat and the pig.

Goats

Besides milk production, goats have a terrific usefulness if you have previously unmanaged woodland, bracken or other invasive species that need clearing. They will eat almost anything and turn it into milk and meat;[6] they will even clear rushes on upland! But as with all animals grazing in woodland, care must be taken that they do not reduce biodiversity by eating sensitive species. Like most other farm animals, they are herd creatures and so need companions.

Goats are particularly effective at controlling invasive weed/shrub species as they have enzymes in their stomachs which destroy poisons such as Poison Ivy. They actually like weeds, briars and leaves, rather than grass. So goats can be sent onto a plot to remove the undesirable vegetation (from a cow's perspective) before letting cows on to graze the grass. The browse line they create in woodland also allows sunlight to penetrate, permitting grass to grow under the brush.

Different breeds satisfy different requirements. Golden Guernseys are kept for their milk, the Boer breed for meat and the Angora for wool. Rare breeds requiring conservation include the Bagot and Golden Guernsey. All goats need a supply of clean water, and about a quarter of an acre per

Figure 8.49 Goats, extraordinarily agile and strong animals, will eat anything that is within reach, preferring branches and leaves to grass.

animal, with extra-special attention paid to secure fencing, but they do respect water boundaries and electric fences.

Their milk has a higher monetary value than cow milk, and can be used to make cheese very easily. Boil the milk, add some synthetic rennet and it curdles. Sieve this out, allow to drain and pat it into shape; salt to taste. Behold, you have haloumi. Repeat the process with the remaining whey and you have a low-fat soft cheese; you can salt this, but if you sweeten it and perhaps add a dash of cinnamon then you have anari, a delicious Greek sweet.

Pigs

Pigs are so intelligent and useful that it is very tempting not to kill them. If that is what you believe then you had best not keep pigs! They are friendly and extremely useful at both processing a lot of kitchen scraps and rooting around to dig up weeds and prepare land for cultivation. Pigs may be used to control invasive species such as bracken and rhododendron, which will be used as bedding litter by sows. They can be kept in woodland like goats, to clear a sward, but not all year round as they will kill trees by stripping bark.

Saddleback or Gloucester pigs are hardier and less prone to disease. Pigs are typically kept for just a few months to be fattened up while doing a particular job before being sent for slaughter: a single carcass will be processed and halved before being transported with the accompanying paperwork to a butcher to turn into chops, sausages and bacon for your own

Figure 8.50 Piglets being used to clear land prior to cultivation, kept in place with an electric fence (organic smallholding, Carmarthenshire). They were sent to the abattoir two weeks after the photo was taken, with regret.

Figure 8.51 Pig belonging to Jasmine and Simon, Lammas.

Figure 8.52 Sheep on pasture at Hockerton Housing Project, Nottinghamshire.

consumption and sale. Keeping them for much longer than this is counter-productive as they will require feeding above the level of their value, as it's unlikely you will be able to provide sufficient organic waste for them.

Sheep

Sheep provide fertiliser, meat, wool and fleeces, but the fleece wool has little value without considerable time input to turn it into either sufficient clean insulation or yarn and clothing. They can provide milk, but not much per animal. Long-wool animals provide the most wool, but a high propor-tion of the wool from a single sheep is commercially unusable as it is either too dirty or not long or fine enough. However, they require much less ongoing care than other stock, except at lambing time. Unusual breeds can provide more valuable, fine, wool but they will produce less meat than a standard breed. Rare breeds such as Shetland are useful because they do not get foot rot, or 'problems with their bottoms' that common breeds do, and they lamb far more easily. Hebridean, Herdwick, Rough Fell or Swaledale can be kept in mature woodland and actually thrive better on relatively poor forage while usually needing little supplementary feeding.

Cows

Cows require milking, and milk can be processed into butter, yoghurt and cheese, providing a predictable, ongoing income stream. In the UK, except for Scotland, milk can be sold unpasteurised to friends at the farm gate as long as it is labelled correctly (see food.gov.uk), but otherwise is subject to regulation and must be treated. Certain breeds are more suitable for upland, acidic moorland with little grass as they will munch on reeds, which standard Friesian cattle, normally fielded on flatter lowland, will not eat. Highland Cattle and Belted Galloways will produce yield (albeit slightly less than Friesans) from land which is otherwise unproductive. Belted Galloways are extraordinary creatures, reminiscent of pandas. They are called belted because around their shaggy middle is a wide white band, while the rest of the animal, front and back, is black. Fortunately, Belted Galloways are a breed that is recovering from the brink of extinction. If the grazing land is poor, remember that horses survive better on poor quality year-round grazing than cattle.

Other animals

Angora rabbits, llamas and deer are just some of the other species that can be farmed for their meat or the value of their wool. For example, Cwm

Figure 8.53 A family of Highland cattle.

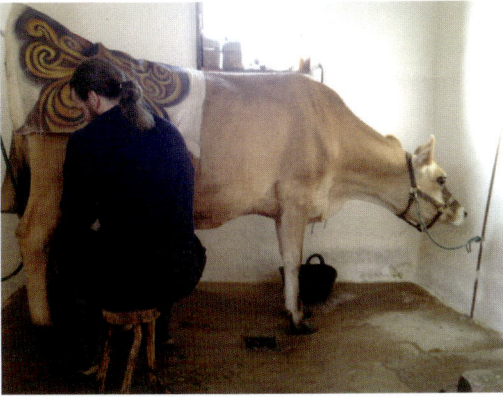

Figure 8.54 Paul Wimbush milking his cow at Lammas.

Figure 8.55 Hockerton lake is stocked with carp.

Coed Farm is a prospective OPD in Powys that is using Angora rabbits to produce their soft wool for sale. Pete Barker notes that 'Angora is a very fine, lightweight and very warm wool' which is 'rare and consequently commands high prices'. The wool will be sold together with high-quality knitwear, predominantly via the Internet. This income will be supplemented by local sales of surplus vegetables, eggs, honey, fruit and timber products, including willow baskets and charcoal, as it is labour-intensive and on its own unlikely to generate profit.

Fish

Fish such as carp can be successfully farmed with little time input. This strategy would work well within an ecological sewage treatment system where the final stage is the output of the purified water into a lake, such as a reed bed or WET system. This is the case at Hockerton where the one acre lake is full of carp which can be and often are net caught and consumed by residents or sold at market. In theory, a lake could be stocked with other species such as trout and access to the lake sold for recreational fishing to generate income.

Further reading

Ryrie, Charlie, *Soil,* Gaia Books, 2001.

Elphinstone, Margeret and Langley, Julia, *The Organic Gardener's Handbook* Thorsons, 1995.

Buczacki. S and Harris K, *Pests, Diseases and Disorders of Garden Plants,* William Collins, 2014.

Laughton, R., *Surviving and Thriving on the Land: How to use your time and energy to run a successful smallholding,* Green Books, 2008.

Larkcom, Joy, *Grow Your Own Vegetables,* Frances Lincoln, 2002.

Larkcom, Joy & Phillips, Roger *The Organic Salad Garden*, Frances Lincoln, 2003.

Dowding, Charles *Organic Gardening: The Natural No-dig Way,* Green Books, 2013.

Fearnley-Whittingstall, H, *The River Cottage Meat Book* (2004).

Notes

1   *Lower Blakemere Farm, Herefordshire HR2 9PX. www.wigglywigglers.co.uk*
2   Sources:
    1   Hessayon, Dr. D.G. *The Garden Expert series*, Pan Britannica.
    2   Elphinstone, M. and Langley, J. *The Organic Gardener's Handbook*, Thorson's, 1995.
    3   *Organic Way,* the member's magazine of the Henry Doubleday Research Association.
3   According to the UN Food and Agriculture Organization. See: www.fao.org/docrep/007/y5609e/y5609e02.htm. Retrieved January 2014.
4   From Mayle, Brenda, *Domestic Stock Grazing to Enhance Woodland Biodiversity,* Forestry Commission, September 1999, available at: http://www.forestry.gov.uk/pdf/fcin28.pdf/$FILE/fcin28.pdf. Retrieved January 2014.
5   Specific information on targeted grazing is available at: www.webpages.uidaho.edu/rx-grazing. Retrieved February 2014.
6   See Mayle, Brenda, *Op. cit.*

Getting from A to B is quite likely to form a large part of your carbon footprint. This is particularly the case if you are living in a rural location where it is probable that public transport is poor and you may have to travel some distance to the nearest town. So the best thing you can do to reduce the environmental impact of your travel needs is to choose a location for your dwelling as close as you can to a good bus service or train station.

After the requirement for south-facing land and accommodation, this is probably the second most important choice you can make regarding location. (On the other hand, people who live over 45 miles from a large urban centre tend to consume less and travel less than those, say, 10–30 miles away, who use their cars the most, according to research.[1])

So what might be the best and worst tactics for reducing the environmental impact of your travel? Here they are, from best to worst:

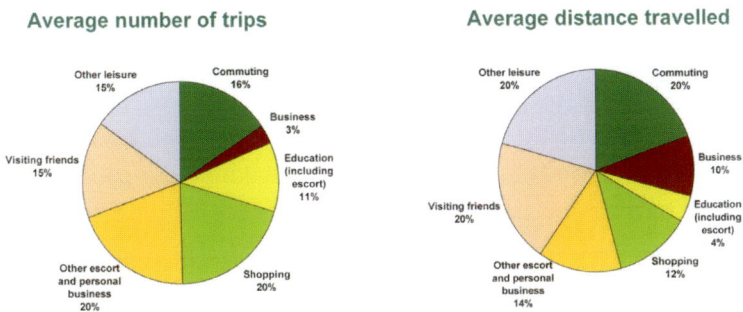

Figure 9.1 Most people's travel needs in terms of distance travelled come from social (54 per cent), commuting and business (30 per cent), followed by shopping (12 per cent) and school runs (4 per cent).[2]
Credit: Great Britain National Travel Survey 2012

1   Avoid motorised transport completely;
2   use public transport;
3   use a car share powered by renewable energy;
4   use a car share powered by petrol;
5   use a car share powered by diesel;
6   have your own small car;
7   have your own larger vehicle and use it for every trip.

Walking and cycling

Walking and cycling are the most common ways to avoid motorised transport. Not only are they healthy, they help you to notice what is happening around you as well as stop and talk to people you meet. Walking frequently along the same route you'll notice all the subtle changes that happen as the seasons rotate. Walking and cycling help to nurture a sense of community.

How should you choose a bike?

When choosing a bike, pick one that is as light in weight but sturdy and with the best quality components, especially gears, that you can afford. Being of light weight and having good gear ratios can make all the difference to your speed and ease of cycling on hills and long stretches. While mountain bikes give more grip on difficult terrain, they will not be as efficient to ride as road bikes on the roads, because road bikes have narrower tyres that produce less friction with the road surface (although some tyres have raised central treads to avoid this). Hybrid bikes are a medium between the two if you think you will be riding as much on the road as off it.

Maintain the bike well, lubricating and cleaning it regularly, and keep the tyres pumped to maximum pressure, as this can make all the difference to the amount of effort required to pedal. Kids can be encouraged to cycle from an early age, firstly with trailers and then with their own bikes.

For conveying goods such as shopping, or taking your produce to your customers, baskets and trailers can be added. There is now a huge range of bikes available that can be used for carrying goods – or children. You could even purchase a rickshaw. In many parts of the world, owning a bike is something the poorest people aspire to; it can make the biggest difference to their prosperity by saving time and bringing them closer to the markets for their produce. Many goods in developing countries are transported by bike in a huge number of imaginative ways!

Figure 9.2 With the right touring bike, you can go anywhere.
Credit: Keithonearth via Wikimedia Commons.

Figure 9.3 Delivery bikes and trailers come in all sizes for transporting all kinds of things – even children!
Credit: Workcycles at en.wikipedia

Electric bikes

Then there are electric or e-bikes, for those who want some assistance. Electric bikes, like electric cars, can be charged from renewable electricity sources, if you have any, or from a 'green' mains electricity charge point. Conventional bikes can even be converted into e-bikes using a kit (see illustration). You don't need a driving licence for electric bikes.

Electric Bicycle made using a retail conversion kit and a standard steel-frame bicycle

Speed controller (housed in smaller canvas bag) is the central hub, receiving connections from the throttle, the motor, and the battery

Thumb throttle (variable speed)

Direct-drive hub motor integrated into the wheel

Battery (housed in larger canvas bag and attached to the frame)

Electrical cable running from the motor to the controller

Standard steel bicycle frame

Figure 9.4 How to convert a normal bike to an electric one.
Credit: Mike Fairbanks.

Electric bikes come in two main types:

1 the 'pedelec': this monitors your pedalling and automatically adds a certain amount of motor assistance;
2 the 'twist-n-go': the motor comes on at the flick of a switch – but you must be pedalling.

Motors also have two main types with the following characteristics, although the technology is improving with every year:

1 hub-mounted in one of the wheels – tend to be quieter but less powerful;
2 mounted in the crank/pedal area – tend to be noisier but better on steep hills.

When choosing an electric bike, check both the quality of the bike and of the electric assistance system. Electric bikes are heavier than the non-electric variety – the battery and motor can double the weight – so it is important to match your choice to the terrain on which you will be mostly using it and to the types of journey you'll mostly be making. If possible, give it a real-world test drive before buying.

Remember that batteries tend to work less well in low temperatures. Lithium batteries are lighter than nickel metal hydride ones. Larger batteries (with more capacity) will give you more power and run for longer. All batteries eventually need replacing. With an electric bike the law says you

can't have more than 200 watts of extra power or 15 mph of extra speed
– otherwise it's a moped or scooter! So batteries won't give more than 250
W. It also has to weigh less then 40 kg, and have pedals. See the section on
batteries in the Energy chapter.

As with all bikes, choose one with good quality gears that are easy to use
and have the ratios that match your needs.

Other electric vehicles

If you're going to have a powered vehicle, the low-carbon fuel choice
is down to either biofuels or electric. If you are generating a sufficient
amount of your own renewable electricity, the advantage of electric vehicles is that the batteries can store the power generated when you don't
need it for other purposes. All electric vehicles are also exempt from vehicle
tax. Therefore they are very cheap to run. Electric vehicles, unlike ones
running on biofuels, also don't pollute the air where they are used and
are quiet. Since there may have been fossil fuels used in the production of
biofuels, electric vehicles running on renewable electricity would also, on
balance, be associated with fewer carbon emissions over their lifetime.

But electric cars are not cheap, even with a (currently) 20 per cent up
to £5,000 government purchase grant for a new model (£8,000 for a van).
Since the fuel may often be effectively free or very cheap, then the further

Figure 9.5 The Renault single-
seater Twizy, one of the most
popular electric vehicles in 2012. It
has a range of up to 62 miles (100
km). At the time of writing, second-
hand versions were available for
around £4,000.

an electric vehicle travels each day, the more cost-effective it is to its owners, as long as they are frequently charged. They are therefore worth buying if a lot of use is to be got from them, for instance for community use in car-share schemes.

Presently, the maximum distance driveable by an electric car on a single charge is around 170 km or 100 miles. In winter, with the heater on and stop-start traffic, this can drop to 60 miles. But there are an increasing number of places where you can charge the battery up in half an hour for free, partly as a result of the British government's Plugged-in Places programme. These places include National Trust properties, some train stations and motorway service stations, where often you will find that renewable electricity generator Ecotricity has installed free charging points.

Figure 9.6 The Nissan Leaf (2012 model), another popular electric car. Credit: Nissan.

Figure 9.7 Ecotricity's CEO Dale Vince standing by a chargepoint at a Welcome Break motorway service station. Credit: Ecotricity.

Many people purchase an electric vehicle for local use only. This may be a two-wheeler or other small, purpose-built, low range, agile vehicle. (At least it can get you to the train station for longer or family journeys, where you might well find a charging point).

Figure 9.8 A Razor eSpark push-type electric scooter.
Credit: AngryJulieMonday on Wikimedia Commons.

Figure 9.9 This Optima Plus electric scooter by Hero Electric has a 250 W BLDC motor and 20 Ah battery and typically consumes approximately 1 KWh from a normal home power supply. The manufacturers claim a maximum range of 70 km on a full charge cycle.
Credit: Viswaprabha.

Smaller electric scooters, motorbikes and delivery vehicles have been around for longer, so it's possible to pick up cheap used models. They vary in size, from the type of scooter a child might use to sit-ons and high-performance models – and milk floats. The bikes and scooters compare well in terms of performance with diesel and petrol models. There are also a couple of internal combustion/electric hybrid scooters on the market. Some models can fully charge in an hour, and one model allows for an easy battery swap so you can charge a battery separately from the vehicle and exchange them when empty. There is even an electric off-road quad bike available now.

Charging

The British government offers a domestic chargepoint grant of up to 75 per cent (capped at £1,000) off the total capital costs of the chargepoint plus associated installation costs. There are four modes or types of charging:

- Mode 1. Domestic AC socket with extension cable: the electrical installation must comply with safety regulations and have a residual current device (RCD) and earth leakage protection. This is the simplest solution. It uses three-pin domestic-style square plugs/sockets certified against BS1363 (rated 13 amp).
- Mode 2. Domestic AC socket, dedicated cable with protection: provided on a single-phase or three-phase network, with the same safety requirements. This solution is more expensive. This and the following two modes can use a three-pin plug or industrial-style blue commando five-pin plugs/sockets (rated 16 A, 32 A or 63 A), certified against the international standard IEC60309. Charging points equipped with Type 2 (e.g. EN 62196-2) seven-pin sockets can only be installed outside at domestic properties.
- Mode 3. AC charging point: As for mode 2, but with the charging control system function on the vehicle charging device and an EVSE control module in the charging installation.
- Mode 4. Direct current (DC) connection: Similar to mode 3, but the AC is converted to DC, which the battery prefers, drastically speeding up the charging time. Requires an AC/DC-sensitive RCD on the network side.

Mode 1 charging points can be installed anywhere. You need a tethered cable and plug (e.g. SAE J1772) installed inside or outside the property. Charging points are typically rated at 3.7 kW (16 amps) or 7 kW (32 amps,

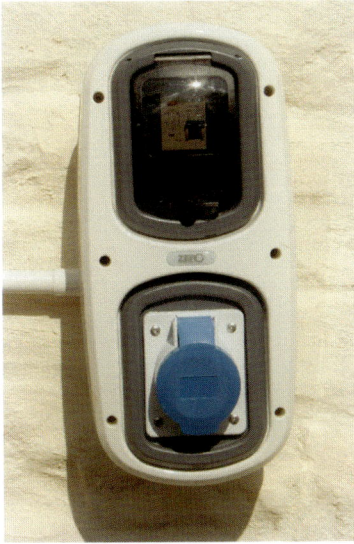

Figure 9.10 A 'Mode 1' domestic chargepoint on a Welsh organic farm that runs off solar panels.

which will charge faster) power output. These are much faster than a standard 3 kW household three-pin connection.

Using dedicated fast or quick/rapid charging equipment offers distinct advantages over using a standard three-pin UK household connection (BS1363):

- They can handle higher electrical currents for longer and are IP rated to withstand weather;
- A 32 amp (7 kW) single phase AC fast charging point can charge an EV typically twice as fast. A 50 kW DC fast charging point can charge even faster, achieving 80 per cent State Of Charge (SOC) in 30 minutes;
- Fitting a dedicated charging point with a high-capacity connection will ensure future upgrades to higher power, faster chargers is made easier.
- Many charging point and energy suppliers offer products that include installation and care packages, taking the stress out of owning a charging point.

Electric cars are relatively new and are slowly improving on cost, range and charging times, helped by improvements in battery technology. They are noiseless and extremely smooth to drive.

For most people the choice will be between a petrol or diesel vehicle, a hybrid or an electric vehicle. The carbon footprint of vehicles can be compared by looking at their emissions per kilometre or their fuel consumption. (European legislation for new cars says that they should not emit more than an average of 130 grams of CO_2 per kilometre (gCO_2/km) by 2015

Figure 9.11 Charging a community-owned Nissan Leaf electric car at Tŷ Solar.

Figure 9.12 A community-owned Nissan Leaf electric car.

(approximately equivalent to 5.6 litres per 100 km (l/100 km) of petrol or 4.9 l/100 km of diesel) and 95g by 2020 (about 4.1 l/100 km of petrol or 3.6 l/100 km of diesel). For vans the target is 175 gCO$_2$/Km by 2017 and 147g by 2020.)

Hybrid cars

Hybrid cars are generally more expensive because you are paying for two different powertrains in the same vehicle. They might be considered if you are going to be travelling further than the range of an electric vehicle on a regular basis. But you also need to consider how it affects the majority of

Figure 9.13 The Toyota Prius (2012 model), the world's most popular hybrid car. Emissions are an average of 96 gCO_2/km and fuel efficiency around 5.3 l/100 km.
Credit: Ifcar via Wikimedia Commons.

the trips you are going to make: usually the electric motor drives the first part of the journey until the battery runs out, at which point the internal combustion engine kicks in. If most of the trips are going to be made using the electric motor this needs to be factored into your calculations. Petrol or diesel engines on some vehicles are now very efficient and for many journeys can be equivalent in terms of carbon dioxide emissions to some hybrids.

Petrol-diesel vehicles – reducing fuel consumption

Of course most people still drive conventional petrol- or diesel-fuelled cars. Is it environmentally better to drive a new car than an old car and keep it running as long as possible? The answer depends on its fuel efficiency, but in general the answer is: newer cars are more efficient. When choosing a second-hand petrol or diesel car, if you don't know what the fuel consumption is, try seeing how much friction there is in the transmission. This means driving the car, then letting it coast either in neutral or in gear and seeing how long it takes to slow down. There is a vast difference between models. The ones which coast for the furthest distance will have the best fuel efficiency.

Driving efficiently

Fuel consumption also depends enormously on driver behaviour. Here are ten tips on how to reduce fuel consumption, some of them obvious, some of them less so:

1   accelerate slowly and smoothly and change to a higher gear as soon as possible;

2   don't drive over 60 miles an hour unless you have to. Driving at 85 mph can use up to 25 per cent more fuel than driving at 70 mph, which uses 8 per cent more than driving at 60 mph. Every car has a 'sweet speed' at which it uses the fuel most efficiently, always in top gear, usually around 50 mph;

3   minimise the use of the brake; do this by looking far ahead and anticipating, and leaving space behind the vehicle in front, so that you can take your foot off the accelerator and decelerate naturally ahead of junctions, and so on;

4   close the windows if travelling over 50 mph to reduce drag;

5   keep the tyres pumped up to the correct pressure;

6   use the air conditioning and heating sparingly;

7   remove roof racks and other additions that can cause friction when they are not being used;

8   don't carry unnecessary excess weight;

9   switch off the engine when stationary for more than a minute;

10 service the car regularly, including cleaning and replacing filters.

Sharing cars

Sharing is a great way to reduce car ownership. There are various ways to share vehicles. If you have a vehicle always try to offer somebody a lift if you can. There are various lift-share websites that aid in this such as liftshare. com. Up a level is car pooling and a level above that is a community-owned car scheme.

Car pools work by members agreeing to let other people use their cars for a fee, usually a payment by the hour. There may be one in your area: check carplus.org.uk. There are instructions on how to set up a carpool on this website.

Community car-owning schemes work by clubbing together to collectively purchase, tax and insure one or more vehicles. Members either pay a share of the overall cost in order to finance the purchase, or take out a loan and repay it with a proportion of the hourly hire fee, which should also cover running and maintenance costs. A booking system (such as Google calendar) is also required. The following additional advice comes from Llanidloes car club:

- Store the key in a secure box with a code lock;
- Evaluate the per-mile charge every three months;
- You will need a bank account, three signatories and an organiser to keep copies of members' driving licences;
- Have a log book in the car to record mileages and general notes such as phone numbers;
- Have a system for undertaking routine maintenance each month.

LPG and diesel

Compared to petrol, diesel vehicles have around 10 per cent lower CO_2 emissions per kilometre travelled because the engines are more efficient. Diesel vehicles also emit lower levels of carbon monoxide and hydrocarbons than equivalent new petrol vehicles but greater levels of NOx. LPG or liquid petroleum gas is a blend of propane and butane, produced as a by-product of oil refining or from natural gas fields. It has broadly the same carbon emissions as diesel but is around half the price. Vehicles can be bought or converted to run on LPG. It costs about £1,500 to convert a vehicle. LPG refuelling sites are now common around the country.

Biofuels

Biodiesel can be used at a 5 per cent blend in existing diesel engines with no need for modification; the same applies to bioethanol in petrol engines. But there have been many concerns about the sustainability of first-generation biofuels, as well as questions about the life-cycle greenhouse gas emissions of all biofuels. These emissions can be reduced in any of these six ways:

1 By growing dedicated energy crops which do not require prime agricultural land;
2 Growing crops which require limited use of fertiliser and other inputs;
3 Growing crops which require less intensive or energy-hungry processing;
4 Growing crops which help to increase soil carbon sequestration on marginal land;
5 Developing more integrated production systems for food and fuel, such as through agro-forestry and the greater use of co-products;
6 Reusing cooking fuels.

Types of biofuels

There are many types of biofuels and none of them are suitable for small-scale production, though at a farm or community scale, it might be possible to use anaerobic digestion to generate biogas. To avoid confusion, it might be an idea to go through the main different types of biofuels.

Liquids

Bioethanol

In the sugar-to-ethanol process, sucrose is obtained from sugar crops such as sugar cane, sugar beet and sweet sorghum, and fermented to ethanol, which is then concentrated. The starch-to-ethanol process requires, in addition to this, the hydrolysis of starch into glucose, and uses more energy than the sugar-to-ethanol route.

Conventional biodiesel

Biodiesel may be produced from soybean, canola, oil palm or sunflower, animal fats and used cooking oil, which are, again, sensitive to feedstock prices. The conversion process uses methanol or ethanol. Untreated raw oils are sometimes used, but this is not recommended due to the risks of engine damage and gelling of the lubricating oil.

Hydrotreated vegetable oil (HVO)

This is produced by hydrogenating vegetable oils or animal fats and is also known as hydrogenation-derived renewable diesel (HDRD). The process has not yet been fully commercialised.

Pyrolysis

Pyrolysis, like gasification (below), involves heating biomass with limited oxygen supply. Pyrolysis oil, or other thermochemically derived biomass liquids, can be used directly as a fuel, or converted to biodiesel, but the process is still in the demonstration stage. In the future, plants such as miscanthus and other energy crops may be used as well as agricultural 'waste' products such as straw.

Pyrolysis also produces biochar, which can be used to improve soil texture and ecology, as well as sequester atmospheric carbon in the soil, increasing its ability to retain nutrients and release them slowly.

Gases

Biomethane or biogas

Biogas (biomethane, CH_4, usually with some CO_2 and hydrogen sulphide present) can be produced through anaerobic (without oxygen) digestion of organic waste, animal manure and sewage sludge, or dedicated crops such as maize, grass and crop wheat. It also produces fertiliser. Anaerobic digestion is becoming popular but has a high up-front cost and needs a reliable, year-round supply of feedstock.

The biogas produced may be used to generate heat and electricity, or upgraded to biomethane by removing the other gases. It is then chemically identical to 'natural gas'. It can be injected into the natural gas grid or used as fuel in natural gas vehicles. The numbers of natural gas vehicles (NGV) have started to grow rapidly, particularly during the last decade.

Bio synthetic gas (bio-syngas or bio-SNG)

Bio-SNG is processed from biomass using gasification, which produces a mixture of gases. To generate biomethane from bio-SNG, it needs to be cleaned, filtered and processed further, using advanced catalytic and chemical processing techniques; these will ultimately combine the hydrogen and carbon monoxide in the gas to form methane. It's an intensive process and not amenable to small-scale production.

Reusing cooking oils

It is possible to run some diesel engines on vegetable oil, new or reused. Legally, anyone can make up to 2,000 litres of biofuel a year for their own use without registering to pay Excise Duty. But the technology as well as the possibility of ruining your engine mean that it's probably not worth trying to do it yourself. If you want to run your diesel vehicle on raw vegetable oil, used cooking oils or fuels derived from them, then you can convert the vehicle to run on biodiesel. Vegetable oil (reused or not) can be purchased from reputable suppliers.[3]

To adapt a diesel vehicle you would need to check first what types of fuel your engine can take and whether you can buy a conversion kit for it. The kits heat the vegetable oil before it goes into the engine, thereby reducing its viscosity. There are several commercially available kits, as well as homemade conversions. Whichever option you go for you're advised to monitor or change fuel filters on a more frequent basis for at least the first six months after the transition, until the system has been cleaned of deposits. Remember that biodiesel is a good solvent and may soften or dissolve rubber parts, so replace these with plastic alternatives.

It's possible to collect used vegetable cooking oil from cafes, pubs and canteens, and process it into a fuel. Usually this is done commercially and you can buy direct from such companies. For those who do wish to explore the possibility of making their own biodiesel from used vegetable oil, training is supplied by John Nicholson's Bio-Power[4] organisation in North Wales. John observes that success depends upon the make and model of vehicle. Many older diesel vehicles will run fine on reused vegetable oil biofuel, especially older Mercedes, Volvo, Land Rovers, Renaults, Peugeots, and so on. More modern engines are designed not to run on them.

Biodiesel can also be used in residential oil boilers, but it's a good idea to consult a professional heating contractor about the requirements of your particular model before doing so.

Livestock

When all is said and done there are always the traditional methods: animals. It's only 20 years since I met my sons' maternal great-grandfather coming into the village from his land in the Greek Cypriot Troidos mountains,

Figure 9.14 Rachel Shiamh's straw bale home (see Exemplary Example) does not have vehicular access, and so all building materials had to be delivered by horse-pulled cart from the road.

Figure 9.15 Henry the horse is used by Dan Moody on his one-planet development near Cardiff for ploughing and extracting timber from woodland.

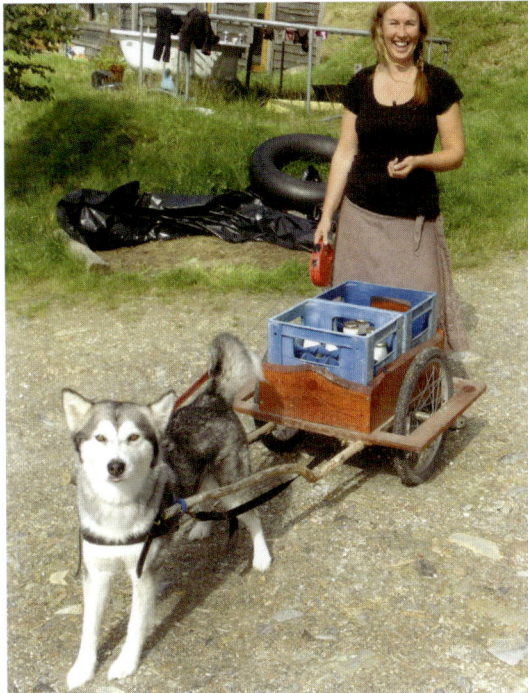

Figure 9.16 Every day Hoppi Wimbush and her husky enjoy delivering milk taken from their cow to other households at Lammas.

leading a goat bearing two baskets laden with freshly picked olives and carob. Animals are still in use as beasts of burden or modes of transport in most parts of the world. Low-impact and One Planet Developments are reviving this tradition.

Horses can be used for ploughing, for pulling carts and for extracting trees from mixed woodland as they were before the huge conifer plantations. Certain breeds of dogs can be used to pull carts, famously huskies.

Mules, goats and donkeys can be used as beasts of burden. In all cases their manure, mixed with straw, is good for the land. And they make great companions.

Notes

1 http://persquaremile.com/2011/07/12/drive-a-lot-housing-density-may-not-be-to-blame and http://persquaremile.com/2014/01/09/carbon-footprint-may-low-think. Accessed January 2014.
2 Great Britain National Travel Survey 2012, tables NTS0401 and NTS0402 at https://www.gov.uk/government/uploads/system/uploads/attachment_data/file/243957/nts2012-01.pdf.
3 See a list for example at www.petrolprices.com/biodiesel-companies.html.
4 Contact John Nicholson at biopoweruk@hotmail.com.

Part Four
Exemplary Examples

10 Exemplary Examples

Contents

1 Hockerton Housing Project

Not far from the minster town of Southwell, Nottinghamshire, Hockerton housing cooperative is the UK's best-known early example of communal one planet living (if you don't count the Centre for Alternative Technology in Wales or Scotland's Findhorn community). Five households have been forging a new way of living there for 15 years that is more sustainable than most in the sleepy next-door village of Hockerton. When I went to see them it was a lovely late summer's day. All of the trees and bushes were laden with fruit.

I was taken on a tour by Bill, a resident who'd been living there for about seven years with his family. We explored the ten acres of orchards and fields

Figure 10.1 The view from the south looking over the lake towards the terrace.

Figure 10.2 Part of the vegetable garden.

Figure 10.3 Looking east from the roof of the terrace. On the left is the earth-covered rear of the homes, which merges into the orchard. To the right is the lake. The chimney is for natural ventilation. At the top of the glazing can be seen the photovoltaic array.

where residents grow 40 per cent of their food, keeping bees, sheep and hens. The community is about two-thirds self-sufficient in vegetables but less for fruit and meat. The hives most years generate more honey than can be eaten so surplus is exchanged. Winemaking makes use of some fruit/ vegetable excesses.

I was taken next to a pond that collects water filtered for use in their washing machines, sinks and toilets. Drinking water is collected from the glass roof of the conservatory in front of the row of houses via copper pipes, which are slightly antiseptic, and stored in a tank with a capacity sufficient to last around 100 days. The water is passed through a five-micrometre string filter, a carbon filter and a UV-light filter. The community is self-sustaining in water and energy.

All of the effluent is purified using an attractive reed bed at the side of the homes, buzzing with dragonflies and other insects, whose outflow enters a long lake situated along the front of the terrace, which is stocked with carp that is harvested for food or sale, and on which the children go boating. The whole is a haven for wildlife.

The houses themselves are partly earth-covered on the north side, for insulation, and constructed of a shell of dense concrete. The idea is to create

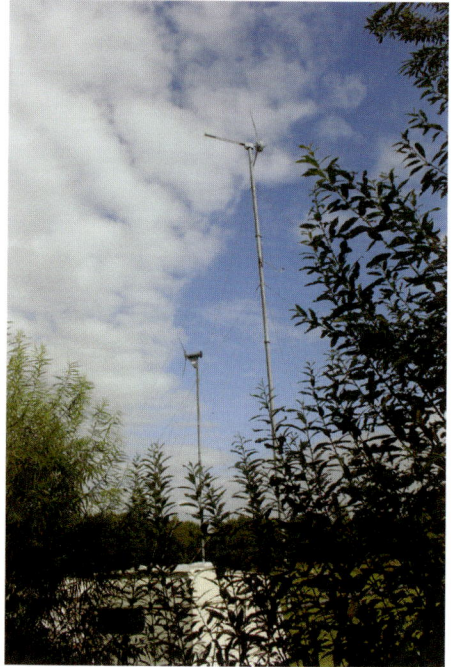

Figure 10.4 The two wind turbines and willow for coppicing.

thermal mass to hold the sun's heat that is captured by the southwest-facing conservatories, which are also used for clothes drying. Nowadays we know more about the carbon cost of using concrete and there are carbon-saving alternatives that do the same job. Each house is 6 metres deep, not so deep that it's dark at the back, and 19 metres wide, fronted by a sunny conservatory accessed by French windows. The rooms at the back are reserved for functions requiring less use and light, such as bathrooms and utility rooms. The homes are spacious, light, warm and comfortable.

Electricity is provided by 7.65 kW peak arrays of PV panels on the roof and new ones on the office to help power that and charge an electric shared car, and by two nearby wind turbines; a 6 kW Proven wind turbine installed early 2002 year (upgraded in 2008) and a 5 kW Iskra wind turbine installed in 2005 as part of the construction of a community building. The wind turbines have produced only 40–50 per cent of their projected output (partly due to turbulence and poorly matched inverters), some heat pumps failed, and energy use has been higher than expected (put down to teenagers, more people working from home and food processing). This is why more PVs were installed in 2012.

The typical energy use for a house is around 10 kWh/day (all electric). The community has on balance more electricity than it needs and the surplus is exported to the grid for profit. Hot water is produced partly via a

Figure 10.5 The view looking directly down across the solar electric panels, a solar water heating panel, and into the small patch of private front garden each dwelling has, with a raised bed and composting area.

heat pump and super-insulated thermal stores, but since they mainly failed, mostly by electricity.

Part of Hockerton's mission is to spread the word about how it is possible to live more lightly on the earth. Although residents own their own homes they are all members of a cooperative and agree to spend 300 paid hours per year supporting a joint business which runs a programme of tours and educational events, workshops and consulting on both new and retrofit energy-efficient building. Finance for the building and land purchase came from the Co-operative Bank & Ecology Building Society. If you wanted to live there it would not be cheap: despite construction costing just 15 per cent more than an average house of comparable size (£95,000 in 1998), recently one of the four-bedroomed homes sold for £500,000.

'My kids love it here,' says Bill. 'And, after the initial suspicion, the local council and residents like us too. In fact, they are very proud of us.'

Planning permission was initially granted – with great difficulty, despite the involvement of senior academics Robert and Brenda Vale, from Nottingham University's Architecture Department, who had built and lived in the country's first autonomous, self-sufficient home in a Conservation Area in nearby Southwell. Permission came with a condition (a Section 106 requirement) whereby, instead of a percentage of food supply to come from the land, as with OPDs in Wales, a fixed number of hours (300 per year per household) must be spent on the land, in addition to the same number of hours spent on the community's business. This condition seems to me to be fairer, more achievable and more manageable, as well as helping to secure the planners' prime directive of preventing such developments becoming owned by people who do not want to use the land, and who will instead commute to jobs elsewhere. 300 hours per year is about 6 hours per week, which is quite do-able and leaves time for other work and leisure, plus the other 300 hours of Co-op work.

The project had to be viewed by the planning department as 'a move towards Sustainable Development', which 'could be seen as complimenting the council's (Newark & Sherwood District Council) own energy / environmental activities'. Account was taken of the social provisions of the scheme – '(it) is not just for the houses in an isolated situation but as a whole living project...the occupants of the dwellings will work on the site towards a system of self-sufficiency through sustainable employment with low impact on the environment'.

Besides owning a shared electric car, some families have fossil-fuel-powered cars, two share one of these, and there are many bikes for local journeys. To improve biodiversity over 4,000 trees have been planted around the site, including willow for coppicing, wild cherries for birds, and oak and hazel. Because of this and the lake/wetland, biodiversity is flourishing, with several pairs of regular breeding waterfowl on the lake, including little grebe. A number of passing bird migrants have been seen, including green sandpiper, hobby and water rail. The ponds are monitored by the local agricultural college (Brackenhurst), who are pleased about a flourishing population of the endangered water vole.

Many people have visited this inspiring place and attended workshops, but so far, despite individual homes being modeled on aspects of the project, no community has yet emulated it in full. Why is this, I wonder. Perhaps it's due to the difficulty of finding the right combination of land, motivated, experienced architects, pioneers and finance. It's notable that three of the community-scale projects in this book – BedZED, Hockerton and Lammas – have been led by visionary architects. We need more of them.

More info at http://www.hockertonhousingproject.org.uk or call 01636 816902.

2 The lessons of BedZED

The next two case studies are here to show how even the best of intentions can miss their targets, and each does so for a different reason. Designers

Figure 10.6 Aerial view of the BedZED terraces showing their use of ventilation chimneys, passive solar design and PV modules.
Picture Credit: BioRegional.

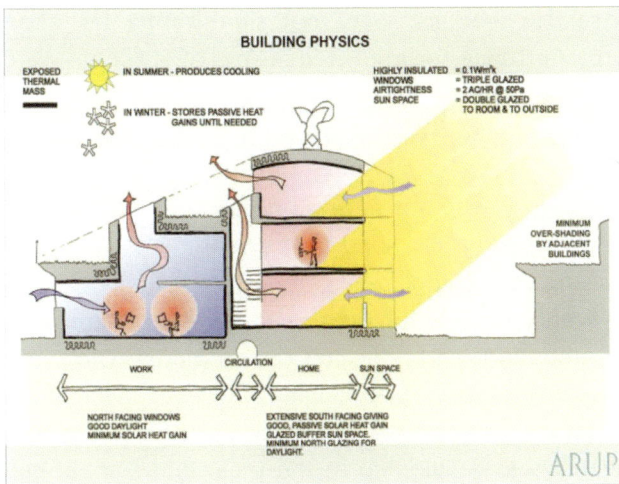

Figure 10.7 The concept design for BedZED by engineering firm ARUP.
Picture Credit: ARUP.

can create buildings which are 'zero carbon' or 'low carbon', but this doesn't mean that the predicted savings of greenhouse gas emissions will be generated. What does? The answers may surprise you.

BedZED, in South London, was a relatively early (for the UK) example of a 'zero carbon development'. It stands for 'Beddington Zero Energy Development'. It was constructed in 2002 by a consortium led by Bill Dunster

Architects for social housing body The Peabody Trust, which included Arup, BioRegional Development, Ellis & Moore and Gardiner & Theobald.
It includes plenty of state-of-the-art features such as:

- 100 per cent renewable energy powered ventilation and heating systems;
- South-facing glazing for passive solar heating;
- biofuel CHP;
- heat-recovery ventilation passively powered by wind cowls;
- water recycling;
- PV and electric cars with a car share;
- superinsulation;
- north-facing workspaces with passive cooling;
- thermal mass energy store;
- roof gardens to provide family outdoor spaces;
- glazed sun-spaces;
- reused steel and timber;
- IT connected e-community.

It sounds perfect. What could go wrong? But a post-occupancy evaluation by BioRegional found that the carbon footprints of occupants, who were predominantly public-service workers, were not significantly less than anyone else living nearby. Certainly, the predicted savings of emissions were not being met.

This was puzzling. They realised that the residents were compensating themselves for their 'green' lifestyles by flying and other perks, perhaps bought with the money saved from not paying energy bills, which effectively wiped out the carbon savings provided by the building. Flying is the most carbon intensive thing you can do.

But this wasn't the whole picture. BioRegional dug deeper, and in so doing uncovered the foundations and principles of one planet living. The organisation's Nick James produced a report, called *One Planet Living in the Thames Gateway*,[1] proposing a zero-energy development east of London, which the UK Government was developing at the time. BioRegional had been set up following the building of BedZED as a not-for-profit consultancy, a charity, that would take forward the lessons learned to implement them on a much larger scale. As the name of the report suggests, they had called this ambitious project one planet living. They knew they had to get it right.

The Thames Gateway covers over 700 square kilometres, including over 1,000 hectares of brownfield (formerly industrial) land, being redeveloped.

As the largest regeneration site in Western Europe, it had, since the 1970s, been proposed as an area in which to meet new housing needs for London, with some 160,000 to 200,000 new homes imagined. While producing the report, the team found that 'Only a small proportion of CO_2 savings, and an even smaller proportion of ecological footprint, could be achieved by constructing very green buildings'.

The proportion is just 4 per cent. The team was shocked. BioRegional's Pooran Desai wrote later[2] that 'By targeting significant CO_2 and water savings in the home by building to BRE (Buildings Research Establishment) EcoHomes 'Very Good' standard (with high insulation standards and fitted with energy-efficient appliances and lighting) rather than simply meeting Building Regulations, we were able to get a 32 per cent reduction in CO_2 emissions from the homes in our model. This level of saving sounds good. However, it translates to an overall reduction in ecological footprint of only 4 per cent.'

BedZED had claimed a 90 per cent reduction in space-heating saving. But this was compared to existing homes. Compared with meeting current Building Regulations, whose rules were tighter, the savings were much less. BioRegional realised they needed to consider instead the marginal or additional benefit of going beyond Building Regulations, and an absolute, not relative measure of performance.

The team went on to crunch more numbers. They wanted to find out how to achieve carbon savings the most cost-effectively. They soon discovered that a 'capital cost saving of one tonne of CO_2 per year varies between £265 for a green transport plan to £28,697 for the same savings from the building fabric (superinsulation and sun-spaces)'. It must be remembered that this is in the city, where it is relatively easy to get a green transport plan together. But even so, it was 100 times cheaper to make CO_2 reductions by investing in green transport than in insulation and so on. Furthermore, of the 'insulation and so on', it was Passivhaus standard glazing that took the lion's share of the cash. Eighty per cent of the extra cost for the building envelope of BedZED was for south-facing windows on the sun-spaces (£282,200 out of the £352,750 for the six-plot terrace).

This meant that superinsulation was much more cost-effective than sun-spaces in cutting carbon dioxide emissions. Moreover, the crunched numbers also revealed that savings to residents of cash and CO_2 in heating bills from both superinsulation and sun-spaces were comparatively small compared to the other measures. PV panels for solar electricity were then more than twice as expensive as nowadays and they too weren't cost-effective. Far more effective were water-efficient appliances, which, by saving hot water, turned out to save as much energy as energy-efficient appliances, not to mention cutting the water bill.

Finally, the team found that the financial payback time for investing in a tonne of annual CO_2 saving (dividing capital cost per tonne of CO_2 saved by bill saving for the 36 people in the terrace), worked out at almost 800 years for the sun-spaces, but only one week for the car club. Surprised? I was – by the extent of the difference. Of course it's because the cost of running a car is high, and cars produce a lot of emissions. Pooran Desai concludes: 'This doesn't mean that I am saying don't bother creating energy-efficient homes. What I am saying is that there is a point of emphasis and of diminishing returns with building fabric. We are getting there, but still have a way to go. If we stop at CO_2 footprint we are not getting a full indication of our contribution to global warming.'

So this is the evolution of one planet living, which, like ecological footprint analysis, attempts to tackle the whole impact of our lifestyles. Greenhouse gas (GHG) emissions are measured as tonnes of carbon dioxide equivalent (CO_2e), but we focus on this gas too much. The largest man-made contributors to global warming are from methane and nitrous oxide emissions and they come from agriculture. It's our agricultural practices that need to change. We need to eat less meat and milk, because methane comes from cattle, and farm more organically and labour-intensively, because nitrous oxides come from nitrogen fertilisers.

The UK government says that the individual carbon footprint of a UK citizen is on average 8.8 tonnes of the gas per year. But if you factor in GHG emissions from agriculture and other sources, it almost doubles to 16.34 tonnes of CO_2e per person per year. So when people quote statistics like '50 per cent of CO_2 emissions come from buildings' it actually means '50 per cent of territorial CO_2 emissions come from all existing buildings and the built-up space between buildings' but it ignores CO_2 emissions from international transport and agriculture. We will never reach sustainability in cities or elsewhere unless all these emissions are brought within safe limits, the limits of what our one, beautiful planet can provide for each of us and our descendants.

3 The Triangle, Swindon

This pioneering project involving *Grand Designs* presenter Kevin McCloud tried hard to make well-built eco-houses affordable. The Triangle is a 42-home housing development in Swindon, comprising 16 two-bed houses,

Figure 10.8 The Triangle, Swindon.
Picture Credit: NHBC.

13 three-bed houses, 7 four-bed houses, 4 one-bed apartments, and 2 two-bed apartments, including homes for Intermediate Rent and Rent To Homebuy – and homes for affordable rent to local people registered with Swindon Borough Council.

It incorporates passive stack ventilation chimneys, and the houses were designed to be very small and open plan. Natural materials and neutral finishes are used throughout, including 350 mm-thick hemcrete walls, wool carpets and cork floors. The hempcrete was grown locally and used for the external walls, and rooms were given higher ceilings to enable more light to flood small rooms and make them feel bigger. Individual gardens were small but a large communal garden was put into community trust ownership and people encouraged to grow food collectively. Overall, 50 per cent of land is for sharing. The houses achieve Code for Sustainable Homes Level 4, and could have met Level 5 with the introduction of photovoltaic panels.

The architects, Glenn Howells Architects, worked with Kevin McCloud's Haboakus development company to design the project, which looked great on paper. But after construction had finished and tenants had moved in, problems emerged. Upset residents complained of water leaks and cracks, and bills higher than they were led to expect. It turned out that the builders, Wilmott Dixon Housing, were not experienced in building with hemp-lime, which must be done by people with proper training who know what they're doing. An expensive lesson, regardless of where the ultimate blame lay. It underscores what I said earlier about the importance of attention to detail.

Despite this, one nice little addition is a touchscreen device in each home that addresses the possibilities that occupants' behaviour can undermine the designers' sustainable intentions. The device lets residents see how much electricity they're using and includes a property log book – a manual for their home. They can also:

- see energy and water use in the home, including 'next bill' information;
- set targets and see how well they do compared to other residents;
- see smart tips to reduce energy usage;
- see a live feed of 'next bus' information at the local bus stop;
- rapidly book the shared community car;
- see cycling or walking information;
- see local car-lift shares;
- see alerts and advice about local community issues;
- see security information;
- see sustainable food sources and ordering.

And it functions as a virtual noticeboard on which messages can be left for the entire community: for example if you want to borrow some garden tools, if you need someone to babysit, or if you want to tell the neighbours about the Saturday vegetable market that locals have already started.

4 Rachel Shiamh's frameless straw bale home

Continuing with the *Grand Designs* theme, here's a success story now, which has nothing to do with Kevin McCloud directly. Rachel Shiamh's delightful house, on the edge of St Dogmael's, a lovely coastal community in Pembrokeshire, Wales, was the first two-storey straw bale building in the UK to be constructed without a frame. The story of how it came to be illustrates that anyone starting from a very low knowledge base can achieve something quite extraordinary. Rachel began with no particular experience or skills relevant to what she was going to achieve – she was a theatre set designer – but her construction was voted the *Grand Designs* building of the year by the TV viewing public in 2008. Her story also demonstrates the enthusiasm some planning officers and building inspectors can have towards low-impact dwellings.

Rachel acquired the land serendipitously and cheaply, but did not move in right away, choosing to live nearby for a while. Although her family was from Wales she herself had not been brought up there. She eventually moved onto the steep-sided, wooded plot when, in her own words, 'I was ready to immerse myself in living in nature, to remember what I was about and what I thought I had lost.' A friend built her a 12-foot shed. 'To begin with I had no water or electricity.' A local planning officer paid a visit and gave her permission to live there while she put her plans together. A friend who was an eco-architect offered to support her in this.

Figure 10.9 Rachel Shiamh's original sketch for her straw bale house.
Credit: Rachel Shiamh.

Figure 10.10 Building the plinth wall and laying the lightweight expanded clay aggregate insulation under-floor insulation.
Credit: Rachel Shiamh.

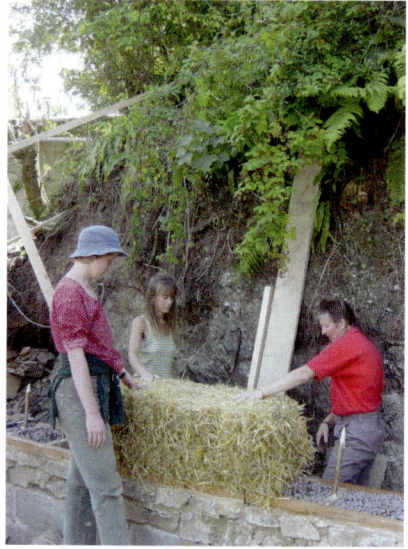

Figure 10.11 Laying the first bales upon the stakes upon the plinth. Barbara Jones is on the right and Rachel Shiamh in the centre. The construction was mostly undertaken by women.

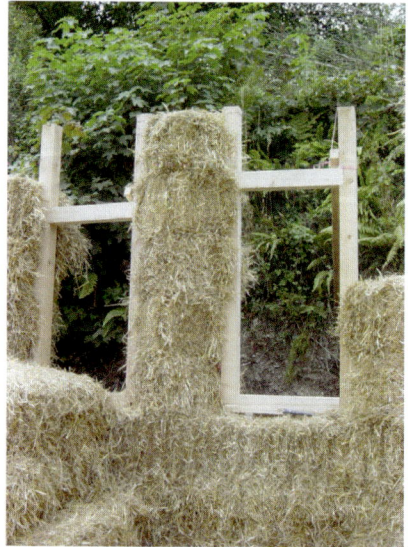

Figure 10.12 Laying the bales around the window frames.
Credit: Rachel Shiamh.

I outlined my vision of how I wanted my home to use natural materials and complement the surroundings. I was told there was a link between the building which was on the site formerly and the Abbey in the village below. I showed my drawings to the senior planning officer. I couldn't get involved in details because I didn't know them; all I had was the inspiration. I had a lovely conversation with her and at the end she said: 'This isn't going to be easy, but I'm going to do everything I can to help'. She stayed in touch. It took two years. She showed me through the process.

Figure 10.13 Where does this one go?
Credit: Rachel Shiamh.

Figure 10.14 Adding the I-beams.
Credit: Rachel Shiamh.

Although the county council was supportive, the village community council was suspicious, but eventually Rachel won them over by finding the courage to talk to them and, besides, the county council officials knew that their concerns were not significant. 'The only way I could get through this was to see it as a learning experience,' she reflected. 'I did not want to feel a victim.' This can often happen to people who feel they are up against opposition. 'I realised [the opposition] was about authority, what we think it is and how we let people make decisions. I had to align myself with the clearest decision I felt I had to make for myself and for the planet, and it was this: to build a natural house. Once I had done this I found that the

Figure 10.15 and 10.16 The roof in position.
Credit: Rachel Shiamh.

opposition presented things I had to work through instead of fighting. If I fought something, everything would stop. My local county councillor at the time was great; he also did not want to see more concrete poured in the countryside.'

Figure 10.17 Lime rendering in progress.
Credit: Rachel Shiamh.

Local opposition is often based on fear: fear of change, fear of some-thing different. This is true of many types of planning application, not just low-impact developments. While it is important to have an open-door policy towards objectors, letting them realise they can come and raise their concerns, as Rachel did, it is even more important to get a dialogue going with your local county councillor, planning officials and building inspec-tors; it is their opinions which really carry the day. In the end, village oppo-sition to Rachel's plans melted away because she followed this strategy. She wrote to each of the members of the council individually, explaining in very personal terms her connection to the place and how passionate she was. These letters went off with the application and it was accepted, in 1998.

It was some time before Rachel started building. First, she had to discover the delights of building with straw bales. 'It was like needlework! Quiet work, forgiving work, gentle, lovely to do.' For her first project she built an extension on her shed. 'Once I'd built it and was inside it, the ambience of that space was so exquisite that I realised this was the closest way I can live in nature, because it breathes. Then the building control officer turned up and he thought it was amazing and suggested I build my house out of straw. So that was when I contacted Barbara Jones.' This was in 2002.

Figure 10.18 and 10.19
The completed house.
Credit: Rachel Shiamh.

Barbara Jones

Barbara is both the pioneer of straw-bale building in the UK and a passionate advocate for women's rights. She is the recipient of a Lifetime Achievement Award from Women in Construction in 2011 and of a Woman of Outstanding Achievement Award from the UK Resource Centre (UKRC) in 2009. She sees straw-bale construction as a way for women to get involved with what is seen as a traditional male preserve. Rather than competing directly with men in their trades, she helps to train women not just in using straw bales but in lime and clay plastering and the use of old car tyres as foundations for buildings. Hundreds of women – and men too – have gained the confidence to start their own building projects by attending these courses. She is fearless in the way she questions why we do

Figure 10.20 The beautiful bathroom, the only room with a stone wall – and a slate floor.
Credit: Rachel Shiamh.

Figure 10.21 Different floorings (earthen floor, limecrete pigmented floor, natural beach slates in glaster limecrete, recycled timber).
Credit: Rachel Shiamh.

things the way we do, but she also insists on learning from architectural and vernacular heritage.

Despite being the subject of jokes at the beginning of her career, she has won huge respect and says, 'I truly believe I have found a way for ordinary people to get involved in building again, through simple techniques and affordable methods.' This approach has produced not only simplified straw-bale building techniques, but simple and cement-free designs for building foundations using car tyres, shallow foundations, flexible and self-draining foundations. These are all legal and approved but, rather shamefully, none are mentioned in UK Building Regulations. Rachel calls Barbara the 'wisdom keeper of natural building'.

Figure 10.22 The chimney from the woodstove heating the large open first floor.
Credit: Rachel Shiamh.

Bill Chaytor, one of the original straw-bale pioneers, must be given credit for sharing straw-bale building with Barbara in 1996; together with Amazonails (her company), Bill and Barbara built a garage, which is where it all began. In 2013 her company Straw Works ran two courses at the Clervaux Trust near Darlington, Somerset, which houses the first straw-bale building in the world to be built with car-tyre foundations. The three straw-bale buildings at the site blend well with the abundant and colourful biodynamic gardens there.

So Barbara was full of enthusiasm for Rachel's project, helping her to design her two-storey building, giving it the distinction of being load-bearing, meaning that no frame is required. (It's called the Nebraska method.) She did not tell Rachel immediately that this would be only the fourth such building in the world but Rachel went along with it. 'I like load-bearing,' she says. 'It saves on timber and skilled labour and more people can be involved in it.' There are quite a few two-storey load-bearing houses now, but this was something of a precedent in the UK. A mortgage was obtained from the Ecological Building Society. In retrospect it was fortuitous that her building control officer, himself quite curious about the process, was so accepting. This experience should give encouragement to any individuals wanting to pursue the unconventional.

In this case the only compromise was the Portland cement used in the foundations, and that 'was because planning permission was running out and we had to get something down quickly'. Rachel would not do it that way again, as the contractors made costly mistakes. Barbara would come and run courses every now and then, the attendees of which helped with construction. On top of the foundations went a 40 cm-high stone plinth wall to stop any splashback. A local stonemason showed Rachel how to build with the stone found on site using lime mortar. 'I had women and children in the village coming up and helping with their rubber gloves and I realised that this is how houses used to be built – communally,' she says. 'It was very empowering. I saw many people's lives being changed and it restored my faith in humanity. We got media coverage and started to be seen as a shining example of sustainability in Wales, which encouraged more volunteers to come and help and transformed the view in the village.' In the two and a half years of the building process (one year to erect and the rest to finish) 200 volunteers attended workshops, helped with construction and left inspired to undertake their own projects.

'It's almost been taken away from us, this building,' observes Rachel. 'It's like it's for other people, but in fact we can do it ourselves. It is common sense, like Lego in some ways. So many more women could be involved.' Most of the materials in her house are sourced locally including slate and limecrete, floorboards from a local mill (green oak and larch), although the cedar shingles came from Canada. The walls are plastered with clay inside, and outside with lime, which Rachel found much easier to work with. The roof is insulated with Thermafleece – sheep's wool. Her woodland is coppiced for some building materials and fuel. A battery bank stores electricity from a 1 kW wind turbine and 500 W of solar panels. She also has thermal solar panels for hot water. The house contains a beautiful bathroom with a toilet serviced by rainwater harvesting and an Aquatron composting toilet. Liquid waste from the Aquatron goes into a soakaway system while the solid wastes are broken down by worms inside. There are other home-made composting toilets in the garden.

Timber frame or not?

Once erected, straw bales take a few weeks to compress under the weight of the structure. This must be allowed to happen before plastering takes place or cracks will develop. It also means that, with a frameless construction, around windows and doors, where compression will not happen, curves may develop in the structure. If the support of the building comes from a frame then, following compression, gaps can occur which must be infilled subsequently. Completely frameless straw-bale buildings have not been in existence for long enough to identify any long-term problems, but so far they appear to be performing very well. Care must be taken to ensure that floors, roofs and so on are horizontal. Ultimately, the choice comes down to a matter of opinion: some people just feel more secure with frames to support the weight of the building, but they are an additional expense, resource use and take more time to erect.

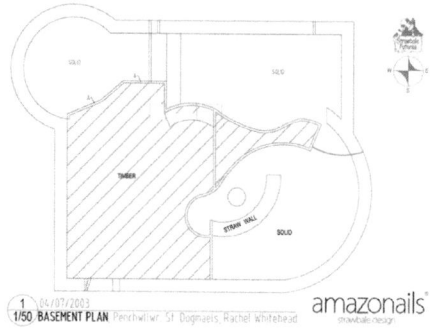

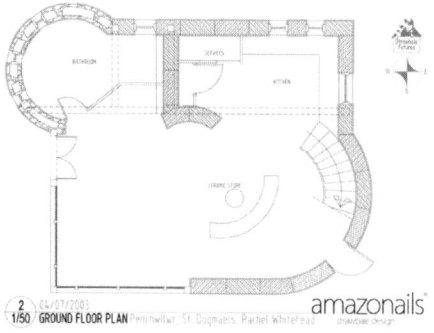

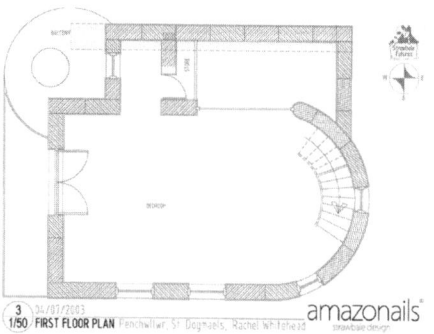

Figure 10.23 to 10.26 Architects' drawings for the straw-bale building: basement, ground floor, first floor plans and an elevation.
Picture Credit: Amazonails

Rachel Shiamh does not think visual impact should be such a consideration for gaining planning permission:

> People have different ideas of visual impact. Eco-building starts with natural materials, and biodynamic horticulture, for example, looks different from conventional agriculture. People take a little while to get used to this. Instead they are used to seeing concrete structures going up, mobile phone masts and so on. The focus for planners should be on sustainability. If a family is living together and growing organically and if it is able to supply the community with surplus produce and beyond in terms of teaching other people about living that way, visual impact – well, what does that mean when up on the hill are lots of new retirement homes? Although we are using traditional building materials we are not going back in time, which seems to be what people are afraid of. For me it's about using old materials but embracing the new technologies, like renewable energy and passive solar techniques, and moving forward.

5 Lammas

When I visited Lammas, the catalyst for One Planet Development policy in Wales, for the first time, I took the long route, across country, through the winding maze of lanes that comprises most of the Pembrokeshire countryside. Undulating and ancient, these narrow, unsignposted ways pass through tiny hamlets and past sheep farms and woodlands, many of which look like they have hardly changed in the last hundred years. Half a mile up a tree-lined lane from the nearest village of honeysuckle-covered cottages lay the entrance to Tir y Gafel, in the north of the county. At first, the plot appeared similar to normal farmland: a new track winding up a hill flanked by pastures where horses quietly grazed. Then the land use abruptly changed: through coppiced willow hedges became visible the variegated quilting of strips and beds planted with varied vegetables, soft fruits and orchards. Amidst this, five people were clambering over a timber-frame structure in the process of construction, close to a temporary house made from bales.

Nothing much unusual in that, you might think: it's just a smallholding. Except that, as Jane Davidson points out in her Foreword to this book, until recently it has been all but impossible to gain planning permission in the UK for new homes to be built on agricultural land in the open countryside. This and eight other smallholdings are taking part in a unique experiment,

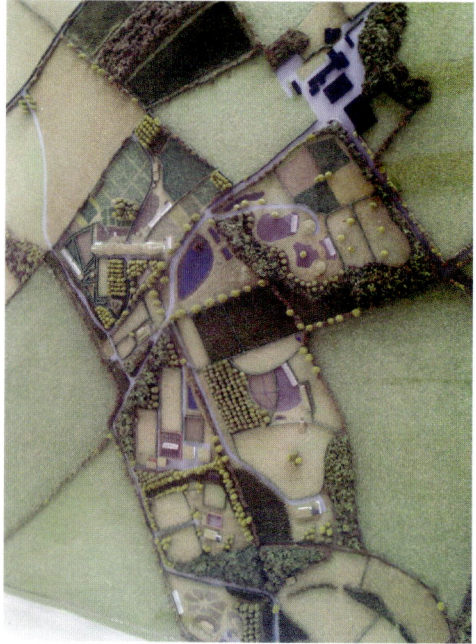

Figure 10.27 A photograph of a 3D model of Lammas on display in The Hub community building, showing how the plots fit within the landscape, The site is accessed from the lane in the top left (easterly edge), down to which it slopes from the bottom (west).

Figure 10.28 The lake at Lammas.

pioneering a way of living that is not only sustainable, but subject to detailed annual monitoring under a legal sanction by the state's planning system, a system that was changed as a direct result of the occupants' efforts. The monitoring will determine if they are allowed to stay after five years, a period that closes just before this book is published but after it goes to press. You may well know if they succeeded, but I do not. If you asked me to bet on the outcome right now, I'd say they will.

Lammas is not really a village; its homesteads are too spread out. Each family has around six acres of what was previously one single sheep farm, comprising mostly upland pasture but with some pine plantation. It's marginal land; some said it couldn't support anything but sheep. It's not been easy for residents but these naysayers have been proved wrong. The variety of produce being squeezed from this land, once the soil has been enriched, is astonishing for such a location. In these six acres the occupants can do exactly as they wish, as long as they provide for at least 75 per cent of their own livelihood from the land and build their own homes. The residents came from all walks of life. Each family paid between £35,000 and £40,000 for their plot and then had to finance their buildings, equipment, livestock, seeds and saplings. In the case of Jasmine and Simon, whose plot is at the southern end of the site, their costs up to 2013 had been:

Plot lease	£35,000
Small house, after building regulations work and other landscaping	£4,000
Trees/plants/fencing	£1,500
Workshop and barn	£1,200
Total	£56,000

Whilst some had experience of low-impact living and natural building, many had none. One of their first collective tasks was to construct a Community Hub building, which they did with the help of many volunteers.

Water, some woodland and most electricity are managed collectively and the plots are largely dedicated to growing food, land-based businesses, growing biomass and processing organic waste. There's plenty about

Figure 10.29 Lammas in early days: a typical pasture file in the process of being converted to vegetable beds.
Credit: Jasmine Dale.

Figure 10.30 Three photographs showing the process of conversion. Credit: Jasmine Dale.

Lammas scattered through this book because of its central importance in the one planet living narrative. In summary, the land-based livelihoods chosen by the residents include: fruit and vegetable production, livestock and bees, woodland and willow crafts, value-added food production, seed production, and vermiculture (the farming of composting worms).

Electrical power is supplied from a 27 kW hydroelectric plant whose power is distributed to the homes, which can supplement this by their own photovoltaic panels. Heating is supplied from passive solar and timber (from woodland management or from short-rotation-coppice biomass plantations). Domestic water comes from a private spring, also distributed by pipes, and other water needs are predominantly met from harvesting rainwater.

'We grow loads of food to sustain all of us here, including all the volunteers that we need to come to help and learn. Because of the vagaries of the British weather, outside, root crops fare well, but aerial crops can suffer, resulting in unpredictable yields, so we do need a polytunnel or greenhouse.' says Hoppi Wimbush.

Figures 10.31 and 10.32 Simon and
Jasmine's first conservatory/greenhouse
under construction and planted up.
Credit: Jasmine Dale.

Polytunnels may not be the most aesthetic of structures (one family abhors
them and has built a cob greenhouse), but they – or some form of greenhouse – are vital for securing a food supply all the year round. Raised beds
are usually planted within them; these require regular, reliable irrigation
from rainwater or other upslope collection. They quickly establish their own
amazing ecosystem: frogs and toads, microscopic wasps that eat the aphids,
ladybirds, and a universe of microorganisms that live within the heated,
damp environment; a whole different world from that outside.

At least two families are building a large shell around the house that
combines the functions of greenhouse and conservatory; besides making

the house more energy efficient and blurring the distinction between inside and outside, a great advantage is that one has to go less far (and not venture into the rain) to obtain the salad, herb and vegetable ingredients for food preparation. This approach typifies that of permaculture, the design philosophy behind Lammas. 'Permaculture is just another word for natural systems that work in symbiosis,' Hoppi explained. 'When you have those symbiotic systems in place and understand them then there is an intelligence that takes over and guides the choices that are being made so that instead of surviving you are thriving on very little money.'[3]

Jasmine and Simon

Jasmine used the Permaculture framework to adapt her vision to the requirements of the planning process. 'Some people have made very detailed plans but not analysed their own suitability to the plans, so their plans have floundered. We were able to map quite thoroughly what we felt we were capable of doing using this process. We haven't necessarily succeeded yet but we have a timetable and a plan, so this tool that we have used is useful in the design process.'

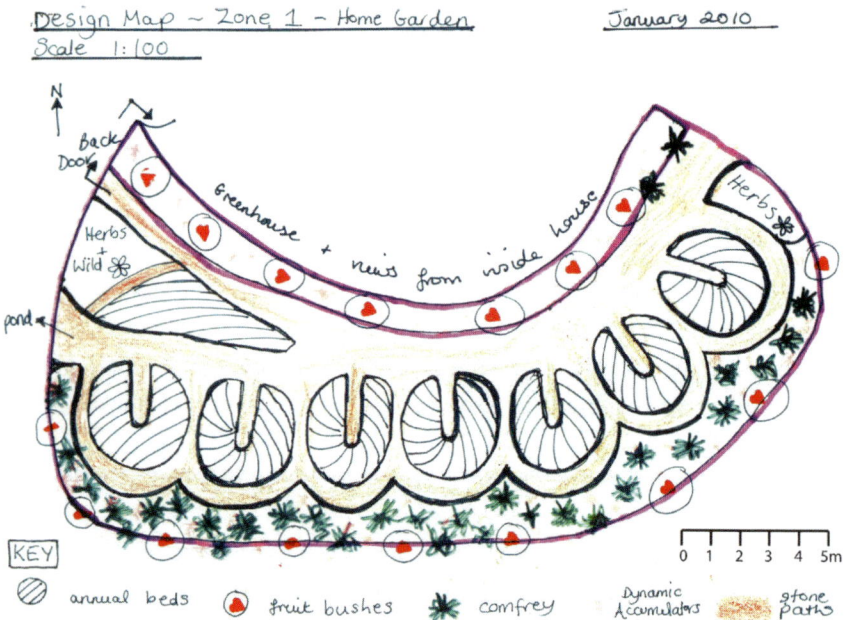

Figure 10.33 One of Jasmine's design drawings for a herb and fruit garden area.
Credit: Jasmine Dale.

Paul and Hoppi Wimbush

Paul (now called 'Tao') Wimbush is an architect, a modest, wise man who is the quietly spoken mentor of many aspiring One Planet novices. The large circular vegetable garden, 'patrolled by ducks', as Paul puts it, is where most of his and Hoppi's produce is grown. A goose house was under construction when I visited. There is an orchard with apples, plums and hazel which, he explains, encircles the garden to form a windbreak and 'create a forest glade effect, which is so much more resilient, in terms of a growing ecosystem', and to raise fertility. 'Around that you've got three fields in rotation for the milking cow and its calf to graze in. There is a pond installed to capture rainwater and rising water that comes up behind the workshop from time to time. It is used to irrigate the polytunnel and the garden.' Paul is building up the habitat of the pond first and will then introduce carp for food. Other ponds satisfy the geese and ducks.

To the left is Hoppi's flower garden, in front of a stone quarry for building materials, with a blueberry patch in the corner, 'because blueberries need something quite specific: acidic soil,' says Paul. He is treating the soil there quite differently to the rest of the plot, introducing limestone and biochar. To further improve fertility Paul is harvesting nutrition from the outer fields where the cow is kept and through a composting process focusing it in the intensive crop area. 'That,' he says, 'is one of the very big benefits of a cow system. Beyond all of that further down the slope is an acre planted with willow for coppicing in rotation, already at one and a half and two and a half years of growth. Eventually that will go into a

Figure 10.34 Hoppi and Paul in the kitchen/living room of their first, temporary, home.
Credit: Paul Wimbush

three- to four-year rotation. I'm anticipating harvesting between three and five dry tonnes a year,' he says. This will be used as a cooking fuel and as a biochar production system in the main dwelling, which is yet to be built. The new house will be wrapped around an insulated dome, which will form 'a guaranteed frost-free space for lemon trees, peach trees and grapes'.

As we approached the cowshed a dove flew out. Paul observed:

> That's one of our doves. They perform two roles, really: the first is spreading peace and love around because white doves are so beautiful, and the second is that they act as cleaners. She will have been cleaning up in the barn any of the seed that the cow will have spilt from the morning milking. The barn is next to the chicken run and they help to clean up that because chickens are notoriously messy. I'm quite meticulous in my cow barn; I endeavour to live without small furry animals.

The cows are kept in the barn every night so that their poo can be collected for fertiliser. There is a separate room for a milking parlour. The council comes and checks that it's all in order. It has to be kept up to a high standard of cleanliness. There is a little bedroom for the calf, enabling him to be shut up at night so that in the morning Paul can collect all of his mother's milk. 'If I let the calf feed twenty-four seven I'm only going to get about five litres a day. By shutting the cow away I bring it up to about fourteen litres a day at the moment. In the peak of the lactation cycle you get as much as twenty; for one cow that's fantastic.' The cow needs two acres of pasture. The milk is delivered every morning to all the other households on site using their dog, a husky, which pulls a little cart containing the milk. 'We rotate the pasture with sheep,' Paul continues, 'because of the complementary way in which they kill each other's parasites. When the cow eats the sheep's intestinal parasites it kills them and vice versa as well as cleaning up the pasture and balancing the different grasses.'

The building where Paul and his family are living now was always intended to be both a workshop and temporary accommodation until the final dwellinghouse is built. It was designed to be quick to erect, efficient in terms of use of materials, lightweight yet comfortable enough to house the family while the rest of the smallholding was established. 'We've been on the land here now three years and three months and we are now over the hill in terms of hard work and we are very much reaping the rewards of our labours already because we are in comfortable accommodation and relaxed.' Each of the plots at Lammas has approached the challenge of getting established in a different way. 'Basically we worked like dogs for the first two and a half years and now we are just settling in and taking time to build up our businesses, such as the marketing strategy and so on.'

The building is timber-frame stud-wall construction supported by concrete pads in imitation of old saddle stones 'to stop the small furry animals from getting into the home'. Each wall was built flat on the deck and lifted into place. This is a really simple method and is how many houses in America were built. 'I have over-structured it deliberately in terms of its ability to withstand high winds,' Paul says, 'because I think we've got some high winds coming.'

Paul's experience of the Building Regulations Inspector was that he came 'in a spirit of trying to find fault rather than of cooperation. The big lesson that we have really embraced is to go private for building control. The private guys tend to be young, open and flexible, whereas the publicly employed officials are the opposite: very conventional, not very open-minded, they want traditional construction and because of that culture in councils, if anything, get very jittery if there is anything that falls outside the box'.

Cassie and Nigel

Cassie comes from a very rural area in Connecticut, so is used to being surrounded by nature. Nigel is from Cheshire initially and then Hertfordshire. They've been together for 27 years since they met at boarding school when they were 17. Cassie's livelihood is mostly growing willow for crafts, sculptures and educational purposes. Before coming here she was already producing living willow sculptures, influenced by the Steiner school and the Dyfed Permaculture farm where they lived previously. She works in schools, makes willow heron sculptures – a blacksmith provides the iron legs for them – and makes 'lots of little things like stars and hearts and baskets, but you can add less money to them because they have to compete in the marketplace with cheap imports'.

Figure 10.35 Willow weaving at Cassie and Nigel's plot, in front of their swimming pool.

Figure 10.36 Some of Cassie's basketwork.

Figure 10.37 and 10.38 Melissa occupies a neighbouring plot to Cassie and also grows willow for basketwork and teaching. This is some of her willow: growing, and harvested.

Cassie planted 1,000 willow rods, which are harvested every year in a 1,500 m² area. This (the fourth) is the first year that she has been able to produce enough willow for her purposes and generate up to £3,000 per year. This is counted against the £10,000 per year basic livelihood requirements for the family of four, which includes clothing, food, car tax, insurance, council tax. 75 per cent of this must be provided from livelihood. They are currently on about £6,500.

She also makes felt crafts. At present Cassie cannot count the felt-craft making as part of her land-based livelihood because she has to import the felt but she plans to get her own Angora goats (two, plus two others that will be for milk) and Shetland sheep (two) and then she will be able to count that too. They will also produce manure. Together with the fruit and vegetable she sells this will reach her 75 per cent. The value of the water, wood fuel and electricity is counted towards this as well. The goats will produce milk, cheese and yoghurt sufficient for their own consumption. Ducks and hens already provide eggs.

Making it real

All OPDs are required to have some educational work, but even if they weren't, because of their commitment and passion, Lammas would still offer their courses, conferences and public tours. The latter occur every Saturday from April to October. An annual conference is held for anyone interested in living a low-impact lifestyle in alignment with the One Planet Development policy but the number of people attending over the last three years has declined. Hoppi Wimbush attributes this to a realisation of both the difficulty of surmounting the planning hurdles and the extreme commitment involved in choosing such a radical shift of lifestyle. 'The dream of living this way is very real in many people's minds, but the knowledge of how to do so is limited. That is what makes Lammas so important,' says Hoppi. 'For both people and planners to understand the systems that have to be put in place. It's a huge investment of time and commitment.'

Simon believes that 'OPD has guided us in the right direction in terms of encouraging us to incorporate land-based livelihood, and to be quite focused about our way of living rather than being more ad hoc.'

Tom, who owns a five-acre plot next door to Lammas and was about to have a pre-application consultation with the council when I spoke to him, said he had put 'dozens of hours' into making his management plan so far. This is very daunting for someone who is holding a full-time job as well. 'It takes a very particular person at this stage in the development of the policy,' said Hoppi. 'It has to come from a burning inner desire. The role of this book is to inspire people and give them some of the tools they will need.'

At Lammas there is a get-out clause: a family can choose to sell up and get out if the going is found to be not good. The planning requirements are attached to the plot of land, not to the individuals owning it. There is a waiting list of people who wish to live at Lammas but so far no one has moved up on it. Were somebody to do so, they would in turn have to come up with their own management plan for that plot of land and have it accepted by the local authority. Personal circumstances change, and some people will not be able to make it all the way through. As with anything in life, there is an element of risk.

Equally, with each family occupying six acres it is possible for them to go through their entire time there without having to see anybody else. There is no obligation for anyone to attend communal events such as meetings, and inevitably a culture emerges, as it does with any settlement of human beings, because we are social animals. And so people do come together for matters of mutual concern, but there is no obligation to do so. Six acres is plenty and feels luxurious, even half of that would be sufficient to support a family, although certain projects might be ruled out, such as growing enough wood for fuel for both cooking and heating. An acre, Paul thinks, might suit a single, fit person living in a super-insulated home pursuing livelihood projects which had a very small footprint such as mushrooms and honey.

6 Hoppi Wimbush: Growing flowers to sell

Hoppi Wimbush generates a small income from selling flowers that she grows. On a beautiful late summer's day, we sat in her flower beds, which occupy 233 square metres, with 70 m² of paths, and, to the soundtrack of purring pollinators, she explained how she went about it.

'My motivation for doing this is love,' she says.

> I love flowers and herbal remedies and learning about them. I take them to the local grocer's and if they sell, great. I'm finding that an income from flowers of about £60 per week is sufficient. The shop also takes fruit that we produce such as blueberries, bilberries and raspberries at the moment. In total I get about £100 a week for a day of pleasure.

First she prepared the land: in March 2012 she covered it with plastic to kill the weeds, and then in October she developed the beds and added

Figure 10.39 Hoppi with some flowers for sale.
Credit: Paul Wimbush

the nutrients that she thought the soil needed. 2013 was her first year of productivity, so the results are tentative.

Which flowers does Hoppi grow for this purpose?

I like the sweet-smelling ones and there are many to choose from. I've been testing different flowers to see which ones the slugs don't like and which ones thrive. I like to grow flowers popular with bees and butterflies, although there is a downside because it means that the flowers go to seed quicker and so need to be harvested in time. I therefore go for the old cottage varieties, many of which are also highly fragrant, such as alliums, foxglove (different coloured ones including white, cream and chocolate), sweet peas, phlox, hollyhocks, carnations, sweet williams, marguerites, marigolds, lilies, peonies, ornamental yarrows, which come in beautiful colours such as terracottas and yellows and delicate pinks.

What I've established is a base of good perennials which provide a stock of good flowers, and then I add annuals to give the pizzazz of colour and productivity: the more you pick the more they flower. Then I have biennial stock, such as honesty, which is amazing for seed pods for winter decoration, spring flowers and hollyhocks.

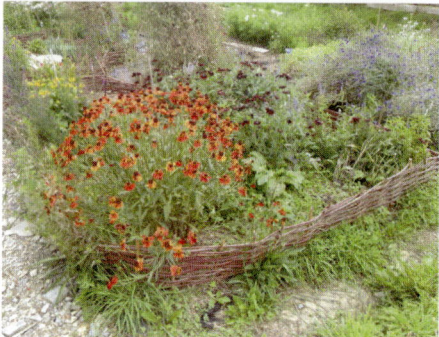

Figure 10.40–10.45 The flower beds.

Figure 10.40–10.45 (*continued*)

Sweet peas[4] are especially valued if they have long stems: the Japanese Oyama's is a good variety. Repeated croppings produce more flowers: plant in October, pot up in November, plant in the ground in January and you get flowering from April onwards. Cosmos and zinnias are annuals and repeat flower. Dahlias are also popular but must be grown in a polytunnel or in combination with ducks, because slugs love them.

There is also a whole range of edible flowers, which includes nasturtiums, calendula, rose, hollyhocks, cornflowers, pansies, hibiscus, chrysanthemum and sunflowers. Some have a very distinct flavour, but others just add colour to salads. 'I tend to sell edible flowers to restaurants,' says Hoppi. 'I have one customer who sells to many different restaurants, which is cost-effective for me. Besides selling direct to florists I am also planning to approach the local organic vegetable box scheme to see if they want to offer a bouquet of cut flowers to be delivered every week. However, it's important to keep it manageable and not be too ambitious. If you plant too much you need to get people in to pick them and then you've got to feed them as well.'

Figure 10.46 Hoppi with a bunch of flowers.
Credit: Paul Wimbush.

Figure 10.47 Another bunch of flowers ready for the market.
Credit: Paul Wimbush.

Herbs can be grown amongst the flowers. Traditional cottage garden herbs include: marjoram, parsley, oregano, sage, thyme, wormwood, catmint, fever-few, lungwort, soapwort, hyssop, sweet woodruff and lavender. These can also be sold, for culinary or medicinal purposes. Hoppi has been approached by people to provide flowers for weddings and hopes to do so in future.

Pricing is relatively simple to predict, but a survey of local prices and markets will be necessary for a management plan. 'I probably sell up to 40 bunches a week from an outside plot of 60′ × 40′ and then 6′ × 10′ in the polytunnel,' Hoppi says. 'There might be three in a bunch sold for £2.50, and 10 sweet pea stems for, in this area, £1.75, but I know they can fetch 50p per stem in cities. They are a hugely popular cash crop because they don't travel well or have longevity.'

For Hoppi, making the step to move to Lammas was a big choice:

It was quite a shift in my mind because I came from a relatively straight world. I'd never done any gardening, ever. I didn't make the connection that the world feeds me and houses me. Houses simply were, food was on my plate and I went to the supermarket! It was very disconnected. I've made a huge transformation. As my consciousness shifts and I start to feel more interrelation with the plants and animals around me it becomes easier to find answers to problems that arise. I feel connected to the landscape, and that is what I feel is the difference. The business side, making money from the land, is actually secondary, because in a sustainable world the driver isn't making money, the driver is the pleasure I get from the interrelationship. What I sell from what I produce is the cream on the top.

Hoppi has provided the following figures. They don't include set up costs or set up labour.

Categories		Year 1 Actual	Year 2 Projected	Year 3 Projected
		£	£	£
Costs	packaging	17	34	51
	seed	21	42	63
	compost	27	54	81
	travel	45	66	111
Turnover		537	1074	1611
Profit		427	878	1194

Year	Profit	Hours	Hourly rate of pay
1 (actual)	£427	70	£6.10
2 (projected)	£878	110	£7.98
3 (projected)	£1194	140	£8.53

'The hours don't change too much throughout the years because the weeding stays the same (or lessens as mulch layers increase and weed stock decreases),' she says. 'The need for planting out reduces as the perennial stock establishes year on year. Harvesting increases though and so does enjoyment year on year... I spent an estimated total of 70 hours on flowers last year in total... including weeding, planting, harvesting... But I spent about 2,000 hours enjoying them!'

Besides love and pleasure, Hoppi says that an additional reason for supplying local flowers is the huge carbon footprint associated with cut flowers imported from abroad. The 100 million roses given on a typical Valentine's Day are responsible for around 9,000 metric tons of carbon dioxide emissions. Many flowers cover vast distances to reach your hands: 83 per cent of the world's cut flowers come from Holland, Colombia, Ecuador and Kenya, and 73 per cent of the cut-flower production is presently imported by the US, the UK, Germany, Holland and France. Most of the flowers found on the British high street are either grown in Africa (Uganda and Kenya) or in intensive greenhouses in Holland, hauled in temperature-controlled trucks across the continent and kept overnight in fridges before delivery to florists. You would think that the Dutch flowers, being nearer, would have the least carbon impact, but research by Cranfield University[5] has found that in fact, because of the energy inputs into the Dutch greenhouses, the life-cycle emissions of the flowers grown in Kenya are six times lower than those grown in Holland. The carbon footprint of cut flowers encompasses not just their transportation but their entire lifespan, from the fossil fuels involved in flower cultivation, their fertilisation processes and their refrigeration.

7 Hoppi and Paul Wimbush: Dairy farming

Hoppi and Paul Wimbush have a single, beautiful Jersey cow, called Sophie, whom they bought from a large organic farm. At the time of writing she has a four-month-old heifer. Every morning she produces about nine litres (sometimes up to twelve) of milk, and between four and six litres in the evening. Bought for £600 when she was in calf, she was cheaper than the market rate because one udder was not working. She gave birth without the need for veterinary assistance. 'There was endless milk every morning and every evening!' Hoppi told me. 'We had to quickly sell it, make butter and cheese.'

Figure 10.48 Sophie, the Jersey cow.
Credit: Paul Wimbush.

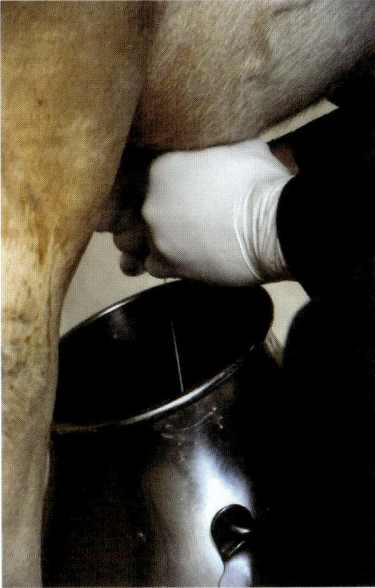

Figure 10.49 Sophie being milked by Paul.
Credit: Paul Wimbush.

Figure 10.50 Hoppi with some of the bottled milk.
Credit: Paul Wimbush.

Raw, unpasteurised milk is legally prohibited from being sold to third parties and must be either bought at the farm gate or delivered directly to the customer. Hoppi takes it round to her neighbours every morning, in two rounds on alternate days, using a trailer she made that is pulled by their beautiful Husky dog, which has been trained from a puppy. A local leather maker made a harness, and it was designed to hold two crates containing glass bottles. The bottles are reused passata bottles for which she sourced new lids.

The milk is sold for 95p per litre. Customers are billed once per month, or some pay upon delivery. Everything is recorded in a ledger. Empties are collected upon delivery, scrubbed and washed and sterilised, together with all the equipment, using the same fluid used for sterilising babies' milk bottles. Hoppi sometimes makes butter from the separated cream, in the kitchen blender. This takes between 30 seconds and two minutes. She has been making yoghurt and cheese for private consumption. The soft cheese is made by pasteurising the milk and adding wine vinegar and lemon juice. More types of cheese could be made if required.

The cow is grazed on three pastures in rotation, and sheep are brought in afterwards, borrowed from a neighbouring farm for a week, who take the grass right down so that it may rejuvenate. It is important to get the relative number of sheep and cows right because, Paul says, 'of the complementary way in which they kill each other's parasites. When the cow eats the sheep's intestinal parasites it kills them and vice versa as well as cleaning up the pasture and balancing the different grasses. So we rotate the pasture with sheep.' A TB check is given once every six months for both the calf and its mother, just in case anyway.

This micro-business is registered as a seasonal dairy with the Food Standards Agency. This is important because if it was registered as a normal dairy then it would become eligible for quarterly tests; as it is only expected

Figure 10.51 Off on the morning milk delivery round.
Credit: Paul Wimbush.

to be producing milk for six months of the year (the rest of the time the cow is expecting) only two tests a year are required.

The FSA inspectors appear without warning every couple of months and check for coliforms at £124 per test. The first test found that the milk achieved exemplary results, with a count of just 25cfu/mL. Up to 20,000cfu/mL are allowed in each measurement of milk. Mass-produced milk has a count of around 400cfu/mL. The difference is accounted for by the fact that Sophie is milked by hand and is not part of a herd, and so there is less risk of infection from the machinery or other cattle. Vets' fees are around £50 per call-out and two were required during pregnancy and to keep an eye on calcium deficiency during and after birth.

Hoppi says that in the normal practice a calf is taken from its mother after, at most, a couple of days, to keep milk production high and to prevent the risk of 'fatty udder' developing as a result of suckling. But Hoppi and Paul have kept the calf with the mother, separating them at night in adjacent stalls in order to preserve much milk production, and, as the calf learns to graze, its consumption of milk tails away. Halter training, to get the calf used to being led, which is important before it grows too large, was gently introduced after the first week.

Figure 10.52 Delivering milk at The Hub building.
Credit: Paul Wimbush.

The production of milk naturally depends on a constant supply of calves, which, since for most people it's not a good idea to keep a bull, depends on artificial insemination. Three months after the birth of a calf is the time to begin thinking about getting the cow pregnant again. Cows have a three-week (17- to 24-day) cycle and are only on heat (known as estrus) for 12 hours. Detecting this is not easy and is dependent on close observation of the animal's behaviour. Signs include a swollen vulva, with secretions, restlessness and calling. The cycle can be reset by a vet with ingestion of progesterone. An AI shot costs £30 and sperm can be ordered; with a little practice and training it's possible to administer it yourself. A cow might come into calf in March and have a milking season until November. Two heifers could be alternated if desired to maintain a year-round supply of milk, provided sufficient grazing is available.

Hoppi cautions that milking and supplying milk is an intense commitment. If a relief worker is available to permit holidays that is a welcome break.

8 Cornerwood: Coppicing as a business

Cornerwood is a square parcel of woodland, 5.9 hectares in area, located close to Cardigan, along a minor road from Llangoedmore to Llechryd. It had been planted with a cash crop of western hemlock and clear felled some 15 years previously. What remained was natural regeneration of mainly birch with overstood hazel and willow coppice interspersed with larger broadleaf standards such as oak. In October 2009 one household (Mel Robinson and Jeff Clarke's family) moved onto the land permanently and about a year later they were joined by Tracy Styles and Ian Critchley's family. To own it, they formed a legal entity called Autonomous Association, a kind of closed co-op, under advice from a Co-operative Development Agency. They then diligently researched and compiled an application for permission to create a sustainable woodland project.

The project will integrate land-based enterprises with low-impact lifestyles. The two families want to grow at least 35 per cent of their own food from the site using horticultural, animal husbandry and foraging skills, prepare their beer, wine and preserves, cook without ready meals, and generate sufficient income from the woodland to meet all their minimum income and food needs. 'The idea of being able to live a low-impact lifestyle with a high standard of living is really exciting,' said Mel. 'I did my own architectural drawings. I'd never done anything like that before since 20 years ago drawing perspective polygons in GCSE art.'

Figure 10.53 A selection of rustic furniture for sale.
Credit: Cornerwood.

Woodlands may be managed for conservation and produce, and often these twin aims coincide. Obtaining value from woodland is a complex procedure because there are opportunities for the manufacture of different types of produce for different markets. With the right mix of skills and imagination it is possible to obtain a range of products from low to high value to support a livelihood in the order of about one person per 2.5 acres (1 ha). It is also possible at the same time to use the woodland and associated crafts and skills as an educational resource which may also obtain revenue and enhance the biodiversity of the site.

Hazel and birch may both be coppiced for rustic furniture and garden and home accessories. At Cornerwood an area of two acres for each species will be harvested and managed every year, employing a loose seven-year cycle, although this is dependent on the product. Coppice is cut from October to January and the wood is stacked alongside the track. The wood is carried out during the cold frosty weather when the undergrowth is lowest and the ground is hard, reducing the amount of work needed and thus increasing profit. The following information was given by Mel Robinson, Ian Critchley and Tracey Styles both on a visit I made and via email.

Hazel

Rustic furniture is an expanding and popular market. The furniture is produced in the workshops from January to September. Products include:

chopping boards, candle holders, bird boxes, bird feeders, planters, obelisks and recycled pallet furniture.

- Bird feeders are made from small rings with the centre drilled out, these are then filled with fat and bird seed, and retail at £3.50.
- The planters and bird boxes are made using offcuts and appealing logs and sold from £5 to £20 at craft fairs, garden shows and on the gate.
- Garden chairs are relatively quick to make (two to three hours per chair) and thus can undercut the price of traditional rustic furniture at £30.
- Chopping boards and candlesticks are made from exceptionally beautiful pieces of timber, and are quick to produce, often only requiring sanding and oiling. Chopping boards sell for £10 to £40, candle sticks £10 to £20.
- Hurdles are produced using a pole lathe and two-year-old willow and hazel rods, they are small, for edging a flower bed, quick to produce and retail at £4.
- Walking sticks are cut from hazel, birch, wild cherry and ash, and are sold for £1.95 as they are, or, whittled and briefly sanded, for £6.95.
- Obelisks are made by planting a large flowerpot with sweet peas or beans. The flowerpots are reclaimed from the local tip and are free and filled with self-made compost. Five two-year-old hazel rods are arranged in a pyramid for the plants to grow up and sell for £6 each.

Figure 10.54 A selection of wood-turned items for sale.
Credit: Cornerwood.

Birch thinnings

Self-seeded birch is a predominate species in regenerated woodland. A sustainable approach to the management should be employed, opting for continual cover. An area in the wood is identified as the current one to be exploited. Trees with dead tops are the first to be felled, followed by smaller trees that are seen to have particularly healthy well-balanced tops, leaving trees that are better formed. Every single part of the tree is used, to make beanpoles, yurt poles, jumps for horseriding, pea sticks, flower stakes, faggots, and brooms. The bottom half is taken for firewood or bean poles.

A set of bean poles, consisting of twelve poles and one long ridge pole, may be sold for £5. Any thinned poles of the correct size may be sold as yurt poles ready for steam bending, for £2 per pole or, post-steam-bending, for £5 per pole. Where there is local demand for horse-jump bundles they may be made from birch tops during the winter season. Three birch tops plus all the side branches make one bundle; these are tied tightly with string and sold for £7 each.

In March any remaining birch-top thinnings become pea sticks for the grow-your-own vegetable market and may be sold for £5 for 10 bundles, a substantial increase in value. The remains of the birch thinnings, the sticks that are neither firewood, bean poles, birch-top bundles nor pea sticks, are marketed as flower stakes for 50p per bundle of 5 stakes. Any remaining twigs are tied up into faggots and sold at 60p. Additionally, brooms are produced in October at the beginning of the coppice season,

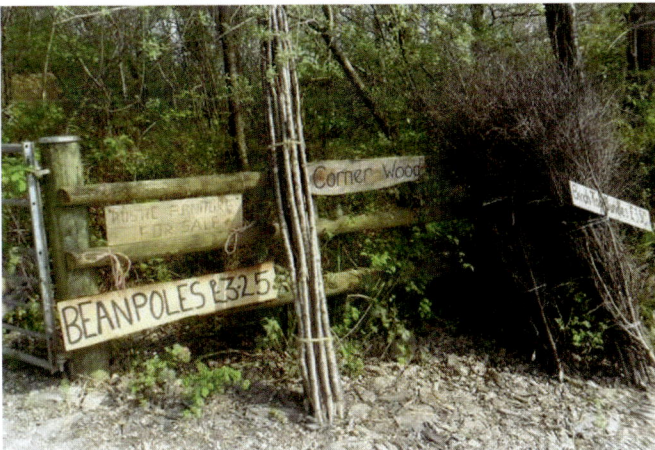

Figure 10.55 Bean poles etc. for sale.
Credit: Cornerwood.

and are made in time to sell for the Hallowe'en market. They are made in a traditional way but slightly smaller for children, and sell for between £2.50 and £5 each.

Willow

Coppiced willow rods are long and straight and can be sold for traditional use (hurdles and thatching spars) as well as to artists for land-based sculpture and for the final stage of a reed bed or wetland sewage-treatment system. Specialist willow osiers may also be planted for basket producers.

Pole lathes

Pole lathes are traditional tools made from green wood used for turning wood to make useful or aesthetic products. They deploy a foot pedal to generate the rotational power. Prior to turning on the lathe, logs are quartered to make billets, which are then rounded off by hand on a shave horse. Pole-lathe workers often find that the majority of products to be sold can be begun during wood-turning demonstrations and then finished in the workshop. Products are sold at craft fairs and in local outlets, or could at a later date be marketed nationally via a website as they are small to post. The price of items varies according to size and time taken to produce and the following is a guide:

Item	Price
Spoon	£5–20
Rattle	£1–10
Dibber	£4–7
Cup and ball	£5–8
Priest[1]	£5–10
Maul (or mallet)	£1–5
Replacement chair rungs for local furniture restorers	£10

[1] A tool for killing game or fish.

Burrs

Burrs are naturally deformed branches often found on trees during thinning or coppicing. They may be separated from the other wood to be

Figure 10.56 Stools and garden furniture for sale.
Credit: Cornerwood.

carved and polished by hand later. The results are beautiful, unique and are sold in galleries.

Buttons, badges, necklaces and pots

Buttons, badges, necklaces and pots are made by sawing a branch into small discs. These are then sanded, polished and drilled appropriately before attaching a cord or brooch backing. This is a quick process. The pots are made by sawing a small branch into short lengths; one length is drilled out and the other adapted to fit using a tenon cutter. These sell at craft fairs for £1 to £2 each, generating a high return for a small amount of wood. Badges, buttons, necklaces, key rings all sell for between £1 and £7 at craft shows, with buttons being additionally sold to local shops. Craft kits may also be compiled for sale, comprising a necklace pendant or badge front, necklace cord or badge back and sandpaper, retailing for £1.50 per badge kit or £3.95 per necklace kit.

Other income-generating activities include selling seeds such as sessile oak (*Quercus petraea*, which grows on site) acorns to a local seed merchant, collected in the autumn, for about £3 per kilo. Seasoned willow makes good artists' charcoal, and charcoal for barbecues can also be produced from other species and sold wholesale for £1.50 per kilo.

Wreaths

For the Christmas market, wreaths may be made in November and December out of holly, cones and evergreen. Ribbons, wire and dried flowers may be bought in at a wholesale price.

Chainsaw sculptures

Larger chainsaw sculptures are made from larger logs, and finished by hand. They are often made from sections of wood intended for firewood that are too knotted to split with an axe, the knot becoming the aesthetic focal point of the piece, suggesting the final shape. The final price depends upon the size. Popular shapes include toadstools, animal heads and birds.

9 Cornerwood: Shiitake production

One of Cornerwood's other livelihood proposals is the production of shiitake (*Lentinula edodes*) mushrooms.

Shiitake mushrooms are delicious and fetch a high price when supplied directly to shops, restaurants and hotels or sold at the gate. The cultivation is relatively simple and takes place in a very small area of land. Shiitake mushrooms are grown on logs that have been inoculated with spores, the drilled holes then being sealed with red wax. After a while they are soaked in water for up to 24 hours, which forces the spores to grow. They must be kept moist while the mushrooms are growing. They may be forced in this way up to three times a year, producing three harvests. The mushrooms will grow on almost any hardwood: oak, birch, chestnut, beech or alder. The spores are ordered from online suppliers. The bark must be intact. The mushrooms must be protected from deer! They can be covered with sheeting which also helps to keep the logs moist.

Cornerwood has begun a 500 log operation, using birch logs (because there is a plentiful supply) of diameter 7 cm–20 cm (3"–8") being about 1.7 metres (5 feet) in length. 130 logs are to be inoculated every year and

Figure 10.57 A shiitake mushroom growing on a log.
Credit: Keith Weller.

Figure 10.58 A stack of birch logs inoculated with the shiitake spoors. The red wax is applied to prevent rot entering the holes where the injections were made.

carried over a four-year rotation with a maximum number of 503 logs (373 fruiting) in the fourth year and continuing for the life of the operation. With good management each log should average 0.9 kg (2 lb) of mushrooms a year (three fruiting cycles) for a total of 2.7 kg (6 lb) over the life of the log.

With an anticipated average price of £5 per 0.45 kg (1 lb), an operation this size could expect to obtain revenue of £1,270 per year from year two, rising to £3,730 from year four onwards. Deducting average expenses might give a profit of £2,600 per year. Cornerwood estimates that it may also be possible to grow mushrooms on brash and use the resulting compost for growing herbs to sell to the same outlets.

10 The Ecological Land Co-operative

Finding available, suitable and affordable land is often not easy. The Ecological Land Co-operative[6] has been set up to buy land that has been, or is at risk of being, intensively managed and lease it to people that have the skills to manage it ecologically and would not otherwise be able to afford do so. The Co-op has three types of membership:

- Investor Members, who have invested money in the co-operative;
- Worker Members, who are employees and volunteers that work at least 30 days a year for the co-operative;
- Steward Members, who either have a leasehold agreement with the co-operative or manage land ecologically within the UK.

How does it work? The co-operative purchases degraded agricultural land and applies for planning permission for low-impact smallholdings with temporary residences. It provides a renewable energy source, water supply, road access, and a shared barn made of natural and local materials. It then sells long-term (150-year) leasehold agreements for the smallholdings at an affordable rate. The first smallholdings have been sold with planning permission for temporary agricultural dwellings for £72,000. One was sold with a rent-to-buy arrangement in which the tenant needed to have £14,400 as a deposit. The remainder is to be paid back over 25 years.

As an illustration, a five-acre smallholding without planning permission was recently advertised for £95,000, and a similar-sized smallholding with a house at £300,000 to £500,000. The net profit for organic smallholders is in the region of £14,000, but if you were to add the value of the food, power and water they produce/generate for their own consumption it would be much higher.

The co-op's first site, at Greenham Reach near Tiverton in Devon, has three plots which are now being developed by tenants. They are partly supported by the Fund for Enlightened Agriculture[7] because the Fund's administrators believe the projects 'have the potential to increase agricultural output, adopt sustainable farming methods, create local supply chains, increase employment and engagement, revive local economies and bring other social benefits'. Temporary planning permission has been granted for five years, during which the project will be monitored to assess the extent to which it delivers on the co-op's objectives of providing affordable holdings for viable ecological land-based livelihoods. In one case special dispensation was given to a particular tenant, to permit his projected income to be less than the minimum wage because he is a pensioner and his income will be subsidised by his state pension. Planning permission was granted within the criteria laid down by the local Development Plan.

If the tenants do not meet the criteria after five years, the (reversible) dwellings will have to be removed. If they do meet the criteria, permanent permission will be granted. The website contains all the documentation regarding the planning process.[8] The annual monitoring reports cover aspects such as the ecological footprints of the residents; the renewable energy generated on-site; the number of vehicle movements; changes in soil quality and biodiversity; visual impact of the dwellings; educational benefits; farm profitability and productivity.

Small is Successful

The co-op has produced an excellent publication, *Small is Successful*,[9] which looks at the economics of growing food on ten acres or less. It contains a foreword by Brett Spiller, the chair of the Royal Town Planning Institute, who makes the point that the Westminster government's Localism and Decentralisation Bill encourages local communities to identify the type of development they want to see. He writes: 'Neighbourhood Plans present an opportunity for both urban and rural areas to support small farms and the creation of sustainable livelihoods'.

The eight case studies examined in detail are all viable businesses with different models, from fruit and vegetable production to shiitake mushroom growing, from a hatchery providing ducklings to Real Seeds, the mail-order seed company, and include the production of cider, apple juice, honey, eggs, lamb and cordials. The evidence shows that, with creativity, sustainable livelihoods can be created on marginal sites, as only one of them, Honey Pot Farm, is on Grade I agricultural land. For example, Real Seeds supports three full-time and two part-time workers on half an acre of

Figure 10.59 Lower Farm, near Bruton, Somerset, a two-acre farm owned and run by Charles Dowding.
Photo: Ecological Land Co-operative.

Figure 10.60 Gary Whiteley of Maesyffin Mushrooms, with some of his produce.
Photo: Ecological Land Co-operative.

semi-improved pasture 100 m above sea level. It concludes that 'the most significant factor' guaranteeing success is 'the mental attitude and approach of those involved'. Characteristics required of individuals pursuing this path include 'commitment, willingness to work long hours, patience, long-term perspective, and creative, solution-focused thinking'.

The key to success, the book notes, is adding value. Every single successful smallholding achieves high yields per unit area by 'intensive and/or diverse cropping', and increases value 'through some form of processing and/or direct marketing'. Having a few different microbusinesses also improves resilience by spreading risk and enabling the more efficient use of land and resources. The most profitable small-scale land-based enterprises are labour-intensive. Growing, harvesting and processing salad leaves, soft fruit, seeds and mushrooms or require careful attention to detail; this is only possible with relatively small acreages. The authors say that horticulture is better suited to this approach than is livestock management, although a dairy serving a local village or community might be viable on under ten acres, particularly if butter, cheese or yoghurt is produced. High property prices remain the greatest barrier to new entrants. The authors have the following key seven pieces of advice for people wanting to earn a livelihood this way:

1 Keep set-up costs low;
2 Add value by direct marketing and/or processing;
3 If possible supply local shops and restaurants which favour fresh, local produce over that available from wholesalers;
4 Consider adding Environmental Health Office (EHO) approved processing facilities;
5 Consider sharing investment in processing facilities between several smallholders;
6 Avoid borrowing money by growing your business incrementally;
7 Ten acres offers little space for economically viable livestock production, unless value is added to the product from making cheese, yoghurt or ice cream.

11 John Hargraves: top fruit grower

John Hargraves grows top fruit from his approved One Planet Development near Pembroke Dock, Wales. Luckily for him, this is on the site of an old plant nursery that already contained mature trees, polytunnels and hardstand-ing. Despite the stringent conditions of being within the Pembrokeshire

Table 10.1 A summary of the case studies in *Small is Successful*.

Name	Size	Main enterprises	Value added products	Sell at	Annual turnover	Net income
Honeypot Farm	5.5 acres	apples and bees	Cider, honey, chutneys, vinegars and elder-flower cordial	Farmers markets, country fairs and own farm shop	£12,300	£7,500
Lower Farm	2 acres	salads	salad bags	small box scheme/direct to restaurants	£34,106	£15,000
Longmeadow Organics	3–6.5 acres	vegetables	–	Green Valley Farm Shop, local markets	£48,000	£16,500
Real Seed Collection	0.5 acres + 2 acres	seed production	seeds	mail order	£188,188	£70,950 (it's a not-for-profit, so shared out)
Bridge Farm	1.5 acre forest garden	fruit and vegetables	–	market stall, restaurants, hotels & shops	£22,000	£10,900
Holly Tree Poultry Hatchery	2.5 acres	ducklings, geese	oven-ready birds, day old ducklings	farm gate, local butchers	£25,000–£30,000	£10,000
Spring Grove Market Garden	6.5 acres	vegetable and flowers	–	local restaurants food outlets, some farm gate sales	£46,900	£23,100
Maesyffin Mushrooms	30 m × 20 m	Fresh & dried shiitake mushrooms	paté	local shops and distributors, restaurants, private customers, website	£8,000–10,000	not yet

Figure 10.61 Young rootstock grafted apple cultivar saplings that will form a new orchard on John Hargraves' site.

Figure 10.62 John watering some of his Mediterranean fruit trees in his polytunnels.

National Park he was able to obtain planning permission for a low-impact development (even though the planners did not like the polytunnels!). The main challenge he faces is obtaining a sufficient income from growing vegetables and fruit since the cost often doesn't match the revenue that can be obtained. 'I should be adding value to my produce,' he says, 'by processing and preserving it.'

Yet he has achieved much, despite being a single parent with a five-year-old daughter. John says, 'My daughter appreciates being on the site and learning. She works in the field and loves it. Far from feeling compelled to do so, she will work on a similar task, for example mulching trees, for several days at a time, and already cycles one mile to the local school.'

Within the polytunnels grow two Mediterranean trees – a peach and an apricot – as well as profuse vines and a cherry tree. Several different culti-vars of apple, including Fiesta and Chivers Delight, are planted, plus a few pear trees, although pear trees do not fare so well in this climate. John opts for rootstock grafting in order to obtain the type of thin-skinned, sweet apples that modern tastes prefer. 'Traditional varieties, having thicker skins, although they like the climate, are not so popular so I graft the thin-skinned varieties onto the traditional root stocks.' The rootstock chosen also determines the size of the final tree.

The main problem with the apples is canker, which he deals with by cutting or carving off the diseased part of the tree and repeatedly applying copper sulphate paint until there is no sign of the canker returning. Bark scar tissue then appears over the wound. Despite the fact that the climate is warm and wet, not a favourite habitat for apples, he manages to obtain a fair-sized crop.

His timber-frame house is to be constructed from Douglas Fir for the frame with larch cladding obtained from Cwm Coed near Cenarth, Ceredigion, not far away. Designed by architect Steve Coulston, it is to be constructed to the Passivhaus standard and insulated with recycled cellulose (Warmcel). Simple to construct, it will sit on gravel sourced from some of the removed hardstanding, to make it, he says, 'look normal', so that visitors will not be put off by an unusual appearance, as it will be partly used for educational purposes.

The site is regularly visited by local children, who enjoy activities such as an Easter egg hunt and just playing amongst the trees. He recognises that sometimes low-impact developments can take a while to be accepted by local communities but his answer to this potential criticism is that new developments in cities also take 10 years to plug into their local communities. 'Like an apple tree they take time to root.' To forge links with the community, John has set up a group called Green Apple, which will hold educational courses, events and workshops. He laments the fact that learning through interaction with nature does not form a greater part of the national curriculum. 'Lots of children enjoy coming here and treat it as a home,' he says. 'The local school comes down. This is as good as it gets: learning while you play. It's not formal learning but it certainly trumps exams.'

Figure 10.63 Ripe grapes at the beginning of October.

12 Phil Corbett: Edible wild flowers and nitrogen-fixing clovers

Phil Corbett operates a mail-order business called Cool Temperate[10] for productive and nitrogen-fixing plants from a smallholding in Nottinghamshire. He has for many years been using land managed by the organic, biodynamic Trinity Farm,[11] which itself runs a box scheme and farm shop. During my visits he was in the process of moving to a nearby piece of land on which he is planting a new orchard, and which he has bought himself.

He explained his business model:

> I buy in wildflower and herb seedlings at 25p, grow them on, and sell them for £2.50. Most of the seedlings are sold by mail order. A wholesaler's order that gets free delivery is made up according to the anticipated demand for each variety. All of my herbaceous suppliers are in the UK. These plants can have a rapid maturity, sometimes being potted on and sold less than a month after having arrived.

His speciality is own-root fruit trees, which is distinct from most of the fruit trees you buy which are grafted onto other roots, and those favoured by John Hargraves above. 'A lot of the characteristics of the grafted tree are determined by the rootstock,' says Phil. 'Not just tree size, but life expectancy, anchorage, fruit size and shape; years to cropping and things like

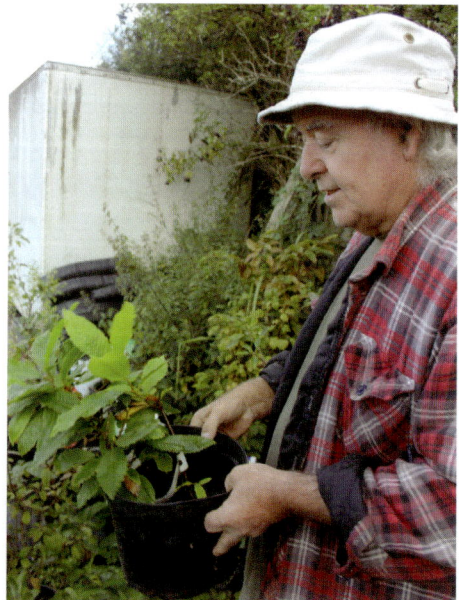

Figure 10.64 Phil Corbett with a pecan sapling.

the ability to cope with cold, drought and flood. But grafting is commonly practised because it is the most flexible way of mass producing planting-size trees quickly.'

Conventionally, the Royal Horticultural Society says that 'rootstocks are used to control the vigour of the plant, allowing the cultivation of trees and bushes in a smaller space than if they were grown on their own roots'. This is because size has been the predominant factor determining choice in an industry happy to use chemicals. But there are plenty of species that do not grow too big, or can be kept smaller, but which have other desirable characteristics, as Phil says, particularly when growing organically.

When I asked him why it is that we don't know after all these centuries what the characteristics of a variety of fruit tree might be in terms of, say, its suitability to a particular soil type or location or climate, his answer was surprising. 'For the last few centuries we've been dealing mainly with grafted trees so we do not know what the roots do. For example, I grew some own-root Katja (*Syn Katy – Malus domestica*), which is a Swedish variety, on a previous site, from young plants. They had grown an additional foot from about 18 inches in a season, and when I dug them up to move them I found that the root system had grown three or four metres during the same period. That is something that you would never know if you only dealt with grafted trees.'

So Phil is slowly building up a database of what he learns about the behaviour of the particular fruit tree species and varieties with which he is experimenting in this bioregion, building on the experience of his mentor, Hugh Ermen, a Kent-based breeder of apple varieties, now, sadly, deceased.

Figure 10.65 Apple Scrumptious on M27 rootstock.

Hugh did the basic groundwork on own-root trees and worked at Brogdale National Fruit Collection[12] near Faversham in Kent, which is home to the world's largest collection of fruit trees and plants: a staggering 3,500 different apple, pear, plum, cherry, bush fruit, vine and cob nut cultivars. Advice is also available to commercial growers from the Farm Advisory Services Team (FAST) based at Brogdale.[13] For example, 'biffins' were large cooking apples that, around Norfolk, used to be dried in parish ovens while they were cooling, causing their flavours to intensify. As they were flexible and chewy they could be packed in hampers and sent to London by stagecoach – a whole industry based on semi-dried apples. 'We've lost a lot of knowledge about fruit but I don't think it's too far gone. It's retrievable. I'm optimistic,' says Phil. Several of his cultivars are pictured in the Food chapter.

Most own-root trees have an enhanced degree of self-fertility, producing more seeds. Hugh Ermen discovered several other advantages, including better health, notwithstanding the susceptibility of the specific variety to disease, the best possible flavour, quality, fruit set and storage life. The typical size of spur-type own-root tree is similar to a tree on m9 rootstock, i.e. three metres tall; non-spur types are typically between M26 and MM106 in vigour; and a few vigorous triploids yield trees between MM106 and MM111. The size of the tree is best controlled by early and regular cropping, which diverts its energy into fruit and away from wood. The most familiar OR trees to be seen are those in hedges and verges where they

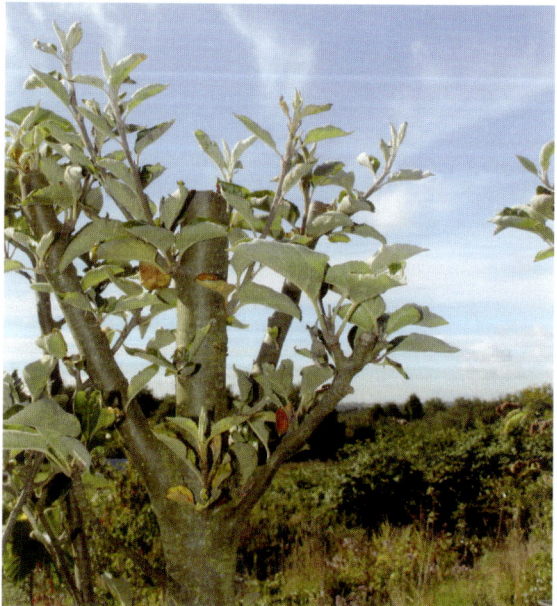

Figure 10.66 A William Crump apple cultivar.

have grown up from thrown away apple cores. They give a good idea of typical tree size, and extra vigorous trees are rare.

Traditional techniques are used to induce early cropping of own-root stock. These include withholding nitrogen (which stimulates growth) and withholding irrigation (except in serious drought), tying down one- and two-year-old branches to the horizontal, summer pruning (which induces fruit buds) and avoiding winter pruning (which stimulates re-growth). Once cropping begins, the tree's energies are channelled into fruit production and growth slows down to a controllable level; a normal feeding and watering regime can then begin.

Figure 10.67 A two-year-old Juglans Exel of Teignton (walnut) – an 'Oscar Winner' among walnuts.

Figure 10.68 A two-year-old tree mallow.

Phil supplies many other plants, including chocolate vines and tree mallow. Britain's biggest wildflower, tree mallows can grow to four metres high. As it grows in compressed stone, it is good for site regeneration. It produces a semi-woody stem material, making it a good bulk biomass producer, a bee plant and is evergreen, so can be cut any time of year and shredded to produce nitrogen-rich green leafy material for mulch. It only lives for a maximum of four years and when it dies its roots, decomposing in rocky ground, create soil. Other highlights he showed me on a fascinating afternoon, included:

- *Elaeagnus umbellata*, also known as Autumn Olive, with its bright red little berries that are juicy and edible, and also make a good dried fruit. Though the fruit are small, the tree bears them abundantly. They are tart-tasting, with chewable seeds. A nitrogen-fixing bush.
- Sea Buckthorn – *Hippophae rhamnoides*. a nitrogen-fixing fruit bush. Grown commercially for juice, this has a high vitamin content and great, lemony taste. It grows on sand dunes around the East Coast but also around the Baltic coast, where it has been developed as a juice and pulp enhancer to high-vitamin preserves, drinks and jams.
- Apricots (he grows a Mormon apricot variety from a high altitude in Arizona – 'the Mormon settlement failed but not the apricots'). 'The problem is not getting them to ripen but keeping the frost off in the spring,' he says.
- His pecan variety comes from the north of their native range in Michigan, and might be grown in the south of England, even further north.

Stooling

Phil also educated me in a way of growing new apple trees from own root trees called stooling. He believes it is more reliable than growing from seeds 'because trees cross-pollinate and you don't know what you're getting. Stooling is a good way of getting a lot out of a small space. Two square feet can produce 40 trees in two years.' A young OR tree is cut almost down to the ground in the winter, the stump dug out and placed in a large container. Come the spring a number of new shoots will come up. When they have grown up to a foot or more, compost is packed round the bottom six inches or so and the whole wrapped around with perforated hard plastic – this keeps the compost in and stops rodents from eating the young shoots. The shoots then start to form roots in the compost. The shoots can then

Figure 10.69 Phil demonstrates his stooling technique.

Figure 10.70 Part of Phil's new orchard.

grow over a metre with more compost added – up to half the height of the shoots. In the late autumn the compost is dug away and the rooted shoots can be cut off. From one young tree you can get 10–20 trees. 'They are layers with a small-root system developing on them, and need growing-on in a nursery bed to develop further for a season before they can be sold.' Phil is experimenting on stooling with a number of apple varieties, but other trees can be stooled too, such as chestnuts: 'hedgehog chestnuts', found on a roadside verge of the A1, which make bushy low trees and crop heavily and readily.

Phil's new orchard contains a row of trees planted two feet apart, for stooling, then other rows spaced wide enough for growth, and laid out north-south. Looking across, there are two rows of apples followed by a row of hazels and nitrogen fixers, followed by a row each of plums and pears; and then another row of hazels and nitrogen fixers and two rows of apples again. 'This helps cross-pollination of varieties – you want to ensure that,' says Phil.

The black sheeting will be peeled back after a year or so when the weeds have died down, so there will be a cultivatable strip between the trees where perennial soft fruit such as raspberries and strawberries are planted in strips between the rows of trees. As time goes by and more land is required the plastic will be progressively folded back till removed completely.

13 Nant y Cwm farm: livestock management

Situated near Cardiff, Nant y Cwm produces lamb, pork, sausages, bacon and chicken, as well as eggs and a wide range of fruit and vegetables. Dan and Sarah Moody and their five children had, in 2013, already been working their 16 acres for four years without planning permission. Their OPD application to the local council was approved in Easter 2014, the first to achieve this under the OPD policy. They told me they aimed to be 'examples of sustainable living like John Seymour', whose book on self-sufficiency has been an inspiration to them.

Having largely been sheep-grazing land for 20 years, soil fertility was poor to begin with. Pigs, horses and cows were used to bring the fertility

Figure 10.71 Sarah Moody selling some of her produce at a market stall.
Credit: Dan Moody.

level up, together with a sprinkling of lime from a nearby quarry. The Moodys began with 20 sheep and a number of pigs; the pigs were used to clear the land. Four years later, when I visited, none were being used in the month of October; instead, I counted ten sheep, two cows, several hens and three horses, but it was planned to purchase two young pigs to fatten up from October for slaughter for Christmas. These would clear up windfalls after harvesting apples and nuts: the only extra nutrition they would need is a few bags of feed. A proposed barn extension will house a milking parlour and a hygiene rated kitchen – 'so we can add value to our food products by turning them into jams, pickles, chutneys, cheese, milk, cream, et cetera,' says Dan.

Henry the horse

Uniquely amongst the places I visited, Nant y Cwm farm has a working horse and two mountain ponies. Henry is a six-year-old Irish gypsy cob bought from a nearby heavy horse dealer. Dan got a farrier to break him and give him tips on how to train him. This involved first attaching reins, then chains and letting him get used to walking around with them. To these were then attached firstly a tyre and then a wheel to get him used to the weight and it bouncing around. Dan then got him used to taking instructions such as go, stop and turn. Finally a cart was attached. At first he ran off with it and Dan was forced to bail out, 'But I immediately got straight back in and took him around the field,' he says. Henry is used to pull a cart, plough, roll trees and harrowing – even several times to take the family on a trip to the pub. The next plan is to purchase a two-wheeled cart to reduce the use of the tractor. The farm has a contract to work the nearby common land where wood is extracted and the land is improved in an environmentally friendly manner. This is a traditional way of managing the land and obtaining firewood.

Figure 10.72 Dan and Henry.
Credit: Sarah Moody.

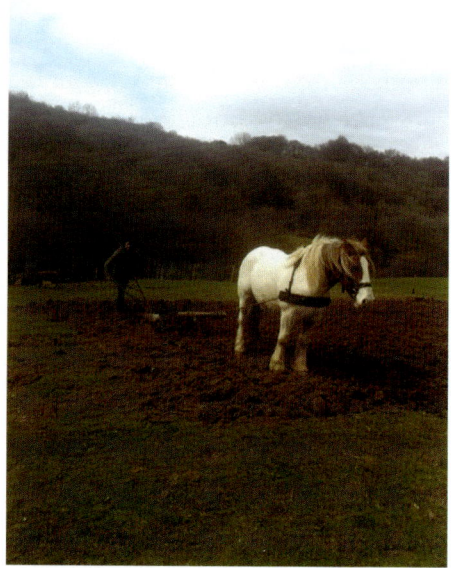

Figure 10.73 Ploughing with Henry.
Credit: Sarah Moody.

Providing fodder

The smallholding has found that growing food for their animals themselves, rather than buying in feed, has drastically cut management costs whilst requiring fewer transport miles.

> The hay/haylage is cut in the summertime (early August to September, after the meadow flowering). There are two or three acres given over to growing fodder. We set aside a field for fodder May–July, and, if we have some, use the pigs to cultivate the soil pre-planting. The crop is then ready December–February. It is stored in the barn if hay, or wrapped if haylage. We would prefer not to wrap but limited storage dictates that for now we must. The hay is then fed to the animals throughout the winter.

Fodder is also grown. The technique employed is to go over the field quickly with a rotovator just once, which only partially turns the soil. Dan says this uses the same amount of fuel as a 10-mile round trip to Cardiff and the advantage is that it allows the seeds to be dropped in without losing the nitrogen-fixing clover already growing in the field. Turnip, kale and swedes are planted by hand and rolled in using Henry the horse. 'We often help ourselves to the fodder crop for family consumption,' said Sarah.

The field is then strip grazed with the sheep, followed by the pigs to clean up. 'The oats and barley have been grown in smaller sections, cut with

Figure 10.74 Logging trees with Henry.
Credit: Dan Moody.

a scythe and left to dry in the late summer sun. This is then kept to feed the hungry animals when there is little other feed or grass around late winter. The oats are primarily used for the working horse for energy. The pigs in particular have benefited from clearing up any vegetables, grain crops and potatoes that have been planted for human consumption and not fully harvested. Animal feed for cats and dogs is included in our shopping bills and is fed to them to top up waste food which is also given.'

Meeting food needs

How has the growing of their own food contributed to the overall food needs of the seven inhabitants of the farm? Since 2009 they have quantified the amount spent on household food. At the beginning it was £5,333. By 2013 this was reduced by £2,000 and is projected to continue to decrease to £1,510 in 2017. Over the same period supermarket trips have decreased by 63 per cent to 90, projected to reduce to 52 in 2017. Concomitantly, the value of the produce consumed from the farm is rising from zero in 2009 to £3,384 in 2013, projected to rise to £5,690 in 2017. Presently the proportion of food produced on the farm is 50 per cent and is proposed to rise to a maximum of 79 per cent in 2017.

There has also, interestingly, been a change in the type of food consumed, as there has been decreasing reliance on processed products, with the exception of cooking oil, confectionery and beverages. In total in 2012, the value of food produced and sold was £10,868.50, the majority of which was meat (33 per cent) and hay and bedding (24 per cent). Deducting costs, this led to a profit of £7,070.30, which is projected to rise to £8,520 in 2017. Lest this be seen as woefully inadequate by conventional standards, the management plan announces that it 'reflects a change in lifestyle in

Figure 10.75 The smallholding has a forge enthusiastically worked by Dan and Sarah's son, Reuben. Credit: Sarah Moody.

which the household costs are minimised as we move towards a sustainable balance of activities'. As a result, by 2017 the minimum household need will be £6,134.86. In other words the proportional needs met from land-based income will rise from 34 per cent in 2013 to 139 per cent in 2017.

It's important that policymakers and planning department officials understand the difference in productivity that arises from land managed in this way compared to modern conventional agriculture. Dan says: 'We have learned that we are able to work the land in an incredibly productive manner and that we are able not only to feed ourselves but also to derive a substantial income from our activities.' A more 'hands-on' relationship between the farmer and the land that is more labour-intensive than conventional farming, being flexible enough to take advantage of opportunities as they are noticed on the farm, and attendance to the quality of the soil are contributing factors to this success.

The importance of community connection

Dan and Sarah also attribute part of their success to being interconnected with the local community and to neighbouring farms. This includes working with a drug rehabilitation charity, Kaleidoscope, to give clients the chance to obtain experience of land-based occupations. Up to seven trainees have been involved at a time including someone training as a green woodworker. It is now well known that working closely with nature has powerful life-transforming effects on people's physical and mental health and can help with rehabilitation. Having been a trustee of a therapeutic garden myself I have witnessed this first hand. Clients and volunteers referred by GPs, young offenders organisations and mental-health charities have often said they appreciate the proximity to nature of working with animals, or looking after plants and watching them grow as they tend them; all of which makes it 'good to feel needed and useful again'.

It might be thought, if you're considering living in this manner: what about holidays? With so little income and so little time because of being tied to the land, holidays can easily be missed. This is true of all land-based activities, but it's always possible to get friends to come and take over for a few days while you get away. Dan and Sarah and family have a sailing boat moored on the coast of the Bristol Channel. Dan says they go sailing 'for a low-carbon holiday. We camped aboard our boat, so no camp fees. We used less than a litre of petrol for the motor and took a load of home-grown food with us from the farm which we cooked on driftwood with freshly caught fish and scallops. Thanks to a mix of great friends and neighbours the farm was still in one piece when we got back!'

14 Jay Andrews: Wetland Ecosystem Treatment

In conventional housing and industrial developments, water and sewerage management are often considered as afterthoughts, as part of an 'out of sight, out of mind' attitude to the subjects. The choice of the technology to be used is purely an economic one; so much capital cost, so much energy consumed for operating the system, so much maintenance cost. Social, environmental/ecological and aesthetic benefits and 'right livelihood' are not a part of the equation. This is almost exactly the opposite to the approach taken in one planet living, where thinking about water flows, soil and waste from the start produces huge rewards.

Figure 10.76 Part of a Wetland Ecosystem Treatment system that treats the sewage of about 50 people. Credit: Biologic Design.

Figure 10.77 Jay Andrews' first Wetland Ecosystem Treatment system that treats very strong and acidic wastewater from a Westons Cider factory – now nearly 20 years old. Credit: Biologic Design.

A natural wetland system is a miraculous thing, a living and productive example of the best that nature can offer to the problems of balancing an ecosystem, whether these problems are caused by human activity (most likely) or not. Natural wetlands form some of the most biodiverse areas on the planet. The chains of complex biochemical processes which occur in these ecosystems can absorb and transform potentially ecologically deleterious compounds into the beneficial inputs of this biological system.

The potential for positive environmental change is harnessed in a type of constructed wetland system called a Wetland Ecosystem Treatment or WET System. This is a multi-species, soil-based constructed wetland which provides a solution to the need to treat and purify effluent. But this is just the start of it, since if designed, planted and managed correctly they can not only purify wastewater but also create a species-rich wildlife habitat and be managed to produce biomass resources – craft materials, fuel, fibre and food.

The key to what goes on in a constructed wetland system such as a WET System is just below the surface, in the soil and in the root zone of the soil – where the soil *mycorrhizal* association of fungi and plant roots plays an active role in the transformations that occur. This beautiful, beneficial, symbiotic relationship is between the roots of vascular plants, which require water and minerals for photosynthesis, and particular types of fungi, called *arbuscular mycorrhiza*, which aid this absorption process. Many other microbes – the fungi, bacteria and slime moulds, as well as the protozoans – all form a vital, living part of the soil root zone and help with the mineralisation of the nutrients found in the wastewater. It is the microbiological processes which occur as a result of this symbiosis which enables the WET System to 'process' and then absorb the nutrients in the water within the system.

WET systems have been pioneered and developed in the UK by Jay Abrahams, who established Biologic Design in 1993 in order to create them for his clients. Jay has created over 150 of them so far, with designs for sewage systems varying in size from the tiny, servicing single homes with just one or two residents, to a caravan park with 400 people, a boarding school with 1,000 pupils and teachers and a recent design for a site with a population of 2,500. Industrial and farm-based systems include cheese-making effluent, dairy farm wastewater as well as the now very well established eight-acre WET System at Westons Cider – which has been purifying the very strong and acidic wastewater from the factory for nearly 20 years. The Westons system was the second WET System Jay designed and it has enabled the company to greatly expand its production capacity since then, whilst saving them millions of pounds over the years, which would have needed to be spent on conventional effluent treatment.

Anyone viewing an established WET System (from about two years after planting) could easily imagine it to be a totally natural wetland that had been there for many years. They are designed to remain in place for hundreds of years. Jay designs both WET Systems and Whole Site Water Reticulation Systems, which harvest and manages rainwater, any water-courses/springs and wastewater flows over an entire site using earthworks and plants to recover resources and which often include a WET System.

Figure 10.79 A Wetland Ecosystem
Treatment system treating the
sewage of 45 people.
Credit: Biologic Design.

Figure 10.80 A Wetland Ecosystem
Treatment in winter.
Credit: Biologic Design.

He calls them both 'low-entropy' systems because 'once they have been created, they require little or no non-renewable energy input. The systems are powered by the sun, as the plants act as "solar collectors", creating through photosynthesis both oxygen and sugars which the soil biota and the *mycorrhiza* employ to help the plants absorb both water and minerals from the effluent and subsoil, and gravity replaces the need for pumps.'

Biochemical Oxygen Demand (BOD) is a standard indicator of water quality and of the effectiveness of wastewater treatment processes. WET Systems can absorb and purify most types of biodegradable pollutants including nitrates and phosphates, and treat severely polluted water with a BOD as high as 20,000. This compares to a BOD value of around 300–400 for domestic sewage. These figures (in milligrams of oxygen consumed by the microbes per litre of sample during five days of incubation at 20 °C) represent the amount of dissolved oxygen needed by oxygen-using organisms to break down polluting organic material.

'Conventional sewage-treatment systems use energy requiring motorised aerators and pumps in order to mix and add the required oxygen to the wastewater, and this is carried out in large concrete or steel tanks – a hugely energy-intensive way of processing the wastewater,' Jay explained to me when I went to see examples of his work in Herefordshire. 'Furthermore, unlike the better-known reed-bed treatment systems, no gravel and very few plastic aeration or distribution pipes are used in their construction. Therefore there is no need to dig up the gravel, nor energy used to bring gravel to the site – WET Systems have a very low embedded energy. We aim to use the earth resources of each site where a WET System is to be created and use the topsoil and clay that is already present.'

Biologic Design's team plant directly into the topsoil of specially created swales a selection of the 45 species of aquatics, marginals and wetland wildflowers produced by Jay's wife on her organically run plant nursery. There is a range of native reeds and sedges that, along with Yellow Flag Iris and Purple Loosestrife, will grow happily and vigorously in various waste-waters. Early season nectar is provided by Marsh Marigolds at the water's edge; Greater Spearwort, Marsh Woundwort and Yellow Loosestrife will spread into drifts of summer colour, and densely rooting wildflowers such as Meadowsweet and Hemp Agrimony are useful for bank stabilisation and shade tolerance as well as providing nectar later in the year.

The topsoil is then covered in locally sourced woodchip, which acts as a weed-excluding mulch, as well as a carbon source for the microbes to inhabit, and derive energy from, as it slowly breaks down and forms new soil. Many different species can be used within the WET System. The species used in any system depend upon the type of wastewater to be purified, what management regime is required, what plants occur in the wild locally, and what yields the owner wishes to harvest. These productive yields can include willow and other wetland trees, fruit trees as well as non-wetland trees that can also be planted around the outer earth banks of the WET System. Willow, of which Biologic Design currently has 55 named basketry cultivars, can be coppiced under a one-year coppice cycle for wands for basketry; two years for hurdle making, living willow domes and tunnels, and binders for hedge-laying; and three years for the construction of other living willow structures and garden furniture. Once seasoned, the coppiced wands may also be used or sold as fuel for wood-stoves and 'rocket-stoves', ceramic stoves, biomass boilers or combined heat and power (CHP) systems.

He took me to view two local WET Systems at very different extremes of scale. The first treated the greywater from a very small restored seventeenth-century timber-frame thatched wattle-and-daub cottage with two residents. (See Fig. 5.26 in Chapter Five.) The occupants use a composting toilet for solid waste. The WET System for the greywater had been in place for just 18 months and, in August, it formed a beautiful triangular bed of about the same area as the tiny cottage. It was a total absorption WET System with no surface water to be seen, with meadowsweet, marsh marigold, ferns and sedges, bustling with dragonflies, butterflies and bees. The couple living there were delighted with it.

The second system was much larger, occupying about an acre, and served a large complex of residential and workshop buildings with a permanent population of between 100 and 150, but which could serve up to 3,500 people for a month during large annual gatherings on the site. (See Figures 5.23 to 5.25 in Chapter Five.) Recently completed, it was not yet fully established. The planting of the marginals had been completed just a month earlier, and the earthworks completed just six weeks before that. Whilst walking around this already beautiful wetland Jay explained that swales form a series of 'channels' which lead the water through the landscape in a very naturalistic looking system. Based on P. A. Yeomans' Keyline system for drought-proofing farms by harvesting rainwater in arid climates, these cross-slope swales harvest wastewater and purify it as it passes through the system. In this instance, each swale is about 45 metres in length and linked by a short length of piping to take the outfall from the one above it. The heavy clay subsoil was compacted to around 4.5 tonnes per square meter using a sheep's foot roller and then covered with uncompacted topsoil – which had been removed and carefully stored whilst the swales were being formed and compacted. The 'shoreline' edges of these swales – where the water and the soil meet – were then densely planted with the marginal species and trees.

Above the field where the WET System is located is a settlement tank for the removal of solids. This concrete tank used to be the aerated sewage treatment system serving the site in the past, and was then full of plastic media, aerated using a large electrically powered compressor. Fed by gravity alone, the outfall empties via a pipe into the top swale, forming a slowly moving pool that is black in colour. Even though the reed-raft has not yet established over the surface of the first swale there was no noticeable smell emanating from it. The water then proceeds through the WET System comprising six further swales; by the time it arrived at the third swale, it was almost clear and a mother duck with ducklings were swimming happily around in it. By the time the wastewater reaches the final polishing pond it is of bathing quality.

The earthworks machinery is the major energy input into the process of creating a WET System, but once completed it requires no further artificial energy input. This conversion of the perennial 'problem' of what to do with human waste – converting it into a positive resource – is just the physical magic. The intangible magic is even more powerful and occurs in the minds of those who perceive the resulting landscape: an immense increase in bio-diversity, of economic value and of spiritual and aesthetic value. These multiple benefits are the direct result of taking an all-encompassing, ecological perspective; of seeing waste and water as an integral part of the web of life.

15 A modular building design

I'm including this because, although small, I believe that the principles can be used to design a building of any size, and with more than one storey. It's my studio, which I designed, and where I wrote this book. The plan is modular in the sense that the studs in the timber frame walls are positioned just 5 mm less apart than the width of the woodfibre batts, which were squeezed between them, both to avoid the need for cutting and to eliminate gaps through which cold air might seep. The plan area can therefore

Figure 10.81 The completed studio.

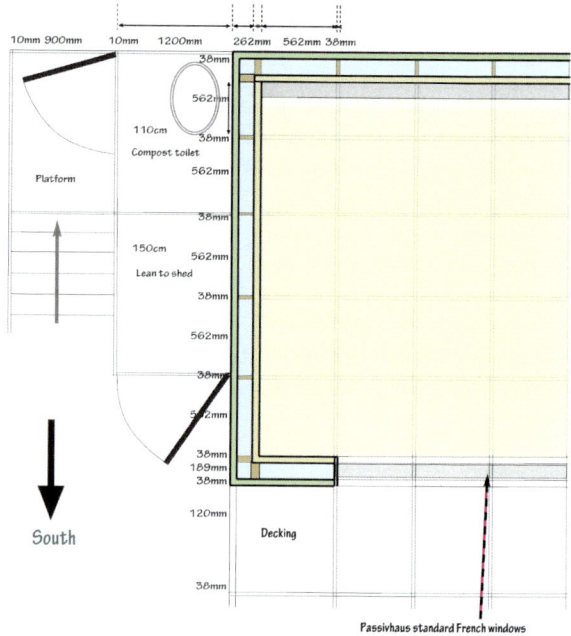

10mm 900mm   10mm   1200mm   262mm   562mm 38mm

38mm

562mm

110cm   38mm
Compost toilet

562mm

Platform

38mm

150cm   562mm
Lean to shed

38mm

562mm

38mm

562mm

38mm
189mm
38mm

120mm

South   Decking

Figure 10.82 Part of the floor plan.

38mm

Passivhaus standard French windows

Figure 10.83 The tyres were laid out in a grid. Reused railway sleepers were laid across them, although in retrospect this was perhaps unnecessary.

be any multiple of this distance in depth or width, to create buildings that are larger in floor area. Structurally, it can take at least another storey.

The building sits on railway sleepers resting on old tyres filled with hemcrete (could be rammed earth or concrete), with no need for foundations. It is timber frame, insulated with wood fibre and recycled newsprint (cellulose) insulation (the cheapest), fitted with south-facing, triple-glazed Passivhaus-certified windows from Germany (also the cheapest but the most still expensive component) to capture the solar heat, lime-rendered and fully breathable. This part is a German system called Steico, from the website ecomerchant.co.uk. The floor has black ceramic tiles to absorb solar heat. The roof slopes slightly backwards from the front. There is guttering at the back.

Figure 10.84 The studio's insulated floor (wood-fibre batts and Warmcel) and interlocking cladding on the outside, sitting on the tyres, before rendering.

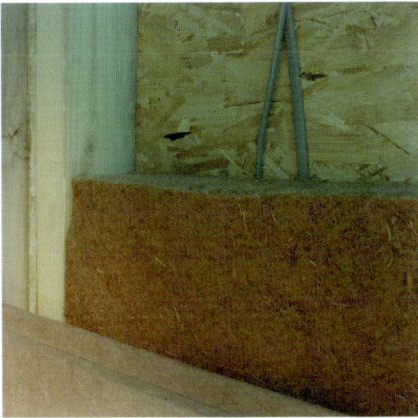

Figure 10.85 The studio's frame, with wood-fibre batts squeezed between the studs, and interlocking cladding on the outside, before the render was added.

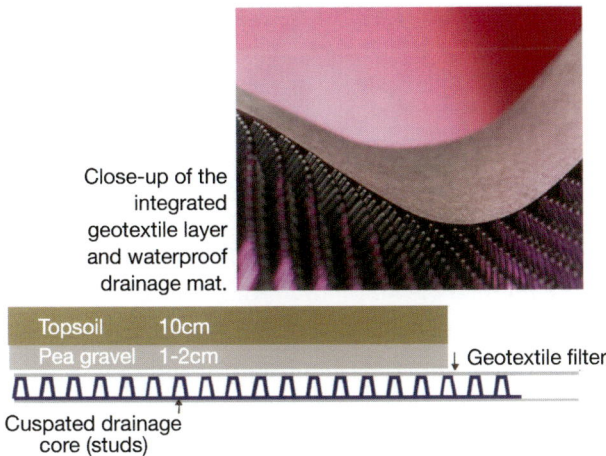

Close-up of the integrated geotextile layer and waterproof drainage mat.

Topsoil 10cm
Pea gravel 1–2cm
↓ Geotextile filter
Cuspated drainage core (studs)

Figure 10.86 Cross-section of the green roof, which consists of the following layers, from the bottom up:
1. roof flashing;
2. EPDM waterproof membrane;
3. GEOfabrics' composite root barrier, drainage mat and geotextile fabric;
4. 2 cm pea gravel;
5. 10 cm poor quality soil (sedums like this);
6. Plants!

Figure 10.87 and 10.88 The interior before and after plastering.

Figure 10.89 The ceiling space before being filled with Warmcel.

The heating is electric, underfloor, but is hardly needed. This was chosen because the supplementary heating requirements are minimal; it is efficient; the building runs on renewable electricity; and not having a wood-stove avoids puncturing the thermal envelope to make a hole in the ceiling (it would also require ventilation to supply fresh oxygen to replace that being burnt!). Thermal bridging is completely eliminated, chiefly by cladding all the way round with tongue and groove wax-impregnated (for water-proofing) woodfibre boards, finished with lime render, itself having a slight insulating property. The building is almost completely airtight (within limits

Figure 10.90 A Passivhaus window installed.

Figure 10.91 Tŷ Solar (solar house), Peters' first prototype.

to prevent me from suffocating!). Ventilation is manual. The cost was about £800 per square meter in 2011, including the sedum roof. Given overheads, the unit cost would be lower if the building were larger. It can be, and was, constructed by a conventional builder who was well supervised.

16 Tŷ Solar

To make a real difference, one planet living must go mainstream. This and the next few examples begin to show how this may be possible. Glen Peters sees his role in this as being to show how it might be possible to supply truly sustainable and affordable housing. Having made a good profit from a solar farm in his field (behind the house) he's putting it to good use by demonstrating a new model for sustainable housing.

Working with a team of architects and designers, he has produced a prototype two-storey detached three-bedroomed house with a radical new take on passive house principles. Called Tŷ Solar (Solar House in Welsh). It is of timber-frame construction and insulated with blown cellulose, and is potentially able to export more electricity to the grid than it consumes itself in a given year. The larch used for the frame and cladding is sourced locally and assembled to specifications that are beyond those required by Building Regulations, giving it a Code for Sustainable Homes 5 rating (out of a maximum of 6). But this doesn't tell the whole story by any means.

By using recycled newsprint (the blown cellulose) as the only insulant around the entire building envelope and local timber, the house is locking up atmospheric carbon in its structure for an indefinite period, unlike buildings that use fossil-fuel-based insulants that have emitted carbon during

Figure 10.92 The landing inside Tŷ Solar.

their manufacture. As with any studio the embodied energy of the house is therefore already very low, an important factor given that for normal buildings between 10 and 20 per cent of their life-cycle energy consumption is used during the phase of extraction of raw materials and construction.

The final purchase price has been set at a maximum of £75,000. The principal watchword throughout the design process that has enabled this to be possible has been simplicity. Almost heretically for passive house construction it eschews ventilation and heat recovery, and the only source of energy is solar: both passive solar through the abundance of south-facing windows and active through reliance on solar photovoltaic panels for electricity and top-up space and domestic water heating.

The demonstration house includes lithium-ion batteries to store 12 kWh of power but is also grid connected to enable the export of unused electricity and the use of the grid as a backup at other times. The battery bank is optional. Glen says: 'A group of 10 or more houses generating in tandem with a local smart grid could form a miniature power station and generate a considerable income, perhaps £1000 per year, for each of the households, or the power could be used to charge electric vehicles which could be shared between them.'

All of this highlights the urgent need for houses of this nature. As Glen Peters says: 'The bulk housing providers in the construction industry are ignoring affordable housing. They say that it doesn't work for them. I say they are missing a trick. We've proved it is perfectly possible to build low-carbon housing that is truly affordable and that gives occupants zero

Figure 10.93 The kitchen.

Figure 10.94 An electric radiator in the landing area.

energy bills.' With energy bills so high on the public agenda it is hard to see how local authorities and housing associations can ignore the potential that this house demonstrates.

Low embodied energy

This successful and attractive-looking house goes against the grain in terms of many of the current developments in sustainable housing. Compared to the Mark Group's demonstration house in Nottingham, BRE's 'Smart Home', in Watford, and Velux's CarbonLight demonstration home in Rothwell near Kettering, it scores very favorably on local sourcing, embodied energy, embodied carbon and simplicity of use. Above all it compares well on price. All of these three supposedly cutting-edge demonstration homes contain extreme amounts of technology and sophisticated materials. They represent corporate attempts to capture a high-end market in low- or zero-carbon housing. The first utilizes an incredibly energy intensive over-specified steel frame. The second uses occupation sensors to control heating, lighting, ventilation, water and security, as well as heat pumps, solar thermal and PV. The third is designed to be iconic in its extremely unusual shape and therefore expensive to reproduce. All of them make heavy use of smart electronics. And this is what puts up their price. Although they may score highly on low operational energy use this does not necessarily make them sustainable.

The real target of sustainable housing should be overall life-cycle impact. This is a prerequisite of the One Planet Life and OPD. It means that, in fact, small homes that are zero carbon in operation, whose materials are sourced locally and are of low embodied energy, preferably built in bulk and

Figure 10.95 The footings and cladding of Tŷ Solar. No foundation digging necessary.

Figure 10.96 The larch cladding.

perhaps in a compact urban terrace or block, will be inherently more sustainable than stand-alone large homes packed with different technologies and comprising a high embodied energy. Even the low pitch of Tŷ Solar's roof is designed to minimize the heated but unnecessary interior loft space and increased requirement for materials that are a result of higher pitched roofs, while still permitting the solar panels which the roof supports to take advantage of solar radiation.

The larch cladding will protect the building for years to come with minimum need for maintenance. The fact that it is screwed on in panels also

Figure 10.97 The straightforward control box.

makes it easier to access the interior of the walls if needed. The Passivhaus certified windows and doors are even made locally rather than in Germany. The house sits on footings raised slightly above the ground to remove the need for unnecessary concrete in foundations.

'Gareth, Jens and I come from very different worlds but we're united in our goal to be a disruptive influence of traditional thinking about building homes. In this, manufacturing becomes a key component and we see ourselves as manufacturers rather than builders,' said Glen. 'We have created a lot of goodwill in our community and hope to continue to do so as we expand, creating local jobs, sourcing locally and above all keeping things small.'

The test is whether from day to day the homes do result in their occupants reducing their energy use and bills. This depends on their habits. To this end simple controls will be easier to manage (see Figure 10.97). Ventilation is controlled just by opening windows when required, and space and water

Figure 10.98 The Passivhaus windows that are manufactured in Wales from Welsh timber.

heating is controlled in the traditional way, with thermostats. There are no other controls.

The house has two floors each of 44.16 square meters and a volume of 254 m³. It has achieved a SAP rated figure of 0.12 air changes per hour. This compares very favorably to the Passivhaus standard of 0.6 air changes per hour or a permeability rate of 3.0 m³/m²h. Over a 200-day heating period, a typical British house with eight air changes per hour and a 100 m² floor area, heated to 20 °C, will cost thirty times more to heat than an equivalent house with 0.3 air changes per hour, according to an energy calculator (SIGA). The SAP-rated space-heating requirement of this house is just 32.39 kWh/m²/year. This high performance is shown by the U-values, which are as follows:

Element	Average / Highest W/m²K	Maximum permitted W/m²K	Passivhaus standard
External wall	0.13	0.30	0.25–0.16
Floor	0.13	0.25	0.18–0.12
Roof	0.14	0.20	0.13–0.09
Openings	0.90	2.00	0.85

It can therefore be seen that the house, according to the SAP ratings, compares favourably with Passivhaus.

LED lights are fitted throughout, making the annual lighting consumption just 371.49 kWh. With no pumps or fans, there are no further electricity requirements over and above that which is used in day-to-day living by a family in any home – for appliances and gadgets. It is therefore predicted by the SAP rating to have a negative energy use of -3253.56 kWh (minus appliance use) and negative carbon dioxide emissions of -596.92 kg/year.

All of this means that the Energy Efficiency Rating on the EPC goes off the scale at 107, with an Environmental Impact (CO_2) rating of 108. In the Code for Sustainable Homes assessment it reaches Level 5. The SAP Assessment also predicts that there will be only a medium likelihood of a high internal temperature, or overheating, in July and August, which can easily be catered for by opening the windows. Future houses could be semi-detached or terraced, and have one, two or three bedrooms, as demand dictates and housing associations or local authorities wish. Glen is now at work on building a small terrace of such houses, a prototype community.

17 Calon Cymru

We need to take all the principles in this book and apply them not just to living in the countryside but to living in urban environments as well. No one, with the possible (but unproven) exception of the Vauban district in Germany (discussed later), has yet achieved this, since it is several orders of magnitude more complex a task than applying the principles to a small number of people surrounded by sufficient agricultural land.

Calon Cymru is an aspiration begun by architect Martin Golder for a network of communities along an existing railway line that passes through 100-odd miles of rural countryside, mostly in Wales. The Heart of Wales line stretches from Shrewsbury to Swansea, stopping frequently at many tiny stations. At many of these settlements there are disused plots of land and a scarcity of employment opportunities. The proposal is for a series of One

Figure 10.99 Artists' impression of Tŷ Hir Pren exterior.
Credit: Calon Cymru.

Figure 10.100 Artists' impression of Tŷ Hir Pren exterior, cutaway.
Credit: Calon Cymru.

Planet Development applications along the line that would take advantage of its transport opportunities. The function of the group that is supporting it, which includes other architects, is to help people looking to start One Planet Developments.

Calon Cymru has already been involved in town regeneration projects and linking them to the surrounding countryside. New developments would include spaces for workshops and offices so that people could work the land and gain employment. One example is Allt Cefn Crug, a 70-acre woodland outside of Llandovery, owned by the Hooper family, who built an A-frame timber house in 2011, and practice sustainable woodland management producing charcoal, construction timber and firewood. They had a retrospective planning application refused, and on appeal, in January 2013 Calon Cymru representatives, along with Llandovery tenants and residential association, all gave support. But because the application was refused the family has sold up. Examples like this are discouraging.

But Calon Cymru is not giving up. It is also acclimatising the communities along the line to One Planet Development principles so that the concepts are not alien to them. 'We'd like to see the railway better used,' says Golder's partner, architect Mark Wagmore. 'In some places along the line there are no towns, so new settlements could be built there. The property market for farmlands and farms is likely to see opportunities because many farmers are approaching retirement and nobody wants to use these farms, so a 350-acre farm being bought for One Planet Development would be an amazing opportunity'. The railway line isn't the only reason – the Tywi valley is good because it's flat and so less energy required than if driving over hills. So the homes have workshops and offices attached to provide livelihood.

There is currently either a huge time cost (for self-builders) or monetary cost attached to new homes for one planet living. So Mark wants

Figure 10.101 Artists' impressions of Tŷ Hir Pren interior.
Credit: Calon Cymru.

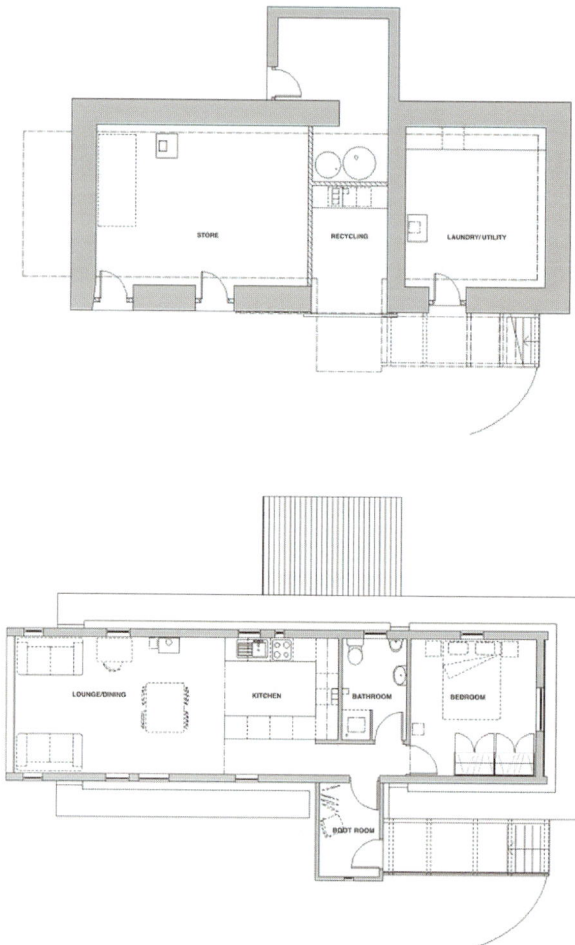

Figure 10.102 and 10.103 Ground floor and upper floor plans.
Credit: Calon Cymru.

to develop 'micro dwellings', which would come pre-specified at a high standard and developed as a product: prefabricated prototypes, assembled on-site, already approved to meet the building regulations, for airtightness and thermal bridging. They will be high-quality units using local timber and able to be easily dissembled for reassembly elsewhere if required when the owner moves. On site, these would be combined with ad hoc structures built with round wood timber, for ancillary workshops, storage and so on. One design has already been developed based on a vernacular style, the Welsh longhouse called Tŷ Hir Pren. Perhaps this is one way in which One Planet Development designs can adapt to fulfill the potential set out in TAN 6 for them to be within existing urban boundaries.

For more information, see caloncymru.co.uk.

18 One Planet City – Brighton and Hove

Calon Cymru is still a semi-rural proposition, far from the environment of BedZED. One planet living is something all urban settlements will have to aim towards in order for the human inhabitants of this planet to live within

Figure 10.104 Sue Riddlestone, CEO and co-founder BioRegional, presents Brighton and Hove Leader, Jason Kitcat, with their One Planet City certificate. On the far left is Thurstan Crockett, the council's Head of Sustainability, who led the process to get the One Planet Action Plan written and adopted.
Photo credit: BioRegional.

their means. Some cities are leading the way as pioneers. As I am a special consultant on a website called Sustainable Cities Collective, a forum for sharing best practice on sustainability in urban environments worldwide and led by urban leaders across the globe, I am witness to some remarkable developments. Let me share some of them.

It would take decades of dedicated work to bring a city's ecological footprint down to a proportionately fair level but that is the aim of the One Planet Brighton policy,[14] decided on 18 April 2013 in Brighton & Hove by the local authority. As an evolution of BioRegional's one planet living philosophy the document agreed on unanimously by council members marks a milestone. The local authority approved a Sustainability Action Plan that would use BioRegional's methodology and embody the city's existing initiatives and climate-change strategy, to be carried out by a wide-ranging partnership.

The strategy utilises the ten sustainability principles put together by BioRegional and the Worldwide Fund for Nature, described in the Introduction. It recognises that it requires step changes in the way problems are solved, in particular in feeding the city's inhabitants, and includes the following objectives among many others:

- year on year to reduce energy use by 4 per cent, to achieve a 42 per cent reduction in CO_2 emissions by 2020 and an 80 per cent reduction by 2050, from a 2005 baseline of 5.7 tonnes per capita;
- to develop 'closed loop' resource management and waste minimisation so that by 2025, 70 per cent of domestic waste by weight will be recycled or composted, with residual waste being reduced by 10 per cent per household by 2025; organic waste to be collected and sent to an anaerobic digestion facility to create energy and fertiliser;
- to promote cycling, walking and low-emission forms of transport so that by 2050 there will be 'zero carbon travel at work', starting from a position where transport contributes 26 per cent of the city's CO_2 emissions;
- the council will use its Sustainable Procurement Policy and Sustainable Procurement Toolkit to control and monitor all contracts for the social, ethical, environmental and economic impacts of the products and services that it buys;
- ultimately to create a circular (materials) economy to replace the present 'take, make, waste' one, including using unused buildings and local reprocessing plants to make reusable materials available, recovering materials currently burned, buried or exported such as mattresses, sofas and tyres;

- to reduce the current element of the ecological footprint related to food from 1.43 global hectares per person to 0.67 by 2025;
- to cut water use by fixing leaks and promoting water efficiency;
- to reduce flood risk and urban pollution sources of drainage networks, watercourses;
- to adopt a Local Biodiversity Action Plan (LBAP) and make the city contribute to the global need for 0.3ha of wildlife habitat per resident somewhere in the world;
- to promote fair trade, a local economy, equity and inclusivity physically and socially, jobs in the green economy and pay a living wage extensively across the city;
- to reduce localised health inequalities, increase access to work and retention of employees with health-related conditions, and to create an environment where employees are able to take personal responsibility for improving their own health and well-being;
- to make it easy, attractive and affordable for people to lead happy, healthy lives within their fair share of the earth's resources.

Food and nutrition

Food is an area particularly targeted for action.[15] In 2013 Brighton & Hove was named 'best community food growing project' in the Big Lottery's Local

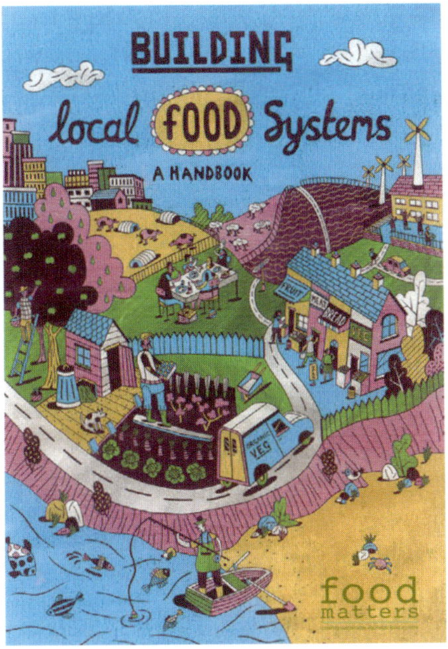

Figure 10.105 Cover of *Building Local Food Systems*, a handbook published by the charity Food Matters, full of ideas for promoting local food in urban areas.
Credit: Food Matters.

Food Awards out of over 500 projects across England. Its strategy, set out in 2012, is called *Spade to Spoon: Digging Deeper*.[16] It includes a drive to get people to eat more healthily with a Weight Referral Service which directs adults and children onto a range of targeted nutrition and exercise programmes, vegetable growing in schools, and another strand addressing food poverty. The Sussex Partnership NHS Foundation Trust purchases food from a local market garden supplier for people using its mental health services to such an extent that its turnover increased by 30 per cent in four years.

New Community Supported Agriculture (CSA) schemes include Sheepshare, in which sheep grazing around the city are brought in as meat to share between residents; Fork and Dig It, which shares vegetables from the local Stanmer Organics site; and Catchbox, in which members pay in advance for a share of the catch of a group of fishermen. Restaurants and cafés are encouraged to source local and sustainable produce. Schools, universities, hospitals and public bodies set up a Good Food Procurement Group to obtain fresh, sustainably sourced ingredients.

Harvest, a city-wide project that encourages more food growing within the city, has recently been awarded 'Best Community Growing Project' from the Lottery's Local Food Fund. According to Harvest's evaluation surveys, respondents reported such changes as wasting less food (44 per cent), composting (41 per cent), and buying more local food (36 per cent). The primary aim is to get people growing their own, in their gardens, balconies, allotments, or even public parks and empty land around housing estates. Training is offered to individuals and community groups, and new community gardens are being developed, financed initially in 2009 by nearly £500,000 over four years from the Big Lottery Local Food Fund. In that time, 51 new growing projects were started on 1.75 acres of new growing space, spread across the city and involving many different types of people, from local neighbours to charities working with vulnerable individuals.

There is a project to collect fruit that otherwise would have gone to waste from trees in private and public gardens which is given to local people, or processed into juice, preserves or chutneys. A Community Composting scheme diverts food waste from landfill. The Big Dig was a celebration of food growing where the community gardens showcased their projects in parks, orchards and forests, to inspire others to get growing too. The Council has published a Planning Advisory Note (PAN) which encourages developers to include space for food growing. Planners in London are now looking to adopt this multi-award-winning model.

To support many of its aims the Council issued an online sustainability checklist for all planning applications to validate themselves for residential

Figure 10.106 Allotment-style food growing on the rooftop of One Brighton.
Credit: BioRegional.

and mixed-use schemes, including food growing, biodiversity, building standards, materials, flood risk, passive design, carbon dioxide emissions, public transport, pedestrianism, parking, waste, job creation and open space questions.

One Brighton

In this context, BioRegional worked with developers Crest Nicholson to develop an example of how this might work in practice with a development called One Brighton. This contains 172 residential units and 10,000 square feet of office and community space on a former locomotive manufacturing site. The 0.39 hectare parcel of land is close to Brighton train station. The development has achieved an 'Excellent' rating under EcoHomes, a now-defunct national sustainability standard assessment for new homes, and was considered to be 'Zero Carbon' under this assessment, by using features such as:

- triple glazing;
- highly insulated breathable walls;
- a biomass community heating system;
- solar PV panels for electricity;
- food-growing space that residents can lease on the sixth floor;
- on-site composting facilities;

Figure 10.107 One Brighton.
Credit: BioRegional/Quantain.

- cycling storage;
- car club with two years' free membership and a 50 per cent discount on rates for residents;
- organic vegetable box delivery points;
- a biomass boiler for hot water and space heating.

The commercial offices and community space are designed to achieve BREEAM (Building Research Establishment Environmental Assessment Methodology) 'Excellent' ratings. A concession by the planning department that they didn't have to provide car-parking space was critical to the financial (not to mention sustainability) success of the project. The on-site biomass boiler and PV panels provide about half the energy requirements; the remainder is bulk-purchased for residents as guaranteed renewable electricity through a One Brighton Energy Services Company.

This is all well and good, but the One Planet Brighton strategy faces many significant hurdles ahead. Two of these are contained in a December 2013 letter written by the planning inspector.[17] She notes the challenge of creating sufficient new affordable and sustainable housing to meet local needs and observes the difficulty in satisfying the social aspect of sustainability. Brighton has stepped out along a brave path into a sustainable future, and must take all of its population with it on this expedition. It is still exploring the route and has a way to go, but has made an excellent start.

Figure 10.108 Solar Settlement in the Vauban quarter in Freiburg (Germany), Elly-Heuss-Knapp-Straße.
Credit: Claire7373 Andrewglaser.

19 One planet living in Freiburg, Germany

One-planet-type developments can be found all over the world, but the planning laws which permit them vary from nation to nation, largely dependent upon how precious or pressured is the demand for land. In areas where land is freely available, there is much greater tolerance towards people doing their own thing, in great contrast to countries like the UK. I'm thinking, for example, of northeastern Germany, an area quite depopulated since reunification. Although much of the landscape is taken up by remotely controlled farming conglomerates, pockets exist where it is relatively cheap to acquire land and create a smallholding with low-impact dwelling. The same is true over large areas of Europe, particularly in the east.

Vauban

But living on the land in this way will neither sustain nor be appropriate for the majority of the world's population. So, besides Brighton, are there other more advanced examples that show how one planet living can work in cities? Yes, and they are perhaps best exemplified by the Vauban district[18]

Figure 10.109 A low-impact dwelling made from a railway carriage on a small-holding by the Baltic coast in NE Germany.

of Freiburg in southern Germany, which possibly checks every box of what a sustainable, liveable city quarter might be like. It's an intentional community, beginning with some squatters who protested about being removed by developers, and took their future into their own hands by negotiation and design. Construction began in the mid-1990s, with the first people moving in in 2000. Shortly after it housed 2,000 inhabitants; now this number has risen to around 5,000, with over 600 jobs in the quarter itself. 'The Vauban district was created through cooperative decision-making, becoming a model of holistic environmental planning and eco-friendly living,' Louise Abellard writes.[19]

Andreas Delleske lives in the first multi-family Passivhaus apartment block in Germany in the town. He was also one of the prime movers of the citizen's organisation, Forum Vauban, involved in the development of the settlement. His involvement began in 1995 when it became clear that the squatted area of the town, a former French barracks, needed to be redeveloped. Like most of the initiatives in this book the impetus for change came from the bottom up via grass-roots activism, which then caused change at the top in legislation and planning. An architect, Michael Gies, and a biologist, Jörg Lange, developed the idea of a people's forum to make sure that the people already living there had their views heard and could determine their future. They also realized there was an opportunity to create a low-impact development and, together with experts in the world-famous Fraunhofer Institute for Solar Energy Systems (Martin Ufheil) and the Passive House Institute in Darmstadt, developed their plans.

The district was planned around green transportation (as with another city known as a global beacon of green urban planning, Curitiba in southern Brazil), because, besides consumption, transportation is the hardest ecological impact of development to reduce. While the district includes streets, cars hardly ever pass through, and car parking is not catered for. Residents who do own vehicles can park in a community lot on the edge of

Figure 10.110 Cycle parking in Vauban.
Credit: www.vauban.de.

Figure 10.111 A grassed tramway in Vauban.
Credit: www.vauban.de.

the district, unsubsidized by the car-free households. Pedestrian and bicycle paths form a highly connected, efficient, green transportation network with every home within walking distance of a tram stop, and all schools, businesses, and shopping centres located within walking distance. 'When moving into Vauban, 57 per cent of the households that previously owned a car decided to let their car go. All in all, 70 per cent of the inhabitants live without a car in Vauban,' Abellard reports.

All buildings must meet minimum low-energy consumption standards of 65 kWh/m²a (i.e. at least half the average German energy standards). Public energy and heat are generated by a highly efficient woodchip-powered combined heat and power generator connected to a district heating grid. Forty-two building units are of the Passivhaus standard, consuming under 15 kWh/m²a. 100 houses adhere to a 'plus-energy' standard, producing more energy than they use, with surpluses sold back to the city grid and profits split between each household. Organic household waste is treated with an anaerobic digester. The place contains a unique ecological sewage system in one pilot project: sucked by vacuum pipes, faeces are transported into this digester, generating biogas, which is used for cooking. Grey water is cleaned in biofilm plants and returned to the water cycle.

Importantly, the project is being monitored using lifecycle and regional material flow analysis with the GEMIS (Global Emission Model for Integrated Systems)[20] software. This is the first time that a complete urban neighbourhood has been analysed with respect to buildings, infrastructure, electricity supply, heat supply, water and waste, traffic and private consumption with a full life-cycle perspective and using regional data. The gathering of local data was possible for all areas except private consumption, for which national average data was used. Through this, the following provisional figures have been developed:

- Energy savings per year: 28 GJ (calculated as 'CER', cumulative energy requirements).
- Reduction of CO_2 equivalents per year: 2,100 t.
- Reduction of sulphur-dioxide (SO_2) equivalents per year: 4 t.
- Saving of mineral resources per year: 1,600 t.

The first house was completed in August 1999 and has been monitored ever since. The results[21] of the monitoring show that the additional cost of making the building so energy efficient was just 7 per cent, which paid

Figure 10.112 Andreas Delleske's Passivhaus apartment block in Vauban. Credit: www.vauban.de.

Figure 10.113 A playground in Vauban. Courtesy of Daniel Schoenen.

Figure 10.114 Vauban street market. Courtesy of Daniel Schoenen.

for itself in 10 years. In Austria, about 300 passive houses have been scientifically evaluated and the extra cost of making them zero energy was anything from no cost to an extra 14 per cent. As with Hockerton and Tŷ Solar, they also found that concrete should not be used, and that individual ventilation with heat recovery systems were not effective for reasons of cost and maintenance. They make the point that combined heat and power is the most efficient form of energy generation to be used wherever there are clusters of buildings, whether for business or residence. This is because there are substantial savings in scale and overheads from community- or district-level plants, which are lost at a much larger scale due to distribution costs and conversion/distance losses. The heat and power are supplied via local networks using an Energy Services Company.

Freiburg

It's not surprising to learn that Vauban is the greenest area of the greenest city, Freiburg, in the greenest province, Baden-Württemberg, in Germany. Freiburg, a city of about 220,000 people and 155 km², is already known as an eco-city, with the Green Party having the strongest presence there of anywhere in the country. Freiburg's citizens are known for their love of cycling, with over 400 km of cycle paths, separate bike paths, and over 9,000 bicycle parking spaces, including 'bike and ride' lots at transit stations. The city has an extensive pedestrianised zone and a tramway network together with feeder buses. Seventy per cent of the population lives within 500 meters of a tram stop, and the trains appear every 7.5 minutes during rush hours, with ticket costs subsidized to encourage use. Waste levels have been reduced by almost two thirds since 1988, with waste minimization, increased recycling (it is very easy to recycle everywhere), anaerobic digestion of organic waste and the residual waste burnt for energy.

The 5,000 hectares of forestry surrounding the town is managed sustainably and organically with certification from the Forest Stewardship Council. The city contains over 600 hectares of parks and 160 playgrounds, providing greenery, recreation, and biodiversity. Changing the lawnmowing schedule from 12 times to only twice a year has 'markedly revived the biodiversity in the meadows'. 3,800 small privately owned garden allotments for the

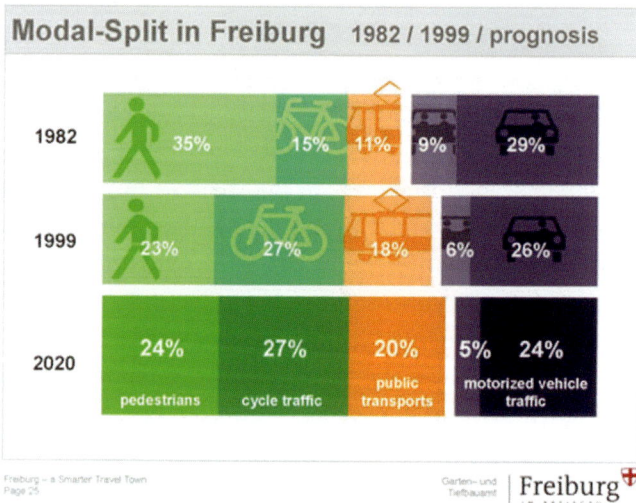

Figure 10.115 Traffic modes in Freiburg showing how cycling and walking has increased and car use decreased, a trend that is projected to continue into the future.
Credit: City of Freiburg.

Figure 10.116 Every building in Vauban has solar panels on its roof. Courtesy of Daniel Schoenen.

inhabitants to grow their own food lie on the outskirts of the city. This number is expected to increase, according to the new Land Use Plan 2020, the writing of which was accomplished by citizens forming 19 working groups to discuss potential construction areas and make recommendations to the city council. Local food is also supplied by farm shops, a farmers' market, a local winery and distillery, beekeeping, butchers, bakers and plant nursery (though the percentage of food consumed in Frieburg that has been produced locally is unknown). Shops and offices are located on the ground floor of the apartment buildings, allowing residents easy access, on foot or bicycle, to their daily needs, so that 'no supermarkets will be constructed on green meadows'. Renewable energy production is encouraged with tax credits from the federal government and subsidies from the regional utility.

In June 1995 Freiburg city council adopted a resolution that it would only permit construction of 'low-energy buildings' on municipal land, and all new buildings must comply with low-energy specifications.

Why is this city so green? Part of the answer lies in the fact that it benefits from an unusually high concentration of specialist professionals working in sustainability, including the ICLEI (Local Governments for Sustainability), ISES (the International Solar Energy Society) and the City Mayors Foundation. Perhaps, for the future of cities to be made sustainable, the only way is for this kind of expertise to be rolled out across every city in the world, through extensive programs of education, training and networking.

This is a role that is already being undertaken by many players, including notably the ICLEI, the World Future Council, the Transition Towns Network and the C40 Mayors network. Some are working top down, while many, notably the hundreds of members of the Transition Towns Network around the world, are working from the bottom up. Together they are creating a gradually expanding patchwork of districts and communities that are becoming greener, reducing their ecological footprints in the process. This is a process that must be encouraged, and we can all play our part.

20 The road ahead to real sustainability

The bulk of this book has concentrated on one planet living in the countryside, because that is where it might be considered easiest for people to begin to do this, and for planning culture to change to accommodate the demand. But we can now begin to see, from the examples towards the end of this book, and from the Foreword by Pooran Desai, how the One Planet Life could one day be led by every citizen. Beyond 'slimmer' zero-carbon buildings, closed-loop resource use and renewable energy supplies, transport, diet and food provision are the main challenges for the One Planet Life, not just in the countryside but in towns and cities.

Communities need to be planned in such a way that walking, cycling, public transport and renewably powered electric vehicles are encouraged as the chief modes of transport. Cities will need to grow much more of their own food, probably using vertical and indoor farms, large buildings that may be passively heated and ventilated, recycling their own water, and allowing crops to be grown and harvested throughout the year.[22] Citizens may also grow some of their own food, as well as having relationships with Community-Supported Agriculture in the hinterlands around their urban areas, as was the case in the past. Community-Supported Agriculture allows growers to sell subscriptions to their services so that they have the capital they need throughout the year to produce a guaranteed food supply for their customers.

As in Freiburg, these districts will see all their organic waste anaerobically digested and turned into fertiliser, renewable gas for fuel, and heat. The gas might power methane-driven fuel cells or be fed into the local gas grid. The circular economy[23] will be widely taken up, with close to zero waste and everything designed so its components can be reused at the end of its life. The calculation of the ecological footprint of towns and cities will need to include all the goods and services that are imported into the area from all over the world, and all flights and travel journeys taken by citizens. Infrastructure will need to be adapted to cope with more regular extreme-weather events too. City ecosystems need to be made regenerative through incorporating, not banishing, nature.

All of this creates exciting opportunities for innovation, community building and healthier lifestyles. This book has shown examples that exist now. If you doubt that change along these lines can happen, just cast your eyes back at the changes that have occurred in our cities and in the countryside over the last 100 years. I believe cities will be equally unrecognisable 100 years from now and that the future will be sustainable or not at all. The One Planet Life is the only resilient life, whatever form it might take.

Notes

1   Desai, P. and James, N., *one planet living in the Thames Gateway: a WWF-UK One Million Sustainable Homes Campaign Report,* WWF-UK, 2003.

2   In Desai, P., *One Planet Communities: A real-life guide to sustainable living*, Wiley, 2009.

3   Here are some productivity figures from Year 4 for Lammas. There are different ways of calculating its productivity; the closest to Pembrokeshire's Policy 52, under which they were granted planning permission, is set out below. It doesn't include income from feed-in tariffs.

   Prior to Lammas the farmer was bringing in between £2,500 and £3,500 from raising sheep on the land. Bear in mind that the site is on a former upland sheep farm of 76 acres, 130–170m above sea level, and is now supporting nine households – 17 adults plus dependents.

   Total household need: £104,517 (averaging £11,613 per household)
   Value of needs met directly from site (fuel, energy, food, water etc.): £41,662
   Income from land-based produce: £19,339
   Total income from educational activities: £6,043
   Total land-based produce: £67,044

   (All figures without agricultural subsidies – none are received.)
   Therefore in their 4th year they met 64% of household needs directly from the land. (The target for Policy 52 in year five is 75%; the target for One Planet Developments in year five is a more achievable 65%.)

4   See: Parsons, R., *Sweet Peas: an Essential Guide*, Crowood Press, England, April 2011.

5   See www.deginvest.de/EN_Home/About_DEG/Our_Mandate/Development_Policy_Mandate/GPR_Reports/Ex_post_evaluation_flower_sector_east_africa.pdf.

6   See http://ecologicalland.coop. Retrieved February 2014.

7   See www.campaignforrealfarming.org/funding-enlightened-agriculture. Retrieved February 2014.

8   See ecologicalland.coop/planning-documentation and ecologicalland.coop/greenham-reach-appeal-documentation. Retrieved February 2014.

9   Maxey, Dr. L., Laughton, R., Rodker, O. and Wangler, Z., *Small is Successful*, The Ecological Land Co-operative, 2011.

10   See cooltemperate.co.uk. Retrieved February 2014.

11   See www.trinityfarm.co.uk Retrieved February 2014.

12   See www.nationalfruitcollection.org.uk Retrieved February 2014.

13   See www.fastltd.co.uk Retrieved February 2014.

14   See www.brighton-hove.gov.uk/sites/brighton-hove.gov.uk/files/PandR%20 version%20OPL%20SAP%283%29%20with%20Forewords.pdf. Retrieved February 2014.

15   See Gouzin, L., Williams, V. and Devereux, C. *Building Local Food Systems: a Handbook.* Brighton: Food Matters, 2013. www.foodmatters.org/flipbook/files/inc/a5854c51eb.pdf. Retrieved February 2014.

16   See www.bhfood.org.uk/food-strategy. Retrieved February 2014.

17   Retrieved at www.brighton-hove.gov.uk/sites/brighton-hove.gov.uk/files/ID-21%20 Letter%20to%20council%20Dec%2013.pdf. February 2014.

18   See www.vauban.de/en. Retrieved February 2014.

19   See www.cereplast.com/vauban-district-germany-when-environmental-planning-gives-birth-to-sustainable-communities.

20   GEMIS (Global Emission Model for Integrated Systems) is a life-cycle analysis program and database developed in Germany, initially as a tool for the comparative assessment of environmental effects of energy, by Öko-Institut and Gesamthochschule Kassel (GhK). Since then, the model has been continuously upgraded and updated. The GEMIS database offers information on: fuel data, processes, materials and transport, and includes the total life-cycle in its calculation of impacts – i.e. fuel delivery, materials used for construction, waste treatment, and transports/auxiliaries. The GEMIS database accounts for each process (efficiency, air and GHG pollutants, solid wastes, liquid pollutants, land use) and can also analyse costs. See: www.gemis.de.

21   Available at www.passivhaus-vauban.de.

22   See Marks, P., *Vertical farms sprouting all over the world*, in *New Scientist* issue 2952, 16 January 2014: www.newscientist.com/article/mg22129524.100-vertical-farms-sprouting-all-over-the-world.html#.Uw3-IPR_uKU. Retrieved February 2014.

23   See the Ellen MacArthur Foundation website for more information: www.ellenmacarthurfoundation.org. Retrieved February 2014.

Afterword
The long and winding road...

Jane Davidson

Congratulations! If you are a person interested in practising one planet living, you have just read a manual which I hope has encouraged you to take that first step to change your life and lower your ecological footprint; if you are a policy/planning official or a politician, this manual could help you develop evidence-based policies for living more sustainably aimed at everybody from government down. Together, the author and the other contributors in word and deed have charted the beginning of a long journey and tried to peer into the future to see what it will be like, or what it could be like if everybody was enabled somehow to reduce their ecological effect.

Getting to this point has already taken a huge amount of time. From the 1970s onwards, there have been powerful and passionate messages about the benefits of self-sufficiency and living lightly on the land. From the early 1990s, the threats of our changing climate and the need to tackle our global emissions have been clearly articulated, but public policy has remained largely resistant.

Politics can move mountains, particularly when passionate grass-roots action is able to influence ministers, as happened with the first Government of Wales Act 1998, which included a unique clause that the National Assembly should set out how it proposed to promote sustainable development in the exercise of its functions to enjoy a better quality of life without compromising the quality of life of future generations.[1] Such an approach was entirely novel and still sets Wales apart today as one of only a very small number of nations across the world with such a distinctive statutory duty. Its potential is huge. Welsh Assembly Members elected in 1999 had a constitutional duty to actively enhance the economic, social and environmental well-being of people and communities not yet born to achieve a better quality of life for our own and future generations.

Under this banner, a number of moves were made to create policies to achieve greater sustainability that were unique to Wales; in my own areas of responsibility, for example, the introduction of Education for Sustainable Development and Global Citizenship (ESDGC) throughout the education system (with all schools encouraged to become eco-schools); sustainability requirements for public buildings, more rigorous planning and energy-efficiency requirements for sustainable homes; charging for carrier bags and legislation to increase recycling, which has seen Wales coming from behind to outperform other parts of the UK.

Others were encouraged to create their own opportunities. Pembrokeshire County Council introduced the radical 'Policy 52', the first of its kind, setting the context for permitting development in the countryside which contributes to the agenda of sustainable development. Proof was required that there would be a positive contribution in terms of the environment, the use of resources, and a combination of social and economic benefits, and that the proposals would achieve a neutral or at least the lowest possible adverse impact. Eight criteria were set, all of which had to be met for a development to be permitted. In addition, applications needed to be accompanied by a management plan and applicants had to agree to the production of an annual monitoring report. Additional guidance spelt out the requirements for both including that 75 per cent or more of basic household needs would be met by means of activities centred on the use of resources grown, reared or occurring naturally on the site. It was expected that this would be achieved within three years – or, in exceptional circumstances, five years.

It appeared, therefore, that the stage was set positively when, in June 2007, Lammas submitted its first planning application for nine family homes with seven acres each and a community hall in Glandwr in North Pembrokeshire, not far from where the 'self-sufficiency' guru John Seymour had lived. The proposed village was to be on a south-facing slope with water and woodland and was supported by the local farmer. The applicants were delivering what government in Wales and the county council said they wanted, but the application was highly controversial. Watching it from afar through press and media reports, I was interested that a modest proposal for nine families to experiment with 'alternative' lifestyles on a site that could only be seen from distant hills was arousing such strong feelings. I was determined that, once it was over, we would develop national planning policy in Wales to encourage similar applications.

It took two years for the application to be finally determined – and by the Planning Inspectorate, not the county council. The UK's first planned eco-village was finally born. The application had, in the end, taken a wheel-barrow-load of paper submissions, three planning applications and signifi-cant bureaucratic and other opposition, including from local newspapers. Only the dogged determination of the applicants to be prepared to rewrite the thousands of pages of their application, and their commitment to win support for their initiative using the planning system prior to development rather than retrospectively, saw them through. This is not how pioneers of a healthier, less wealthy lifestyle should be treated by those who profess to want to deliver the same outcomes.

The introduction of One Planet Developments into national planning guidance in Wales – Technical Advisory Note 6: Planning for Sustainable Rural Communities 4.15[2] – therefore owes a great deal to the negative experience of the planning system by the families at Lammas. Grass-roots action on its own is not sufficient because it needs to be supported by legislation, and top-down legislation or regulation won't work on its own unless there is buy-in on the ground. So, for the One Planet Life to be an option for the majority, this local partnership between the political and the personal needs to work and be encouraged and the experience shared.

Once the Lammas' application had succeeded, I met for the first time with those who had been involved to understand the key planning barriers from their perspective to inform our new national policy for low-impact developments. It was an interesting meeting. I am a passionate believer in not allowing unfettered development in the countryside and using the planning system to develop and maintain strong rural communities. So were the Lammas applicants. I am a passionate believer in creating an effec-tive and fair planning system that is responsive to ecological challenges and encourages innovation. So were the Lammas applicants. We all agreed that if we want more people to live more sustainable lifestyles, governments need to make that the norm.

So how do we make it the norm? In Wales, there has been progress towards hardening the understanding of that optimistic commitment in the first Government of Wales Act in 1998. 'One Wales One Planet' was published in 2009 with a vision of putting sustainable development at the centre of government delivery, and encouraged others similarly to embrace sustainable development as their central organising principle. The vision of a more sustainable Wales is one where Wales '*lives within its environmental limits, using only its fair share of the earth's resources so that our ecological footprint is reduced to the global average availability of resources, and we are resilient to the impacts of climate change'.*[3]

The intention was to ensure that within the lifetime of a generation, i.e. by the middle of the century, Wales would be using only its fair share of the earth's resources, approximately 1.88 global hectares per person as measured by ecological footprinting. To achieve this goal by 2050, there will need to be a reduction by at least two thirds of the total resources we currently use to sustain our lifestyles. In energy, this means a 80–90 per cent reduction in our use of carbon-based energy over 40 years, resulting in a similar reduction in our greenhouse gas emissions; all new buildings will need to be zero carbon; electricity should be produced from renewable sources; we will need to become a zero-waste nation, to live and work in ways which have a much stronger connection with our local economies and communities; to source more of our food locally and in season; to manage ecosystems sustainably and do all of the above in ways which make us a fairer society. In other words, to be a 'One Planet Society'.

Introducing 'One Wales One Planet' the Rt. Hon Rhodri Morgan AM, the redoubtable First Minister of Wales, said,

'I want a Wales fit for generations to come … What motivates me is doing my best to ensure a brighter more sustainable future for my grandchildren and their grandchildren and every other child growing up in Wales today. Top of the list of our priorities which will continue to improve the quality of life for people today and in the future is sustainability.'[4]

As each year goes by without the necessary changes being made, the public-policy challenge of responding to our changing climate becomes ever harder, but the number of people from all walks of life who have become interested in food growing, in more sustainable buildings, and in creating more sustainable futures for their children, is growing steadily. We have to take comfort from this and continually encourage those who want to actively make a better future to do so either for themselves or by lobbying others for better public policy.

This year in Wales a Future Generations Bill will be enacted which will translate the duty to 'promote' sustainable development as contained in the Government of Wales Act 1998 and translate that into a duty to 'deliver' sustainable development – with the likelihood of the ecological footprint at the heart of the legislation. This gives further government support to encourage more sustainable living, with the added bonus of a new Commissioner for Future Generations independent of government to act as a critical friend providing annual reports to government. I am hopeful that future Welsh governments will make more considered policy decisions as a result.

Wherever you are and whoever you are, I hope your life has been challenged by what you have read. So I leave you with a short manifesto to support more of us living more responsibly for the future.

1   Take immediate actions to make your life greener. Measure your own ecological footprint – your food, home, travel and stuff – at the WWF site (http://footprint.wwf.org.uk/home/calculator_complete) and follow the seven-day plan for bringing your footprint down – and then get a friend to do the same thing. With the UK average being in the region of three planets, mine is 1.79 and there is still more I can do.

2   Campaign to support the idea of One Planet Development applicants being supported as pioneers in the planning system. Local councils across the UK should develop local policies to encourage such developments, including making space available for them in their local development plans. Provided the applicants contract to deliver on an agreed management plan, they should be treated as permitted development. In return, the applicants should be prepared to have two open days a year – one in winter, one in summer – to share their experiences with others. Low-impact dwellings could be a key to contributing towards a better future and enable young people to have access to affordable housing with land in the countryside.

3   Join the One Planet Council (http://www.oneplanetcouncil.org.uk), which supports those who are making the transition to this more sustainable way of life by providing guidance and tools. It works together with all those with an interest in One Planet Development: Local Planning Authorities, policymakers, academics, landowners, and those already living on and planning to live on One Planet Development sites.

This book has come about because of grass-roots action and political support for a vision. The road has been long and winding but there is now a collection of stories and experiences across the world of people living happier, more fulfilled lives within a fairer share of the earth's resources. Nelson Mandela said, '*Vision without action is just a dream, action without vision just passes the time, vision with action can change the world.*'

So – what are you waiting for?

Jane Davidson
April 2014

Notes

1 Government of Wales Act 1998 section 121 'Duty to promote sustainable development).
2 PPW Technical Advisory Note 6: Planning for Sustainable Rural Communities section 4.15.
3 'One Wales One Planet' the Government's Sustainable Development Scheme published May 2009.
4 Introduction by the First Minister to 'One Wales One Planet'.

Index

Page locators in italics refer to figures and tables